ADULT EDUCATION IN INNER LONDON 1870–1980

To Nan

ADULT EDUCATION IN INNER LONDON 1870–1980

W.A. DEVEREUX

OBE, BSc (Econ), DPA, Hon MA (OU)

SHEPHEARD-WALWYN

IN COLLABORATION WITH

Inner London Education Authority

© Inner London Education Authority, 1982

This edition first published 1982 by
Shepheard-Walwyn (Publishers) Ltd.,
12/13 Henrietta Street,
Covent Garden, London WC2E 8LH.

ISBN 0 85683 059 3

Devereux, Wm.A.
  Adult education in Inner London 1870–1980.
  1. Adult education—London (England)—History—
  19th century   2. Adult education—London (England)—
  History—20th century
  I. Title
  374'.9421   LC5256.G7

ISBN 0-85683-059-3

Typesetting by Colset Private Ltd, Singapore
Printed and bound in Great Britain by Biddles Ltd, Guildford and King's Lynn

Contents

Illustrated section between pages 150 and 151

Acknowledgments

I am grateful for the opportunity to discuss the outline of this book with Dame Margaret Cole in 1979, a year before she died. I thank Sir Harold Shearman for the opportunity of a similar discussion and for the loan of two relevant government publications.

I am indebted to the published research of my friend, Dr Thomas Kelly, on which much of the early part of the first chapter is based.

I acknowledge gratefully the help I have received from many people. The principals of adult education institutes showered me with all the log-books and records they had; past principals – Miss Ivy Back, Miss Muriel Cookes, Miss Edith Ramsay and Miss Dorothy Plastow (former principal and ex-ILEA assistant education officer), Mr Alec Auerbach and Mr Stephen Hunt – reached back into their memories and also gave me valuable photographs and other records. I am further indebted to Miss Ramsay for allowing me to use and quote from her various letters to friends.

I wish to thank Mr Peter Clyne, assistant education officer, ILEA Community Education and Careers Branch and Mr Peter Lincoln, his deputy, for their helpful comments on the draft; the staff of CEC Branch and, in particular, Miss K. Leavis and Miss Betty Walker for their patient and helpful answers to my questions; Miss Heather MacLeod for transmitting manuscripts, books and documents; Miss Dolores Webb, a former colleague, for reading and making valuable comments on the first draft; the staff of GLC Records and of the History Library; Mr Neate, in particular for his courtesy and ready helpfulness; the staff of the Education Library and Mrs H. Bennett who transcribed the tapes and typed the greater part of the manuscript. I thank my wife for helping me to select the photographs and for her constant support and encouragement throughout all stages of the project.

For permission to reproduce the photographs between pages 150 and 151 I am grateful to The Greater London Council Photograph Library, Miss Muriel Cookes and Christopher Devereux.

Foreword

The story of adult education in Inner London over the past 110 years is an absorbing one in which three elements recur.

The first is that, from the earliest years, the education of adults has been seen to have two related aims: to satisfy the needs of the individual and to promote the well-being of the community at large. Initially, the two aims came together in such obviously important tasks as teaching English to the waves of immigrants that settled in London towards the end of the last century. But since then, as the later chapters of this book show, the two aims have been pursued with increased resources and undiminished vigour in widely different and innovative ways.

The second recurring element in Inner London's Adult Education Service is that those who have led it, taught in it and administered it have consistently fought the notion that the education of adults is in any way incidental to the main tasks of an Education Authority. The fight has not always been successful. There have been set-backs as well as advances. But no-one who studies the final chapters of this book can doubt that adult education in Inner London ended the 1970s in a position of great strength: well-organised, well led professionally and well supported by voluntary bodies, by the Education Authority and the public alike. For the ILEA's Service to be so placed at the end of a decade which has seen a sad decline in the nation's commitment to adult education is an achievement in which it can reasonably take pride.

The third recurring element in the history of London's Adult Education Service has been the way in which it has engaged the whole-hearted commitment and brought out the best in many who have been charged with shaping its course. Pre-eminent amongst these was the Rev. Stewart Headlam. It was his vision and determination, in the later days of the School Board in the early LCC years, which gave the Service the high morale and sense of purpose which it has retained ever since. Later, a succession of distinguished principals of institutes, and chairmen and members of committees have carried the work forward. The Service has been fortunate, too, in the inspectors and officials who have worked for it. One such official was the author of this book. Between 1962 and 1975, W. A. Devereux was the Assistant Education Officer responsible for the Adult Education Service. Its development in those years owes much to him. The Service is also in debt to him for producing a comprehensive account of its history. The book is one which, in recalling past achievement, should serve to inspire confidence in the future.

P.A. NEWSAM

Preface

Throughout the last ten years of my service with the LCC and ILEA I urged colleagues, about to retire from the adult education service, to fill the gap in the history of adult education in Great Britain by writing an account of the London service. Although one or two of them began the task, retirement enveloped them and they turned to other interests. When, therefore, at a party to mark my own retirement from the Adult Literacy Resource Agency, I was asked if I would be prepared to be commissioned by the ILEA to write such an account, I felt unable to refuse. My own direct involvement with that service for over twenty years and my belief that, for more than fifty years, the adult education service in inner London had been pre-eminent, nationally and internationally, were added incentives to tackle the task. Such incentives had their disadvantages; they could overlay objectivity and personalize the record. I have tried to avoid these dangers and no doubt in the process have eschewed personal anecdotes and comments which might have enlivened the text.

Those who helped to build the service – members, officers and principals – have been embarrassingly reticent. Two or three principals only set down limited accounts of their work and these were written in the 1930s. With the exception of T.G. William's memoir of the City Literary Institute, no one appears to have written the story of any particular institute or an account of the many individual success stories of their students. Indeed, not until the ILEA evidence to the Russell Committee was there any published review of the work of non-vocational institutes. I have therefore been particularly grateful to those anonymous writers of reports to committees who, from the time of the School Board for London, have maintained a standard which I doubt can be surpassed in any other local authority. Happily, too, despite the ravages of the second World War, there are still some early departmental records which illuminate reports prepared for the public eye.

Whilst I have referred to the adult education work of voluntary organizations, the University of London and the WEA, this account is concerned primarily with the provision made by the statutory body of the time – the School Board for London, the London County Council and the Inner London Education Authority. The work of voluntary organizations in this field deserves separate study. Also, except where the sequence of events made it necessary, I have not covered the statutory youth service.

Today there is much discussion about the validity of the term 'non-vocational', and there is an increasing tendency to blur the distinction between vocational and non-vocational education. The discussion is not new and it is still true that it is the student who determines whether a subject is vocational or non-vocational to him or her. The history of the London service, however, illustrates the effect which size of demand in an urban area can have on the development of separate establishments geared to a particular method of teaching and a curriculum unrelated to the demands of an examination syllabus or particular job requirements. In an area as large as inner London it has always been possible to group and specialize. Attractive as multi-discipline establishments may seem, institutes with 10,000 part-time day and evening students attached to equally large colleges of full-time and part-time vocational students, present major problems of accommodation and organization, to say the least.

This book is, therefore, unashamedly an account of the development of non-vocational adult education institutes in inner London. It is the story of men and women who have many latent interests and talents not directly related to their job or means of livelihood. These interests offer a touchstone for the informal further education of the individual. From being a relief from the rigid discipline of the mainly vocational programme of the early evening continuation schools, non-vocational classes grew into literary, men's and women's institutes and, later, adult education institutes. The record shows how London led the way to a widespread understanding that teaching methods, relevant to adults, and an adult ambience for classes, were all-important. The work of the institutes, during and after the 1939–45 war years, were a testimony to their resilience and flexibility. With the old communities dispersed, they responded to the widening tastes and changing mores of the 1950s and 1960s with a tremendous development and broadening of the curriculum.

Finally, reviews of its education provision by the ILEA in the late 1960s and early 1970s pointed to the need for the education service to reach out to the greatly changed multi-ethnic community. Reports show how the institutes responded and how, despite increased financial restraints, the ILEA continues to recognize the vital role of non-vocational adult education institutes in the education of the whole community.

W.A.D.

1.   Before 1870 – a Perspective

The development of a public education system in England and Wales owes much to the devoted efforts of private individuals and voluntary groups who, from a religious or social motive or simply the desire to pass on knowledge to others, saw a need and tried to meet it. To describe a period of statutory endeavour, particularly in the field of adult education, without some indication of the ground work would be to ignore the substantial progress made and, perhaps more important, the extent of the concern for educating adults which existed long before the first public Education Act in 1870. It would also tend to give credence to the too often held view that adult education is something which began with the WEA and the University Extension Movement.

Universal education was foreshadowed by Sir Thomas More and many other 'utopians' but few saw the education of adults as a natural concomitant of the education of children. Samuel Bott in *Nova Salyma* (1648), James Harrington in *Oceana* (1656) and Gerrard Winstanley in *Law of Freedom* (1652), propounded education systems which provided for adults. Winstanley, in particular, one of the leaders of the 'Diggers', who believed in the common ownership of land, developed in his writings a political philosophy, which Professor Sabine said, 'spoke with the authentic voice of proletarian utopianism, giving expression to the first stirring of political aspiration in the inarticulate masses and setting up the well-being of the common man as the goal of a just society'.[1]

Political developments on the ground took the form of a remarkable expansion in the number of teachers of mathematics, astronomy and navigation in the early part of the seventeenth century, much of the instruction being given privately, either individually or in classes. There was also extensive provision in London at this time for the teaching of foreign languages which the following passage, quoted by Dr Kelly from *Annales* by J. Stow, (1615), well illustrates:

> There bee also in this Cittie Teachers and Professors of the holy or Hebrew Language, of the Caldean, Syriake, and Arabike or Larbey Languages, of the Italian, Spanish, French, Dutch (German) and Polish Tongues. And here be they which can speake the Persian and the Morisco, and the Turkish and the Muscovian language, and also the Sclavonian tongue, which passeth through 17 Nations. And in briefe divers other Languages fit for Ambassadors and Orators, and Agents for Merchants, and for Travailers, and necessary for all Commerce or Negotiations whatsoever.

In the eighteenth century, religious societies under the aegis of the Society for Promoting Christian Knowledge (SPCK) began to tackle the education of the adult illiterate. The religious revolt of Methodism and the emotional appeal of lay preachers made a dramatic impact on the working classes. Dr Kelly, in his *History of Adult Education in Great Britain*, points to the significance for adult education of the success of Methodism 'first and foremost because of the great moral reformation which it brought about in those who came under its influence . . . it is certain that thousands of working men and women, who, because of the poverty and hopelessness of their situation, had become idle, drunken, and dissolute, were given new hope and put on the way to being honest, sober, and industrious citizens.' The structure of the Methodist Societies themselves greatly assisted the process of self-improvement. 'The lowest unit in the organisation was the class meeting, which incidentally provided a model for later forms of working class political organisation. The weekly meeting for mutual examination and encouragement in the faith was a great training ground in the arts of democracy. Even the humblest and most illiterate might aspire to the position of class leader, and many a working man rose from class leader to local preacher, from local preacher to itinerant minister.'

The latter part of the eighteenth century was a time of great social and economic change following upon the increased industrialization and growth of factories. The Sunday School Movement was a direct response to these changes in which Methodism played an important part. The shift of population to the industrial centres, together with a dramatic increase in the total population due to improved sanitation and medical knowledge, intensified the education problem. The existing educational provision of grammar schools, private schools, charity schools and dame schools was quite unable to cope with the tremendous influx of population to the new industrial centres. Universal education, the subject of utopian treatises in the last century, now began to be urged as a practical necessity by radicals such as Tom Paine and eminent writers such as Adam Smith and Malthus. The sheer ignorance and squalor in which the poor lived in the new, industralized economic conditions prompted a new education movement on religious and humanitarian grounds. From this developed the Sunday School Movement. By 1787 Robert Raikes could claim that there were a quarter of a million children in his schools. Adult schools, having as their object the instruction of adults in reading the scriptures, made an attack on illiteracy. Not everyone approved the teaching of reading to adults. Thus Thomas Pole, writing in 1814, said, 'In prosecuting the plans for instructing the adult poor to read, we have, as might naturally be expected, met with a variety of opinion on the practicability, the propriety, and even the dangerous consequences of the scheme; and the idea of instructing persons far advanced in age, has excited even the ridicule of prejudiced individuals.'[2]

Instruction in writing as part of literacy teaching in Sunday Schools raised considerable doubts. The propriety of writing on the Sabbath as distinct from reading was strongly questioned by some. Pole's answer to such criticism would be greatly appreciated by present-day adult literacy tutors. 'We have been fully convinced that the practice of writing is an excellent mean of improving them in spelling, and consequently of greatly facilitating their learning to read; and the main force of our arguments in favour of teaching adults to write, rests upon this ground.'[3]

Equally, Dr Pole's advice on the teaching of adults would find great favour among good adult education tutors today:

> In the instruction of adults, it is not only necessary that we should feel a con-
> sciousness that Christian kindness and benevolence are the spring of our
> actions, but the whole of our conduct and deportment should be such as would
> demonstrate to them that we are their sincere friends. A softness of manners, a
> patient forebearance with the weakness of some of their capacities, or the
> occasional slowness of their comprehension; zealous and persevering endeav-
> ours to explain what they cannot at once understand, will gain their regard,
> and at the same time encourage their best efforts to overcome the difficulties
> they may meet with. But an austere deportment, the use of authoritative
> language, or impatient rebuke, will have a discouraging tendency, and frus-
> trate both their laudable desires, and the object of our own labours.[4]

Dr Kelly, from his research into Martha More's Journal, later published as *The Mendip Annals* (1859), tells the story of two redoubtable and deeply religious sisters, Hannah and Martha More. In the 1790s they overcame the opposition of Cheddar farmers to the education of their employees and established, in the Mendip villages, Sunday Schools, day schools, evening schools as well as benefit clubs for the women. The very limited aims of such workers is shown in Hannah More's description of the Schools: 'My plan for instructing the poor is very limited and strict. They learn of week-days such coarse works as may fit them for servants. I allow of no writing. My object has not been to teach dogmas and opinions, but to form the lower classes to habits of industry and virtue.'[5]

There were, however, breakaway groups from the Sunday Adult Schools who set up adult schools in which instruction was given not only in reading and writing but also in arithmetic, drawing, geography, natural history, etc. Despite the limited approach of many Sunday Schools their attack on the illiteracy of adults was a substantial leap forward. Secular education in the eighteenth century was mainly the concern of the literate middle and upper classes and, as the churches expanded their concern beyond literacy, so the two streams began to come closer together.

Coffee houses and clubs, often formed from weekly diners' meetings, sprang up in London and provided a framework for a range of varied educational activities. The demand for newspapers and books grew although the former was savagely controlled by the newspaper tax and the paper tax made both something of a luxury. Circulating and subscription libraries rose to meet the demand for books and periodicals by the new middle classes, wealthy from their commercial and industrial enterprises. A plethora of societies – literary, antiquarian, art and musical, debating, political and religious reform – grew up. Most of them were middle class in character but the London Corresponding Society (1792) was a deliberate attempt to mobilize working-class opinion. Francis Place, who was to be the mainspring of so many reform movements, joined it in 1794 when he was twenty-two and said of it:

> The moral effects of the society were very great indeed. It induced men to read books instead of spending their time at public houses; it induced them to love their own homes, it taught them to think, to respect themselves, and to desire to educate their children . . . The discussions in the Sunday afternoon reading and debating associations held in their own rooms opened to them views to which they had been blind. They were compelled by these discussions to find reasons for their opinions and to tolerate the opinions of others. In fact, it gave a new stimulus to a large mass of men who had hitherto been but too justly considered, as incapable of any but the very grossest pursuits and sensual enjoyments. It elevated them in society.[6]

The Society for the Encouragement of Arts, Manufactures and Commerce, later the Royal Society of Arts, was founded at a meeting in a London coffee house in 1754 by William Shipley, a drawing master from Northampton.

The scientific developments in industry, hitherto restricted to the Royal Society, became of widespread interest to the educated. Lectures involving experiments abounded. In London the Gresham lectures, begun in the sixteenth century, continued and included astronomy, geometry and physics as well as mathematics and chemistry. A Dr Desaguliers, a leading figure in the English Masonic movement, was a notable London lecturer of the first half of the century. He lectured regularly on mathematics and natural philosophy from 1712 until his death in 1744. In 1724–5 he gave a course of twenty-two lectures covering mechanics, hydrostatics, pneumatics and optics which he delivered on Monday evenings at a fee of two-and-a-half guineas; there was also a separate morning course of sixteen lectures on astronomy. In the second half of the century a group of itinerant lecturers made regular tours of provincial towns, giving popular lectures on the physical sciences, illustrated by quite spectacular experiments, models and demonstrations. The audiences were usually middle class and by no means exclusively male. The Professor of Natural Philosophy at Glasgow University was required, under a statute of 1727, to give a course in experimental philosophy especially designed for the general public. John Anderson, the holder of that office in 1757–96, turned this into an applied-science course for the benefit of 'the manufacturers and artificers of Glasgow'. The course met morning and evening on Tuesdays and Fridays throughout the University session at a fee of one guinea. Anderson claimed that it was attended by 'townspeople of almost every rank, age and employment'; he is alleged to have distributed free tickets to 'gardeners, painters, shopmen, founders, bookbinders, barbers, tailors, potters, glass-blowers, gunsmiths, engravers, brewers and turners.'[7]

The Spitalfields Mathematical Society, founded in 1717, was perhaps the first scientific society for the working class. It had a membership limited to 'the square of eight', mainly working men and principally weavers of Huguenot descent. It met from 8–10 p.m. on Saturday evenings, at first in taverns and later in its own rooms. In the first hour each member engaged in some mathematical exercise and, in the second, in an experiment in natural philosophy. The society acquired apparatus (air pumps, reflecting telescopes, reflecting microscopes, electrical machines, surveying instruments, etc) and a considerable members' lending library.

A witness before the Royal Commission on Hand-Loom Weavers testified, in 1840, to the extraordinary number of cultural societies which had existed in the Spitalfields area. Apart from the Spitalfields Mathematical Society there were an historical society, a floricultural society, botanical society, entomological society, recitation society, musical society and a columbarian society which gave a silver medal as a prize for the best pigeon of a fancy breed.

In the first half of the nineteenth century, therefore, it could be said that adult education was flourishing in a great variety of ways and to a limited extent at all levels. There had grown up all through the seventeenth and eighteenth centuries a widespread interest in science, stemming from the application of science to industry. This technological interest gave an impetus to the study of science for its own sake also. The universities and grammar schools were still geared to the classical tradition and little science was taught there.

During the first half of the century scientific societies sprang up in London and the provinces. The Geological Society (1807) the Royal Astronomical Society (1820), the Zoological Society (1826), The Royal Geographical Society (1830), the Royal Botanic Society (1839), the Chemical Society (1841) were national societies. In London the London Institution (1805), the Philomathic Institution (1807) and the Russell Institution pursued the study of science in the general context of science, literature and art; many provincial societies followed a similar pattern. Essentially they were societies for the general improvement of their own members but the Royal Institution in London (1799) had the wider purpose of 'defusing the knowledge and facilitating the general and speedy introduction of new and useful mechanical inventions and improvements, and also for teaching, by regular courses of philosophical lectures and experiments, the application of these discoveries in science to the improvement of arts and manufactures, and facilitating the means of procuring the comforts and conveniences of life.' In the event the Royal Institution did not develop on the lines of its declaration. Its

attempt to provide residential technical education for young mechanics in 1801 –
a time when there was serious concern about the radicalism stemming from the
French Revolution – was judged to be a 'dangerous political tendency' and was
abandoned. For many years the Institution's main activities were public-lecture
courses delivered by such men as Humphrey Davy, Michael Faraday and Sidney
Smith who attracted brilliant, fashionable audiences. But it was the chemical and
electrical researches of Davy as Professor of Chemistry from 1802–12 and of
Faraday who held that office from 1833 until 1867 which won for the Institution
an international reputation. The Royal Institution inspired similar bodies in the
provinces, the most notable being the Liverpool Royal Institution and the Royal
Manchester Institution. These institutions provided a focus for a good deal of the
lecturing on science that had previously been carried out under other auspices; but
there were still a great many independent public lecturers who were more and
more giving their lectures to a wider sector of the public. The ground was being
prepared for the establishment of institutions similar in organization to the
literary and philosophical societies – but geared much more to the working class.

   This reaching down to popular audiences by itinerant lecturers, together with
the establishment of working men's libraries, book clubs and mutual improvement societies in the eighteenth century, were the natural forerunners of a most
remarkable adult education movement – the mechanics institute movement. As
well as being an extension downwards to the working class of the more elite
philosophical and literary societies, the mechanics institute movement was an
expression of the upward thrust of the economic and political aspirations of the
working classes. In addition, the massive growth in population and the concentration of the working classes in the new industrial areas, together with the need
for better educated workmen to cope with the demands of the rapid technological
changes, provided a climate in which the mechanics institutes could grow dramatically. The term 'mechanics' did not, as now, mean a machine operative, but
rather a craftsman; it was to the skilled craftsman, of whatever trade, that the
education offered in mechanics institutes was first directed.

   The Spitalfields Mathematical Society and the Mechanical Institution, founded
in London in 1817 by Timothy Claxton, a Journeyman Mechanic, and a number
of mutual improvement societies, had already been operating for some time when
the London Mechanics Institution was founded in December 1823. Dr George
Birkbeck was its first President. Dr Birkbeck had been Professor of Natural
Philosophy at Andersons Institution, Glasgow, from 1799 to 1804. In 1800 he
established a special course 'abounding with experiments, and conducted with
the great simplicity of expression and familiarity of illustration, solely for persons
engaged in the practical exercise of the mechanical arts'.[8] Whilst he doubted
whether the course would contribute much to scientific discovery, he was
convinced 'that much pleasure would be communicated to the mechanic in the

exercise of his art, and that mental vacancy which follows a cessation from bodily toil, would often be agreeably occupied, by a few systematic ideas upon which, at his leisure, he might meditate'. The subject of the lectures was 'The mechanical affections of solid and fluid bodies'. The fact that seventy-five mechanics attended the opening night and that, by the fourth Saturday evening, the audience had risen to 500 says much for Dr Birkbeck's skill and the interest of the workmen. The course was repeated annually until he came to London in 1804. It was no surprise therefore that, in 1823, Birkbeck, now a successful London physician, was a natural choice for President of the London Mechanics Institution. The manner of its founding is of particular interest since it set the pattern for mechanics institutes throughout the country.

J.C. Robertson, editor of the newly founded *Mechanics Magazine* and Thomas Hodgskin, his associate editor, proposed the establishment of the London Mechanics Institution. Birkbeck was one of the first to come forward in support of the proposal and he played such a prominent part in it that he has come to be known as its founder. Robertson and Hodgskin sought the assistance of Francis Place and, in so doing, affected fundamentally the course of the mechanics institute movement. Place, although invaluable as an organizer of working-class support, also brought in middle-class Whigs and radicals – Henry Brougham, J.G. Lampton (later Lord Durham), J.C. Hobhouse, Sir Francis Burdett, Jeremy Bentham, James Mill, George Grote – and so gave, not only to the London Mechanics Institution but to the whole mechanics institute movement, a reputation for radicalism which it was difficult to live down. Place's influence was to have another important consequence. Robertson and Hodgskin were firmly against launching a public appeal. Hodgskin, later to become known as one of the pioneers of English Socialism, had already written in the original manifesto announcing the project, 'Men had better be without education – properly so called, for nature of herself teaches us many valuable truths – than be educated by their rulers; for then education is but the mere breaking in the steer to the yoke; . . .'[9]

Place was sure that, without an appeal, working men could not secure the necessary funds to establish the Institution. Birkbeck, as chairman, supported him. After much acrimonious debate it was agreed to launch a subscription appeal; the constitution of the institution, however, provided that two thirds of the managing committee must be working men. This decision by the London Mechanics Institution to combine self-government with support from the well-to-do was widely adopted elsewhere.

The 'Rules and Orders' of the Institution set out its objects as 'the instruction of the Members in the principles of the Arts they practise, and in the various branches of science and useful Knowledge'. There were to be lectures on science, literature and the arts (especially science); classes to teach the various branches of mathematics and their application; a reference library, lending library and reading room; a museum of 'machines, models, minerals and natural history'; and a workshop and laboratory. In his opening address Dr Birkbeck declared 'all intention of interference with political questions we do therefore disclaim . . . If indirectly we shall be supposed to exercise any influence, – and education may extend the views of the Mechanic, – I am persuaded we shall invigorate the attachment which must ever exist to every wise and well constructed system of legislation . . .'[10]

The growth of mechanics institutes spread with astonishing rapidity, especially in London where whole clusters of institutes grew up in the suburbs. A special group of institutes known as literary and scientific institutes sprang up to cater for commercial and professional people. A powerful factor in the rapid growth of mechanics institutes was a pamphlet by Henry Brougham, entitled Practical Observations upon the Education of the People, which was published in 1825 and ran through twenty editions before the end of that year. Brougham appealed to employers to assist generously the new movement and many of them did so. Alexander Galloway, a well-known engineer, was a prominent supporter of the London Institution and people like George Stephenson at Newcastle and Josiah Wedgwood at Hanley were also notable supporters. The development of mechanics institutes was very strongly opposed by the Tories; the Church either stood aside or openly opposed them. Such was the growth of institutes that Dr Hudson, writing in his *History of Adult Education* in 1850, gives a list of some 610 institutions (of which twenty-eight were in London) with 102,050 subscribing members possessing 691,500 volumes in their libraries. If the smaller mutual improvement societies, Christian and Church of England institutions and evening adult schools were added, the total number of adult education institutes for England was 700 with a membership of 107,000. The London Mechanics Institution, according to Hudson, owed a good deal of its success, if not its continued existence, 'to munificent patronage'. The number of members in the first eight years, the most important period in the history of the Institution, ranged from 750 in 1824 to a peak of 1477 members in 1826 which, by 1831, had fallen to 941. From Hudson we also learn that the letting of the Institution's hall on Sundays made it the forum of the Owenites, the Cobbettites, and Huntites and the Anti-religionists, Carlisle and Taylor. By 1831 it became apparent that a considerable change had taken place in the class of persons subscribing to the Institution:

> Each quarterly meeting was rendered notorious for undignified scenes of boyish boisterousness and disorderly debate: the attorney's clerk out-talked and ultimately out-voted the working mechanic. In the first and second year after the formation of the society the working mechanics of the Metropolis formed a large majority of the subscribers; but from 1830 to the present time

(1851) not more than 200 members, on the average, had been working men, or that class distinguished as receiving for their labour weekly wages, and for whose benefit the institution was specially established.[11]

For some years up to 1851 the institution had been little more than an association of shopkeepers and their apprentices, law copiests and attorney's clerks.

The motives that inspired the founders of mechanics institutes were varied. Employers such as Alexander Galloway sought better-educated and more industrious workmen; politicians and radicals like Brougham saw the institutes as a training ground in self-government and philanthropists like William Wilberforce hoped that they would alleviate the poverty and misery of the working classes. Only a very few regarded the institutes as Birkbeck did, that is, as agents of cultural education by liberating the mind and enriching the understanding. For most of the workers who flocked into the institutes 'Knowledge is Power' were their watch-words. But they came with a genuine interest in learning for its own sake as well as for knowledge as an instrument of personal advancement. People like Henry Hetherington and William Lovett in London saw the institutes as a means of effecting a radical reconstruction of society.

Like the London Mechanics Institution most mechanics institutes reached their peak in 1826 and, from that time on, their forward development declined. Their working-class members, often ill-educated and exhausted (or at least tired) at the end of a long day's work, could not absorb the long and systematic courses of lectures in chemistry, mechanics and hydrostatics such as the institutes attempted in their early days. Lecturers who could explain and illustrate their material were scarce and, even if available, were too expensive for most of the institutes to engage. The institutes also suffered from their almost exclusive preoccupation with scientific education. Many of their members were not really interested in science; they were interested in literature or in politics and economics but these were almost universally barred as controversial.

After a long day many people wanted something more in the nature of relaxation and social life. The early institutes made no such concessions; newspapers were excluded from the reading rooms and fiction from the libraries so the average working man returned to his public house or his club or his mutual improvement society. Whilst it is true that the institutes failed to capture and hold the interest of the masses of the working people, namely the unskilled workers, they changed their approach considerably after the mid-1820s and systematic lecture courses in science gave way to education in groups, that is, in classes, and to greater attention to literature, art and music. Lectures and short courses on the history of art and architecture became common and the lectures and classes by Benjamin Hayden from 1835 to 1839 were a highlight in the early history of the London Mechanics Institution. Art with its implications for industrial design was given an important place in mechanics institutes and similar bodies. The select committee on arts and manufactures appointed by the Government in 1835 led to the sponsoring by the Government of the establishment of special schools of design in London and a number of provincial centres. One of these was the Normal School of Design in London, later to become the Royal College of Art. These schools of design developed for the most part independently of the mechanics institutes and were absorbed into the system of technical education under the auspices of the Department of Science and Art, established in 1852. Programmes of single lectures and short courses on a variety of topics were frequently interspersed with musical entertainments, parties, concerts, excursions and exhibitions.

The mechanics institutes also had an impact on middle-class education and the literary and scientific institutions established in London in the 1820s to cater for commercial and professional workers became prototypes for the 'Athenaeums' of the Provinces, such as the Manchester Athenaeum founded in 1836. These institutions were soon monopolized by employers and professional men and combined club facilities with a more popular form of adult education than that offered by the literary and philosophical societies. Similarly, facilities for hearing and studying music were everywhere increasing. London had its Concert of Antient Music founded in 1776; the Philharmonic Society, founded in 1813; and the Sacred Harmonic Society founded in 1832, as well as English and Italian opera. For the working classes, mechanics institutes arranged the occasional cheap concert or they combined music with refreshments in a public house or in one of the casinos or music saloons. John P. Hullah, a composer and organist, and John Curwen, a congregational minister, gave a great impetus to choral singing in the 1840s by their popularization of the Sol-fa notation. In February 1841 Hullah opened a singing school at Exeter Hall, London intended for teachers in day and Sunday schools but all kinds of other people flocked to join it. The establishment of successful classes for singing led to a demand for elementary instruction in other subjects like writing, arithmetic and drawing. A move in the House of Lords to secure a Government grant for Hullah's work was rejected on the grounds of the Bishop of London's suspicion of classes without provision for religious instruction. Despite the success of Hullah's notation, after years of great rivalry it was Curwen's simpler, tonic Sol-fa system which was eventually adopted throughout the educational world. This had been publicized by his own publishing business and the establishment of a Tonic Sol-fa Association and a Tonic Sol-fa College (1879) for teachers.

Alongside the institutes there sprang up a host of other bodies, very similar in purpose and organization, in the form of mutual improvement societies. One such society arose under the auspices of the Young Men's Christian Association, founded in London in 1844 on the initiative of a young drapers' assistant, George Williams. Its purpose was defined as 'the improvement of the spiritual condition of young men engaged in the drapery and other trades by the introduction of religious services among them'. Within a year, however, in order to widen the appeal of the Association and bring in young men who might not be attracted by the religious approach, the definition was altered to read 'the improvement of the spiritual and mental condition of young men engaged in houses of business by the introduction of family or social prayer, bible classes, mutual improvement societies, or any plans strictly in accordance with the Scriptures'. In 1848 a library and reading room were opened in Gresham Street and lectures and classes were organized. In 1850 there were already 500 members and classes were held in French, German, Greek, Hebrew, arithmetic, mathematics, book-keeping, history, essay writing and psalmody. Each winter the Association organized a series of large-scale, popular lectures in Exeter Hall which ultimately became the headquarters of the London YMCA. By 1851 there were already eight London societies as well as sixteen provincial branches.

Adult Schools

Adult schools, with the object of teaching the adult poor to read the scriptures, had a period of intense growth between 1811 and 1818. In 1816 there were 135 such schools in England of which sixty-three were in Bristol and twenty in London. But with few exceptions they were short-lived. Dr J.W. Hudson in the first *History of Adult Education*, published in 1851, recalled that 'nearly all the adult schools which were in operation in 1815 to 1818 have long ceased to exist. The London institutions had a shorter career than others owing rather to the apathy evinced by the labouring population than their superior intelligence.'[12] Despite their brief existence they made a considerable impact on the problem of adult illiteracy, computed in 1815 to be '1,200,000 grown persons who from poverty or negligence of their parents had never been taught to read'. Hudson estimated that 'upwards of 30,000 of the poor in England have acquired the power of reading the New Testament'.[13]

In the 1850s it became apparent that mechanics institutes, the literary institutions and the Athenaeums were all failing to meet the needs of those for whom they were designed. 'The warehousemen, the packer, the carter and the millhand shun the society of the clerk and the foreman and they in turn quit the institution which was established expressly for them.'[14]

Lord Brougham's assertion in 1837 that 'education was less provided for in the large towns than in country districts'[15] is borne out by the abundance of mechanics institutes and literary societies in quite small country towns compared with the comparative few in densely populated, urban areas.

The growth of London's population and the failure of mechanics institutes and public societies to cater for the needs of the working man was causing considerable concern. Admittedly, a few of the crowded public houses and beer shops made newspapers available and some set aside nights for political discussions or, as in the Kennington Road, for lectures in astronomy. In 1840 an improvement society for the religious, moral and intellectual improvement of men engaged in 'manufactories', by means of a library and lecturers, was established in Lambeth. In 1846–9 the society extended its influence by setting up auxiliary societies in Vauxhall, Westminster, Shadwell, Bermondsey, Millwall and Southwark but, despite an appeal for membership to seventy manufacturers, only 250 members enrolled. Many of the large linen drapers set up libraries for their young employees. That at Messrs Sewell and Co. in 1850 exceeded 1000 volumes and a few others in London, including Messrs Hitchcock and Rogers and Swan and Edgar, had libraries and reading rooms and occasional lectures and discussions for their young men.

The disappointment at the failure of the Reform Act of 1832 to emancipate the working classes led to a concentration on political objectives in movements and societies quite independent of, and sometimes in opposition to, the mechanics institutes. Francis Place, William Lovett and Henry Hetherington in London were active in the work of mechanics institutes; Thomas Hodgskin who, with J.C. Robertson, inspired the foundation of the London Mechanics Institution, used that institution for his anti-capitalist lectures, afterwards published as the *Popular Political Economy*. Most mechanics institutes, however, were so anxious to avoid the taint of radicalism that they virtually excluded politics and political economy. Nevertheless, the programme of the Hampden clubs and the early co-operative movement, for example the London Co-operative and Economical Society and the British Association for the Promotion of Co-operative Knowledge founded on the ideas of Robert Owen, all had a considerable educational content. Lovett and Hetherington formed the National Union of Working Classes; in 1836 this became the London Working Men's Association and gave a high priority to education. Lovett tried to carry his comprehensive educational ideas into the fast-developing Chartist movement but lacked the means to carry it through.[16] Nevertheless, the contribution to working-class education by the Chartists was considerable.

Despite the growth of educational and social institutions in the first half of the century they lacked the amenities or ambience to attract the unskilled or labouring classes. For the youth leaving 'the free schools (National, British and Congregational) the cheap academies and the Sunday schools for work' there was no provision.

> The youth who leave these schools have acquired a taste for learning which should not, as at present, be obliterated from their minds as soon as they are introduced as apprentices, or assistants in shops and manufactories where crowded assemblages of human beings work in close contact and exercise a

powerful influence over the future career of the noviciate, and upon all who are so associated. The establishment of *free* circulating libraries, of *free* newsrooms and cheap evening schools, might effect much good, at little cost, when that cost is measured by the generosity of the wealthy. [17]

This comment by Dr Hudson in 1851 comes to the heart of the matter. Despite all the progress made, and undoubted progress there had been throughout the seventeenth and eighteenth centuries, and the intense activity in the nineteenth century, the efforts of the many voluntary organizations were patently failing to deal with the great problem of the increased populations of urban areas. In particular, they were not providing for those who had virtually no basic education and felt unable to avail themselves of facilities which were primarily the concern of craftsmen and the better educated. Indeed, it may well be true that there were more adults able to read and write in the eighteenth century than there were in the intensely industralized urban population of the nineteenth. As early as 1837 the farsighted Lord Brougham had seen that voluntary organizations could barely cope with the educational needs of the existing population and could in no way deal with the additional demands which stemmed from the rapidly increasing populations of the urban areas. In the same year William Lovett and the Chartists proposed their comprehensive plan of public education. The great majority believed, however, that the education of the people was a matter for voluntary effort.

The first grant of £20,000 by the State towards the education of the people was made in 1833 – £20,000 equalled the amount set aside for the upkeep of the Royal Stables in that year. The money was distributed by the Treasury on the advice of the two principal voluntary organizations, namely, the National Society for Educating the Poor in the Principles of the Established Church (founded in 1811) and the British and Foreign Schools Society (founded in 1814). From then on grants from the State were gradually increased. There was, however, no general belief in the value of education for its own sake and child labour was so much a part of the working life of the poor that parents were loth to forego the income, pitifully small that it was, which children of the tenderest years could provide.

In 1840 the first two of Her Majesty's Inspectors, appointed by the Committee of the Privy Council in Education, began to report on the education of the people, including 'night schools'. The Rev. W.J. Kennedy, HMI in his report for 1848 was highly critical of the use of child labour which caused children to leave school at an early age and urged that night schools should be encouraged in which 'youths should systematically carry on the education which they have commenced in the elementary school. The same buildings would serve. What is wanted is the masters and funds to pay them. I see no way to bring about this vital measure except by large special assistance from the Committee in Council.' [18]

From 1851 the Committee agreed to grant-aid evening schools but was insistent that teachers should not work three sessions a day and so endanger their day-school duties and, in particular, their supervision of the evening studies of pupil teachers. Grants were given to enable an additional teacher to be employed so that a certificated teacher could take charge of the evening school without working three sessions. Fees had to equal the amount of the Government grant. Outside large towns these conditions made the development of evening schools difficult.

Reference has already been made (page 10) to the support given by the Government to the teaching of art to improve industrial design. In 1856 the Science and Art Department of the Board of Trade and the Education Establishment of the Privy Council were brought together in a new Education Department. The two divisions remained in their separate headquarters: the Science and Art Department in South Kensington and the Education Department in Whitehall. A Code, issued annually by the Education Department, set out the conditions and criteria for grants; the Science and Art Directory, published annually from 1860, served the same purpose for the Science and Art Department.

In 1861 the Education Department issued its Revised Code, introducing the system of payment by results. Managers of schools received grants on the attainments of children as assessed at the annual examination in reading, writing and arithmetic. In 1862 the regulations for evening schools were brought into line and payments were made to managers of evening schools (and to individual teachers) on the attendance and attainments of evening-school pupils assessed at an annual examination in reading, writing and arithmetic. The regulations which restricted day-school teachers from teaching in the evening school were withdrawn. The Instructions to Inspectors, which accompanied the Revised Code of 1862, set out the functions of the evening school as follows:

> The evening school should differ in nothing from the morning or afternoon meetings except in the scholars who attend. Its business is not secondary but continued elementary instruction. A few scholars here and there may be fit for more advanced instruction and may be glad to find at the evening meeting a room in which they can study and obtain assistance . . . As the object of attendance in the evening is to fix and perfect elementary knowledge, scholars who have passed under Standard VI are not precluded from being examined and bringing grants to the school by their examination. [19]

The Science and Art Department set out to organize a system of evening-science schools. From 1862 it based its grants on the attendance and attainment of the students at an annual examination. An important difference in the allocation of grants was that they were paid to the individual teacher qualified to teach under the Directory. The classes could be held in any suitable premises, many being held in ordinary evening schools alongside those operating under grants from the Education Department. A class had to meet for at least forty lessons, examinations in each subject in the Directory were held in May of each year, a separate evening being assigned for each examination; the question papers were prepared by the Science and Art Department and sent from South Kensington by post and the work papers returned there to be marked. Teachers received a grant for each student of the industrial classes, that is, those who received weekly wages and were below the level of income tax, to whom he had given at least forty lessons. Five pounds was paid for each first-class pass, £4 for a second-class pass, £3 for a third, £2 for a fourth, £1 for a fifth and nothing for a failure. The Department did not organize classes; it acted as an examining body which administered grants.

G.T.C. Bartley, an examiner in the Science and Art Department, assessed the work of the Department from 1857 to 1869 in the *Schools for the People*, published in 1871. He considered that the plan in operation since 1860 had been successful because it had offered enterprising teachers the opportunity to form classes without irksome conditions.

> The plans from 1853 to 1860 all seemed to aim at awakening the locality to a sense of its duties and responsibilities, to perform the task of educating its artisan classes, not only without profit to itself, but as a sacrifice of both time and money. The new plan held out pecuniary inducements direct to teachers. It said, 'If you will qualify yourself to teach, passing such and such an examination, the state will remunerate you for every artisan you can succeed in educating up to a certain standard; the amount of the remuneration to be in proportion to the instruction imparted; if, on the contrary the teaching is deficient and brings forth no fruit at the annual examination, no payment is to be made'. The country desired science instruction for its artisans and it obtained it at first cost without the establishment of any expensive machinery. All the risk of success, the chief work of organising the schools and getting the pupils together, fell upon the teachers, whose pecuniary interest it was to make the classes successful.[20]

So much for the artisan and for those who had had some form of basic education. The majority of evening schools, however, were concerned with the elementary education of young people and adults who had never been to day school or who had attended day school and largely forgotten what they had learned there. Of these schools Bartley says that they were usually for adults or those over the ages of seventeen or eighteen who:

> . . . feel their extreme ignorance and have an earnest desire to improve their condition . . . The subjects taught are almost exclusively reading, writing and arithmetic, though writing is usually the favourite. Those who attend regularly are often very energetic in their endeavours to get on . . . Many pupils, however, only attend for a few nights and get totally disheartened by the discovery of their own ignorance. In a flourishing evening class at the Parochial School, Shoreditch, out of 1300 who have attended in eight years, no fewer than 300 left before they received a week's instruction. This can hardly be

wondered at. Young lads and even girls of 18 or 19 who, up to that age, have been taught nothing, find the drudgery of going through the rudiments very great, and almost unbearable.[21]

In addition, there were evening schools for those boys and girls who were 'excluded from the regular Sunday or day school in consequence of their ragged and filthy condition and also the great numbers who constantly infest our streets and alleys to idle, to steal or do mischief'.[22] These, the Ragged Schools, established in 1844, were evening schools open on one or two evenings of the week. As the work was extended some of them were open on every night of the week and, in addition to teaching basic skills, 'industrial classes' were added. By 1870 there were 217 of these night schools in London attended by 10,000 older boys and girls, meeting on two or three evenings a week.[23] Supported entirely by voluntary funds and helpers they were often the means whereby many well-known figures of the late-nineteenth century received their first introduction to the conditions of the poor by working as helpers. Dr Barnardo, as a medical student, helped with a Ragged School in Stepney; in the same year Quintin Hogg began his work with London working boys in a Ragged School just off Charing Cross.

The evening schools for artisans, those which provided an elementary education; those associated with co-operative societies and mutual improvement societies which provided mainly for the political education of the working man; and those like the Working Men's College which provided a general and informal education, all grew up in their quite separate ways, appearing to have little contact with each other. Most of them, however, were hampered by their students' lack of basic education and were attempting in the evening a task which should have been done largely by an organized system of education in the daytime. Meanwhile the demand for a more comprehensive system of State aid for education gained ground. The introduction of payment by results in the revised Code of 1861 had been followed by a sharp fall in State grant from £813,000 in 1861 to £673,000 in 1865.[24] Voluntary organizations were clearly unable to do more than strive to keep pace with the rising population. Whilst there could be arguments about the actual statistics there was no doubt about the growing educational destitution in the great cities and nowhere was this more apparent that in the great metropolis of London.

In 1870 W.E. Forster, Vice-President of the Committee of the Council, firmly backed by Gladstone as Prime Minister, introduced his Elementary Education Act which aimed to fill the gaps which the voluntary system left unfilled. One major obstacle to the setting-up of an education system had been the absence of any adequate units of local government capable of raising and administering local funds for schools. The original intention was to set up School Boards comprised of representatives from borough councils and parish vestries but the Bill was amended and the Boards recruited by direct election with funds raised by precepts on the vestries. The Boards, in the absence of large units of local government, represented a bold experiment in directly elected institutions. It had not been intended to apply the 1870 Act to London, the original intention being for the metropolis to be dealt with in a later Bill which would divide the capital up into small units of administration based on the workhouse-school districts and the vestry boundaries. In the event an amendment by Mr W.M. Torrens, MP for Finsbury and a member of the first School Board for London brought London under the Bill and designated the area of the Metropolitan Board of Works (114 square miles) as the area over which the School Board for London would have jurisdiction. London was divided into ten electoral divisions; the City, Southwark, Chelsea and Greenwich divisions returned four members each; Lambeth, Tower Hamlets, Hackney and Westminster five members each; Finsbury six and Marylebone seven. Each elector could cast as many votes as there were seats in his division. The vote could be used cumulatively, the voter could cast all his votes for a single candidate if he wished or spread them through the list. The voting was by secret ballot – anticipating the Ballot Act for Parliamentary elections.

The fact that the School Board was an authority charged with the sole purpose of developing a single service attracted people who were specially interested in education. By common consent the quality of the candidates was high. For the first time women were allowed to stand for election and two distinguished women were elected to the School Board for London, Miss Emily Davis and Dr Elizabeth Garrett, later Mrs Elizabeth Garrett Anderson, the first woman doctor. They were to be the first of a long line of distinguished members of the School Board and councillors who have played a notable part in London's education service. Thomas Gautrey, in *Lux Mihi Laus: School Board Memories* (1937), gives a fascinating sketch of some of the members whom he described collectively as 'liberal minded men and women filled with confidence and buoyant hopes'. He himself was connected with the Board throughout its thirty-three year life as teacher, union leader and member. Religious denominations were represented in strength; the Anglicans included two future bishops and later the Rev. Stewart Headlam who combined Christian socialism with a passion for evening schools; the Free Churches had as their spokesman Dr J.H. Rigg, Principal of the Wesleyan Training College in Horseferry Road, Westminster; and the Roman Catholics, who had not contested the elections as a body but had benefited from the cumulative vote, included Father (later Bishop) W.F. Brown who represented Southwark.

London had gone to the polls for the first time to elect an education authority in an atmosphere which was described as almost euphoric. The School Board for London met for the first time at the Guildhall (by invitation of the City) on 15 December 1870. Lord Lawrence, a former Viceroy of India, was elected as its first Chairman. The Board set up an administration with £25 in the petty cash. There were eighty-nine applicants for the top job of Clerk with a salary of £800 a year, the successful candidate being George Croad, a Cambridge graduate who had taught for ten years and at the time of his appointment was Secretary of the Bishop of London's Fund. He held office for almost the whole of the period of the Board's existence, retiring in 1902 on grounds of ill-health. As the senior administrative officer he managed the Board's affairs but was in no sense a Director of Education or an Educational Adviser since this was not a function which the Board recognized. Mr Thomas Smith, the Headmaster of Hampton Gurney Church of England School, Marylebone, became the first Clerk to the all-important School Management Committee and Mr Thomas Spalding was appointed, and remained, Secretary to the Chairman throughout the life of the Board. He later wrote a highly informative record of the Board's work for presentation at the Paris Exhibition in 1900.

London's education service had begun.

2. The School Board for London: 1870 – 1904

It is an unusual occurrence in the history of English institutions that a local authority should be called into existence without having any predecessor to whose duties it succeeded and that its existence should be of short duration. The School Board was the creation of the Act of 1870 and its extinction is due to the Act of 1903 . . . It was compelled to break entirely new ground, and to solve a problem which had perplexed Parliament for the greater part of the Century.[1]

There is no doubt that the task which faced the School Board for London was immense. Section 67 of the 1870 Act required that within four months from the appointment of its Chairman, the Board should submit a return to the Education Department containing such particulars in respect of elementary schools and children requiring elementary education as the Department might demand. The information required was very comprehensive. The Board appointed agents to analyse replies from over 3000 schools and to give the estimated population of London in each of the ten electoral divisions of the metropolis.

With the aid of information from the April 1871 census made available to the Board's enumerators, somewhat reluctantly, by the Registrar General, the Board calculated that the population of London on 2 April 1871 was 3,265,005. Of this, 681,000 were children between three and thirteen years, of whom 97,307 were being educated at home or in schools which charged 9d. or more a week and were therefore not of the social class for whom elementary schools had to be provided. Another 9,101 were inmates of institutions. This left 574,693 for whom elementary schooling was required.

The second part of the operation – determining how many children were already in school and whether the schools were efficient – was a most complicated task. The Board appointed local divisional committees who, in turn, appointed superintendents and enumerators. The task of assessing efficiency was subcontracted to HMIs seconded for the purpose by the Education Department.

Eventually it was calculated that 95,975 children could be said to have valid excuses for non-attendance and the estimated total number of places required was therefore 478,718. An arbitrary deduction of 5 per cent to allow for legitimate absentees brought the total number of places required to 454,783. There were 1399 schools, partly or wholly efficient, which provided accommodation for 350,920 pupils, leaving a deficiency of 103,863 places. Two children in every nine were unprovided for.

There is no doubt that the Board, aghast at the task revealed, was anxious to present the lowest possible figures. In their Final report (1904) the Board indicated that the shortfall of places had been nearer 250,000. Their task was not to lighten with the years. Between 1871 and 1904 the population of London increased from 3,265,000 to 4,536,000. The increase in population alone was greater than the combined population of Manchester and Liverpool in 1901.

In 1870 London wàs lagging behind the rest of the country in school provision. Even with Government subvention the voluntary system had been unable to cope for some time. In London it was certainly true that between 1837 and 1868 there had been no improvement in the proportion of school places to school children. The main cause was the cost of sites. 'In the heart of a crowded city the price of land runs up to a figure which is prohibitive to the charitably inclined and it is precisely where the population is densest that school buildings are most required. The task had become impossible save by a state or municipal effort, coupled with the power of acquiring sites compulsorily in districts where school accommodation was needed.'[2]

Between 1871 and 1904 the Board was to provide 559,667 places in 475 permanent schools – a staggering achievement.

Speaking on the first reading of the Bill which was to become the Elementary Education Act of 1870, Mr W.E. Forster said, 'We are aware that by no Bill dealing with this matter can we hope to effect real good unless it be a Bill which does not merely meet present necessities, but is also capable of development so as to meet the necessities of the future. Indeed no Bill would really meet the needs of today unless its provisions are likewise adapted to meet the needs of tomorrow.'[3]

The Act lacked two definitions of prime importance – it did not define 'a child' or the scope of elementary education. Neither did it indicate the times at which a child should be educated. Certainly in the minds of those who drew up the Act, elementary education meant Reading, Writing and Arithmetic. Also, the Education Department's Code for 1870 which determined whether grant should be paid or not was very limited; it recognised Reading, Writing and Arithmetic only for all Standards and one specific subject for children beyond Standard 6.

The first draft of the Bill made twelve the maximum age for the permissive compulsion which Boards could apply. The age was raised to thirteen during the committee stage of the Bill.

The role of the Education Department had little relationship to what we have come to expect of a central Ministry. 'We look through the 1870 Act in vain for any suggestion that the Education Department was to perform a function even remotely similar to that of a modern Minister of Education in promoting the education of the people . . . the role of the 1870 Education Department was to be more that of a central paymaster than that of a Ministry.'[4]

Initially, the lack of definition in the Act of 1870 enabled the School Board for London to extend the conception of elementary education: ultimately it was to be the cause and occasion of its demise.

High Hopes and Failure: 1870–82

The Elementary Education Act 1870 did not specifically empower School Boards to provide evening schools; but, since it did not define the hours during which schools should be open, there was nothing in the Act to prevent their establishment. Moreover, the Education Department for some time had recognized evening schools run by voluntary agencies and had assisted them with grants limited to the teaching of Reading, Writing and Arithmetic. The Act did not define the maximum age at which a child should cease to attend a school although it did make it illegal to compel the child's attendance after the age of thirteen.

It was the intention of the Board to establish evening schools concurrently with day schools primarily to provide opportunities for those children who for a variety of reasons could not or were not likely to attend during the day and to reinforce the instruction given at day schools. The evening school which had existed previously to 1870 was a school in which young persons who had passed school age, and were earning their living during the day time might obtain those rudiments of education during the evening which they had failed to acquire in their childhood. The instruction given was usually one of the most elementary character and the idea of the evening school as an institution in which well instructed youths could continue and expand the education of their school days was not even conceived. The uneducated were too many and the half educated too few for such a plan to be practicable. It could only be dreamt of as a future possibility when the day schools had raised a more educated generation.[5]

When the establishment of evening schools was being considered in 1872 the Department's Code of that year defined the maximum age of scholars in both day and evening schools as eighteen. It was not clear whether this was a bar to earning grant or a more general prohibition of expenditure on the education of people over eighteen. The Board's solicitor advised the Board that if it educated people over eighteen without charging a fee which covered the whole cost of their education, the Board was liable to have the cost disallowed by the Local Government Board. The Board, acting upon his advice, resolved that, without incurring any expense, it would grant the use of school rooms to properly constituted committees for the purpose of carrying on evening schools for persons over eighteen.

There is little doubt that this aspect greatly inhibited the Board in establishing evening classes. Nevertheless the Board's Committee on the scheme of education said:

. . . evening schools are of great importance, partly as a means of providing elementary education for those who, for various reasons, fail to obtain sufficient instruction in elementary day schools and partly because it is easy to connect with such schools special classes in which a higher kind of instruction than that contemplated by Standard 6 can be given to the more intelligent and elder scholars. In this manner the advantages of further instruction may be secured for those scholars who are unable or unwilling to go into secondary schools, but who are both able and willing to pay for instruction of a more advanced kind than that given in primary schools.[6]

The Committee advised, and the Board agreed, that the curriculum for evening schools for young persons under the age of eighteen should be of the same character as in day schools and the managers of evening schools were advised to adapt the instruction given to the requirements of the localities in which the schools were situated and to establish where possible science and art classes in consultation with the Science and Art Department. Following an early approach by the Science and Art Department (Kensington) the Board in 1873 resolved that all permanent schools could be used for science and art evening classes provided that the cost was met without demands on the Board's funds.

The Board, already conscious of the potential demands on its funds and the doubtful legality of expenditure on adults, passed this resolution 'under the influence of the enforced prudence which immediately precedes a triennial election'.[7]

In its initial enthusiasm the Board instructed the School Management Committee to consider and report on the desirability of opening evening schools during the winter of 1871–2. Managers were urged to establish evening schools wherever possible. The notice was short and managers were fully engaged in a reorganization of day schools. Very few evening schools opened. A request by the Board to the School Management Committee that more should be done to open more evening schools brought a stalling reply from the Committee that they were prepared to consider any requests properly recommended by a duly constituted body of managers. It was clear that in the pressure of school work 'evening schools were evidently being crushed out of consideration'.[8]

The final blow to the Board's first attempt to establish evening schools came in a resolution of the Board in 1873 that 'no evening school should be opened unless at least 40 names were entered on the register or continued if the average attendance at the previous month fell below 20'.[9]

For frank comment one can do no better than turn to the chapter on Evening Continuation Schools in *The Work of the School Board for London* produced in 1900 for the Paris Exhibition. S.E. Bray, the Inspector of Evening Continuation Schools, said:

. . . the plan which had originally been proposed was somewhat ahead of the requirements of the time. To bring it to fruition, and to attract pupils to the schools, a long period of nursing was essential. The evening schools required to be forced into popularity. To refuse to establish such a school because 40 scholars could not be enrolled, and to insist upon closing such a school because the average attendance fell in any one month below 20 was to deny the scheme a chance of success. The attendance at an evening school must of necessity be irregular, the scholars attend, after a long day's labour, and many of them, under pressure, are compelled to work overtime at their callings. It is no evidence of waning interest in their evening studies if they sometimes, or even frequently, fail to attend at the evening class.[10]

Evening schools could not develop in such a climate. Their end came in an odd manner. In June 1875 the School Management Committee, on what could only have been a pretext, recommended that evening schools should not be created to meet the needs of half-timers and that the resolutions of the Board for establishing evening schools be rescinded; that no evening schools should be conducted directly by the Board but that use of the Board's schools should be granted for evening classes to voluntary organisers at a small charge for rent.

The Committee's recommendations were adopted by the Board apparently without challenge or debate and the press appears to have taken no notice of the resolution!

This sudden waning of the Board's initial enthusiasm can only be explained by the fact that, at the time, it was under considerable and persistent criticism for alleged lavish expenditure and it resolved 'to destroy, with as little publicity as possible, a branch of the work which was costly without being popular'.[11]

The Board did not return to the question of evening schools until 1882.

Hope Renewed: 1882–1904

Towards the end of the 1870s there was a growing feeling that, although the Board had spent vast sums on elementary education, their scholars had been left high and dry afterwards. The period immediately after leaving school it was felt, was one of the most dangerous periods in a child's life, and evening schools could be well-nigh self-supporting. On 5 November 1879 the Board resolved on the motion of Thomas Heller, seconded by Sidney Buxton:

That the School Management Committee be instructed to consider and report generally upon the state of higher elementary education in the Metropolis; and to bring up such recommendations as may seem desirable for the improvement and extension of such education, more particularly by all, or any, of the following means:
(1) the establishment of higher elementary schools;
(2) the grading of existing elementary schools;
(3) the establishment of night schools and night classes in connection with the City and Guilds and other voluntary agencies, such classes to lead up

to the proposed technical schools and colleges;
(4) the insertion in the Government Code of four or five additional higher standards. [12]

The resolution was supported by the Hon. Lyulph Stanley who was to become one of the stalwarts of the Board.

The School Management Committee did not report. On 21 July 1881 the Board resolved, again on the motion of Thomas Heller, 'That a special committee be appointed to consider and report upon the best means of organising evening classes for ordinary and science subjects in the schools of the Board.' On 20 July 1882 the special committee whose Chairman, not surprisingly, was Thomas Heller reported and asked for powers to establish classes in:

(a) elementary instruction under the conditions of the Code (elementary classes);
(b) instruction in subjects recognised by the Science and Art Department and by the City and Guilds of London Institute and in such special subjects that the Board may from time to time approve (advanced classes). [13]

The committee also determined that a responsible teacher be appointed at a fee of 12s. a week or 4s. an evening and an assistant (where the average attendance exceeded thirty) at 7s. 6d. a week or 2s. 6d. an evening. The fees for elementary students were 3s. a term or 3d. a week; advanced students paid 2s. 6d. a winter session of two terms or 5s. a winter session of two terms in any three subjects. [14] The advanced classes had, for some time, been taught by persons who rented the Board's rooms.

For the next few years the classes were conducted in the following manner:

Your Committee think that the cost of establishing and maintaining these classes other than that arising from the use of rooms, cleaning, fuel, gas and educational appliances should be met by the fees of the scholars, the Government grant and such other assistance as may be applied from voluntary sources. It is further necessary to state that in the working of classes not recognized in the Code no charge whatever can be made on the school fund. [15]

Or, as S.E. Bray put it, 'The Board, in the spirit of its motto "Lux mihi laus" determined to dispense a little light in the evenings as well as during the day.' [16]

A Successful Second Start: 1882–90

Eighty-three evening schools, forty-three for men and forty for women opened in various parts of London in 1882 and 9000 students enrolled. Men outnumbered women by two to one. The evening schools were purely elementary in character, miniature reproductions of day schools and subject to almost the same conditions with Standard distinctions and Standard examinations by HM Inspectors with restrictive regulations as to class and specific subjects of instruction.

The graph (Appendix A(i)) shows the progress that was made in the years following.

In 1883 – 4, to encourage the teaching of commercial subjects of science and art the Board allowed, at a nominal fee, the use of school buildings to responsible teachers and others who might wish to provide classes in more advanced work, especially under the regulations of the Science and Art Department (Kensington). The Board exercised little supervision over these classes and no financial responsibility. Higher education work was thus left to individual and unofficial effort. Supported by the demand for study of science and modern languages, particularly by young London teachers, and the fees and substantial grants from the Science and Art Department, the provision of more advanced classes made a fairly successful beginning with 1300 students.

The session 1884 – 5 more than recovered the drop of 38.6 per cent on 1883 – 4 attributed to poor publicity and the novelty which attended the opening of evening classes after twelve years absence. A more liberal allocation of staff, reduction of weekly fees, the introduction of prizes for regular attendance, the establishment of French classes and a general encouragement of a closer connection between elementary and advanced classes were special features of this session.

In 1885 the London Trades Council asked the Board for recreative and practical subjects (such as musical drill, singing, drawing, modelling, carving, cookery, sewing, etc.), oral teaching and object lessons illustrated by 'the lantern' to be introduced into evening schools. The Board consented to these suggestions and also accepted voluntary help in the schools. The Recreative Evening Schools Association was formed in that year – a voluntary union of educationalists to give 'an impetus to class enterprise by introducing into the curricula, at their own cost, such subjects of instruction of a semi-recreative character as would more effectively appeal to those young people, who suffering from physical exhaustion after a heavy day's labour, either had no inclination for evening study or having such inclination, desire mental food of an easily digestible nature'.[17]

The Association began to carry out some of its proposals in the second term of 1885 – 6. The Board welcomed the co-operation of the Association and the Evening Schools Committee expressed their appreciation of the Association's help in its annual report to the Board. Over a period of seven years the Association supplied evening schools with musical instruments and portable apparatus for musical drill, with lantern and slides to illustrate instruction in geography, history and popular science. It also introduced vocal music, clay modelling, wood carving and domestic economy. Without doubt the Association gave an impetus and lasting impression to evening school work which broke the stranglehold of the limited Education Department Code and the consequent restriction on grant which it imposed on the Board. After seven years of vigorous extension of its work it dissolved itself when it judged the Board was in a position to continue the work it had begun. There is no doubt that the leap from 9300 students in 1884 – 5 to almost 14,000 in 1885 – 6 was due to the impact of the Association and the boost it gave to teachers in the evening schools.

It is only fair to say that the Board itself had tried to expand and liberalize the work of the schools. 'The conditions of the Education Department Code prevented the Board from accomplishing the chief purpose of an evening school. Consequently they asked the Education Department to alter the Code in such a way as to admit the establishment of a type of evening school which would be more suited to the needs of pupils who were becoming better educated year by year in the day schools.' [18]

In December 1884 the Board asked that there should be special schedules of subjects and that the ground to be covered by students in one year should be reduced since 'the requirement of the Department that an evening school scholar should cover as much ground as a day school scholar was unreasonable'. [19]

The Board also added that attendances of students should be recognized for grant without the need for them to submit themselves for examination in the standard elementary subjects. They wished students to be presented in the Standard as low as Standard 2, however.

Apart from the addition of elementary drawing no changes were made in the Code and in 1887 the Board made representations to the Royal Commission on the working of the Education Acts urging that students above Standard 4 (instead of Standard 7) should be allowed to take additional subjects. In 1889 the Board presented a 'memorial' to the Prime Minister and Lord President of the Council embodying points already made and urging that, as recommended by the Royal Commission on the working of the Education Acts, evening continuation schools should be made an integral part of the elementary system of education and 'adapted to the needs of boys and girls so as to attract and interest tired children and prepare them for activities of life'. [20]

During 1886 – 8 both elementary and advanced classes gained in numbers, strength and importance. In 1888 the order to disallow expenditure on adults over twenty-one years in elementary classes was a considerable setback. The Board had at first refused admission of such adults to elementary classes, then admitted them at a high fee and eventually decided to show its disapproval of the Education Department's uncertain guidance on the legal age of admission by admitting adults as students on the same terms as younger pupils. A few months afterwards the Board took an important step in counteracting the setback in development by appointing nine organizers whose duty it was to supervise classes and advise the Board on the best methods of obtaining increased efficiency in the evening schools. The organizers, however, had other duties during the day and could only devote their evenings to the work. The wide field of their duties also prevented them from fully concentrating on particular weaknesses of organization of teaching.

Nevertheless, in the session 1889–90, there was an increase of 4000 in the elementary classes alone and instruction in the French language was taken up with great vigour. For the first time classes showed such vitality that evening schools were permitted to extend their courses until July instead of ceasing at Easter, a practice which has continued ever since.

Attempts were being made about this time to promote a Technical Education Bill which would give School Boards power to provide technical education in day and evening schools. The London School Board urged the Education Department to support such a Bill. The Bill was made unnecessary, however, by the Technical Instruction Act of 1889 which authorized the London County Council and the other multi-purpose county authorities created by the Local Government Act 1888–9 to raise a penny rate for technical and manual instruction.

The School Board for London in a variety of moves including, in 1890, being appointed as a local committee for the operation of the Science and Art Directory, fought a strong rearguard action to retain and extend the provision for commercial subjects and science and art in its evening continuation schools. But the writing was already on the wall and the process by which the new authorities would eventually replace the School Board by the end of the century had begun.

Before that was to happen, however, the evening schools of the Board were to experience a period of development and intensive growth. In February 1890 the Board made a further attempt to induce the Education Department to modify the Code. It joined with the Leeds School Board in a deputation on the subject. At the same time the Recreative Evening Schools Association prepared a 'memorial' and asked the Board to adopt it or a modification of it. The Board submitted a memorial to the Education Department asking for amendments they had previously requested, quoting in support the final report of the Royal Commission on the work of the Education Acts (the Cross Commission)

> . . . on the need for evening schools to fix and make permanent the day school instruction and for more money for such schools: the thorough revision of the system which would enable local managers to submit special curriculum and schedules of standards suited to the needs of the locality; fixed grants instead of grants in individual examinations; the abolition of the need for evening school students to pass in the three elementary subjects as a condition of taking additional subjects; the removal of superior age limits; the organising of evening schools chiefly as schools for maintaining and continuing the education received in the day school.

At last the persistent representations were heeded and, in 1890, the Education Department's Code was radically changed to accord with the recommendations of the Cross Commission which the Board had quoted in its memorial. So radical were the changes in the Code that the Code was in danger of repealing, if not the 1870 Act, then previous definitions of elementary education derived from the Act; a Bill was prepared and rushed through Parliament to authorize what had been stated in the 1890 Code.[21]

A Real Advance: 1890–99

The Education Act declared that Section 3 of the 1870 Act (which provided that elementary education should be the principal part of the education given in schools) should not apply to evening schools.
Other changes included:
1. Book-keeping, German, shorthand, needlework and laundrywork which were added to grant-earning subjects;
   Science and art, manual training and physical exercises were recognized as part of the curriculum though no grant was given from the Education Department;
   Latitude was allowed in the teaching of English, geography, elementary science and cookery.
2. It was no longer necessary for students to be examined in the elementary subjects (Reading, Writing and Arithmetic) in order to earn a grant on special subjects of instruction.

The first change enabled the Board to take sole responsibility for the management of advanced classes which had been growing in importance year by year. The second allowed the student to be examined in a particular subject without the drudgery of an examination in the three elementary subjects (the three Rs).

In 1890–91 as a consequence there was a dramatic increase of 12,000 students over the previous year. A good part of the increase was due to the inclusion of swimming for the first time as a subject of instruction specifically encouraged by the Board.

In 1892 the Recreative Evening Schools Association, which had done so much to liberalize the curriculum of evening schools, no longer felt justified 'in continuing to throw on a few generous contributors a burden which might now be legally met by an insignificant addition to the rates.'[22] It asked the Board to purchase its stock. This the Board did, resolving, 'That the best thanks of the Board should be accorded to the Recreative Evening Schools Association for the valuable assistance which they have rendered to the Board's evening schools during the past seven years.'[23]

In 1893 a separate Education Code was issued for evening continuation schools – a name which was adopted by the Board in place of evening schools. The new Code gave freedom to managers and teachers in the organization of schools and allowed students liberty in the number and wider choice of subjects. It recognized the attendance of adult students at evening schools and substituted inspection of schools for the former examination of individual students. One of the special features of the Code of 1893 was the introduction of a syllabus on 'the life and duties of the citizen'. The extent of the change in the approach of the new Code is illustrated by some preliminary notes to this syllabus: 'The object of the teachers should be to proceed from the known to the familiar, such as policemen, the rate collector, the Board of Guardians and the Town Council, to the history of, and reasons for, our local and national institutions, and our responsibilities in connection with them.'

In the event this course attracted a meagre response despite the use of special lecturers by the Board. History, including literature, also failed to attract many students but those subjects which students considered to be of practical use were more strongly supported. Needlework, which included dress-cutting and dress-making, was very popular. Similarly, the demand for typewriting caused the Board to increase its hiring of twenty-four typewriters in 1894 to ninety-six in 1897. Whilst students were inclined to take subjects which would assist them in their occupation, a substantial number of students also took up vocal music which, as a result of the new Code, the Board could offer in evening continuation schools and 'at centres where it was possible to combine the various voices'.[24] Small beginnings were also made in teaching the violin, gymnastics, life-saving and first-aid.

The Ship Masters Society told the Board that ship-wrecks and other disasters at sea were frequently traceable to a lack of technical knowledge among officers of the mercantile marine and suggested that 'a class should be opened at one or more schools on each side of the Thames, where the sons of watermen, pilots, masters, mates, marine engineers and seamen of all grades might have an opportunity of acquiring a theoretical knowledge of navigation'.[25] The Board decided to offer navigation in the Gill Street, Limehouse Day School and also at two evening schools; 'but the experiment in the latter schools was not successful as those who needed the instruction were not long enough on land to be able to attend the classes with credit'.[26]

The tables (pages 34–38) show the growth of the curriculum during the period 1889–1903.

The era of advanced work (that is, post-elementary) had now really begun. Science classes increased in number and gradually grew into science schools; commercial subjects were becoming more popular every year. 'Workshops were being multiplied and utilised in evening education, wood carving was receiving more encouragement, laundrywork was being taught at centres and vocal music in mixed classes was taken up with considerable enthusiasm.'[27]

By 1894–5 the grouping of students at specially equipped centres, initially limited to practical subjects, was being extended to instruction in history, literature, gymnastics, and citizenship, both history and citizenship being illustrated by lantern slides. Specially qualified teachers were appointed for the purpose, most of whom succeeded in awakening an intelligent interest in these subjects.

The pessimism of the earlier comments in 1884 when inspectors seemed greatly oppressed by the low calibre of most students gave way to enthusiastic optimism at the lifting of the restrictions. Until 1898 the general concern of the Board and its officers was to observe the working out of innovations, consolidate the evening-class work and make the evening schools centres for the mental, physical and social well-being of the students. With the abolition of fees for day schools the Board abolished fees for evening continuation schools for the session 1898–9. The number of students enrolled increased from 57,586 in 1897–8 to 109,121. Commercial schools for commercial subjects only were established and science and art classes were similarly consolidated in schools of that name. The teachers in these schools were specialists in their subjects and were paid higher salaries. In 1898–9 there were ten such schools with 6588 students; by 1902–03 there were fifteen more schools and the student roll was 17,581. By 1903–4 there were thirteen commercial schools, ten science and art and commercial schools and four science and art.

The teaching of ambulance and home nursing by medical practitioners was introduced and lecturers appointed 'to create and foster an appreciation of literature';[28] mechanical drawing was taught as a stepping stone to machine drawing and building construction. The Rev. Stewart Headlam, Chairman of the Evening Continuation Schools Committee gave a prize for the best class in dramatic literature in the session 1898–9 and the competition has been held annually ever since.

The previous ratio of men to women of two to one was now being substantially altered and the enrolment of women increased considerably. The number of students over twenty-one was 23,062 as compared with 7776 in 1897–8, the number under fourteen was 8004, significantly less in proportion to the 11,531 in 1897–8. The total number of students represented an increase of 51,535 over the previous session. The table (page 30) showing the growth of the curriculum in evening schools from eighteen subjects in 1889–90 to forty-six in 1897–8 illustrates vividly the tremendous development which had taken place. The reports of the Board and its committees reflect the pride and excitement at the progress made. The evening continuation schools were seen as a yardstick of the progress made in the day schools. The gloomy forecast of the early days when it was doubted whether few pupils of the elementary schools would reach Standard 7 gave way to the excitement of the more advanced classes in commercial science and art subjects. The needs of students in the different localities determined the characteristics of the evening schools and, until 1889, there was no official distinction between one school and another. After that date commercial and science and art schools, schools in poor districts and schools for the deaf, all of which differed from the majority, were established.

In most of the schools an attempt was made to teach adults in separate rooms from younger students but, until 1897, no attempt was made to open separate schools for different age groups. A successful experiment in that year led to many schools being opened for juniors (generally under eighteen years) and seniors.

The ages of students ranged from twelve to seventy or even eighty. No restrictions were placed on the upper age although there were restrictions on the lower age. Government regulations recognized for grant only the attendance of those exempt from the legal obligation to attend day schools. Entries in log-books of evening continuation schools, at the time show that students under the age of fourteen not only had to be recorded in the log-book but also had to be seen by the HMI before their attendance was approved. It is noticeable from the figures given above that the number of students under fourteen in 1898–9 (8004), despite the 51,535 increase in the total number of students, dropped from 20 per cent to 7 per cent. Although the majority of students were still below eighteen the number over twenty-one was steadily rising. Before 1889–90 the attendance after Easter was so unsatisfactory that classes were closed; after 1889–90 the session was extended to July. Schools usually met on three evenings a week between 7.30 p.m. and 9.30 p.m. but commercial and science and art schools met on four and sometimes five evenings a week. Classes such as cookery, laundrywork, manual training and gymnastics were usually held at centres and were taught on 'off' evenings when the whole schools were not meeting. The Board did not restrict evening schools to their own building but, in co-operation with the managers, used voluntary school premises from 1899 onwards. (Twenty such schools with a responsible teacher appointed from the school staff were operating in 1902–03.) In 1899 six sub-inspectors replaced the nine organizers appointed in 1886–8.

Evening classes met in the ordinary buildings of the Board designed primarily for the accommodation of day-school children and, says the watchful Mr Bray,

> . . . inconvenience has arisen in connection with evening education on account of the scholars desks which, being constructed for children between the ages of 7 and 14 do not quite conform to the physical proportions of those of maturer years. This difficulty has been minimised by the supply, in some cases, of special portable desks and in others, by the introduction of a new form of dual desk which better suits the convenience of both day and evening class pupils.[29]

Most teachers in evening schools were teaching during the day, 'a gain in many respects, yet there are some disadvantages associated with the practice. Jaded energies on the part of both teachers and taught are distinctly unfavourable conditions for the acquisition of knowledge'.[30] This frank, percipient comment is followed by the suggestion that a partial remedy would be to work only half-time in day schools. There is, however, no evidence that this was ever put into practice by the Board.

Nearly all schools have an intellectual physical and social side, some however lack the last. These are the worst attended, the least vital and the most colourless schools in London. The reason does not lie far away. London has not the cohesion, that dove-tailing of municipal and local authority and influence, that characterises well managed provincial towns and continental cities. There is more individual and family isolation in London than perhaps, in any other city in the world. Social life for the poor is practically non-existent except through the instrumentality of local philanthropists, ministers of religion, educational centres and the various 'settlements' that have sprung up. The student therefore feels that he needs a recreative side to his existence and he quite naturally thinks and expects that this should be developed in connection with the institution which has voluntarily undertaken the training of the other sides of his nature. Indeed many poor hard-working factory girls openly say that some of the happiest hours of their lives have had their source in the evening continuation schools of the Board. [31]

The log-books of evening continuation schools bear testimony to their well-developed social side. Most schools had a social committee of students and interested staff. Entertainment, usually musical or dramatic, in the winter months; cricket, cycling, tennis or rambling clubs in the summer. Reading rooms with newspapers and magazines were gradually being introduced. Text-books, supplied by the Board, could not be removed from the school but students were encouraged to buy books at reduced prices. Prizes for regular attendance were awarded for many years as well as certificates for proficiency. Students were encouraged to take the external examination of the Society of Arts, the London Chamber of Commerce and the Civil Service Commission. In 1899, 1200 students took the Society of Arts examinations in French, German, Spanish, Portuguese, book-keeping and shorthand. In the main they did so because their employers valued this evidence of their progress.

A particular feature of the London scene in the 1890s was the development of the 'centre system'. It was the outcome of the need for special equipment in certain subjects for a limited number of students who wished, or who were qualified to receive, instruction in them. 'Kitchens of spotless cleanliness and cheery brightness, laundries with modern appliances, workshops with benches' [32] had been established in certain school buildings to which students from surrounding schools and evening schools went for instruction. Similar provision was made in 1899 for repoussé metalwork, engineering and, at one school in a district where there were iron-working firms, an engineer's workshop was fitted 'with all appliances incident to the trade, motive power for lathes was supplied by a steam engine' [33] and a forge which students used to make their own tools. Ambitions for the development of technical education are shown in the comment, 'as the apprentice system is decaying it is in the highest degree desirable that these work-shops should be multiplied – workshops in which the theory and practice of the great industries in the district shall be taught'.[34]

Evening continuation schools were open to all those exempt from the legal obligation to attend day school. 'No test of nationality for newly arrived Russians, Poles, Germans, French or Spanish and many others of foreign extrac-tion and birth are to be found in the East End schools, struggling with praise-worthy zeal, and with the aid of Yiddish speaking teachers, to master the elements of the English tongue.'[35]

The Board's evening continuation schools were seen primarily as a means of supplementing or continuing the education of day-school pupils. Responsible teachers of evening schools were drawn from the staff of the day school in which the evening school operated and, wherever possible, teaching staff were drawn from other local schools. Systematic efforts were made to secure the immediate attendance of all scholars leaving day school and certain schools were seen as con-tributing to certain evening schools. Head teachers were encouraged to make evening facilities known to their pupils and required to make quarterly returns of school leavers. Those named on the return were contacted by the responsible teacher in charge of the evening school. Despite a consistent policy and practice to co-ordinate the work of day and evening school there were many difficulties. The distance between place of work and home, the demands for overtime and long hours of work hampered the commencement at evening school and continuity of attendance if a start was made. Head teachers in day schools were allowed a free hand in the choice of subjects and the schools in a particular district often chose their own higher subjects for the more advanced pupils. Not every school had an evening school on its premises. Home study was often impossible for many students either because they were too exhausted after a long journey and long hours of work or because of the crowded conditions in which they lived. One hundred and nine thousand enrolled students from a total population of about 4 million was still very small but, comparing the number of school leavers in 1902 (49,000) with the number on roll in evening classes between the ages of fourteen to fifteen that is, 31,685 – it would seem that well over 60 per cent of school leavers were joining evening classes. Moreover, the figure of 25,386 enrolments by fifteen to sixteen-year-olds in that session indicates that 50 per cent of school leavers continued their education for at least two years.

Growth of the Curriculum 1889–1903

1889–90	1902–3
Algebra	Algebra
Arithmetic	Ambulance
Book-keeping	Arithmetic
Botany	Art
Chemistry	Book-keeping
Cookery	Botany
Domestic Economy	Building Construction
Drawing	Chemistry
Elementary Science	Commercial Correspondence
English	Commercial Knowledge
French	Composition
Geography	Cookery
History	Domestic Economy
Magnetism and Electricity	Domestic Science
Mechanics	English
Physiology	French
Reading	Geography
Writing	Geology
	Geometry
	German
	History
	History, including Literature
	Hygiene
	Laundrywork
	Life and Duties of the Citizen
	Machine Construction and Drawing
	Magnetism and Electricity
	Manual Training in Wood
	Mathematics
	Mechanics
	Mensuration
	Navigation
	Needlework and Cutting-out
	Physical Exercises (Life-saving, Swimming, Gymnastics, Drill, etc.)
	Physics
	Physiography
	Physiology
	Reading
	Recitation
	Science of Common Things
	Shorthand
	Sound, Light and Heat
	Steam
	Violin
	Vocal Music
	Writing

Subjects Taught 1902–03

All classes except those held under Divisions II and IV of the Regulations of the Board of Education, South Kensington

Subject	No. of Schools	Total no. of pupils who received instruction during the session · excluding those who attended for one evening only	Total no. of pupils who received 14 or more hours instruction during the session [14 is the minimum number for which grant is paid]
Accountancy and Auditing	1	24	17
Algebra	11	383	159
,, and Arithmetic	2	100	42
Arithmetic	177	11,225	3799
,, Commercial	33	2150	869
,, and Composition	1	108	31
,, and Mensuration	1	50	19
,, Reading and Writing	136	10,915	4284
,, Commercial, Reading and			
,, Writing	1	52	15
,, and Writing	32	2304	967
,, Commercial and Writing	1	90	51
,, Writing and Composition	2	170	85
Book-keeping	309	16,554	8142
Brushwork	1	45	13
Chemistry	18	911	213
,, and Light, Practical	1	49	24
,, and Light, Theoretical	1	49	12
,, as applied to Photography	3	76	34
Cookery	179	5623	2582
*Correspondence, Commercial, and			
Office Routine	47	2009	764
Domestic Economy	7	233	69
Drawing (see also Mechanical Drawing)	141	6628	2058
English Citizenship	4	91	21
English Language	27	1162	478
English Literature (taught by special			
lecturers)	53	1825	718
,, ,, (taught by ordinary			
teachers)	25	993	389
Ethics	1	32	10
Euclid	1	30	17
†First Aid (taught by medical prac-			
titioners and ordinary teachers)	189	6482	2421
†First Aid (taught by ordinary teachers)	6	161	41
French	195	10,488	4947

Geography		132	6761	1733
,,	Commercial	27	1298	508
,,	and History	61	4214	1138
,,	Commercial	2	115	48
Geology		1	32	14
German		36	1387	772
Health		2	66	33
History		66	3572	938
,,	Commercial	9	318	120
,,	Contemporary	7	321	114
†Home Nursing (taught by medical practitioners and ordinary teachers)		85	2274	1066
†Home Nursing (taught by trained nurses)		57	1597	584
†Home Nursing (taught by ordinary teachers)		3	36	15
Horticulture		1	54	45
Housewifery		4	42	16
Italian		4	104	65
Latin		10	173	78
Laundrywork		66	1304	530
Law, Commercial		12	225	127
Machine Construction		3	62	48
Machinery of Business		3	96	49
Magnetism and Electricity		19	775	240
Manual Training in Metalwork		30	879	435
,, ,, in Wood-carving		139	4527	2274
,, ,, in Woodwork		203	11,130	4938
Mathematics		12	435	164
Mechanical Drawing, Preliminary		55	1663	730
Mechanics		2	28	11
Mensuration		7	275	104
Metalwork (Elementary Leadwork)		4	118	50
,, (Repoussé)		22	652	336
‡Millinery		49	2158	1015
Music, Instrumental		24	846	460
,, Theory of		2	52	27
Nature Study		2	73	3
Needlework		1	17	17
,, (including Dress-making); see also Millinery		227	15,286	8406
,, (including Dress-making and Millinery)		10	952	538
Physical Exercises—				
§Swimming and Life-Saving		291	11,961	872
Gymnastics		276	20,343	10,207
Drill, etc.		90	5948	1925
Physics and Chemistry		6	161	74
Political Economy		5	69	30

Précis Writing	1	40	15
Portuguese	1	18	7
Reading	29	1173	384
,, and Composition	8	642	328
,, and Recitation	10	429	162
,, and Writing	68	5451	1672
,, Writing and Composition	2	112	23
Recitation	8	198	89
Russian	2	30	14
Science (Elementary)	10	431	92
,, (Experimental)	15	487	284
,, (Natural)	4	44	36
Science of Common Things	24	1686	364
*Shorthand	315	28,729	16,082
Spanish	11	273	176
Tailoring	3	83	49
*Typewriting	62	2829	1673
Violin	11	314	140
Vocal Music	235	14,590	6515
Writing	1	37	9
,, and Composition	86	6285	2013

Classes held under Divisions II and IV of the Regulations of the Board of Education, South Kensington

Subject	No. of Schools	Total no. of pupils who received instruction during the session excluding those who attended for one evening only	Total no. of pupils who received 14 or more hours instruction during the session [14 is the minimum number for which grant is paid]
Art	54	3079	1996
Biology	2	25	19
,, Practical	1	51	41
Botany	7	298	188
,, Practical	2	100	71
Building Construction	14	396	246
Chemistry, Inorganic, Practical	27	852	468
,, ,, Theoretical	25	737	333
Geology	1	22	15
Geometry, Practical, Plane and Solid	12	365	191
Heat, Advanced	1	14	6
Hygiene	10	525	346
,, Practical	1	28	22
Machine Construction and Drawing	12	557	376
Magnetism and Electricity	10	306	138
Mathematics	17	752	427
,, Practical	1	8	3

Mechanics, Applied	1	56	25
,, Theoretical, Fluids	1	13	5
,, ,, Solids	3	67	34
Physiography	10	249	143
,, Practical	1	23	15
Physiology, Human	11	746	491
,, Practical	5	145	85
Sound, Light, and Heat	3	40	23

Reproduced from *Final Report of School Board for London 1870–1904*

N.B. In these tables a student has been counted for as many subjects as he, or she, studied, and may therefore appear more than once. The figures are approximate, as the return from one school was not received.

*Typewriting formed generally a part of a course of instruction in shorthand or commercial correspondence.

†The course of instruction covered a period of about three months.

‡Millinery was also taught under the title of needlework

§Instruction in this subject was given mainly in the summer months, the lessons were necessarily limited in duration to about half an hour, and their total number was, of course, comparatively small.

The Final Years: 1899 – 1904

In 1899 – 1900 the School Board for London was at the height of its power. As far as evening continuation schools were concerned the curriculum was wide and varied. There were no less than 395 evening schools with an enrolment of nearly 147,000. From 1893 onwards the Board offered more subjects; by 1900 it had greatly increased its commercial and science and art subjects and more advanced work generally. At the other end of the spectrum the Board had developed particular evening schools in a number of the poorer districts conducted in such a way as to induce the rougher element of the neighbourhood to attend. No fees were charged and the curriculum for a men's evening school was gymnastics, swimming, history, geography, drawing, first-aid, metalwork, elementary science, reading, writing and arithmetic. Students in such schools included 'labourers, stablemen, coster-mongers, bricklayers, watermen, car men, milk boys, street orderly boys, boys employed in telegraph works, soap works and candle works; boys on barges and errand boys'.[36]

For women – the curriculum included needlework, dress-cutting, gymnastics, cookery, laundrywork, singing, reading, home nursing, writing, composition. The students were employed in 'cap making and packing, card, fancy and tie box making, machining blouses, trousers and buttonholes, envelope folding and stamping, paper bag making, sock making, bookbinding, sewing and folding, cigar making, cigarette packing, show card making, carpet sewing, toy making, packing perfumery and washing perfumery bottles, sieve making, feather curling and making umbrellas'.[37]

An HMI report on a men's school refers to the admirable conduct of 'this difficult school' and the undoubted 'highly beneficial influence' on the students. A similar report on a women's school says 'the marked feature in this school is the improvement in the behaviour and appearance of the very rough class of girls that attend it, and reflects great credit on the responsible teacher'.[38]

Over the years the Board had built up a remarkable day and residential provision for handicapped children. The great advance was marked by the transfer of the nine evening schools for the deaf with a total roll of 433 students from the School Management Committee to the Evening Schools Committee in 1901; another such school was opened in 1904. Evening classes were held in the same building as the day school for the deaf and attendance in the evening was recognized as an attendance in the day school. Students were those under sixteen who were still in day classes and those over sixteen who had left day school or had become deaf in later years. The instruction given was designed to improve the students' speech and lip reading. They could also take subjects selected from: arithmetic, cooking, drawing, English language, first-aid, manual training in wood, metalwork, needlework (including dress-making), physical exercises (swimming and gymnastics), reading and writing.

The payment by results system of grant operated for a substantial period of the Board's existence and the grant based on attendance, introduced later, made it almost inevitable that the curriculum of evening schools should be closely controlled. It is to the great credit of the Board and its officers that, with such limitations, it nevertheless broadened and liberalized the curriculum in the way it did. Throughout its existence it encouraged both innovation and quality. The tables (pages xx–xx) show the choice made by students from the wide variety of subjects. Of particular note is the interest in languages stemming not only from immigrants but from the development of Britain's commercial interests. Russian was first taught voluntarily in one school but, in 1902–3, the Board met the cost of two classes. A special appointment of an organizing teacher for French was made in 1900 and only those teachers who had obtained the Board's First Class Certificate in French were permitted to teach the subject. An illustration of the close control exercised by the Board is given in its consideration of the teaching of Gaelic. In 1903 the Evening Schools Committee decided to open a class in Gaelic but the Board resolved that the class should not meet until it had given its sanction. A memorial was received from the Catholic League of South London asking that Gaelic might be taught and adding that it was already taught in evening schools in Manchester. The Evening Schools Committee thereupon proposed to open a class in the Greenwich Division. The Board, however, rejected the proposal by twenty votes to nineteen. One cannot help wondering whether the example of Manchester affected the Board's decision.

The impact of the London County Council's Technical Education Board, set up in 1892–3, is to be seen in the agreement between it and the Board. In 1899 it was agreed that the Board's evening schools should no longer offer instruction in steam, applied mechanics, advanced building construction, advanced machine construction and drawing and advanced magnetism and electricity in order to avoid overlapping with evening schools in technological subjects and instruction specially intended for university degrees.

The Board made special efforts to create and foster interest in literature and special lecturers were employed to give 'oral descriptions' of the work of poets, dramatists and prose writers. Instruction in vocal and instrumental music was greatly developed in the last few years of the Board. In 1897–8, eighty schools offered vocal music; in 1902–03 it had increased to 235. In 1902–03 133 teachers obtained the Board's School Teachers' Music Certificate and twenty-four schools offered instrumental music mainly in the violin. There were also a considerable number of orchestral classes. These, with the choirs from vocal music and students from the dramatic literature classes, were the mainstay of the social activities which were strongly supported by students and their friends.

The most popular development was, however, in physical exercises. Prior to 1898 gymnastics was only taught in a few schools but, in that year 13,986 students enrolled for such tuition in 135 schools and, by 1902–03, it was offered in 276 schools to a total of 20,343 students. As a rule each class took place in the school hall which was equipped with parallel bars, horizontal bars, vaulting horse, dumb-bells, bar-bells, and Indian clubs. Their contribution to the social and physical well-being of many who lived and worked in over-crowded conditions was considerable. Extracts from the reports of two instructors give a vivid insight into both instruction and pupils:

> Most of the pupils are at work in factories and workshops in the neighbourhood of the school. More squad drill than gymnastics has been taken as so many of the girls suffer from anaemia and round shoulders. Last year the class at Carlton Road won a Silver Challenge Cup in a competition . . . Girls are sent to class by doctors and instances can be given where pupils suffering from anaemia have been cured.
>
> The class at Gopsall Street was comprised of boys drawn from the slums of the district. They were at first much opposed to discipline or anything in the shape of order; it was certainly the most 'raw' class that he [the instructor] had ever seen. In the mass drill the boys were hardly able to distinguish from left and right and could not, even with a run, vault over the low horse from the springboard. At the end of the season, the results were very satisfactory. The boys could perform marching mass drill with a great precision and in better style than he [the instructor] has seen in some gymnasia where the classes have been composed of older pupils and where they have had two nights a week instruction. The apparatus work improved in like manner.
>
> Students were carefully examined and measured at the commencement of

the session. Some few had to be rejected and others with spinal curvature, hollow chest, weak heart and lungs were given suitable work. The season's work has been very beneficial and in some cases, quite beyond expectation, having regard to the adverse conditions of work and home surroundings. The greatest increase in chest measurement was $3\frac{3}{4}''$ and in lung increase 57 cubic inches and there were in cases increases of $2\frac{1}{4}$ and $30''$ respectively. The pupils show a much better carriage of the body, greater strength with a high degree of health and quicker growth in all parts and there was a great improvement in their conduct and moral tone.[39]

Swimming was first taught in 1890 and supplemented by life-saving in 1898. Although no government grant was paid for physical exercises after 1900, the Committee thought the Board of Education might be willing to aid instruction in life-saving as part of first-aid, but the Board of Education declined to sanction instruction which involved the teaching of swimming. The School Board nevertheless continued with it. The number of students increased from 3500 in 1897–8 to 11,961 in 1902–03 – undoubtedly encouraged by the London Board's decision to pay the charge for admission to the baths. In the first few years of the existence of evening schools no record of physical education other than musical drill introduced by the Recreative Evening Schools' Association exists. Until 1890 the government recognized military drill but in that year substituted 'suitable physical exercises' and from that time drill of some kind was taught in most schools. Dancing was also introduced in some schools in response to a suggestion in the Government Code: 'My Lords will be interested to learn from the reports of HMIs that . . . the evening continuation schools have been rendered more attractive, e.g. by means of . . . gymnastics or other employment of a more or less recreative character.' By 1901 dancing had been approved by HMIs in twenty-four schools. This did not prevent the Vice-President of the Committee of the Privy Council on Education (Sir John Gorst) commenting unfavourably on the teaching of dancing in a speech in the House of Commons on 7 May 1901. It was dropped from the school curriculum in 1901–02.

THE SOCIAL LIFE OF EVENING CONTINUATION SCHOOLS

Although the Board was unable to spend money on promoting the social side of evening schools, from 1892 they encouraged teachers in this direction and in that year allowed free use of premises for social gatherings to be held not oftener than once a month on an evening when the school was not meeting. It is clear that the Board attached considerable importance to the role of evening schools in improving social life. In its final report the Board pays tribute to the teachers who had established friendly relations with students by vocal and instrumental-music recitals, recitations and readings, dramatic recitals, exhibitions of work and dancing and clubs for cricket, football, tennis, cycling, country rambles and outings to places of interest, as well as study circles in French.

PRIZES AND CERTIFICATES

From the beginning the Board encouraged the good attendance and diligence of students by the award of certificates and, from 1884, prizes. From 1887 students who passed the annual Government examinations were awarded prizes in the form of books, educational instruments, etc. within the sum of £50 for each school. It was recognized that for many schools £50 was inadequate but it was hoped it would be supplemented by recruiting subscriptions from voluntary organizations. This did not happen, however, so the scheme was amended without a defined total but prizes of particular value were awarded under specific conditions until 1893. In that year prize money was supplemented by a scheme of prizes from 4s. to 10s. for those who passed in science and art examinations. Teacher students were debarred from prizes in 1899. From 1894, to conform with the Government Code and grant system, certificates were awarded to those pupils who had received at least twelve hours instruction in a subject and made diligent progress. In 1900 prizes were awarded to students over sixteen (except teacher students) for passing certain examinations of outside bodies and those held by responsible teachers – good attendance was also required. The value of prizes in 1902–03 was £860.

THE DAY-TO-DAY OPERATION OF THE EVENING SCHOOLS

It is clear that, from the beginning, the School Board for London regarded evening schools as an integral part of elementary education and saw them as closely connected with the development of day schools. Accommodation for evening schools as well as staff was provided initially by day schools and it was not until later that evening schools used premises outside the ordinary day-school accommodation and employed specialist staff who were not necessarily teachers in day schools. The Board recognized that the accommodation designed primarily for school children was not ideal for adults so it took steps to improve the situation by modifying the design of furniture used in day schools to make it more suitable for adults. Teachers employed in evening schools were engaged sessionally under a separate contract. The Board expected a considerable amount of initiative from responsible teachers to publicize the courses, to keep contact with employers and, as far as possible, to relate their work closely to the work of day schools. The latter proved particularly difficult because the freedom given to heads of day schools to determine curriculum was difficult to follow through in evening schools. Nevertheless, the provision for specialist subjects such as handwork, woodwork, metalwork and cookery and domestic crafts in the day schools led to specialist accommodation which was used by evening schools as soon as it became available. Similarly, as science, art and technical work in day schools developed, evening schools followed suit. The concern of the Board to integrate the work of evening continuation schools with the day schools is seen particularly in the control by management committees of the appointment of teaching staff and the question of fees.

LOCAL MANAGERS

Originally only one body of managers for each division was set up except in the Greenwich and Tower Hamlets division where day-school managers also acted for the evening school. In 1885 the divisional system was abandoned and bodies to control smaller areas were formed and steps taken to secure the services of day-school managers, local employers and working men and women. It was believed that the latter would be willing to serve since representatives of the trade societies had assured the Board of the interest felt by working men and women in the evening school movement. In the Greenwich division, but not in Tower Hamlets, the day-school managers continued to act for the evening schools; later on, similar arrangements were made for schools in other divisions. It is interesting to note that there appears to have been no difficulties in the use of day schools. Possibly this was because the school management committees were also in charge of evening schools but more likely because teachers of day schools were strongly committed to evening schools.

The duties of managers were to visit the schools to see that the regulations of the Board and the Government were carried out, to nominate teachers, to inspect the registers and generally to promote the success of the schools. At first one of them acted as an honorary correspondent but this was later taken over by organizers and correspondents appointed by the Board and, in 1895, was transferred to the correspondents of day schools. All of the above indicates that day schools were associated with, and anxious to promote the development of evening work, saw it as a natural continuation of their work and were anxious that there should be the closest co-operation. Log-books indicate that not all head teachers were as conscientious as they might have been in publicizing the work of evening schools although they were all obliged to send lists of school-leavers once a quarter to the Board for transmission to responsible teachers.

After 1898 there were deviations from the pattern of management for commercial and science and art schools. Some of these had no local managers, others had managers without power to nominate teachers and two or three such schools had visiting managers only.

There is plenty of evidence that managers took their duties seriously and log-books show that they frequently visited the schools, inspected the registers, signed reports in the log-book originated by HMIs and generally gave strong, local support to the development of evening schools.

TEACHING STAFF

Responsible teachers were selected from the day school, usually that in which the evening school operated. Head teachers, were not excluded from being responsible teachers and some were so appointed but the number diminished in the later years of the Board.

A responsible teacher was paid an inclusive sum of 4s. an evening for two hours in 1882; by 1902–03 it was 8s. 6d. to 16s. an evening plus extra remuneration based on average attendance. The more highly paid teachers were those who were in charge of special schools and they worked for about three hours an evening. Assistant teachers were paid 2s. 6d. an evening in 1882 and by 1902–03 this had risen to 4s. to 10s. 6d. an evening for assistant teachers and instructors; doctors were paid a guinea for a two-hour session. The principle was to pay teachers a fixed sum and add to it an amount depending chiefly on the attendance in the schools or classes. Instructors as opposed to assistants were paid a fixed sum determined mainly by the subject they taught.

Schools with an average attendance of sixty-five had three assistants and those with an average attendance of 140 had six, excluding the responsible teacher. Teachers of certain subjects in which comparatively small numbers could be taught at a time were counted as half-teachers. If the students fell away then the staff was reduced; a school with three assistants would be reduced by one assistant when the numbers fell to forty-five for two weeks and one with six assistants would be reduced by one assistant when the numbers fell below 120. The teachers whose service could best be spared received the notice to leave; for a time the system was that the teacher last appointed had to leave but since this sometimes involved losing a teacher who could least be spared the previous system was reverted to.

FEES

In 1882 a uniform fee of 3d. a week or 3s. a quarter was charged to all students of evening continuation schools. In 1883–4, until the abolition of fees in 1898, the number of schools charging 2d. or 1d. a week was increased almost every session. The normal fee was 3d. a week. The term or quarterly fee of 3s. at schools with 3d. a week fee was reduced to 2s. in the second session and a corresponding reduction made where a lower weekly fee was charged. The higher fee of 6d. a week imposed in a few schools did not remain in force. An extra fee was charged for

French in five sessions and an extra fee for cookery in one or two sessions. For a few weeks in 1888–9 a fee of 1s. a week was charged to adults. This was immediately after the Auditor and Local Government Board had challenged the Board on whether it could legally instruct adults in evening schools and the Evening Schools Committee *acting in recess* agreed to charge a fee of 1s. a week to cover the cost of instructing such students. When the Board reassembled it decided that adults should be admitted on the same terms as juniors. Meanwhile, the number of adult students fell off considerably and the loss was not recovered until two or three years later.

Schools were freed from fees in 1898 but before that the Board had made several attempts to abolish fees. On 9 July 1891 it was resolved 'that in the event of the Free Education Bill now before Parliament becoming law in all schools of the Board . . . all scholars shall be admitted without requiring any fee from and after the day the Act shall come into force'.[40] In other words they could not wait to get rid of fees. From the beginning the Board had imposed fees only because it would have been illegal not to have done so. As it was they took every opportunity to secure exemptions for special circumstances and generally regarded fees as a hindrance to the attendance of the people who most needed the service they were providing. In the event, their impatience to be rid of fees had to be contained and the suspension of fees did not take place. In 1893–4 fees in two schools were abolished on the grounds that the young people of the neighbourhood could not afford them and the end-of-term report showed that attendance had increased although percentage attendances had fallen off. A proposal to extend free admission to two schools in each division was rejected. A number of alternative suggestions were considered including the deposit of returned fees in the Post Office Savings Bank to pupils who made a certain percentage attendance. This was opposed by the Board of Education and Local Government Board as illegal. At the suggestion of the Board of Education the School Board for London decided to charge no fees in the second part of the session to those students who had made a certain number of attendances in the first part. This operated for only one session, 1897–8, for in the next session, 1898–9, fees were abolished. Tuition at evening schools remained free until 1902–03.

In 1901–02, as a result of the Cockerton Judgment (see page 51), the South Kensington branch of the Board of Education took over the administration of the evening schools, formerly supervised by the Whitehall branch; it intimated that it would not recognize schools in which no fees were charged but it was prepared to consider remittance of fees for individual schools. The Evening Schools Committee appointed a sub-committee to receive evidence and make recommendations on the whole question of fees. The Board came to the conclusion that the present system of free evening schools had worked well and should not be changed but, if fees were to be imposed, then they suggested:

1. no scholars under eighteen should be charged;
2. pupils attending certain schools in poor districts should pay no fees irrespective of age;
3. in remaining schools a sessional fee should be charged to persons over eighteen years of age as follows:
   (a) ordinary schools: 1s.
   (b) commercial schools: 2s. 6d.
   (c) science and art schools: 5s. a session.

The Board of Education demurred at free education of scholars under eighteen years but eventually sanctioned the scheme with the substitution of sixteen for eighteen. Subsequently, soldiers in uniform were admitted to all schools free of charge. In commercial and science and art schools, students of science and art subjects under Divisions II and IV of the Regulations of the Board of Education were charged 5s. a session and 2s. 6d. for other subjects. In schools for the deaf no fees were charged. In 1902–03 there were seventy-six schools in which no fees were charged and 289 where fees were charged.

LOG-BOOKS

A glimpse of life in the schools themselves is given by the diary or log-book which the responsible teacher was required to keep – some of which are still in existence. The firm and detailed control exercised by the Education Department and the view of evening schools as an extension to day schools are well illustrated by the 'Extract from the New Code 1882' which is pasted in the front of one such log-book.

> The managers are held responsible by the Department for the conduct of their schools, for their maintenance and efficiency, for the provision of all needful furniture, books and apparatus and in particular of –
> (a) suitable registers;
> (b) a portfolio to contain official letters;
> (c) the code for the year;
> (d) a diary or log-book.
>   The log-book must be strictly bound and contain not less than 300 ruled pages. It must be kept by the principal teacher who is required to enter in it from time to time such events as the introduction of new books, apparatus or courses of instruction, any plan of lessons approved by the Inspector, the visits of Managers, absence, illness or failure of duty on the part of any of the school staff or any special circumstances affecting the school, that may, for the sake of future reference or for any other reason deserve to be recorded.
>   No reflection or opinions of a general character are to be entered in the log-book.

Doubtless as a result of this, the log-books portray responsible teachers as fairly colourless people in awe of authority, constantly visited by honorary and paid correspondents, members of the management committee, members of the Board, officials of the Board and HMIs whose approval was paramount if the grant was to be paid. 'The summary of the inspector's report after his annual visit or any visit made without notice and any remarks made upon it by the Department, must, as soon as communicated to the managers, be copied verbatim into the log-book and signed by the correspondent of the managers.'

High Street Evening School, Female Department, Stoke Newington opened on 28 September 1885. Miss Mary J. Wilkes, the responsible teacher, apparently marked the registers herself. Since the numerous visitors all seemed to 'test' and initial them it was clearly not a task to be left to others. The 'orderly and industrious' pupils to whom she refers are evidently young women who either still attend or who have left school. By 12 November 1885 the average attendance was 52.3 and two additional teachers, in addition to her deputy, were in process of being appointed. The preoccupation throughout is with the attendance and the weather. The 'bad state of the roads' in January and consequent bad attendance reminds us that, in those days, crossing sweepers were necessary to enable pedestrians to cross roads without walking in deep mud. On Wednesday, 12 February 1886 the class was dismissed early owing to an anticipated riot in the neighbourhood. The activities of the Recreative Evening Schools Association was apparent in March 1886 when a concert for High Street and Oldfield Road Schools was arranged at the Abney Chapel lecture hall. Perhaps it was to support the hope of the honorary correspondent that attendance at the concert 'will be reckoned as one of the evenings of attendance of the class' that the responsible teacher records 'the class will attend at Abney School for an entertainment on Friday 19th inst'.

The report of the HMI, duly recorded and signed by the correspondent, was 'This evening school is well taught and the scholars have passed a satisfactory examination'.

In October 1886 Miss Wilkes lost her voice and was away all week and a Miss Yates came 'on supply'. She apparently was a quiet and careful teacher and 'took much interest in her work'. The French class commenced on Friday, 22 October. By December music drill had been added to the curriculum and from then on magic-lantern shows by one of the managers before classes caused the classes to start later than usual. In the session 1886–7 passes in reading (fifty) writing (forty-eight) Arithmetic (thirty-four) English (thirty-eight) French (one) represented a pass rate of 88 per cent.

The log-books record the bare outline of staff additions, illnesses, visitations and inspections against the general background of deep concern for attendance and the resultant grant earnings. The weather, epidemics, long hours of work of students and local happenings such as the prospect of a local riot in Stoke

Newington in February 1886 and the School Board Fete at Crystal Palace in April 1890 claim a place as the natural enemies of good attendance. In the year 1880 the numbers for each evening school are small, between 100 or 200 on the roll, and it is apparent that growth was due to the opening of more schools than to any rapidly increasing rolls in individual schools. Basic subjects at this time are reading, writing, arithmetic and English. Curriculum and examination procedures are those of the day school with a number of schools offering French and musical drill. The majority of students are between fourteen and sixteen. Not until towards the end of the session 1885–6 do we see references to a light-hearted activity in the shape of a concert or magic-lantern show; these reflect the impact of the Recreative Evening Schools Association. HMI reports, faithfully recorded and signed by the correspondent, are terse and generally encouraging.

There are little signs of any great initiative on the part of staff or students, indeed the latter appear to rate for no other comment than that they are 'industrious and well-behaved'. Visitors are frequent and regular and even in the bare recordings of the log-book there are some whose close attention begins to indicate a supportive roll. The struggle against the impeding weather and long hours of work is obviously taxing. Despite the close contact with schools and school leavers and notes to students who show signs of falling away, overall attendance is around 50 per cent. January and February are the bad months when the weather and illness play havoc with classes and staff. With the 1890s more subjects are added to the curriculum. There is a great demand for shorthand and examination certificates from the Royal Society of Arts. The log-books become rather more animated and there are even references, creditable and discreditable, to particular students. The Rev. Stewart Headlam, a member of the School Board for London and a regular visitor, comes to the High Street, Stoke Newington Evening School on a Monday evening in 1893 to present a book to Ada Moore as a prize for shorthand. On 8 November 1895 one Olive Penny was expelled from the same evening school 'for misbehaviour, constantly turning out the gas on stairs and rudeness to her teacher'. Vocal music, which allowed men into women's evening schools and women into men's schools, became a feature of evening school work and there are increased references to lantern-lectures by individual managers and others on a variety of foreign cities. History, geography, singing and drawing, swimming and life-saving are now a part of the curriculum.

Some HMI comments appear to be more critical by the end of the 1890s and there are even signs of a dialogue, for example, 'HMI Thomas visited – suggested introduction of games prior to marking of registers. This will be adopted as an experiment during present term.' There is no further reference in the following term which suggests that duty, having been done, it was quietly dropped. Certainly there are indications of increased social activity and more participation between students and staff. The suspension of the ordinary timetable on a Thursday in February 1898 at Matthias Road Male Evening Continuation School for an experimental lantern-lecture brought the comment in the log book 'Quite a success. The matter of having such lectures fortnightly or monthly was referred to the students for consideration.' We are not told what happened. In May 1898 'The swimming class to meet at Hackney baths Wednesdays 8 p.m. to 9 p.m. Tickets to be distributed 7.45 p.m. to 8 p.m. Free!' Significantly, this is the first and only exclamation mark to appear in the sober records.

By the session 1898–9 'many adults and still more students . . . are really in earnest about their work' and 'great difficulty has been experienced with those *under 14* who were allowed to attend last year and who are not allowed to attend this' reflect the enlarged and more appealing curriculum to older students. Under fourteen students were only admitted exceptionally and after being seen personally by the HMI and his approval recorded in the log-book. The numbers of students under fourteen at this evening school dropped from ninety-three in 1898 to fifteen in 1899, and to four in 1902–03, in a total roll of about 300.

The curriculum covered writing and composition, arithmetic, English, geography, history, French, book-keeping, ambulance, shorthand, manual instruction and physical exercises.

The subjects offered in the *men's* school were arithmetic, book-keeping, drawing, French, geography, history, science, shorthand, woodcarving, woodwork, writing, gymnastics, swimming, vocal music and violin; in the *women's* school they were reading or recitation, writing or composition, French, German, commercial arithmetic, book-keeping, commercial geography, vocal music, ambulance, home nursing, shorthand, needlework, cookery, English literature, swimming and gymnastics, drawing and other recreation subjects classified under recreation. Despite the range of subjects the total roll at the men's school was 301 and at the women's school about 270. There is no doubt, however, that the increase in the number of students had been mainly in those subjects related to their work namely, the commercial subjects such as shorthand, book-keeping, etc. The momentous events of 1902–04 by which the London County Council assumed responsibility for evening schools are recorded by the laconic entry on 9 May 1904, 'Received rubber stamp – London County Council'.

The Power Conflict – the End of School Boards

The distribution of central-Government grant for education, first begun in 1833, was the responsibility of a Committee of the Privy Council on Education or the Education Department (Whitehall) as it was called from 1856 onwards. Its spokesmen in Parliament were the President and Vice-President of the Council. It administered grants according to a Code issued annually which set out the rate of grant and conditions for payment for a specified curriculum or lists of subjects.

The scope of the Education Department was ill-defined as were its relations with other providers or grant-making bodies such as the Endowment Commissioners which became the Charity Commissioners who, by endowment, supported many grammar schools providing a secondary education. The Science and Art Department of South Kensington, an offspring of the Board of Trade, constituted a separate department in 1853, examined pupils in, and gave grants to, a wide conglomeration of educational establishments in respect of their instruction in science and art subjects. Its funds came from a quite separate vote from that of the Education Department (Whitehall) and it administered them as a quite separate department according to the conditions set out in the Directory of Approved Subjects.

There was therefore no clearly discernible pattern of inter-related elementary and secondary education and certainly no coherent central administration of education. Added to this, the 1870 Act itself lacked important definitions. The 'religious question', rather than education, dominated the debates during the Bill's passage through Parliament and the Act emerged as a compromise between the principles of the voluntary providers and the new State provision by School Boards. The Science and Art department (South Kensington) was not mentioned in the Act and, as indicated earlier, the Education Department (Whitehall) was seen as a paymaster rather than a policy-maker.

From the outset therefore the scene was set for eventual conflict. The School Board for London saw its educational goal more broadly based than the teaching of the 'three Rs' to children. From time to time the Education Code of the Education Department reflected the developments HMIs saw from initiatives in the field, but the Education Department was in a very difficult position in walking the tightrope of ill-defined legislation. If it adopted a too-forward-looking policy it came dangerously near repealing parts of the 1870 Education Act. Nowhere was this more apparent than in the administration of evening schools which, both on grounds of students' age and control of curriculum, were certainly not specifically covered by the 1870 Act.

Time and again the Government Auditor had challenged the legality of certain items of expenditure by the School Board for London and thus checked development. In the climate of encouragement which followed the Code of 1890, the increased support of the Education Department on the reasonableness of the expenditure questioned, caused the Local Government Board not to uphold the decision of the Government Auditor in a number of cases, or to remit the surcharge. This central support, together with the removal in 1891 of the major obstacle, namely, the applicability of Section 3 of the 1870 Act to evening schools, gave a tremendous impetus to this side of the School Board for London's work.

In the meantime, however, the London County Council had been established. In 1893 when the Education Department issued a separate Education Code for evening continuation schools which recognized for grant purposes the attendance of adults, the LCC decided to use its powers under the Technical Instruction Act of that year and set up a Technical Education Board (see pages 55–59). Its very existence, the funds at its disposal and the inevitable developments which began to flow from them, threw into sharp relief the activities of the School Board for London in the science and art and technical education field and the overlapping provision which was likely to result.

The undoubted success and achievements of the School Board for London; the threat to other educational bodies which the development of evening schools since 1893 gave; the size of its operations and of its precepts on the rating author-ities for the metropolis, brought a crop of critics and active opponents.

Foremost among the latter was the new political head of the Education Depart-ment from 1895 (Sir John Gorst). Although the active encouragement of local initiative by the Education Department under Sir George Kekewich, its Perma-nent Secretary since 1890, continued throughout the 1890s, Gorst was busy seeking ways in which the power of school boards could be checked and education brought under the control of the more conservative county authorities. As early as 1896 Gorst introduced an Education Bill to give financial support to voluntary schools and achieve a measure of local co-ordination. The Bill was subjected to heavy attacks even from the county authorities and was finally withdrawn, but it foreshadowed events to come. The occasion for the inevitable confrontation came, or more exactly was contrived, in April or May 1899. William Hales, a solicitor and a governor of Camden School of Art, on behalf of that school and others and ratepayers, before the District Auditor, L.R. Cockerton, objected to the School Board for London's expenditure on science and art schools and classes. Cockerton decided against the School Board and surcharged its members with expenditure they had sanctioned. In addition, Hales in his private capacity as a ratepayer and unsupported by the other parties challenged all the School Board for London's expenditure on evening schools. Cockerton allowed this expenditure, rejecting the challenge, but Hales appealed to the Local Government Board. This particular challenge was never followed through.

On the first issue, the School Board for London appealed and a test case was brought in the Queen's Bench Division of the High Court. The Court upheld the decision of the Auditor. It declared this teaching to be secondary education and outside the scope of the Elementary Education Acts. The Board appealed against the High Court's decision but the Court of Appeal concurred in the judgment of the High Court and further declared that it was also illegal to conduct evening continuation schools for persons who were not children at the expense of the school fund.[41]

The Cockerton case has long been an illustration to elected members and officers of local authorities and students of local government that:

1. a local authority can only do those things which an Act of Parliament empowers it to do;
2. the ratepayer has the right to challenge expenditure through the District Auditor; and
3. the District Auditor has the power, through the sanction of surcharge, to ensure that public money is spent legally.

What is not always so readily appreciated is that the Cockerton case was contrived in order to put an end to the threat that the School Board for London was making to the development of advanced and technical education by the Technical Education Board of the London County Council. Had the School Board not objected strongly to the application of the Technical Education Board in 1898 to be the residual authority for secondary and technical education under Clause VII of the Science and Art Department's Directory; had they also not indulged in such a sweeping interpretation of the Act of 1890, they would not have played so directly into the hands of their arch-enemy, Gorst. Nevertheless it was Dr Garnett, the Secretary of the Technical Education Board, who initiated the challenge to the School Board's accounts through the District Auditor and the Camden School of Art. He it was who played a notable part in advising Hales in the conduct of the challenge. Garnett and Gorst both made no secret of their wish to be rid of school boards and the School Board for London in particular.[42]

It is interesting that the issue with which we are concerned here, namely, the legality of the Board's provision for evening schools was accepted by the District Auditor and supported by the Education Department. The only person who pursued this aspect inexorably was Hales as an individual ratepayer and even he did not take his appeal beyond the Local Government Board. Only on appeal from the High Court was the illegality judgment given.

The Government recognized the difficult and serious position in which the school boards were placed by these decisions. A short Act, known as the Cockerton Act – its official name was the Education Act of 1901 – was passed. This enabled School Boards, with the consent of the county and borough councils, to continue for a period of one year, to maintain training schools and classes which they had maintained at any time during the twelve months proceeding 31 July 1901, to the maintenance of which the school fund was not lawfully applicable.

The passage of the Bill through Parliament was bitterly contested in long debates. Although it was a simple enabling Act, the reasons for the bitterness were not difficult to discover. The 1901 Act allowed only for the continuation of schools or classes already in existence. Where evening school work was expanding rapidly, as in London, this was a serious restriction. The Boards were also at the mercy of the local authority who could refuse to agree to certain classes which threatened those they intended to develop. Also for Boards with proud records of achievement, such as the School Board for London, to have to go 'cap in hand' to seek permission to continue what they had done so successfully was felt to be a poor reward for all their endeavours.

The debates in the House during the passage of the Bill showed the remarkable duplicity of the whole affair. Using the very low-age limit of fifteen, Gorst argued that the number of pupils in day schools affected by the judgment was less than 1000 but, since there were some 225,000 students over the age of fifteen, about half of whom were in London in evening schools, the number was substantial. Since, after 1890, neither the Department nor the School Board had ever doubted the legality of the evening school work, any illegality could scarcely be other than that induced by the Education Department and the Science and Art Department. Gorst attacked the work of evening schools as 'cheap, shoddy education' as shown by the poor attendance and trivial work and the 'serious overlap' with the work of the Science and Art Department and the Technical Instruction Committees. The attack called forth a sharp rejoinder from the School Board for London in the shape of a memorandum which was sent to the Board of Education and Members of Parliament.[43] The Board pointed to the growth of evening classes in polytechnics and schools of art as shown in the report of the Technical Education Board of the London County Council. It referred to 'the favourable reports of HM Inspectors on individual schools and drew attention to the high rate of grant received by the schools and pointed to the percentage of passes in science and art as a proof that the work in schools was efficient'. In reply to Gorst's statement that, with some exceptions, most of the schools were purely recreative, the Board commented that 'the bulk of the work done in the evening continuation schools consisted of instruction in subjects recognised and paid for under the Code' and that as encouraged by that Code 'experiments had been tried in order to render the schools more attractive but in not more than 20 schools, out of 395, was dancing taught and in these instances it had been approved by HMIs'.

One result of the Cockerton Judgment was that the work of evening schools was no longer regarded as elementary education and responsibility for it was transferred from the Board of Education (Whitehall) to the Board of Education (South Kensington). The operation of the enabling Act (1901) was extended by the Education Act 1901 (Renewal) Act 1902 to 31 July 1903 and further extended by the Education Act 1902 and the Education (London) Act 1903. Acting under powers conferred upon them by this latter Act, the London County Council authorized the continuance of evening education schools by the Board until the appointed day set by the Education Act of 1903, namely, 30 April 1904.[44]

3. Towards a Comprehensive Education Service

The Crystal Palace Exhibition of 1851 and that of 1862 brought an increased awareness of industrial competition and, with it, a greater awareness of the need for technical education. The severe trade depression of 1884–6, together with the report of the Commission on Technical Education appointed in 1882, which prepared the way for the Technical Instruction Acts of 1889 and 1891, gave an added impetus to the movement of technical education in the last quarter of the nineteenth century. With the passing of the Local Government Act of 1888 which created county councils and county borough councils, leading men of both parties saw that technical education could be developed by giving the new authorities educational powers. In 1889 the Technical Instruction Act empowered these local authorities to supply or aid the supply of technical education out of the product of a penny rate. In 1890 certain Customs and Excise Duties, raised by Parliament with the intention of compensating publicans, were not applied for that purpose and were distributed to local authorities under the terms of the Local Taxation (Customs and Excise) Act 1890 (Whisky Money). After allocating £300,000 to Police Superannuation, about £750,000 was granted to local authorities for technical education or relief of rates. The LCC's share of whisky money for 1890–91 was £142,727.

For the first three years of its life, the newly created LCC was so concerned with the development of its own administrative machinery that it felt unable to undertake additional educational duties. In 1892, however, with the election of a new Council there was a determined move to implement the Technical Instruction Act and tackle the vast and complex problem of a technical education service for London. The prime movers in this direction were Mr Sidney Webb and Mr Quintin Hogg, the founder of the Regent Street Polytechnic. In addition to the central incentives mentioned above another factor was important in influencing the decision to provide technical education. Under the terms of an Act passed in 1888 a number of old City charities, the original purpose of which had become obsolete, were diverted to educational purposes. Already the threatened attack on city companies' funds had impelled them to steer some of their interests into educational channels. The City and Guilds of London Institute (1878) which led to the Engineering College in South Kensington as well as the Finsbury Technical College and some minor institutions, resulted from some of these diverted City parochial funds. Further developments were being considered in the shape of

54

endowments for a scheme of polytechnics for London. The time was therefore ripe for the LCC to avail itself of the provisions of the Technical Instruction Acts of 1889 and 1891. In 1892 the newly elected Council set up a special committee on technical education to explore how best the Council could administer the powers to promote technical education, aided by the 1890 whisky money. Wisely this exploratory committee commissioned Mr Hubert Llewellyn-Smith (later Sir Hubert), Secretary of the Voluntary Committee of the National Association for the Promotion of Technical Education, to survey the complex scene. Llewellyn-Smith had been one of Charles Booth's assistants in the latter's great survey, *Life and Labour of the People of London* (1891).

Llewellyn-Smith's masterly survey was presented to the Council in July 1892. In the short space of six months he had produced a most remarkable account of the state of non-elementary education in London. The survey analysed the needs of a wide range of industries and the existing provision or lack of technical education for them. Six months later the Technical Education Board was set up, consisting of twenty members of the Council and fifteen other members of whom three were appointed by the School Board for London, two by the City Parochial Charity Trustees, three by the City and Guilds of London Institute, three by London Trades Council, one by the Headmasters' Association, one by the National Union of Teachers, while two were to be co-opted. Sidney Webb, at whose instance the Technical Education Board had been promoted, was its first chairman and remained so for several years.

In the autumn of 1893 Dr William Garnett was appointed Secretary to the Technical Education Board and the Board was given almost independent status and complete control of the residue grant from whisky money. The appointment of Dr Garnett was to be of quite unusual significance. A man of tremendous energy and vision as well as of high academic attainment he came to the post as one who had already achieved national status and respect. His work in establishing the Durham College of Science had earned him the name of 'William the Builder' and, as the representative of provincial colleges on the Royal Commission of the 1851 Exhibition since 1890, he had been in contact with the best-known men of science such as Lord Kelvin, Professor Huxley and Sir Henry Roscoe who were also members of that Commission. Perhaps more importantly, he had been in touch with many leading figures of the London scene who were seeking ways in which to use the funds of the City Parochial Charity Trustees for the development of technical education in London. His acquaintance with the broad educational scene meant that he came to London with decided views on the development of education generally and of technical education in particular. The Llewellyn-Smith report confirmed his own views that technical education in London, as in other places, consisted largely of 'congeries' of nearly independent classes held together by an office organization. He feared any extension of this in the use of City Parochial funds. Moreover his own experience of the payment-by-results system and its effect on some of his brilliant students had made him an implacable enemy of the system and he was determined to bring it to an end as soon as he could. The appointment to the Technical Education Board came at a time when his experience, vision and personal inclinations were just right. He established himself in a small office in Spring Gardens with a staff of one woman organizer, a male clerk and a boy.

The story of the work of the Technical Education Board over the eleven years of its existence must be told elsewhere. Its major significance for us is that not only did it revolutionize the provision for higher and technical education in London but also, through its scheme of scholarships to secondary-school pupils, it established a means whereby pupils from secondary schools could advance to higher education. The administration of the Junior County Scholarship Scheme brought Garnett into close contact with secondary schools and their headmasters and staff in an encouraging and supportive role. Similarly his close contact with the City Parochial Charity Trustees and the combined use of funds from this source and from the Council commended him to the governors and principals of polytechnics and technical institutes. His tremendous industry and that of his chairman, Sidney Webb, had by 1903 completely transformed the higher and technical education scene of London. The number of polytechnics and technical institutes had risen from eight to twenty-six. The number of day classes had been trebled whilst the number of student hours worked by evening students of mechanical and electrical engineering, carpentry and joinery, plumbing and building, experimental physics, chemistry and mathematics had increased four-fold. The London Day Training College and the Central School of Arts and Crafts had been built and centres set up for photo-engraving and lithography, carriage building, typography, leather dyeing and tanning. No less than fifty laboratories, twenty-five science-lecture rooms and eighteen workshops had also been created for boys' secondary schools and the teaching of science and botany in girls' secondary schools was richly enlivened by similar measures. Nationally, Sidney Webb and his colleagues and the Technical Education Board had made two notable contributions. Firstly, at a time when England's prosperity of the 1870s had diminished and the United States of America, Germany and even the Eastern countries had begun to oust her from her former premier position in world markets, the Technical Education Board gave heartening indications of a system of technical and higher education which could become the envy of the world. Secondly, through its relations with secondary schools it had demonstrated that, as a committee of a county council backed by the power and prestige of that authority, it could control secondary education and also develop higher and technical education in a co-operative way with voluntary organizations and with an astute use of voluntary funds. There is no doubt that the lesson of the

Technical Education Board of the LCC was not lost on those in Government who, for some time, had been concerned at the lack of progress towards a comprehensive education service. The success of the Board was also a decisive answer to those who doubted that a large authority such as the LCC could, among all its other commitments, cope with the business of education.

It is not difficult to see the inevitability of Garnett's part in the demise of the School Board for London. The views he held when he first came to London had been reinforced in a quite remarkable way by his work at the Technical Education Board. Moreover, as the architect of a large, technical and higher education system with its secondary school scholarships he became one to whom many persons, influential in the national scene, came for advice. His friendship and association with R.L. (later Sir Robert) Morant, M.E. Sadler's assistant in the Office of Information and Exchanges and a one-time resident at Toynbee Hall, enabled him to provide the documentary evidence and arguments for allocating educational functions to the new counties. More importantly these arguments were passed to, and effectively used by, the new Vice-President of the Committee of the Privy Council for Education, Sir John Gorst, also a frequent visitor to Toynbee Hall. The story of Garnett's involvement in the Cockerton Judgment and the eventual determination of the LCC as an education authority is told in Bernard Allen's *A Memoir of William Garnett*.

Following the withdrawal of Gorst's contentious Education Bill in 1896, the Science and Art Department in 1897 introduced a clause into the Directory or Code of Regulations. This clause VII aimed at decentralizing the work of the Science and Art Department, as recommended by a departmental committee which had recently reported, gave local authorities the responsibility for distributing the Department's grants among the individual schools. This clause assumed that counties and county boroughs were to be the bodies which possessed 'an organisation for promotion of secondary education'. School Boards maintained that these words attributed to those bodies powers which they did not legally possess. The county councils and county boroughs were able to point to the fact that they had, for several years, promoted education in secondary schools by aiding the teaching of all subjects which could be brought under the definition of technical education. This definition, incidentally, was wide enough to include all school subjects except literature and the classics. The work of the Technical Education Board certainly entitled the LCC to claim such powers.

The LCC took no action in 1897 because the progressive majority on the Council was not anxious to offend the dominant party on the School Board which was led by the Hon. E. Lyulph Stanley (later Lord Sheffield), the most active and energetic of all the School Board champions. In the spring of 1898, however, the LCC elections resulted in a dead heat and the chairmanship of the Technical Education Board was given to a member of the moderate party, Mr Edward

Bond, MP. Soon after his appointment he asked whether it was not now time for the Board to do as other local authorities did and seek recognition under clause VII of the Directory. It was Dr Garnett's recommendation to the Board that it seek authority under clause VII that precipitated the clash with the School Board for London. The suggestion aroused intense antagonism in the Technical Education Board and of course, opposition by the School Board's representatives. The LCC received the Technical Education Board's report on 6 December and, at the same time, received a letter from the School Board asking the Council to appoint representatives to discuss the whole question with representatives of their own body. This was done and the Council decided to seek recognition under clause VII. In order not to prejudice the question of the constitution of the future authority for secondary education the Council decided that the Technical Education Board should make the application to the Science and Art Department. In later years Dr Garnett commented on these events: 'The ball which had thus been set rolling by the Technical Education Board in the Autumn of 1898 did not stop until the Education Acts of 1902 and 1903 had revolutionalised the administration of education throughout the country'.[1]

The School Board decided to appeal to the Science and Art Department. The hearing took place before Sir John Donnelly, the Head of the Department on 1 February 1899 at South Kensington. Dr Garnett prepared the memorandum for Sir John's guidance and the Hon. Lyulph Stanley opened the case for the School Board, expressing grave concern at the effect of clause VII on the activities of the School Board. It was a threat by Dr Macnamara, another member of the Board's delegation, which alarmed the meeting and shaped future events. He said that if the Council's application were granted the Board would deliberately introduce further overlapping and would open new schools and classes in the proximity of existing institutions. Dr Garnett advised Sir John Gorst that the School Board's accounts could be challenged by a ratepayer and that this was the way in which the legality of the Board's operations could be tested.

At a later date, in 1903, the passage of the Bill which would give the LCC the control of education was in jeopardy. Responsibility for the control of water supplies had been given to a separately constituted Metropolitan Water Board and there were real fears that the other services of the LCC would be dismantled. Dr Garnett later wrote:

In 1903 all the representatives in Parliament of London's constituencies, with the exception of two or three were members of the Unionist Party. They formed among themselves an association for the consideration of Parliamentary questions. In the confusion of diverse proposals the Government referred the question of the Education Authority for London to this Association of London Unionists members for advice and on a certain Friday the present writer received an SOS in the form of a letter from the Vice-Chairman of the

Association, the Honourable W.F.D. Smith, afterwards Lord Hambledon, stating that the matter would come before the Association on the following Tuesday; that a member of the House of Commons who was regarded as a very high authority on education, had persuaded other members that it was impossible for the Council to add the work of the School Board to its existing duties; and that this view had greatly influenced members of the Association and that the decision would go against the Council unless the writer could submit before the meeting such information as would convince the members to the contrary.

Garnett responded to the appeal and wrote a memorandum enclosing a copy of a scheme of education he had drawn up for the administration of London's education system. This memorandum was addressed to each of the nineteen members of the Association as a personal letter from Dr Garnett. This letter later found its way into the columns of *The Times* and, despite the fact that he and some leading members of the Council explained that it was an unofficial document and could not be regarded as committing the Council, it gave offence to many not only on the general ground that it was concerned with educational politics but also more particularly because his scheme proposed to assign to the borough councils a larger share in the administration of education than they were prepared to grant them.[2]

The Bill became law and from 1 May 1904 the London County Council became the education authority for London. The Education (London) Act 1903 abolished the School Board for London and transferred its powers to the Council which also received, subject to various conditions, the responsibility for maintaining the voluntary schools. Moreover it gave to the Council a new general power 'to consider the educational needs of London and to take such steps as seemed to it desirable, after consultation with the Board of Education, to supply or aid the supply of education other than elementary and to promote the general co-ordination of all forms of education, and for that purpose to spend such sums as it thought fit.'[3]

The Council thus became the first public body in London able to deal with education as a whole. Sidney Webb whose energy, ability and tact had done so much to bring this about said of the new powers, 'To the London County Council is given the power and the duty subject to few conditions and practically no limitations, of equipping London with a complete educational system.'[4]

4. The London County Council as Education Authority

'Education as education becomes a function of the local authority – not the education of the poor alone or the education of craftsmen; not elementary education merely or technical education, or any other grade or kind of education, but just "education".'[1]

The only substantial departure from the Education Act of 1902, as applied to the rest of the country, was that the London County Council was not limited to the expenditure of a twopenny rate upon higher education and that the metropolitan borough councils were given the power to appoint two thirds of the managers of provided schools and to be consulted on proposals to purchase sites. The style of operation of the new authority had been set by Sidney Webb as chairman of the Technical Education Board. Whereas not a pane of glass fell from a School Board for London school without its replacement involving some committee or other, the style of the Technical Education Board was to determine principles and policy rather than interfere in the day-to-day management of colleges. They delegated a great deal to governors of establishments and left detailed management to officers within broad lines of policy which they had determined. The Council was also anxious to avoid watertight departments and took steps to ensure that the Education Committee and Education Department did not have the isolated independence of the Technical Education Board. The administration of the new department was therefore committed to three principal officers: Mr (later Sir) Robert Blair as Executive Officer, Dr William Garnett as Educational Adviser and Mr H.J. Mordaunt as Chief Clerk attached to the Department of the Clerk of the Council.

This unusual arrangement, 'dictated partly by personal considerations, soon produced a crop of difficulties, despite the best endeavours of the officers concerned, which ultimately resolved themselves on the personal side into a battle royal between the Clerk of the Council and the Executive Officer.[2] A special sub-committee was appointed by the General Purposes Committee 'to consider and to report in all particulars if the education service of the Council could be conducted more efficiently and economically than it is at present'.[3] In their report on 7 July 1907 the Committee's conclusions were 'based upon the conception of the Education Service being different in its character from other municipal services and comprising a vast heterogeneous mass of detail not appertaining to any other service'. Mr Blair was appointed Education Officer and made responsible for the whole service of education. As regards the Educational Adviser, a position which was personal to Dr Garnett and not continued after he subsequently left the service, it was made clear that he was 'solely an advisory and intelligence officer and that he had no executive or administrative duties'. The Clerk of the Council was no longer to act as Clerk of the Education Committee and his duties were strictly limited.[4]

Despite the development of technical colleges and polytechnics, including commercial departments and domestic-economy departments, the Technical Education Board had made little or no impact on the evening schools of the School Board for London, apart from an attempt to ensure the absence of any overlapping in the higher realms of technology. For the first few years the new authority had a similar lack of impact. The Education Officer's annual reports were concerned almost exclusively with school and other matters and it was not until 1912 that a report by the Education Officer, *Eight years of Technical Education and Continuation Schools (mostly evening work)*, was presented to the Education Committee.

It was apparent from this report, however, that a careful scrutiny had been going on over the years by inspectors and teachers generally and that there had grown up a consensus of view that evening schools needed to be carefully surveyed and reorganized. During 1908 and 1909 a conference of officers and teachers had spent a great deal of time considering evening school problems and had submitted a valuable report to the Education Committee. There had been a sustained effort over the years to raise the standard of teaching and provision generally in evening schools. An appendix to the report lists thirty-eight published reports on technical education and evening schools between 1892 and 1912 including *Art Teaching in Evening Schools* by Lethaby and Christie (1904); *Teaching of Literature in Evening Schools* (1905); *Teaching of Physical Exercises in Evening Schools* (1905); *Social Gatherings and Recreation in Evening Schools* (1906); *Report of Conferences on Evening Schools* (1909).

The changing face of London, its greatly increased population, its role as the capital city, commercial centre and major port called for special educational facilities. In 1912 manufacturing businesses had to some extent been driven from the centre, their place being taken by commercial offices and dwellings. Whole areas had been transformed by building development and transport systems which now were needed daily to carry increasing numbers to and from work. The 1912 report makes the point that a quarter of all the clerks in England and Wales were engaged in London and that one fifth of the United Kingdom shipping was covered by the Port of London. On the other hand, a quarter of all the men and boys over fourteen were engaged in unskilled employment and only one third of school leavers entered skilled employment. One quarter of a million found employment in the making of dresses and clothing and a fifth of a million were engaged in food, drink and lodging. Seventy per cent of the dock labourers were born in London. The compelling attraction of London meant that one third of the population of London consisted of newcomers from the provinces or abroad. Significantly – 'newcomers are often preferred by employers to London born workers; and their children are in turn in danger of being neglected in favour of more newcomers'.[5]

It is not surprising therefore that the emphasis of the report is on the need to co-ordinate and concentrate commercial education in specialist institutions and ensure an orderly progression from junior to senior institutions. What the Technical Education Board had done for day-time technical education was now needed for evening education.

A major preoccupation of the report was the attendance of students. In 1910–11 there were:

25,000	evening students in polytechnics
10,000	evening students in technical institutes and schools of art
30,000	evening students in commercial centres
100,000	evening students in ordinary evening schools and an estimated
30,000	evening students in other institutions such as University Colleges, the Working Men's College, Morley College, YMCA and settlements and clubs
195,000	Total

An exhaustive examination showed that when all allowances had been made for the difficulties of evening study of the 130,000 students in commercial centres and ordinary evening schools it was reasonable to regard only 90,000 as serious students. In other words nearly one third, 40,000 out of 130,000, had to be regarded as ineffective. Class registers showed that even where classes survived, teachers often changed so much that class teaching became impossible and good students suffered and became indifferent. Evening work was a struggle against poor attendance. The energy of teaching staff

> . . . which otherwise might be directed into purely educational channels was disrupted in the struggle with idle or indifferent students. The strain of anxiety as to falling attendance has driven many responsible teachers and assistants to spend too much time and care in the mere whipping-up of laggard students who possibly under better class conditions might need less incentive to good attendance and mental activity. It is quite possible that less solicitude for mere attendance and more optimism as to programmes of work, presentation of subjects and general class management might secure better attendances as a by-product. But the subject of poor attendance is an old and very difficult one and there is a strong body of opinion that nothing short of compulsion will successfully cope with 40,000 ineffectives.[6]

This reference to compulsion reflects an admiration for the German technical education system and, in particular, the contact that Mr Blair and others had with the Director of Technical Education in Munich. In the light of the record of day-release in this country over the last fifty years the references to compelling students to attend evening classes seem strangely sanguine. Talk of compulsion was another indication that the major concern was commercial and technical education.

At the time of the report there were thirty science and art and commercial centres, 234 evening schools of which fifty-one were free and eleven schools for the deaf. The commercial centres grew out of the evening schools and, as we have seen, the large increase in the number of students over the previous ten to fifteen years had been in the commercial education sector. It was clear now that such a centre was considerably hampered 'by their performance of unrelated duties, legacies of the time when the evening school, the only institution of its kind, was necessarily all things to all men'.[7] Among the ordinary institutes themselves there were those that dealt primarily with commercial subjects such as shorthand, book-keeping, typewriting, arithmetic, etc., those that dealt with the higher commercial studies, those that dealt with foreign languages and those that dealt with a miscellaneous collection of subjects comprising literature and domestic subjects, physical exercises, technical subjects, etc. Some idea of the concentration of commercial and technical subjects can be gained from the fact that, of the 5000 teachers in evening schools, 3000 were specialists drawn from occupations in which it was hoped they had gained qualification and experience. Dressmaking and millinery teachers, for example, were mostly drawn from workrooms. Two hundred medical practitioners and a few nurses gave instruction in home nursing, first-aid, infant care, health, maternity and nursing and midwifery. One thousand teachers of shorthand and book-keeping were drawn from business houses and government departments and many teachers of drawing came from architects' offices. For the variety of general subjects day-school teachers were usually employed but, as the report says, it was 'unfortunate, however, that the traditions of the day school have been allowed to a large extent to govern evening class procedure, so far as the ordinary evening schools . . . are concerned. It is essential that these traditions should be laid aside. The teachers do not all realise that these evening school students have entered into a new life since leaving the day school, and that they need the guidance, the knowledge and the treatment that are appropriate to it.'[8]

Throughout the report there is steady support for the evening student and the need for the work of the various institutions to be so related to him or her as to encourage his progress, for example, by providing courses in ordinary evening schools and other centres in preparation for the more advanced courses. The report pays a tribute to the great variety of subjects in evening schools.

Students as various as teachers and civil servants, clerks, salesmen, saleswomen
and foreign correspondents, agents and caretakers, van boys and commercial
travellers, policemen, domestic servants, dressmakers and midwives, telephone operators and maternity nurses, all find special provision made for them
. . . There are classes for those that work, for those out of work, and for those
who do not work. There are schools for those who can pay and schools for
those who cannot. There are classes in Welsh, in Irish, in Yiddish and in
Japanese; and classes in English for aliens. There are choral unions and social
evenings and there are classes in which clothes are made up, and some even in
which the weekly washing is put through. Neither politics nor religion is
taught, but there is much that the student of politics or religion may learn.[9]

The section of the report concerned with ordinary evening schools was written
by S.E. Bray, District Inspector, whom we first encountered visiting the evening
continuation schools of the School Board for London in the 1880s. Whilst he
shared the concern on the need for more stable attendance his steady support for
the work of the ordinary evening school through various vicissitudes and major
handicaps shines through his comments. He detected signs that more and more
young men and women were becoming more and more aware of the benefit of
further education, and that greater demands were being made on the individual
and on a rising generation which craved half-consciously for something it could
not define. One feels that he regretted the lack of initiative in many evening
schools in that, despite substantial changes in the shape of London and its needs,
they remained very much the same with no marked changes either in methods or
organization, other than to meet needs as they appeared to the people on the spot.
Nowhere was this more evident than in the surge forward in commercial subjects.
He saw the activities of clubs and settlements as making an important contribution to the scene and not a subject for regret 'that they have captured lads and girls
who would otherwise have attended evening schools'. He had not the same
charitable thought towards 'picture theatres'. Once again he reminded the
authority that evening education was heavily hampered by the conditions under
which it was carried on. Students and teachers had done a hard day's work and the
evening schools were in session during the most inclement part of the year. The
short duration of classes in the evening meant that students and staff had a rush to
get there and to get home. There was little or no continuity between one evening
school session and another. The evening school started almost as a new school
each session.

There were two types of schools, those with a commercial bias which constituted the great majority and those with an industrial or domestic bias in which
the sexes were taught separately. In the latter type the lads were usually engaged
in unskilled labour and factory girls formed the bulk of the students. Practical
subjects aroused most interest and more consistent attendance.

It is the minority, here or elsewhere in evening schools that prove their grit and form the backbone of the institution. Not a few female students show an affectionate regard for their evening school: they realise the good that has been done — the light that has been brought into their lives. The 'course system' is, as a rule a failure in these schools . . . Too much is attempted in this connection considering the arduous labour which most of the students have to perform during the day and which, at certain periods of the year, is prolonged, to meet the pressure of business. Most of these schools are doubtless doing valuable work. The struggle, however, is always uphill, and the progress is not always exactly measurable. But humanising work — the best work — can never be exactly gauged.[10]

Predictably, of the fifty subjects offered in the fee-paying schools, that is, those situated in good or fairly good neighbourhoods, the most popular subjects were shorthand, book-keeping, dressmaking and arithmetic whereas in the free schools, that is, those in difficult and poor neighbourhoods, the order of demand and appreciation was very different — the first four being gymnastics, dressmaking, the three Rs and woodwork. All the evidence pointed to the need for a co-ordinated system which would avoid the senseless competition between competing establishments, provide for the grouping of subjects and for passing students on to more advanced institutions.

Highly critical as the 1912 report was of the existing system of evening school education there was one feature which it found pleasing, namely the pattern of student ages which, in 1910–11, was 49,000 students between fourteen and seventeen years, 36,000 students between seventeen and twenty-one, and 44,000 students over twenty-one. The report lists the number of adult students from the session 1893–4 to 1910–11 and points to the tremendous growth from the 4436 adult students in 1893–4 to 44,000 in 1910–11. These figures did not include adult students in the evening classes at university colleges, polytechnics, technical institutes, schools of art, etc. Taking account of these the report said that there were over 70,000 students over twenty-one, 46,000 between the ages of seventeen and twenty-one and 60,000 under seventeen.

The report reflected the fieldwork and survey which had taken place against the background of two major aspects, the interest in, and study of, the German system of technical education and the realization that if the UK was to compete against German industrialism a more effective commercial education was essential. An appendix to the report described the compulsory, continuation schools of Germany and the system of compulsory release from work in the day-time for those under eighteen. The second influential feature of the background to the survey was the place it gave to the Working Men's College, Morley College, the work of settlements and clubs, the Workers Educational Association and the University Extension Movement. Of the Working Men's College it said that 'the college holds a unique place in the system of evening education; it is a centre of a strong social and intellectual movement, successfully fulfilling the object of its founders'.[11] Of Morley the report said it appealed, like the Working Men's College, to older students. 'The college has a most important place to fill in the scheme of education for South London as a really equipped college of the humanities for adult working men and women.'[12] It went on to indicate that it was more than a mere centre for teaching but also had a very extensive and vigorous social life with numerous clubs and societies connected with classes and groups. It hastily pointed out that they were not just recreational – in many cases they formed a nucleus for additional study and that there was both the need for, and possibility of, expansion as much as on the purely educational side. On settlements it listed the fifteen best known[13] and referred to the social work carried out by residents of the settlement in the form of advice centres and general social work and to the organization of classes, usually to enlarge the outlook of those who came in contact with the settlement as citizens. Many special classes in dancing, home nursing, etc. were conducted by residents. Clearly the writers of the report were impressed by the association of teachers with the taught and the discussions and debates which arose from this association and which contributed to the formation of many societies within the settlement. 'It would be difficult to over-estimate the influence of such institutions on the thought of London or to fail to recognise their share in promoting the advance of evening education work within the county.'[14]

Bearing in mind the comments and statistics of the working population of London to which the report referred earlier, namely, that one fifth of school leavers went into unskilled employment and that 70 per cent of dock labourers were drawn from the London population, it would seem as if the writers were looking to the voluntary sector of the educational provision to tackle the more obdurate problem of the working man and woman of low educational attainment. It is doubtful, however, whether the Working Men's College or Morley College were in much contact with this type of man or woman or, for that matter, whether the approach of this kind of establishment was likely to attract such people. One cannot escape the suspicion that the concern to promote the well-being of the vocationally motivated students threw into sharp relief the absence of provision for the non-vocational student of which there was not a clear conception or understanding. The emphasis given to the accommodation available at the Working Men's College and Morley College, together with that at the settlements which provided for more than tuition in the classroom, almost suggests the recognition that day-school accommodation was unlikely to attract such students without social and recreative facilities.

The report provided a basis for the reorganization which was the subject of a substantial report to the Education Committee on 13 May 1913.

The Great Reorganization of 1913

The reorganization of evening education which followed in 1913 was a landmark in the history of London's education. Whilst it reaffirmed the view of the School Board for London that evening education was an integral part of the London education service it did so with very important differences. The School Board for London, from the beginning, regarded evening education as an extension of the work of day schools and many of the Board's evening continuation schools reflected the organization and approach of the day schools. Moreover, the great majority of students were under seventeen. The aim of the reorganization of 1913, as expressed in the Education Committee Report of 13 May 1913, was 'to lift evening education to another plane', recognize the substantial growth in the number of adult students and 'infuse freshness and attractiveness into the system'.

With this approach went the most important recognition that students had to be attracted to the facilities and, having enrolled, had to have this interest sustained by stimulating teaching and surroundings which refreshed their often tired minds and bodies.

No longer were evening education establishments to be 'schools': henceforth they were to be known as 'institutes'. Perhaps most important of all for the future development of London's evening education service, the reorganization introduced the distinction between 'vocational' and 'non-vocational' education. It recognized that, whilst large numbers of men and women sought to improve their *vocational* qualifications – their education for work – others came to classes out of interest for a particular subject or from sheer love of learning.

In later years much was to be made of this distinction and much debate was to take place about the term 'non-vocational'. It is therefore of interest to note how the division and term came about in London.

Having identified and regrouped those technical, commercial and other subjects related directly to the vocational needs and aspirations of the students, there remained two sizeable groups. The largest of the two was that of health and domestic subjects which were studied by women preparing for work in trades predominantly reserved for women, or by housewives and mothers. They were subjects sufficiently specialized to require special provision and facilities. The other group – general education subjects – was for those students who wished to improve the level of their school attainment or general education as a base for further vocational or cultural education.

In addition, the report identified a need to provide specially for those who wished to pursue a subject out of interest or for purely cultural purposes or love of learning. For these students it was proposed to set up non-vocational institutes. It is of note that this term 'non-vocational' was not just the obverse of 'vocational'; it envisaged a quite different teaching approach, based on the work of settlements and other voluntary providers in which there was a strong student participation in determining the scope of the study of, predominantly, the humanities.

The major part of the reorganization was devoted to regrouping the vocational, commercial and technical subjects and courses on the basis of the occupation of students, their ages and the vocational course appropriate to them in establishment specifically geared to their needs. This was done by establishing:

1. fifty junior commercial institutes with a two-year course of instruction, to link with one of the twenty-seven neighbouring senior commercial institutes; and

2. twenty-two junior technical institutes to provide the rudiments of a technical education and the preparation for entry to the higher technical institutions (polytechnics and technical institutes) to which they were to be linked.

The large body of work, partly domestic (cookery, laundry, housewifery) partly health (first-aid, home nursing, infant care, etc.) and partly needlework (needlework, home dressmaking, home millinery) were to be grouped and organised in thirty women's institutes. Three such institutes were to be associated with the three girls' trade schools and in those institutes the teaching of modern languages would be permitted. In the other institutes non-vocational subjects could also be provided. It is interesting to note that the work of women's institutes in the domestic and needlework crafts was not regarded as non-vocational. Certainly the women's institutes were not regarded as non-vocational institutes at that time.

In those districts not large enough or sufficiently well defined to demand one or more schools with single objectives such as a junior commercial institute or a junior technical institute or a women's institute, there were to be twenty-five institutes covering more than one department such as junior commercial and junior technical institutes or junior commercial and women's institutes.

In certain parts of London where only one institute was needed, general institutes, about forty of them, were to provide for all classes of students in the best possible way.

Approximately twenty-five free institutes, at which a general but not a commercial education would be given, were also to be set up. Again it is interesting to note that general education was not considered to be either vocational or non-vocational. The eleven schools for the deaf were to continue as before.

One of the stated aims of the reorganization was that whilst it would be necessary to put restrictions on the type of establishment and course which the under-eighteens would be permitted to join, as few as possible restrictions would be put on such matters for those over eighteen. Better provision was to be made for the needs of the large number of students who sought education other than vocational. To meet this it was proposed to set up twelve non-vocational institutes which were to be limited to non-vocational subjects; the students at such institutes should be over eighteen.

The Education Committee were at some pains to spell out what teaching should be undertaken in these non-vocational institutes. Their view was that, in the past, the failure of evening schools on 'humane subjects (especially history) in our opinion is due largely to a carrying over of the day school methods to evening school pupils'.[15] They felt that

> . . . history and geography, some appreciation of architecture, art, music (for a popular not an expert audience), something of local and central government and of the general arrangement of the country's business, the value of institutions like Labour Exchanges . . . how London is fed; London's water supply; . . . museums, libraries, picture galleries, their accessibility and value; ought to form an integral part of the curricula of evening institutes and ought to be approached directly not through the text book but from the living event. A few events of importance in 1912 could have been used as matters of engrossing interest, by means of which much history and geography at least, could have been introduced. What is wanted is interesting (and well illustrated) talks on 'living' events: a live point of contact between the student and the world in which *he* lives.[16]

The Education Committee commended pamphlets produced by certain elementary schools for their school journeys which they thought could bear imitation in evening institutes. The work of the WEA, the University Extension Board, the settlements and the Working Men's College in the Education Officer's report of 1912 is praised: 'Humane subjects in the evening school need men and methods similar to those employed by the WEA and the University Extension Board, by the Settlements and the Working Men's College' and, again, 'There are probably a good many men and women among the 25,000 teachers in the Council service who have both the knowledge and the capacity for applying WEA methods, suitably modified to the conditions of varying classes of evening school pupils.'[17] Although the Committee felt that headmasters and headmistresses should not be responsible teachers at evening institutes, they felt that they could very well make a contribution in this area. They went on to say, 'there is too much disposition to think of evening education in terms of repairs to the defects of an elementary education or of aids to employment. Whole sections of the adult population are unaffected by the existing organisation. Something is done for the working man by the WEA – mainly social science and economics. Something for the middle classes by the University Extension Board'.[18] They saw the role of the twelve non-vocational institutes catering for students over eighteen as giving instruction 'which should be limited to lectures on the lines above indicated, to subjects of a non-vocational character. These should fill in blanks by the WEA and the University Extension Board, the Working Men's

College and Morley College and so on.'[19] For good measure they added that 'lectures on the British Empire and South America – their history, traditions, science, art and literature – would come as a revelation to the people of London'.[20]

Classes in five other non-vocational subjects were to be limited to a total number for the county as a whole, as follows:

music (vocal instrumental)   160
gymnastics   170
handicraft   150
first-aid (men and boys)   100
gardening   20

The last four subjects should be available in a certain number of buildings so that juveniles under eighteen following a course might join a class. Art classes generally were to be confined to art schools but, where there was too great a distance from the area of demand to the art school, classes were to be run as a branch of the art school, polytechnic or technical institute. There was evidently great sensitivity about vocal music. There had apparently been criticism from HMIs that there was too little systematic instruction in theory and voice production; there had also been a great difference between attendance in the first hour and the second hour. The Committee therefore felt that a vocal-music class of two hours was too long and that it should be one and a half hours in future; there should also be a smaller number of classes which would tend to make them more efficient. The lack of homogeneity in the teaching, they felt, called for some central oversight: 'We think it desirable that every music class should be inspected at least once in two years.'[21] They recognized that to do this would occupy inspectors three or four evenings a week during the winter and that under present staffing conditions this was impossible.

WOMEN'S INSTITUTES

The Committee's view of women's institutes is of particular interest in view of the fact that they were not regarded as non-vocational. Instruction was to be mainly:

1. domestic
2. needlework
3. health
4. humane subjects
5. light physical exercises

Although courses could be organized they would not be insisted upon and would be regarded as optional. More important still 'we propose to apply in these women's institutes some of the features of the clubs which have shown the evening schools the need for developing a social side. We think there should be better cloakrooms and washing accommodation.'[22] There should be simple refreshments at a minimum cost which the Council would aid in the same way that they aided secondary schools. One hall, each night, was to be furnished and equipped as a combination of library, reading-room and writing-room and another was to be set apart on some nights for tutorial work, homework and preparation of lessons. Attendants were to be women wherever possible.

Probably the most important decision that the Committee made towards the future adult education service was when they decided that responsible teachers of women's institutes 'wherever the institute was large enough should be whole-time' on the grounds that 'her initiation and supervision of social gatherings, clubs, magazines, excursions and so on, would be fully as exacting as those of the responsible teacher of a commercial centre'.[23] In one of a number of flashes of intuitive understanding of the difficulties of evening work, the Committee said 'to furnish a hall as a combination of library, reading room and writing room between 6 p.m. and 10 p.m. and leave no mark of it the following morning and no cause for complaint on the part of the day school staff, will not be an easy task, but it should not be beyond the capacity of capable women to reduce the disadvantage to a minimum'.[24]

As far as free institutes for women were concerned it was felt that they should be run as far as possible on similar lines to ordinary women's institutes. It was recognized, however, that this would rarely be possible since women at such institutes (whether young or middle-aged) 'can rarely spare either time or energy for subjects other than those pressingly required for some home purpose such as how to cook a meal or how to make and mend clothes'.[25]

STAFF

Any service stands or falls on the quality of its staff and it was the recognition by the Committee of this that made a most important impact not only on the service of the day but on its future. In a generous tribute to the work of teachers in the past they said that, considering the conditions, the work of responsible and assistant teachers in evening schools had exceeded all expectations,

> . . . but it is obvious that men and women who teach 10 half days in a day school and three or four and sometimes five evenings a week . . . cannot do justice to either day or evening or themselves. The system which requires such efforts is bad for the day schools, and bad for teachers concerned. The evening institutes want freshness and the conditions of appointment of responsible masters and mistresses should include generous recognition of that requirement.[26]

They went on to recommend that seventeen commercial institutes with over

50,000 student hours in 1911–12 should have whole-time responsible teachers, that is, completely free from day work, and that reconsideration should be given to a whole-time appointment if student hours fell below 40,000 in two successive sessions. For women's institutes, as indicated above, they appointed twelve whole-time responsible teachers who were entirely free from day work, like the responsible master of the larger commercial institutes. They went on to recommend that a large number, not exceeding 100, of responsible masters and mistresses should be half-time only in their day schools and that their half-time evening institute and half-time day school be one whole-time appointment. This would set them free to visit day schools to 'catch the leavers' and visit employers. It would also give them some time for recreation and for enlarging their own views: 'Freshness of mind and width of outlook are necessary qualifications in responsible teachers. Under present conditions such qualifications are generally unattainable.'[27] Interestingly, the committee also added that evening staff appointments should not be held for too long and that, at the end of ten years, the appointment should be reviewed. It appears, however, never to have been implemented. Full-time day teachers should do no more than three evenings a week as assistant teachers; all so employed should undertake to do no additional evening work, a regulation that still stands today although from time to time a shortage of teachers in specific subjects has necessitated its temporary suspension.

TRAINING

All instructors appointed to posts in evening institutes who had not had one year's experience in some form of school teaching were, whenever required, to attend a course of ten lectures and demonstrations at the London Day Training College or some other approved institute. As far as possible the courses were to be open to all others who cared to attend. Arrangements were made for special lectures to teachers in evening institutes on the methods of introducing a wide conception of teaching English, including history, literature, current affairs, etc. in evening institutes.

CLOSING NUMBERS

In a determined attempt to give responsibility to the new staff that they wished to see in charge of evening institutes the Committee swept away the existing regulations which governed opening and closing numbers of classes. Under the existing regulations a class, as a rule, closed as soon as its average attendance fell below a fixed number, six to twelve, according to the subject. 'It is usually the faithful few – the best students – who are transferred or dispersed when a class is closed. The rule acts as a deterrent even to good students at the beginning of the session.'[28] The existing regulations were suspended and in their place an opening number determined for each subject, under six schedules of subjects, for example, nine for advanced subjects, twelve for more practical subjects, fifteen for the general run of subjects and twenty for physical exercises, vocal music and so on. Classes were to be opened on the enrolment of the required number and were to be reviewed at the end of each term, the responsible teacher having the duty of closing such classes as necessary. 'We think the responsible teacher, having classified under reasonably good conditions in September should alone be entrusted to exercise the responsibility as to closing before Christmas,'[29] said the Committee. Implicit in the new arrangement was a greater discrimination in enrolling and establishing classes at the beginning of the session than had hitherto been the case. Short courses were to be introduced at reduced fees after Easter at all institutes where the responsible teacher was half-time and after Whitsuntide where the responsible teacher was whole-time or half-time.

In the past assistant teachers had been engaged by the evening. The conditions of appointment authorized by the Committee determined that they should be offered a term's engagement subject to a fortnight's notice during the term and to payment of a proportion only of the term's salary if their services were dispensed with before the end of the term. This was another remarkably forward-looking decision which, like that concerning closing numbers, was abandoned some years later and which the advent of mechanized accounting and the computer succeeded in preventing being reintroduced.

FEES

Fees in general institutes and women's institutes were 2s. a course or single subject (1s. for a term and, in the case of general institutes, 1s. for each additional subject). Extra-county students who worked in London were to pay the in-county fee plus 25 per cent and extra-county students the in-county fee plus 50 per cent. Responsible teachers were given authority to grant, provisionally, free admission or admission at reduced fee to students unable to pay the full fee.

INSPECTORS

Mindful of the role of people like S.E. Bray, the Organizer and, later, District Inspector with the School Board for London and the LCC, it was natural that the Committee would wish to ensure that the new organization had the benefit of inspectorial advice. The previous practice had been that inspectors covered both day and evening work; not surprisingly, they found themselves considerably overworked and often it was the evening work which suffered. It was therefore recommended that an additional District Inspector and two additional assistant inspectors be appointed, and that three assistant inspectors be seconded to complete the evening school reorganization. As soon as the reorganization was completed all inspectors were to share both day and evening work. These recommendations were accepted and appointments were made. It is of interest to note the salaries of whole-time responsible teachers, sessional responsible teachers and District Inspectors of that time. A District Inspector was paid an annual salary of £400 and an Assistant Inspector an annual salary of £250. Whole time principals received an annual salary of £200 – 250.

The table below gives the salaries of sessional responsible teachers in ordinary evening schools and colleges of commerce and schools of art:

Salaries of Sessional Responsible Teachers

No. of evenings	Grade	Ordinary evening schools Student hours	Sessional salary	Grade	Commercial and science and art centres Student hours	Sessional salary
3	I	Under 11000	£40	I	Under 30000	£75
	II	11000–15499	£45	II	30000–41999	£82 10s.
	III	15500–19999	£50	III	42000–53999	£90
(£5 for each additional 4500 student hours				(£7 10s. for each 12,000 student hours)		
4	I	Under 14500	£53 6s. 8d.	I	Under 40000	£100
	II	14500–20499	£60	II	40000–55999	£110
	III	25000–26499	£66 13s. 4d.	III	56000–71999	£120
(£6 13s. 4d. for each additional 6000 student hours)				(£10 for each 16,000 student hours)		
5	I	Under 18000	£66 13s. 4d.	I	Under 50000	£125
	II	18000–25499	£75	II	50000–69999	£137 10s.
	III	25500–32999	£83 6s. 8d.	III	70000–89999	£150
(£8 6s. 8d. for each 7500 student hours)				(£12 10s. for each 20,000 student hours)		

The general effect of the reorganization was to exclude from higher institutions unprepared students under seventeen years and therefore to exclude from junior commercial institutes and junior technical institutes all students over eighteen years, and to pass on to the higher institutes all students who had taken a two-year course. The reorganization excluded commercial and technical subjects from all the ordinary women's institutes but at first, and with some exceptions, placed no age limit on the students admitted to them. General institutes on the other hand were free of restrictions either as to age or curriculum and so charged with the general duty of providing instruction for students of whatever age in the subjects for which there was a demand. It was hoped that the careful distribution of institutes, together with the influence of the standing conferences of principals which were also set up, would eliminate all fear of competition as to the mere number of students and student hours and would leave those responsible for each institution free to pursue without distraction the educational aims of their particular institute.

Advisory committees took the place of management committees and they were expected to become a body of persons assisting the responsible teacher in maintaining the objects of the institute.

The Education Committee's report of 7 May 1913 was a remarkable statement of the philosophy of evening education. It was the result of a number of years' careful investigation and scrutiny of virtually every kind of establishment from polytechnics to voluntary clubs. It did not limit itself to statements of broad policy but went on to examine every aspect of day-to-day teaching and administration which would enable that policy to be implemented. In removing instruction in commercial and technical subjects from the ordinary evening schools and concentrating them in commercial and technical establishments, it took the essential step necessary to ensure the concentration of qualified teaching staff and thus develop specialist departments so important to the raising of standards of teaching.

Similarly, by concentrating tuition, under whole-time or half-time responsible teachers, in domestic, health and craft subjects in women's institutes; by giving authority for instruction in five non-vocational subjects and emphasizing that attention should be given to the social amenities in such institutes – firm foundations were laid for the future non-vocational women's institutes.

In modern terms the programme envisaged for the non-vocational institutes was extremely limited. They were, however, the forerunners of the literary institutes and, together with the women's institutes and the free institutes, were the foundation of the future adult education service.

The list of evening institutes to be opened in the session 1913–14 was published on 30 June 1913 and showed that there were forty women's institutes, ten of which were free. Eight of the twenty-nine free institutes were for men and eleven were for both men and women. Non-vocational institutes were opened at Lavender Hill, Battersea; Santley Street, Brixton; Kingwood Road, Fulham; Halstow Road, Greenwich; Enfield Road, Hackney; Yerbury Road, Islington; Beethoven Street, Paddington; Woods Road, Peckham; Dingle Lane, Poplar; King and Queen Street, Walworth; Toynbee Hall, Whitechapel; and Conway Road, Woolwich.

The New Era

Two hundred and forty-two evening institutes opened in September 1913 in their new guises. For the most part they had new names, redefined functions and specific educational aims.

Reviewing the effect of the organization, the Higher Education sub-committee was able to report to the Education Committee on 13 May 1914 that, generally, the reorganization was working well. The need to seek a substantial supplementary vote for part-time salaries led them, however, to increase the opening numbers for several groups of subjects. The opening of all classes in future would require the approval of the Inspector and the Education Officer. Classes in different standards of the same subject were to be held on the same evening. With these safeguards, despite the evidence that in many instances responsible teachers had not used their discretion wisely and had kept a large number of classes running which should have been closed, it was decided to continue to leave the responsibility for closing classes to responsible teachers for another session. The Education Officer had obviously made it clear to responsible teachers that, unless their discretion was more wisely used in future, they would cease to be trusted with it.

The number of free institutes had been reduced by the reorganization but they were being used by some students as a way of securing a cheaper technical education. Students who were unable to afford a fee had, apparently, spent 'sizeable sums' on materials for woodwork classes. A few free institutes therefore were converted to fee-paying institutes and a registration 'fee' of 6d. was charged at such institutes to give 'some guarantee that a student is serious'. All institutes were to become 'evening institutes' and the non-vocational institutes 'literary institutes'. The provision for instruction in the three Rs at general, free and women's institutes was to be extended to literary institutes.

The number of whole-time appointments was increased from twenty-nine to thirty-seven. Since commercial institutes 'have been made definitely the higher institutions for commercial instruction in London' the responsible teachers of such establishments were in future to be known as principals – a title which it was felt would be more likely to impress the business firms with which they had to deal.

A proposal to reduce the eleven institutes for the deaf to five 'regional' institutes and pay tram fares of students came to nothing after the Finance Committee questioned the proposed cost.

The result was that, for the 1914–15 session, there were thirty-one instead of thirty-seven general institutes, twenty-six instead of twenty-nine free institutes and thirty-three instead of thirty women's institutes. There were nine literary institutes.

The Rev. Stewart Headlam, the LCC member for South-West Bethnal Green and a strong supporter of evening education, predictably opposed (although unsuccessfully) the closure of a junior commercial, junior technical and women's institute at Knapp Road (Bow and Bromley) and the closing of Lollard Street General Institute. More surprisingly, he opposed the changing of Cranbrook Road (Bethnal Green) free mixed to a free men's institute.

Mr Gautrey and Mr Nicholls tried, without success, to extend the title of 'principal' to responsible teachers for women's institutes and the Rev. Stewart Headlam also, without success, tried to improve the provision of clerical assistance.[30]

5.   The 1914 – 18 War

By the beginning of the next educational session the First World War, or what one entry in a women's institute log-book called 'The War of All the Nations', had begun.

There is no doubt that, despite the references to non-vocational work, the reorganization of 1913 was predominantly a reorganization and strengthening of vocational work. It presaged the eventual concentration of commercial and technical education in commercial colleges, technical institutes and polytechnics. The strengths of the reorganization were to be underlined during the war years and its weaknesses obscured.

The grouping of domestic and health subjects (of particular concern to women) in women's institutes, the encouragement they were given to develop a social and informal education framework and a close association with voluntary clubs and schools were all aspects which could flourish in wartime. A male – less or heavily diminished male population provided a direct incentive for women to tackle tasks to which they had either been denied access or which had been regarded as exclusively male. Voluntary effort in clubs, associations and settlements came to the fore in wartime as the means of tackling day-to-day problems of the 'war effort' and of sustaining morale amidst wartime bereavement and shortages. There is plenty of evidence that women's institutes, girls' clubs and voluntary organizations worked closely together throughout the war years.

Early in the war courses were geared towards the war effort. In November 1914 special classes for women were authorised at Cosway Street Women's Institute in health subjects, with particular reference to food values, and literature and social legislation affecting women for which special course fees were set. Special classes for men of H.M. Forces were authorized at Woolwich with lectures in history and the geography of the war and a weekly vocal-music class. The presence of 8000 territorials in camp at White City prompted a Board of Education request for an educational programme which was solemnly approved by the Education Committee on 11 November 1914 as follows:

twelve lectures of about forty-five minutes each in –
1. simple French conversation
2. simple German conversation
3. health hints
4. history and geography of the war
5. weekly vocal music (including patriotic and marching songs in two parts)
6. lessons of one-and-a-quarter hours every evening on (i) sewing and darning

(ii) drawing and sketching (iii) woodcarving (iv) repoussé (v) leather work (vi) camp cooking – at Ellerslie Road School.[1]

The Committee were later informed that enrolments were as follows: French (472), German (78), drawing and sketching (78), woodwork (53), woodcarving (17), history and geography of the war (66), camp cooking (46), camp needle-work (23), leather work (26) vocal music (191) health hints (59).[2]

Whilst the technical and commercial colleges and institutes tackled the special-ist technical education needs of wartime London, women's institutes ran emer-gency first-aid and home-nursing courses, wartime cookery and nutrition classes and, by dressmaking and handicraft, enabled women to clothe themselves and their children and keep their homes and families going whilst the men were at 'the Front'. Women's institutes were, however, much more than this. Through a network of affiliated club classes held in girls' clubs and elsewhere they were providing specialist expertise in the informal setting of the club and a valuable framework for the social education of women. In their own centres, too, they were providing a social centre in which physical and cultural interests could be pursued by women of all ages, often for the first time.

Regular students' social evenings and exhibitions of students' work, physical exercise displays, dramatic art and vocal and orchestral music recitals continued throughout the war with educational visits and special lectures.

Zeppelin raids and the need to take cover from falling shrapnel necessitated classes gathering in a ground-floor hall or corridor, protected from the latent danger of blown-in windows. Naturally, this caused disruption from time to time. Bright moonlit nights favourable to Zeppelin raids and sleepness nights after raids, played havoc with attendances but, as the Education Officer said later in his report on the war years, 'Zeppelin raids created comparatively little damage or alarm.' The great majority of the reorganized institutes therefore remained open through the war years, providing for a diminished student body, but one sizeable enough to enable the reorganization to be tried and tested.

In March 1915 classes for teachers included a number expressly for teachers in evening institutes, e.g. class singing, conduct of evening institutes, etc. In February 1915 Her Majesty the Queen visited an experimental furnished flat in the Guinness Trust Buildings in Bermondsey. This flat was connected with the domestic-economy scheme for evening institutes by which women's institutes had begun one of their significant contributions to the war effort in training some 2500 army cooks in domestic-economy centres throughout London.

After two sessions of the reorganization the Higher Education sub-committee (12 May 1915) felt that no major changes were necessary. It is interesting to note that the number of women's fee-paying institutes reverted from thirty-three to thirty and women's free institutes from eight to eleven. The number of whole-time responsible teachers rose to forty-two. Possibly through the Rev. Stewart

Headlam's efforts a scale of clerical assistance was adopted, based on average student hours during October and February. An average of 800 hours weekly secured one attendance of a clerical assistant for three hours; 900 hours, two attendances; 1000, three attendances; 1200, four attendances and 1500, five attendances.

By the 1916–17 session the number of women's institutes had dropped to twenty-nine, free institutes to twenty-one, the literary institutes to two and institutes for the deaf to one. We find Rev. Stewart Headlam opposing the closure of institutes in Bethnal Green and Finsbury and the literary institute in Greenwich. Session 1917–18 opened with thirty-six women's institutes, both free and fee paying, ten free institutes (men and women), two literary institutes and one institute for the deaf. 1917 was a bad year for air-raids. Daylight aeroplane raids, a feature of 1917, caused considerable damage. In June 1917 a bomb fell on a Poplar School killing eighteen children and injuring many others. The log-books of institutes as far apart as Newington Green Women's Institute and Goodrich Road Women's Institute, Dulwich, indicate frequent air-raids and air-raid warnings throughout September, October, January and February of the 1917–18 session.

Throughout 1917 discussions on the education of the adolescent intensified. These discussions followed the setting-up in 1916 of a departmental committee under the chairmanship of J. Herbert Lewis, MP and Parliamentary Secretary to the Board of Education, to study juvenile education in relation to employment after the war. On 24 October 1917 a report by the Higher Education sub-committee, submitted to the Education Committee, set out in detail the contents of a French draft bill for education of adolescents – Projet de loi sur l'education des adolescents – as presented to the Chamber of Deputies on 12 March 1917 and printed in the *Revue Pedagogigue*, April 1917. Perhaps even more surprisingly, the report to the Education Committee included a very full statement on the reform of education in Germany, taken mainly from the *Padagogische Zeitung*, January 1916–July 1917. The report quoted discussions between teachers' organizations on the removal of the isolationism of pre-war years which had surrounded elementary education in Germany. In a year when eighteen children had been killed by a bomb dropped on a Poplar School and there was no sign of the war coming to an end, consideration of proposals for the reform of the enemy's educational system seems, at this distance, remarkable or even bizarre.

The enthusiasm of the Education Committee and the Education Officer for the proposals in the Fisher Act of 1918 was very apparent. The LCC made clear its support to Mr H.A.L. Fisher and proceeded with its plans for twenty-two day continuation schools. The proposal in the Act for such schools and the provision whereby local education authorities could make attendance at them compulsory for all young people between the ages of sixteen and nineteen had implications, of course, for evening institutes. All institutes in some way or another had been providing for young people of this age group and the Education Officer's report of 1912, which preceded the reorganization of 1913, had a great deal to say about the difficulty of attracting this age group to evening classes. It had referred to the compulsory day-release of young men in this age group in the city of Munich (and generally throughout Germany) and had indicated that whatever could be done in evening education was a poor second to the introduction of compulsory day-release. The introduction of twenty-two day continuation schools to London was likely, therefore, to remove a considerable number of evening students to these day schools. The Act, however, required the submission of a scheme to the Board of Education before such schools could be established and, in the event, it was to be January 1921 before they were established.

A report to the Education Committee of 1 May 1918 indicated that, despite difficulties, some 100,000 students, two thirds of whom were women and girls, had made an average attendance each of fifty hours throughout the war years. In view of tram, bus, railway disruption and darkened streets, air-raids, etc. this, as the Committee said, was very commendable. Some 170 courses of instruction had been conducted specially for groups of employers and some employers had asked for classes of a more recreative type. Commercial institutes had been diversifying their programme with periodical lectures on commercial and technical subjects and the report of the Higher Education sub-committee indicated that, in the 1918 – 19 session, the scope of these lectures should be extended to include the humanities. They still thought it right to exclude handicraft, music, cookery and needlework from commercial institutes but thought that an occasional break from vocational subjects by periodical lecturers would be of great educational value. A report by the Education Officer was promised later. In the meantime it was thought that the practice of the previous two sessions should continue. These required (a) that returns of enrolment and attendances were made to the Education Officer at stated periods with a view to concentration of classes where necessary and (b) that instructors were not engaged unless the number in the enrolment week indicated that the required number in the schedule for those particular subjects would be reached. Also the responsible teacher or principal was required to submit a scheme giving the teaching time allocated if enrolment was low. In other words the fairly tight control by the Education Officer over enrolment and the concentration of classes was maintained. Of the 190 institutes approved in the sessional arrangements for 1918 – 19 there were thirty-six women's free and fee-paying institutes, ten free institutes (men and mixed), two literary and one deaf institute.

In February 1919 a resolution was proposed by Mr Cotton and seconded by Mr Claque that when the reorganization of evening institutes came before the Higher Education sub-committee, the question be considered of extending the curriculum of women's institutes to commercial and technical subjects. The committee decided that there should be no change in the curricula of women's institutes except for letter-writing and arithmetic at Bath Street Women's Institute. It was no doubt thought that the introduction of occasional non-vocational subjects in commercial institutes might affect the enrolment at women's institutes and therefore justify some relaxation of the exclusion of commercial and technical subjects from them. Clearly such a development would have considerably weakened the purpose of the reorganization of 1913 and the committee was firm in rejecting such a proposal.

6. Post-War Reconstruction: 1919 – 29

With the signing of the Armistice on 11 November 1918 and the cessation of hostilities, the process of re-establishing family life and resettling returning servicemen began. Despite an influenza epidemic and a railway strike, enrolment and attendance at evening institutes in the session 1918–19 exceeded that of 1913–14. The numbers enrolled at women's institutes, free and fee-paying (28,028) exceeded that of 1913–14 by 7700. The two literary institutes had a 54 per cent increase in the number of students over the previous session. The report presenting these statistics to the Education Committee (10 March 1920) stated that ex-servicemen were joining mainly vocational classes and, with astonishing blandness, commented that 'among the demobilised soldiers some were not persevering students'.[1]

It was clearly time to implement some of the provisions of the 1913 reorganization which had been sabotaged by the war. Meanwhile, the Adult Education Committee of the Ministry of Reconstruction was considering the national provision of adult education.

The Final Report of the Adult Education Committee of the Ministry of Reconstruction[2]

On 4 December 1919 the Higher Education sub-committee noted the receipt by the LCC of the final report of the Adult Education Committee of the Ministry of Reconstruction. This remarkable document, as the first national survey of adult education undertaken by Government, was the fourth report of a committee, chaired by the Master of Balliol (Arthur L. Smith), which included Albert Mansbridge (then a member of the LCC Education Committee), R.H. Tawney and a number of other members of the LCC. It had as one of its secretaries, Arthur Greenwood, later to be Minister of Housing in the first Labour Government.

The Committee's first interim report completed in March 1918, about industrial and social conditions in relation to adult education, found that the main reason underlying the demand for adult education was a growing appreciation of the responsibilities of citizenship. The second interim report completed in July 1918 was on education in the army and was principally directed to assisting soldiers to turn themselves again into citizens in the critical period between the Armistice and demobilization. The whole question of libraries and museums was the subject of the third report completed in May 1919 which supported the proposal to transfer the administration of public libraries to the local education authority and recommended the union of educational and library administration, especially in England and Wales.

The final report was predominantly concerned with university, tutorial and extension classes, the WEA, settlements and other voluntary organizations. The Adult Education Committee's survey showed that local education authorities were primarily concerned with children and with vocational further education. 'But adult education . . . requires a freedom and initiative on the part of students, which is foreign to the highly centralised administration of the local authority.' The local authority also laboured under other handicaps: 'Schools do not make attractive meeting places for adults. The equipment and seating accommodation are planned for young people. There is, moreover, a certain shame-facedness about "going to school".' The Committee were also sharply critical about the attitude of many elected councillors 'who are unable to understand the desire for education of no direct utilitarian value, unless it be for purposes of personal accomplishment and who suspect dark motives in the minds of those who desire such education. More especially is this so where the demand is for the study of problems which are controversial. It is within our knowledge that there are even today town councillors to whom the term "economic" is synonymous with "socialism".'[3] So far there had been little demand made upon local authorities by adults for classes in non-vocational subjects. The Committee attributed this not so much to lack of desire as to lack of knowledge of the possibilities and lack of confidence in educational established methods.

To all this the London County Council was the splendid exception. Rather more than one page of the six pages devoted to local education authorities, in the two hundred and fifty pages of the survey of adult education in Great Britain, was devoted to an account of 'the departure from the older traditions' by the LCC in its women's institutes, general institutes and 'of special interest, the two literary institutes'.

As far as London was concerned the final report of the Adult Education Committee was a striking confirmation of the philosophy expressed in the Education Officer's report of 1912 and a commendation of the steps taken in the 1913 reorganization (and subsequently) which had established London as the pre-eminent authority in this field. No wonder Sir Robert Blair, the Education Officer, chose to end his report on the war years 1915–19 by quoting the passage from the Master of Balliol's letter, submitting the Adult Education Committee's report, to the Prime Minister, Lloyd George. 'The necessary conclusion,' said the Master of Balliol, 'is that adult education must not be regarded as a luxury for a few exceptional persons here and there, nor as a thing which concerns only a short span of early manhood but that adult education is a permanent national necessity, an inseparable aspect of citizenship and therefore should be both universal and life long.'

In 1919 Sir Robert could quote this now famous passage with pride and conviction in its truth and belief in its early acceptance. So often, subsequently, it has been quoted as a high-water mark and goal from which successive governments have fallen short.

The Education Officer's report on the Adult Education Committee's final report was presented to the Higher Education sub-committee on 22 January 1920.[4] In it he outlined the main aspects of the report and recorded, but made no comment on, the recommendations by the Committee that universities should set up extra-mural departments with extra-mural councils on which should be represented other adult education providers; that universities should be the main source of supply of adult education teachers; that tutor's fees for one class a session should be not less than £80 and a full-time tutor's salary not less than £500.

The main points to which he directed the Committee's attention were:
1. the question of the desirability of making separate provision in the Council's scheme for non-vocational adult education;
2. the question of making special grants to the University of London for an increase provision for tutorial classes;
3. the Adult Education Committee's recommendation that non-university work should be controlled by an Adult Education Joint Committee comprising representatives of the local education authorities, voluntary educational bodies and universities within the area of the local authority; and
4. further steps necessary to increase classes in 'humane subjects' in institutions providing technical or vocational education.

There is no record of a further report by the Education Officer on these particular aspects but it is clear from other records that a good deal of consultation took place on the Adult Education Committee's recommendations between representatives of the London County Council and various interested bodies. Several meetings took place between representatives of the University of London and the LCC on the need for closer co-operation on facilities for extension, tutorial classes and increased financial support. The London Head Teachers' Association reacted favourably. In a resolution dated 17 December 1920 the Association endorsed the opinion of the Council that one of the most significant features of the present time was the growing demand for adult education; welcomed proposals of the Council to support the adult education movement through the University of London and indicated that they would cordially support a policy which aimed at:
1. bringing into co-operation with the University all grades of educational activities throughout the metropolitan area; and
2. extending further local facilities for the education of men and women particularly in the outlying districts.

But in June 1921 the London Head Teachers' Association said, 'LHTA is of the opinion that the wisest, safest and most suitable form of adult education is through the medium of, or under the governing influence of the universities and that in cases where such adult education is recognised by university it is worthy of the financial support of the LEA as well of grant earning capacity under the Board of Education.' Reading between the lines it is clear that the introduction of adult education classes into secondary schools and the prospect of this being extended by the introduction of more literary institutes was not absent from the minds of the drafters of these particular submissions from the LHTA. Both December and June submissions were duly received by the Higher Education sub-committee with no comment.

At a conference with representatives of the University and the LCC at least one representative seemed to think that the universities should be responsible for non-vocational education and for the appointment of all tutors. The view was expressed that the opening of literary institutes had considerably complicated matters! However, at a conference in Cambridge attended by representatives of local education authorities and universities, opinion generally was against a university take-over of non-vocational adult education. The idea that universities had a special prerogative in non-vocational education died hard, however, and more than once the suggestion came from universities that they had a special role to perform in the training of all tutors for non-vocational adult education – a view which went along with a somewhat restricted view of adult education, namely, that adult education was concerned only with the teaching of the human-ities. It persisted until the 1950s and possibly later among some university extra-mural staff.

Meantime, the University of London sought increased support from the LCC for its tutorial classes and in 1923 submitted an application for a grant of £1500 which was an increase of £400 on the previous year. Blair asked the Chief Inspector to arrange for tutorial classes to be visited so that the authority would have first-hand information on them, particularly on those run in conjunction with the WEA. He asked

1. are they attended by manual workers?
2. are the attendances satisfactory?
3. is sound work being done?

Some of the reports of inspectors on the visits which followed make interesting reading. G.D.H. Cole tutored a course on the 'history and problems of labour and modern history'. At one of his classes observed by an inspector, the class took the form of a meeting of the National Railway Wages Board. Cole himself acted as Chairman of the Company and the class secretary acted as the Chairman of the employees. There were six black-coated workers and eight middle-class women. Of the thirty-one original students, fourteen were clerks and none of the others, apart from possibly a storekeeper and a trade-union organizer, were manual workers. The inspector noted that, 'Mr Cole's qualification as a teacher and knowledge of the subject is beyond dispute. His opinions are of course famous if not notorious. [The last four words had been deleted and 'very well known' substituted!] 'On the present occasion no tincture of party bias was to be observed and as a matter of fact he put the employers "case" with an ability which a great many employers would, doubtless, envy.' Favourable reports were also made on an economic history class taken by Mr Pringle in which thirty-two students had enrolled and, apart from two or three postmen, most of the students were post-office sorters. At a genetic-psychology class at Mary Ward Institute where the students were clerks and professional people the lecturer, apparently stung by the inspector's questions, retorted that they might be clerks but they were on small salaries and were financially no better off than manual workers. In a philosophy class conducted by Dr C.E.M. Joad, the students were not manual workers but 'working people'. One can imagine the inspector and Dr Joad locked in verbal combat on 'it depends what you mean by manual workers'.

In 1918–19 the number of students in tutorial classes, was 3300 for all the universities in the country. The number of students in extension classes and tutorial classes of the University of London was in the region of 6000; voluntary establishments such as Morley and the Working Men's College had just over 1000 students each and Toynbee Hall just under 500. The number of students at women's institutes (free and fee-paying) amounted to 28,028 and the two literary institutes in 1918–19 session had about 500; these last two figures exclude, of course, the substantial number of students who were enrolled in non-vocational classes in vocational institutes.

Literary Institutes

In a bold move to strengthen non-vocational education the LCC approved the opening, in September 1919, of five literary institutes – Plumstead and Woolwich, Marylebone, Dalston, Peckham and the City Literary Institutes.

Just how bold this initiative was can only be appreciated if one recalls that, in the streamlining of existing evening institutes in the 1913 reorganization, a number of classes in the humanities did not fit in comfortably with the commercial, technical, women's or general institutes. Moreover, studies in the humanities were the province of the university extension or tutorial class, the WEA and the other voluntary organizations. With the notable exception of Morley College and, to a lesser extent, the Working Men's College they were subjects studied in small, usually isolated, groups of the extension or tutorial class system, in which there was little or no collegiate interchange or cross-fertilization. Such was the emphasis on study in depth and the achievement of university standards that it was tacitly accepted that substantial numbers of men and women would not reach these standards. Yet here was a local education authority providing not one but five institutes which would be devoted to the humanities. Two principals of literary institutes, writing considerably later, bore testimony to this bold initiative. T.G. Williams, appointed as a whole-time responsible master of the City Literary Institute in 1920, records:

It was a pure act of faith. It cannot be said there was any public demand to which the local education authority was responding, at any rate no coherent and specific demand. It is almost true to say that full-time principals were appointed before a single student was enrolled; their duty was first to create and afterwards to organise demand and it may well be thought that the boldest decision of all was to choose a site for one of the literary institutes in the heart of business London, the square mile altogether dedicated, as it might have been supposed, to the pursuit of material, rather than ideal, ends. However, there it was and the limited expectations that were entertained for the City Literary Institute may be estimated by the modest extent of the accommodation and equipment provided. It consisted of four rooms of a building scheduled 25 years before as sub-standard, but still in use as a Teachers Training College. Because of its needs our access was limited to three evenings a week after 6 p.m., by which time, of course, the neighbouring streets were silent save for the incessant throb of the printing presses.[5]

Fred Burbidge, the first head of Plumstead and Woolwich Literary Evening Institute, writing in 1933, said:

The literary institutes were a new departure. No one knew what was expected of them; no one had any clear idea of the nature or scope of their work, no one was specially enthusiastic about them – they were just given their chance, and perhaps this is the best way of launching an experiment. Fortunately, at the outset, they were hampered by very few restrictions. Their members were to be over 18 years of age; their work was not to conflict with established commercial or technical institutes or polytechnics. Beyond this they had a fairly clear field. One other new departure must be noted; one that contributed enormously to their success. They were housed, where possible in the Council's well equipped secondary schools. In the first place they were not welcomed by the staffs and governors of these schools; they were perforce put up with. But the perhaps natural latent opposition soon died down. Inevitably problems and difficulties do arise wherever dual contact operates, but no serious impasse has arisen and although the literary institutes are not even now wildly welcomed by the schools concerned, they are regarded as quite creditable lodgers.

As the 1919 reconstruction report indicated there was still considerable suspicion of the motives of any working man or women who sought to study any subject which was not strictly utilitarian. Personal scholarship or interest had still to be excused under the utilitarian umbrella of a greater interest in citizenship or international affairs.

T.G. Williams found the discussion beset with clichés. 'One was that the values of adult education were attainable only under a ''voluntary'' system.' The 1919 report certainly felt it was difficult for an LEA to offer that essential freedom of choice of subject, tutor, etc. to the student which was available in university and other voluntary provision.

> Another cliché which obscured realities was that the standards of adult educa-
> tion were and should remain academic, and that its highest aims were attain-
> able only by the traditional university methods of lecture, discussion and essay
> work. Further it was said that it was a form of education which appeals only to
> a limited number of students so that there was need for caution lest, as a result
> of association with non-academic forms, it should suffer a dilution of standards
> – this in a TUC pamphlet! . . . The claims always seemed to me to be based
> on a number of non-sequiturs. It did not follow that merely because classes
> were organised, administered and grant aided under adult education regula-
> tions and because the University was associated with them, the classes were
> going to do work of University quality. It did not follow that students
> enrolled in such classes, even though of three winters duration and following
> an approved syllabus, were ipso facto intellectually equipped to meet demands
> which are implied by the discipline of University studies. Again it did not
> follow that when a student came starry eyed with gazing on the social millen-
> nium – the 'student with social purpose' – he was divinely marked out as
> one equipped for studies of University standard. Yet as I scanned the references
> to adult education in books, pamphlets, journals and reports I found that all
> those non-sequiturs were commonly accepted without examination.[6]

The clue to the goal to which the new literary institutes were aiming is perhaps enshrined in the following: 'It seemed to me that a system of adult education was good if it took the adult as it found him and started from there. It should provide him with the kind of stimulus and training which he needed *at his own level*. That means that adult education has to adjust its methods and its standards to a wide variety of types and conditions of men.'[7]

Fred Burbidge was appointed as a sessional head which meant that he carried on his ordinary day-school work and devoted the evenings and practically every Saturday and Sunday to the new institute. In the following session he was appointed a whole-time head in charge of both Plumstead and Woolwich Literary Institute and the new literary institute at Eltham. Woolwich was perhaps the least suburban of London suburbs – it was more like an independent industrial town. In the past it had been so dominated by the Arsenal that it would have been true to have said that, in 75 per cent of its houses, lived an Arsenal employee. Whilst in 1919 this was no longer true there was an homogeneity about the Woolwich area not present in other suburban boroughs. Moreover, in 1919

Woolwich had a generally prosperous population. In the first session the enrol-ment of the literary institute was about 700, by much the largest of any of the literary institutes. Just about the same time as the principal was appointed, the Royal Arsenal Co-operative Society, always a very powerful force in the Woolwich district, appointed a new full-time educational secretary and, in 1920, the Society purchased Shornells, a mansion standing in extensive grounds on Bostall Heath. This house, with its subsequent extensions, was to become the centre for the social-educational and recreative sides of the Society's work. The principal of the literary institute worked closely with the educational secretary and there seems little doubt that his influence led to the promotion of a very much wider educational programme by the RACS than might otherwise have been the case. Purely cultural subjects such as literature, psychology, appreciation of art, architecture, music and so on were introduced into the RACS programme and the classes more often than not were held in RACS premises, so much so that it became increasingly difficult to justify the Kings Warren School as the head-quarters of the institute.

The enthusiasm of Mr Burbidge, head of the two institutes, Plumstead and Woolwich and Eltham, shines through his reports. Eltham, however, was a very different story from Plumstead and Woolwich. Of Eltham Fred Burbidge said:

The county secondary school, Deansfield Road is a pleasant enough building situated in a remote and inaccessible part of the district. To compensate for this, arrangements were made to open certain classes in the Roper Street School. This is the old village school, well and centrally situated but hopelessly unsuitable for adult work and very inadequately heated. As will be gathered from reading my annual reports on this institute Eltham was for many years somewhat of a lame duck. Some quite excellent work was done but there was not enough of it. The want of suitable centrally situated premises hampered possible development and the widespread nature of my work made it physically impossible for me to give close personal attention. Indeed for many years, the work during the evening was perforce directed – most unofficially but also very efficiently – by my wife. The character of Eltham – or perhaps the want of it also made things difficult. It is a rambling amorphous place with a very rapidly increasing population: a clumsy shapeless body superimposed on what was, even up to the time of the war, a compact, delightfully situated and very healthy village. With a quite charming high street that has been most scandalously and effectually destroyed and vulgarised. The soul of Eltham to begin with was the niggling, sniffy, patronising village branch variety. It is doubtful now if it has a soul at all: it is disintregating into a dormitory suburb and possibly its only hope is the literary institute.[8]

T.G. Williams, head of an institute sited in a part of the City almost without residential population except for some Temple barristers, had a very different task from that of Burbidge in Woolwich. His clientele were workers in the City who were only too anxious to rush away in the early evenings to their suburban homes.

> When I came on the scene after the first term of session 1920–21 there were some 180 students on the roll, and nine weekly classes were in progress; about three or four of them were vigorous growths, the rest were weaklings. How to proceed from here? My first step was to have printed a thousand copies of a single leaf timetable of classes. Then I set out on a tour of the Fleet Street and Holborn offices, seeking out staff officers, and with an eye for staff notice-boards. I tried to 'sell' the idea of the City Literary Institute which I described as a place where adventures of the mind and spirit might be undertaken in the congenial company of like-minded people, and in an atmosphere of freedom. It was difficult at first to persuade people to believe that there were no preliminary tests, no final examinations, no certificates or diplomas to be won. But the message sometimes got home, and, mainly as the result of a large, though unexpected, summer term enrolment, the session ended with 430 students on roll.[9]

For some years he was without a telephone and typewriter and clerical help was allowed for three hours on each of two evenings a week. There was a postage allowance of 3d. per student enrolled per annum. In the next session the numbers were again nearly trebled to about 1200 and Williams had to set about borrowing accommodation – Birkbeck College and neighbouring schools, Dr Johnston's house in Gough Square and Prince Henry's Room in Fleet Street. He organized some classes for staff on their own premises, as at the Accountant General's Department at the GPO North. 'Somehow or other classrooms were found to match the growing demand. By 1924–25 the 2,000 mark was passed; after another two years the 3,000 mark and so it went on until in 1928–29 we reached 4,000.'[10]

By September 1920 the number of literary institutes had increased to ten of which six were supervized by three whole-time heads. The five new institutes were Eltham, Dalston and Poplar, Holloway, Fulham and one in the East End, all in secondary-school premises. Reading rooms were to be established at all literary and general institutes.

Men's Institutes

One obvious gap in the 1913 reorganization was the omission of any form of non-vocational institute for men. Although women's institutes were not regarded as non-vocational, they had always had a club-like atmosphere, taught non-vocational subjects and approached instruction informally. As we have seen the war emphasized the importance of women's institutes and masked, through the absence of men on war service, the lack of provision for men.

In seeking reasons for the omission one notes the emphasis given in the confer-ences and discussions, leading to the 1913 reorganization, to courses of study, diligent application to studies and response to demand. The purely non-vocational institutes – the literary institutes – bold innovation that they were, sought to respond to the demand for cultural development which had already manifested itself. Support for the work of settlements, the WEA, the university-extension classes, the Working Men's college and Morley College was similarly based. There is little evidence to indicate that Sir Robert and his team thought that simple recreative past-times could do other than provide occasional relief from the more serious business of education.

It was the Rev. Stewart Headlam, the man who had started a drama competi-tion for evening institutes by offering an annual prize, and the man who was probably the most assiduous visitor and consistent supporter of evening education since the early days of the School Board for London, who sought to secure facili-ties in the statutory sector for working men.

Headlam and Sir Robert Blair frequently did not agree. F.G. Bettany's bio-graphy of Stewart Headlam gives some revealing glimpses of the antagonism between the two men. As the former Chairman of the School Board for London Evening Schools sub-committee, Headlam had expected to be co-opted to the first LCC Education Committee as one of the ex-School Board members. He was not co-opted and was therefore not in the first triennium of the LCC or its Educa-tion Committee. He stood for Bethnal Green in 1907 and was elected. 'On my return, I found what I might call the "R. Blair rubber stamp" supreme. The Education Officer of the Council was a very able but also very masterful man and he worked education as if it were a machine. Everything had to be done through him and the Committee's function was merely to approve.'[11]

On the death of Stewart Headlam, Harold Hodge, a fellow member of the Higher Education sub-committee, wrote:

> What will the Higher Education Sub-Committee do without him? How flat the proceedings without the passages between Headlam and the Education Officer! It was a saving interlude when the two got at cross purposes – the driving Scotsman trying to force Headlam's fiery spirit and intangible ideals into the channels in which 'the Office' had decreed all London education must flow. No wonder a good deal of hot steam came off. I remember Headlam exclaiming 'I will read any document which is not signed "R. Blair".' Yet Sir Robert Blair whose ability everyone recognises, had the greatest regard for Headlam.[12]

The different approach of the two men is perhaps summed up in a sentence of Sir Robert Blair's own tribute to Stewart Headlam. 'His sympathies did not lie with vocational education . . . I stood for . . . a course of instruction related to that which interested the evening students most, their occupation.'[13] Headlam's sympathy, however, always went to the 'down and outs'. 'This is all very well,' he said, as he studied the Blair schemes for commercial and technical instruction, 'but what are we going to do with the rough lad, the van boy, the errand boy and their type?'[14] Whilst Headlam recognized that many of the reforms were necessary he dreaded the effect of the 1913 reorganization 'on those who are not lucky, not very earnest or who are engaged in occupations which they do not want to be reminded of in the evenings'.[15] He hated the idea of the elimination of some 30,000 of the 130,000 students in the interests of efficiency. He campaigned unceasingly for those whom he claimed the 1913 reorganization had ignored.

Stewart Headlam was to get his way. At the meeting of the Higher Education sub-committee on 25 March 1920 the Chairman, Mr Henry C. Gooch, referred to a suggestion by the Rev. Stewart Headlam for establishing non-vocational classes for men and stated he was in favour of establishing a limited experiment of five or six institutes for men over eighteen to provide instruction in non-vocational subjects. The institutes were to be separate from the existing evening institute system and to be conducted with as few rules as possible. The Education Officer was instructed to submit detailed proposals on the lines laid down by the Chairman. The Education Officer reported on 22 April recommending five institutes, each with a whole-time responsible master, for men students, in areas then served by general or free institutes at Battersea, Bethnal Green, Deptford, Stepney and Walworth. Admission to the institutes was to be free and there was to be no restriction as to the numbers required for classes. Free admission was later withdrawn and the fees for women's institutes substituted. The whole was to be an experiment and progress was to be considered before the end of the first term in December 1920.

In view of the manner in which the report came about it is interesting to note the argument put forward in the brief report to the Education Committee of 28 April 1920 by the Higher Education sub-committee for the establishment of men's institutes. It was based on the Education Officer's report and showed the same unwillingness to do other than respond to a demand even if that demand had to be imagined. 'Before the war noticeable interest was taken by working men in municipal and national affairs – the war has extended it to international affairs. There now appears to be an opportunity to attract into appropriate classes a type of student who has hitherto not attended institutes in appreciable numbers.'[16] The report went on to indicate that the curriculum should be English (in attractive form), physical exercises, music, handicraft and popular lectures in subjects such as economics, the laws of health and citizenship. Great stress was laid on the need for whole-time responsible masters who should be relieved of day work. On 22 December 1920 a report of the Higher Education sub-committee, based on a return for the week ending 25 November 1920, gave the following information:

Name of institute	Students enrolled	Percentage attendance	No. of classes
Battersea	242	41	16
Bethnal Green	156	56.3	16
Deptford	225	54.3	13
Stepney	306	67.3	26
Walworth	272	50.1	22

The order of popularity of subject was as follows: handicraft, gymnastics, first-aid, music (vocal and instrumental), lectures in economics and social subjects. The one subject which attracted little interest was international affairs.

These results fully justified the Education Committee's decision and this quite remarkable educational advance was under way. To see it as a natural step to offer those educational facilities to men, which the women's institutes already offered to women, is to ignore the particular characteristics and mores of that large body of working men who had finished with education at fourteen. Together with minor commercial and other non-manual groups of workers they constituted the largest section of the adult community of whom very few had undergone courses of instruction in further or technical education; fewer still had had specifically secondary education. Their aptitudes and tastes were very different from other sections of the community. S. Myers, the head of the Deptford Men's Institute, illuminates the background:

> There is, firstly, the energy that shows itself in an urgent desire to *do* things – to build sheds and kitchen tables, to paint woodwork, tinker with taps, clocks, wireless sets and motor cycle engines, to breed and rear chickens, rabbits and canaries, to perform horticultural prodigies with packets of seeds and wheelbarrows – all on top of a day's work. Accompanying this, there is a marked tendency towards getting together on matters of common interest; hence poultry clubs, cage bird societies, allotment associations – all serving the double purpose of fostering some hobby or interest and of providing opportunities for talking over other matters such as the shortcomings of Wolverhampton Wanderers or Chelsea, the amazing exploits of Herr Hitler, or what the foreman said last Tuesday. Sometimes these ends are served in the informal brotherhood of the public house . . . One soon deduces something more than a desire to do and to meet. A vigorous altruism runs through English working-class life making a man's fortunes and misfortunes not altogether his own. The most terrible condemnation of a man by his comrades in the army during the war years when the writer knew it was to label him with the sentiment ' – you Jack: I'm alright'. A thief was more readily forgiven than this one . . .
>
> Add to the picture the so called working class vices notably the 'bob each way' on the big race, 'one over the eight' now and again and for the women folk the sinful cinema. It is difficult to be strongly moved when these vices are thundered against. The workingclass has few real vices. Those forms of vice

which constitute social dry-rot are not characteristic of this group. Their development demands not only original sin, but also the means to do justice to it . . .

As to the social and economic facts, for practically the whole of this group the salient fact is clothing, feeding and housing the family, often a grim enough business.[17]

The Education Officer and Inspectorate rightly judged that if the experiment was to succeed the responsible master, or heads as they were later called, of the institutes would need to have tact, sympathy, resourcefulness, untiring energy and patience and, above all, a large amount of discretion. It is to the great credit of the Council that such men were selected and given both the discretion and flexible administrative support that was so necessary. The manner in which the task was tackled and the difficulties which were overcome were without doubt one of the most remarkable educational achievements of the Council.

The heads distributed posters and handbills to friendly tobacconists and general shopkeepers and secured the interest of clergy and ministers of religion, heads of schools, employers, trade-union officials, co-operative societies, etc. but it soon became apparent that normal methods of publicity would not reach the people they sought. 'In the public houses the results were, on the whole, better. The publicans in these areas exhibited the LCC posters with something like pride. The street corners proved still more fruitful although suspicion as to the motives of the propagandists was frequently displayed. 'What do you do of an evening?' asked the head of one institute after a little friendly back-chat. 'What the Hell's that to do with you?' was the reply. Very little effective publicity could be done until the institutes were open and the plain truth is that they had first to establish themselves and then succeed by virtue of their own success. Most of the publicity in connection with men's institutes was done then, as it is still, by personal contact in the streets, but the first hundred members were the corner stone on which each institute rose to success.[18] The institutes were conducted in elementary school buildings and this did not appeal to many of the men.

It had to be demonstrated that this was not going back to school; that if a man wanted to smoke there was nothing to stop him; that if a man did not want to do sums he need not; that, in short, he could do the sort of thing he wanted to do, such as argue about politics, bring the Rhode Island Red cockerel which had mysteriously expired in the back yard for a post mortem examination, hang by his hocks on the rings and ropes or blow his cornet on the top floor of the building far above the house tops and away from the remonstrances of the 'lady up stairs' at home. If interested, he could later go more seriously into these and kindred matters with the expert who was at his disposal. If a man could not squeeze into the little desks, he could have a chair. Or if he preferred his lessons standing up, he could have it that way. 'All for a bob a term' – the fee for each of the three terms being one shilling – became a slogan. There were some who did not want to hear lectures but to give them. To them the answer was: 'Very well. Give a lecture,' and very interesting some of them were. One proved that the earth was flat, another that millions now living will never die, and another still that Herbert Spencer has solved all our religious, social and economic problems. It is only fair to add that, although free speech was never denied, it was always exercised at one's peril. There was never a real 'rough house' but comment was extremely forcible even when good humoured.[19]

The institutes were continued experimentally year by year from 1920 to 1924 when they were placed on a permanent basis. By that date the men had become very active partners in the whole enterprise, they had grouped themselves into clubs and societies with chairmen, secretaries and committees.

There were poultry clubs, male voice choirs, brass bands, orchestras, sketch clubs, social study circles, etc. each forming the nucleus of a class held yearly in those subjects. The clubs were co-ordinated by a students' central council in each institute and were conducting their own affairs. It was this distinctive manifestation of democratic feeling which, encouraged by the heads of the institutes, did more than any other single cause to promote the growth and success of the institute.

Several institutes had central committees of students which included representatives of all the classes and clubs and which the heads found valuable consultative agencies in many of the problems arising in the course of their work.

The successful establishment of men's institutes owed a great deal to the remarkable men who were their first heads. They had to be well known in their districts and to be in close touch with various men's clubs and societies. They had to secure the entire confidence of the men who attended their institutes, to be interested in their problems and in sympathy with their various activities. Students invariably referred to the head of the institute as 'the governor', a good form of address which covered their appreciation of his role as organizer, troubleshooter, counsellor and friend. The term persisted long after men's institutes had disappeared. The report to the Education Committee recommending the permanent establishment of the institutes was able to say that 'men's institutes have now become an integral part of the educational activities of the districts served by them, and, as there appears to be every reason to expect further development, we are of the opinion that they should be placed upon a permanent basis'.

In 1926 a report on the work of men's institutes was prepared by HMIs for the information of the Board of Education and the local education authority. In its introduction the report referred to the remarkable experiment of 'men's institutes'.

No similar institutions are known to exist. They differ in their object and methods from all previous enterprises, not because they are intended to take the place of other efforts, but because they are attempting to fill a gap in the educational system. . . Universities and public authorities have also from time to time extended their functions in ways which have brought higher education within the reach of an ever wider public. . . But whatever the type of interest to which appeal has been made, almost all previous enterprise in adult education has aimed at reaching the more intellectual sections of the community. It has always been *higher* education that has been offered. The novelty and significance of the experiment which is the subject of this report lies in the fact that another side of the problem has been considered. It can hardly be denied that there are large numbers for whom *higher* education is impossible; but they have other needs, and to neglect them is to leave unsolved one of the most serious problems of a great city.[20]

The report paid a well-deserved tribute to the London education authority on 'its unique experience of experiments and its pioneering role in many directions'.

In setting up men's institutes the LCC had taken an important step in closing a gap in its own adult services, but more than that, it had demonstrated that a public authority could provide an adult education service for all sections of its adult community. LCC literary institutes had shown that a local education authority could meet the demand for cultural subjects. Nevertheless, literary institutes, like most adult education provision of the day, were concerned with the intellectual, or exceptional individual.

The publication of the 1926 HMI report gave a national significance to the London experiment. Moreover, the report noted that existing methods and provision left untouched vast numbers of ordinary men and women; a means had to be discovered by which a beginning could be made. This was a radical change of front which did great credit to the writers of the report. 'It may be asked,' said the HMIs with characteristic understatement − since it was most certainly asked by a good many then and now − 'Why offer education to people who do not want it?' The best answer they said 'is to be found in the work accomplished by the Institutes in the few years of their existence. Some thousands of men have been taught how to use their leisure to better advantage; they have discovered new interests and new powers in themselves. Their recognition of the benefits they have derived, and their attitude towards the teachers and others with whom they have been brought into contact, are in themselves a testimony to the civilising influence of the Institutes.'[21]

The heads of men's institutes did not of course 'offer education' − they set out to involve the working men of their area in finding ways to enrich their lives. Education was by stealth and the pragmatic opportunism of the heads and the staff they recruited. In the words of the HMI report:

Hundreds of young men who would otherwise be 'running to seed' are submitting to the healthy discipline of physical training, and are learning to conduct their contests in a spirit of true sportsmanship. Hundreds of men of all ages, amongst them many young married men, are practising handicrafts such as home carpentry with a persistence which must react beneficially upon their character. Incidentally the practice of such a hobby by men whose daily work is often of a casual nature induces a feeling of self-respect and a pride of achievement hitherto lacking in their lives. In every Institute men are learning the possibilities of the rational employment of their leisure. Activity is the key note. Music appeals to them if they can take part in making music. Hence every Institute has its 'band', and after the first year or two its orchestra, with subsidiary classes for learners. Hobbies of many kinds are cultivated. Photography is studied under the guidance of an expert, and the chemistry of photography arouses an interest in the wonders of science. Interest in 'wireless' gives an opening for classes in elementary physics. Interest in motors brings groups of young men, some of whom are engaged as drivers in the day time, to classes in 'petrol engines' and kindred branches of the science of engineering, all conducted on a simple and practical plane. . . Classes for the study of economics, or social problems in current events are not, as a rule, a strong feature; although each Institute has one or more of these.[22]

Exhibitions of work showed that many students had a spirit of craftsmanship and a natural gift for artistic expression. A warehouseman, a house decorator, three deckhands waiting for a ship and a haddock smoker were the nucleus of a class which, after a year's instruction, gave an interesting exhibition of original drawings and paintings in a Bethnal Green Museum.

In the first year the enrolments in each institute had reached about 350. By the third year they had grown to an average of 500 in each institute. It is significant that the attendance at the institutes was remarkably stable and remained fairly constant at three hours a week; this indicated that students were attending for more than one night, many of them for up to four nights a week. At the time of the HMIs report in 1926, 30 per cent were attending classes in physical training; about 25 per cent were in handicraft classes, chiefly woodwork, and about 12 per cent were involved in musical classes; about 7 per cent followed a variety of hobbies. The remaining 26 per cent were distributed in a wide variety of classes such as English, literature, economics, citizenship, elementary science, Esperanto, mathematics, first-aid, drawing and painting, general knowledge and law. Apart from the Battersea Institute 'general education' was not a prominent feature of any institute. Interest in abstract knowledge, even in connection with politics and economics, was rare. Activity was the key note: 'the man who spends his industrial life in uninteresting repetition work finds joy and satisfaction in making – from beginning to end – a stool, a bedstead, a cradle, a pair of steps, in beating out an ash-tray or metal picture frame, in potting and repotting plants, in making or remodelling a wireless set, and so on. To act in a play or even to read one is an extension of self for any man, and not least for those whose lives are without much variety and colour . . .'[23]

There was no doubt that the institutes were attracting labourers rather than artisans, 'Busmen, bakers, barmen, bricklayers labourers, butchers, barge-builders, carmen, crane drivers, blacksmiths' labourers, cable makers, fish curers, sausage makers, grooms, porters, hawkers, gas workers, factory hands, lighter men, lavatory attendants, messengers, news vendors, plate layers, carriage cleaners, rivet heaters, rag and bone dealers, packers, stokers, scaffolders, store-keepers, tram women, wine tasters, warehousemen, etc, etc.'[24] were the unskilled manual.workers who found in the institutes a congenial atmosphere in which to discover themselves and extend their interests.

The institutes carried on many social activities. On Saturday evenings, tea-parties, dances, concerts and other gatherings were open to members and their wives and friends. As early as 1926 at least one institute organized an annual dinner attended by several hundreds (and subscribed for in advance) – a practice which was to become widespread in later years. Placing responsibilities upon a large number of the members for the management of various functions; appoint-ing committees; enlisting the services of class secretaries and forming societies to promote hobbies of an educational, even a profitable, type, were all ways of carrying out, quietly and unobstrusively, valuable social education.

'They are a civilising agency in every district in which they are placed. They prevent moral and intellectual wastage among a class living in some of the least favourable surroundings of urban life, employed for the most part in low skilled manual and even casual employment. They have inspired confidence and respect for a public authority among many who previously regarded education as at best a bugbear.' The institutes had brought together a number of features which are normally difficult to combine. 'The aimlessness of a mere club is avoided by the presence of actual pursuits organised by experienced teachers. On the other hand, the element of club life is there to provide social amenities. Intellectualism is not banished; but it is not allowed to monopolise an undue share of attention whilst other important interests are ignored.'[25]

It is of note, too, that the club atmosphere which was such an essential part of the success of men's institutes was brought about, for the most part, in ordinary, elementary school accommodation. Battersea and Bethnal Green Insti-tutes, although used for day continuation schools and junior instruction centres, were adapted later to provide common-rooms, reading-rooms, workshops and gymnasia. The Kentish Town Institute shared a disused elementary school with a public assistance committee non-residential training centre. For the rest there was no accommodation available other than that to be found in the ordinary elemen-tary school. Here and there a decline in school population temporarily freed a classroom for the special use of the institute but, for the most part, common-rooms and reading-rooms had to be made out of classrooms in which the desks had either been removed or stacked round the walls and then replaced by tables of the collapsible type supplied by the Council. Myers, writing in 1933, says mildly that the problem of accommodation 'tends to be troublesome'. Apart from the damage to treasured school objects such as goldfish and plasticine models, other claims on the building had to be considered such as the requirements of the day school for social purposes and games outside school hours, old scholars' clubs, election and other public meetings and lettings of various kinds. The Council sensibly referred applications for lettings made by outside bodies to the heads of the institutes for their views; nevertheless, creating a 'club atmosphere' in an elementary-school building was no mean achievement. Heads of men's institutes had to be capable of overcoming all kinds of difficulties. 'It is remarkable, however, how much can be done even in these circumstances by the exercise of good-will and initiative. The sympathy and forebearance of the teachers in the day schools deserves notice.'[26] Undoubtedly they were remarkable men!

Junior Men's Institutes

Whereas young women between the ages of fourteen to eighteen could join women's institutes their male counterpart were not so privileged since men's institutes were for men over the age of eighteen. Mounting concern for the continued education of boys not definitely engaged in commercial or technical occupations, the undoubted success of men's institutes and, in particular, the attraction they had for young men of eighteen led the Education Committee on 13 May 1925 to approve a proposal to set up five institutes for boys on the same lines as men's institutes. As with the inception of men's institutes the five institutes were to be experimental. Fees were to be the same as free institutes, that is, there was to be a registration fee of 6d. per session. There was to be a special curriculum and no restriction on numbers required for the opening of classes. The experiment was successful and, from 1926 – 7, junior men's institutes were established, sometimes alongside men's institutes; the responsible master of the men's institutes was in charge also of the junior men's institute. The experience of men's institutes had confirmed the importance of a whole-time responsible master and whole-time responsible masters were therefore appointed to junior men's institutes.

In the Council's own handbook, *The London Education Service*, men's (junior) institutes were described as institutes

> . . . to meet the problem created by the large number of lads between 14 and 18 years of age, who are not able to obtain regular or skilled employment . . . The institutes are organised on lines similar to those adopted for the men's institutes; care has been taken so that they will not adversely affect the

admirable work of many of the boys clubs, nor usurp the influence of club leaders, and that organised study elsewhere shall be safeguarded. A registration fee of 6d. is payable on admission. At each institute a clubroom is open every evening; newspapers, magazines and games are available and the institute library can be used by all students. Students committees are formed for organising sport's clubs, gymnastic displays, boxing competitions, concerts and social evenings. The subjects taught include English, in the form of topics of interest to boys; wood and metalwork, hobbies, hygiene, gymnastics, first aid and boxing.

Self help, co-operation and initiative are stimulated. The lads are encouraged to plan their own educational and vocational needs, the institutes providing expert instructors for the subjects decided upon. The institutes have established friendly relations with neighbouring clubs and associations devoted to the social welfare of boys.[27]

The task to be tackled by this experiment was as challenging as that which faced the men's institutes in 1920, for the problem was as old as the evening-school system itself and greatly aggravated in the 1920s by widescale unemployment. The comprehensive system of further education developed by the LCC provided for almost every kind of educational need. The women's institutes had gone a long way in providing for young women of fourteen to eighteen but young men of that age proved more difficult. Despite the efforts made in general institutes and in, junior commercial and technical institutes there remained a large section, the junior counterpart of those in men's institutes, who were for the most part incapable of systematic study. The success of the men's institutes was the major inspiration and encouragement to try 'the new approach' in the junior men's institutes. Nevertheless, the appeal had to be made to those young men who had no wish to 'continue' their further education. The evidence of successful men's institutes undoubtedly helped. They helped to quell innate suspicions of 'school' and 'education'. What was good enough for the men was worth trying by the boys. In the first year 2700 young men enrolled. From then on it was a question of trying virtually anything which appeared to have appeal and then, by trial and error, selecting a programme. Subjects or pursuits were successful according to the 'allegiance' attracted by the teacher. They had to be very special people who could inspire support and interest. Many day-school teachers, adapted well to the challenge; equally, many people who were not teachers proved to have those qualities of sympathy and craftsmanship which gained the respect, loyalty and affection of the students.

As with the senior men, students were unobtrusively encouraged to play a large part in helping to run the programme. Although there was a wide diversity of support for particular subjects in the various institutes within a comparatively short time there was a remarkable similarity in the curriculum offered at all junior men's institutes. This was due not simply to the close contact that heads had with each other but to the universality of demand from the students themselves. Practical subjects and physical training and those subjects involving manual dexterity had pride of place but the skill of the heads and their teachers was to be seen in the support given to a range of general education subjects.

In 1931 the Board of Education published *London Men's (Junior) Evening Institutes*, a report by HMIs on five years' work and judged to be of such interest to those concerned with 'Adolescence and Adult Education' as to demand wider circulation.[28] 'At the time of the report the five new institutes had been at work for five years and two others for three years. The institutes under review were:

Name of institute	No. of boys in attendance
Bethnal Green ('Stewart Headlam' with branch at Rochelle Street)	1526
Rotherhithe (Herold's Institute with branches at East Lane Cobourg Road)	1284
Battersea (Shillington Street with branch at Eltringham Street, Wandsworth)	971
Islington (Gifford Street)	930
North Kensington (Middle Row)	462
St Pancras (The 'Kentish Town')	588
Southwark (Sandford Row)	556

Inspectors set out to answer six main points:
1. have the institutes actually reached a class or section of youths who would otherwise not have come under educational influence at all?
2. by what means have these youths been attracted?
3. what sort of curriculum has been found feasible?
4. has the curriculum any permanent significance, and is it capable of improvement or development?
5. what other influences are of importance?
6. what is the relation of schools such as these to other parts of the educational system?

The report was a valuable analysis of the first five years of junior men's institutes. Clearly it was not possible to say that all who needed the institutes had been reached but HMIs felt able to say that all who had been reached were of the types for whom the institutes were intended and that it was extremely unlikely that these young men would have gone to any other educational institution. The fact that, in the session 1929–30, 6317 had enrolled, each with an average of seventy-five hours a session showed that some came regularly three or four evenings a week. They came because the institutes offered a congenial atmosphere in which they could follow a range of pursuits that interested them and in which they had had a part in selecting. HMIs stressed the importance of the right kind of staff. 'The success has been due not merely to missionery zeal, nor to gifts which create a certain sort of popularity, but to a combination of qualities of character and mind peculiarly valuable for this task. With less good leaders the enterprise might easily have been a complete failure.'[29] The report listed the subjects they found in all, or almost all, the institutes. There were two main groups: the first included all practical subjects 'involving manual dexterity rather than theoretical knowledge' and physical training; the second group consisted of those subjects 'most nearly akin to school subjects, calculated to prepare for a more academic type of education'.

I. – 1. Physical training, games and boxing
        2. Home carpentry and woodwork
        3. Metalwork
        4. Hobbies involving handwork, e.g. leather work, basket work
        5. Boot repairing: care of clothes and home tailoring
        6. Cookery (domestic and camp cookery)
        7. First-aid
        8. Photography
        9. Drawing and painting
     10. Music: vocal; instrumental
     11. Popular science: petrol engines, wireless, etc.
II. – 12. Library and talks about books
     13. General education (reading, composition, arithmetic, etc.)
     14. Lectures on current events, travel, etc. (usually illustrated)
     15. Literature (sometimes dramatic literature with preparation of plays)
     16. History and geography
     17. Debates

The following tables reprinted from the report indicate the age of students and preferences expressed for the different subjects. The Roman figures at the head of the columns in the first table refer to the institutes; in the second table the subjects are grouped in order of attractiveness as measured by the attendance calculated in total hours.

Age at enrolment	I	II	III	IV	V	VI	VII	Total
Under 14	38	36	66	24	22	47	51	284
,, 15	448	214	217	361	120	150	141	1651
,, 16	350	360	250	208	115	136	135	1554
,, 17	333	409	249	159	111	174	121	1556
,, 18	268	265	178	178	89	62	108	1148
,, 19	89	—	11	—	—	19	—	124
Total	1526	1284	971	930	462	588	556	6317
Total student hours	85,514	114,535	76,627	74,277	45,241	45,396	34,364	475,954

	I	II	III	IV	V	VI	VII	Total
Average hours per student	56	89	79	80	98	78	68	Av. 78
Percentages in subjects								Av.
Physical Training	29%	27%	20%	22%	28%	29%	28%	26%
Woodwork	9	20	25	25	20	14	25	20
General education	19	15	20	20	9	32	11	18
Hobbies	17	11	5	—	2	3	13	7
Music (vocal and instrumental)	5	12	5	4	7	9	2	7
Boot-repairing	3	3	10	11	6	5	4	6
Science	1	1	6	5	9	2	7	4
Miscellaneous	17	11	9	13	19	6	10	12
	100	100	100	100	100	100	100	100

Physical training took first place in almost all the institutes with an average percentage overall of 26 per cent; woodwork alone accounted for 20 per cent and if there had been more facilities would have occupied an even larger place. Although the HMIs were clearly concerned that there was such a small demand for literary or theoretical subjects they had no doubt that any attempt to stress the importance of the literary side might easily 'defeat its own object and impair the value of the experiment'. HMIs paid special attention to physical training since it was

. . . the one subject in which the work done might reasonably be expected to compare favourably with that of boys of equal age in any other schools. This expectation is realised, and it is gratifying to find that as a result of the teaching these boys can hold their own with any others. If the institutes had done nothing else, their existence would be justified by the fact that they have enabled some thousands of youths, just at the period when they most need it, to obtain systematic training under qualified teachers.[30]

An appendix to the report gives rather more detailed advice on the development of physical training and one passage in particular gives us a vivid picture of the type of students and the very basic difficulties with which the institutes were faced.

A serious handicap to the work is the very general practice of wearing the ordinary clothing during the lessons. Many of the exercises cannot be properly performed in ordinary clothing, boots make jumping and vaulting except of the most elementary kind impossible or very risky, and strenuous exercise without a change is neither conducive to comfort nor helpful in teaching hygienic habits. The difficulty of securing a change of clothing, even of footwear, is considerable; it may be hoped that a way will be found.[31]

There is little doubt that, particularly in areas such as the East End where boys' clubs were numerous, the junior men's institutes were seen by some clubs as 'poachers' of members. The heads of the institutes worked closely with club leaders and where appropriate facilities existed in club premises, supplied teachers for classes in the clubs. Where such facilities, particularly for practical work, were not available, classes for club members were provided in the institutes. In such circumstances the club atmosphere of the institutes challenged that of the club. In the words of the HMI report 'many difficult and delicate questions arise in such a situation'. Nevertheless, despite the club-like atmosphere, the justification for the institutes was educational and they were meeting an educational need which was not being met to the same extent by the clubs. On the other hand, club classes seemed to be more successful in popularizing dramatic literature; with the notable exception of one institute (Bethnal Green), which won the Stewart Headlam Shakespeare Association Annual Exhibition of scenes from plays, dramatic societies did not flourish in junior men's institutes.

One expectation of the original experiment did not materialize. The hope was that young men would move from the junior to the senior men's institutes at about eighteen years of age. There was a certain amount of flexibility in the admission arrangements which permitted a young man of seventeen to join a men's institute and a young man at a junior institute to stay on for a short period after reaching eighteen. In 1930, however, a large number of young men of eighteen preferred to remain in the junior institute, to which they had become accustomed and there was little transition from junior to senior institute. HMIs felt that too much importance could be attached to this aspect: 'It is right that the way should be open and every encouragement offered, but it is not a sign of failure if the period of intermission occurs between 19 and 22 or 23 instead of a few years earlier.'[32]

A major distinction between the work of the junior men's institutes and other types of institutes was that, whereas in the latter the social side was often sharply divided from organized formal work, in the junior men's institutes it tended to permeate the whole institute. There was, however, considerable social and recreative activity outside the normal hours of opening, in the shape of outside sports, Saturday games and matches, competitions, concerts, social evenings, dances, meetings of a variety of hobby societies and holiday camps. Groups of students spent a week or fortnight at some of the permanent boys' camps at Oxford and elsewhere.

The 'gang' spirit which made leisure so dangerous for many of the boys was channelled by the heads and staff of the institutes into loyalty and pride in their institute. HMIs felt able to say that, in a few years, the institutes had brought about 'a general "civilising" effect, upon even the roughest boys' . . . and

. . . improved standards of behaviour . . . and taught some thousands of boys a better use of their leisure. The institutes have certainly succeeded in reaching a section of the adolescent population which no other schools have touched in large numbers. They have succeeded by a combination of personal, almost missionary, effort, and of practical ingenuity in devising and adapting a suitable curriculum. They have maintained a moral influence comparable to that exercised by the voluntary agencies concerned with the welfare of boys of this age. The new institutes have filled a gap, but they have done much more. They have thrown light upon the character and the extent of a problem whose existence has long been known. The experiment is still in its infancy, but if it proves, as it already promises, to be a notable contribution to one of the most difficult educational and social problems, not only of one great city but of all cities, it will be owing to the human qualities of disinterested zeal, intelligence, insight and sympathy displayed by all who have taken part in it from its inception.'[33]

Women's Institutes

In the session 1925−6, when there were six men's institutes and five junior men's institutes with a total enrolment of 7727 students, there were thirty-seven women's institutes with an enrolment of 30,194 students. The reorganized institutes established in 1913 had been given an additional impetus by the war. The war made heavy demands on the services of women and gave them a new status to which the women's institutes responded magnificently. The fact that, in 1925−6, there were twenty-four whole-time heads of women's institutes (from June 1925 the designation of responsible master or responsible mistress was replaced by the term of 'head of institute') was itself an indication of their development. Heads of women's institutes were whole-time if the institutes had achieved over 30,000 hours of registered attendance over a period of three consecutive years; half-time heads were appointed when the registered attendance was over 20,000 and sessional heads when it was below 20,000. Institutes with full-time heads therefore had an enrolment of between 600 and 700 students with a number of branch institutes meeting in buildings apart from the main premises.

Apart from heads and deputy heads the staffs of all types of evening institute, both men's and women's institutes, were drawn from panels formed by the Education Committee. There were panels of part-time instructors (and assistant instructors) in a large variety of subjects, of pianists and of clerical assistants. Apart from a pedagogic course, at a small fee, for specialist teachers in evening institutes who had little or no teaching experience, and training in the teaching of physical exercises, the Council did not train people for part-time teaching in women's institutes although less than half of them were professional teachers. Applicants for admission to the subject panels were required to have recognized academic qualifications. On the whole, little difficulty was experienced in recruiting suitable candidates. Two very experienced and dedicated principals, Miss Edith Ramsay and Mr S. Myers, writing in 1936, said it was not so easy to find instructors who, having the necessary qualifications, had, in addition, 'temperamental qualities suited to the work in men's and women's institutes. Stewart Headlam – who sat for 30 years on teaching staff selection committees in London – called them 'qualities of heart,' and he had in mind patience, sympathy with the materially and intellectually (as well as morally) less fortunate, tenacity of purpose, social zeal in its altruistic sense, willingness to give oneself, and the pioneer and missionary spirit'.[34]

By 1930 when the HMIs were reviewing the junior men's institutes, there were ten men's institutes and seven junior men's with a total enrolment of 15,777 and 974,864 student hours, and thirty-eight women's institutes with an enrolment of 34,449 and 1,613,420 student hours. After a substantial decrease from 35,573 in 1920–21 to 27,936 in 1921–2, attributed to the opening of compulsory day continuation schools, the revision of fees and the trade depression, enrolment at women's institutes had steadily increased.

The women's institutes had many of the characteristics of the men's institutes. They had the same broad objectives of helping to satisfy the creative instincts of students who had little opportunity elsewhere to do so; encouraging new, and extending existing, interests and involving students in the organization of the institutes. Although the tuition was informal, one has the impression that it was rather more structured and formalized than in the men's institutes and that student determination of subject matter taught was in the demand for a particular class rather than in the actual class teaching. The instructors of dressmaking, for example, knew what they wanted to teach and gave a good deal of individual tuition. The organization, whilst flexible and responsive to demand, seems to have been firmer. There were a number of aspects of women's institutes which may have contributed to this. In the first place, the numbers of students under eighteen in women's institutes at this time was nearly 50 per cent of the total overall. It varied from institute to institute according to the area and the relationship of the head with local schools. Also, from their inception the institutes had maintained a close association with girls' clubs. Indeed the numbers of students in 'club classes' (classes held on club premises) – the paid teacher being supplied by the institute – was substantial. Again they varied according to the area and whether the institute was free or fee-paying but, for example, at Keetons Road Women's Institute (Bermondsey) an entry in the log book for 13 April 1927 (when the institute closed for the Easter vacation) records that there were 337 students in club classes out of a total enrolment of 519.

Heads of women's institutes took their responsibilities for the fourteen to eighteen age group very seriously. They attended the after-care conference for girls at senior girls' schools, a school leavers' meeting at which the girl about to leave, accompanied by her mother or a responsible adult, was seen by a representative of the LCC Children's Care Organization, the Juvenile Employment Exchange and the headmistress of the day school. The object was to inform the girl and the parent of facilities offered at women's or other institutes. The conference would record a recommendation to attend an evening institute and send a copy to the care office and the head of the appropriate institute. The forms contained particulars of the girl's school, medical record and other useful information. On receipt of this information the head of the institute would write to all the girls, many of whom already knew of her through having seen her comings and goings to and from the school or through their friends who were already students. Sometimes the head of the institute would invite the girl to tea or to look around the institute. Often this would be the first letter the girl had received through the post. It was therefore an indication of a newly acquired status and an approach which undoubtedly encouraged a substantial number of girl school-leavers to join the women's institutes.

The emphasis in women's institutes was decidedly domestic. Popular subjects included cookery, needlework (dressmaking, etc.), embroidery and design, home-handicrafts, home-nursing, home-tailoring, laundry, care of children and the home, child health, first-aid, dietetics, home-hygiene, housecraft, millinery, domestic arts and crafts and simple woodwork. Physical exercises and gymnastics, still called drill in some log-books in 1927, and vocal music had always played an important part. Swedish gymnastics were replacing the old-style drill but 'Keep Fit' had not yet arrived. Greek dancing and country dancing increasingly appeared in programmes and dramatic literature and elocution in dramatic classes provided some formal speech training. The social life of the institutes was considerable, through meetings of various societies, physical exercise displays, concerts, exhibitions, etc. Exhibitions, usually annual, were becoming the main means of institute publicity and attracted many hundreds of visitors.

An indication of the growing popularity of women's classes is to be seen in the demand that arose from women who worked in central London but who lived in outlying London suburbs. St Giles-in-the-Fields Women's Institute (Shaftesbury Avenue), whose boundaries extended from the Bank to Regent Street and from Oxford Street to the Embankment, covered an area in which the residential population was steadily decreasing but in which there was a concentration of Government offices and other semi-public bodies. The programme published in 1920 when Mrs M.A. Vallis was the sessional responsible mistress listed twenty-five classes of which ten were taught in four buildings separate from the main institute. In 1922–3, the first session after Mrs G.P. Shaw, MBE had been appointed whole-time responsible mistress, there were 498 students on roll and the institute was open for three days a week. (In 1921 the institute had been restricted to two days a week as part of the economy measures due to the depression of that time.)

In 1931–2 there were 1682 on the roll and the programme for the following session, 1932–3, lists ninety-six classes at twelve centres in addition to the main institute. This list appears to exclude classes such as that for policewomen held at New Scotland Yard, classes at St George's Home and club classes at five other centres. The programme includes no less than nineteen first and second year cookery classes, twelve dressmaking, thirteen arts and crafts and nine physical exercise classes excluding country dancing (two) and Greek dances (two). Mrs Shaw indicates in her notes that a further eleven classes were approved and that, of the total, only fifteen did not open. Despite the proximity to the City Literary Institute, classes in citizenship, dramatic literature and elocution, musical appreciation and modern literature were well established. In her notes for the session 1929–30 Mrs Shaw gives an interesting analysis of the students' enrolment as follows:

physical training	567	students
arts and crafts	401	,,
cookery	394	,,
needlework	394	,,
health	124	,,
literature and citizenship	83	,,
music	78	,,

She adds that 'practically all the students are adults and of secondary school type living outside the area. Greek dancing and home decorations, both new subjects in 1929/30, have been most successful.' Incidentally, about 3000 visited the annual exhibition during the three hours it was open.

It would seem that the pre-eminence of physical exercises had at last been overtaken at this institute by cookery. A note under session 1932–33 confirms this and gives the reason: 'There is a big drop in physical exercises due in a large measure to an organisation, well advertised, known as The League of Health and Beauty. It has no value but draws girls as they pay lesson by lesson.' Mrs Shaw and a number of other principals of women's institutes certainly did not approve of Prunella Stack and her League of Health and Beauty. Time was to show that women's 'Keep Fit' in LCC institutes was to have a greater staying power.

Throughout the 1920s the women's institutes had shown a steady development. They began the post-war years with the distinct advantage of having consolidated the 1913 reorganized form throughout the war years. By 1920–21 a women's institute had been set up in most areas of London and the majority had whole-time responsible mistresses which enabled them to establish relationships with schools and girls' clubs as well as to fashion a curriculum to meet the needs of women generally. With literary institutes, men's institutes and junior men's institutes the LCC by 1930 had established a non-vocational service unique in Great Britain and the world.

A Triumph over Odds – or Because of Them?

The initiatives and achievements referred to in this chapter are all the more remarkable because of the period in which they took place. The high hopes and idealism of the 1919 reconstruction report were quickly followed by a slump in trade and the Geddes Act which sliced into education in the 1920s. Nationally negotiated teachers' salaries were reduced by 5 per cent and economies were demanded of the institutes, as with other sectors of the education service. The hours of opening of evening institutes were curtailed in 1921 and 1922.

The Education Act of 1918 which had embodied so many LCC views concerning the education of those aged fourteen to eighteen required authorities to submit a scheme to the Board of Education on this aspect. The LCC draft scheme planned twenty-two compulsory day continuation schools to open in January 1921. Fourteen to sixteen year olds were to attend for eight hours a week, in two sessions of four hours, for a course of general education; this would be extended in 1928 to the sixteen to eighteen age group, for whom vocational courses would be provided. Each school was to have 360 places and to be open from forty-four to forty-eight weeks a year. There was to be a rapid build up of 15,000 students a quarter to a total of 120,000. Some 800 instructors were to be appointed in the first year and another 800 in the second year at an initial estimated cost of £247,500, rising to £1 million.

In January 1921 day continuation schools were opened, operating in old school buildings and hired premises. Heads and staff overcame early difficulties by extensive improvizations and tried to build up relationships with employers. Despite growing doubts cast upon the effectiveness of the operation by the inactivity of surrounding authorities, by February 1922 the Higher Education sub-committee received an enthusiastic report that thirty-five schools had opened and were housed in ninety-five buildings, fifty-nine were hired by the LCC from private owners. Some 47,000 students had enrolled and the operation was heralded as a major breakthrough in the education of the fourteen to sixteens. Unemployment was, however, rising and the slump brought the inevitable crisis in public finance. Employers in London compared the position in London with that outside where other local authorities had failed to enforce the day continuation clauses of the 1918 Act. In such circumstances compulsory day-release in London was regarded as a tax on juvenile labour which was not applicable to employers in neighbouring counties and boroughs. Not only did employers object to what they regarded as discrimination but parents feared that attendance at day continuation schools might prejudice the chances of their sons and daughters getting scarce jobs. Whereas London's example might have encouraged less-enlightened neighbours, with the Government announcement, that, as part of the economy measures, the day continuation sections of the 1918 Act would not be enforced, the LCC Education Committee was in an extremely difficult position.

After discussions in June 1922 with H.A.L. Fisher the LCC Education Committee decided not to reopen the schools after the summer holiday. The existing scheme was brought to an end and a more modest scheme for ten day continuation colleges on a voluntary basis substituted. Day continuation schools were retained in the City, Westminster, Islington, Greenwich and Woolwich, Battersea, Homerton, Brixton, Hammersmith and Southwark and Bermondsey. The schools provided for students released voluntarily by employers; young people awaiting employment could attend up to half-time. Even so numbers were encouraging, although slow in building up. By the autumn of 1922 there were 4071 students and 4678 and 4941 for the first two terms respectively of 1923. In the winter of 1923 the LCC began to organize instruction in recreational centres for unemployed youths of sixteen to eighteen at the request of the Ministry of Labour which paid three quarters of the cost. Although 3700 unemployed young people attended as the spring and summer drew on, the numbers fell off and only four centres were kept open.

In 1926 Kenneth Lindsay, a research worker who was later to become Parliamentary Secretary at the Board of Education in the immediate pre-war years, published a book entitled *Social Progress and Educational Waste*. The book was a sociological study of secondary schools in London and a number of other provincial cities and countries, undertaken under the guidance of R.H. Tawney. Lindsay carried out the survey whilst holding a fellowship at Toynbee Hall. The study criticized the uneven distribution of secondary-school places throughout the country and drew attention to the fact that, whereas in England and Wales as a whole, 9.5 per cent of elementary-school leavers went on to secondary schools, in London only 6.4 per cent went on to grammar schools; in London itself there was great disparity in the distribution of scholarship places between rich and poor areas and between individual schools. During the years 1914–23, Bermondsey won 309 scholarships compared with 1373 in Lewisham and 1489 in Hackney. Of that total, Keetons Road and Alma schools in Bermondsey won 114 and individual schools like Stillness Road won more scholarships than all the elementary schools in Bermondsey.[35] Lindsay's analysis also showed that some 40 per cent of the fathers of grammar-school pupils were skilled workers, 35 per cent came from official and clerical classes and 10 per cent were shopkeepers; the other 15 per cent were the children of widows (just over 10 per cent) and unskilled workers. The most under-represented group was the dockers and general labourers whose children were virtually absent from the scholarship lists.[36] The report was published in 1926 when there was serious juvenile unemployment and 15 per cent of the fourteen to sixteen year olds in Bermondsey were out of work. Moreover, those who were able to get employment became errand boys with nothing much to hope for except unemployment later on. In the same year the Hadow Report on 'The Education of the Adolescent' was published, presaging the reorganization of primary and secondary education into separate successive stages. In 1924 London had begun its own reorganization into junior and elementary schools with a break at eleven, as a result of the usual conferences and working groups prompted by Sir Robert Blair.

There can be little doubt that the success of non-vocational adult education owed a great deal to the high level of unemployment in the 1920s. Initiatives were taken to reach labouring men and their junior counterparts which might not otherwise have been made. The fear of some of the consequences of unemployment added a social impetus to the setting up of men's institutes. The success of these institutes and the failure of so many other ventures to tackle the problems of young men paved the way to the establishment of junior men's institutes. The 1920s were, for the most part, a period of disillusion and disappointment − a 'land fit for heroes', after four years of blood and misery in the trenches, was still far away. Almost paradoxically, for London it was a period of outstanding educational advance which provided the basis for a comprehensive adult education service of quite remarkable educational and social breadth.

7.   The Changed Scene: London in the 1930s

A new chapter in London's adult education service began in 1930. Two reports published in that year had a particular relevance to the development of that service.

The first – *The New Survey of London Life and Labour*[1] – brought up-to-date the findings of the monumental inquiry undertaken by Charles Booth some forty years before and published in the years 1889 to 1891 as *The Life and Labour of the People of London*.[2]

The second – *The Scope and Practice of Adult Education*[3] – was published as Paper No. 10 of the Adult Education Committee, constituted by the President of the Board of Education in 1921.

As we have already seen the impact of adult education depends on the understanding and appreciation, by those who shape its provision, of social conditions, the needs of the time and an effective response to them. *The New Survey of London Life and Labour* reviewed the changes in the social and economic conditions of the population of London since Charles Booth's inquiry and gave a valuable picture of those conditions in the late 1920s. The survey was undertaken by the London School of Economics and Political Science and was directed by Sir Hubert Llewelyn Smith who chaired a Consultative Committee which included Mr G.H. Gater who had succeeded Sir Robert Blair as Education Officer in 1925 and Lord Passfield, formerly Sidney Webb. Llewelyn Smith with Ernest Aves, both residents of Toynbee Hall, had assisted Charles Booth in the original survey. Llewelyn Smith had already played a notable part in London's education by the preparation of the survey of employment and industry which led to the appointment of the Technical Education Board of the LCC. The London County Council was very closely associated with the *New Survey*.

Charles Booth's inquiry which began in 1886 took place at one of the critical periods in the economic and social history of this country. 'The era of unquestioned predominance and of unbroken and rapid expansion of British trade had given place to a difficult period of transition marked by long and often painful readjustments to meet the new conditions of commercial rivalry and economic nationalisation with which British traders were everywhere faced in their former overseas markets.'[4] The 1880s were times of disillusion and depression. The search for new solutions led to an unprecedented number of official inquiries, the formation of English socialist organizations and the beginning of socialism as a definite political creed in this country and to movements, such as the university settlements, to study social conditions in the poorer districts of London.

Charles Booth launched his inquiry to probe into the problems of London poverty and, in his own words, 'to show the numerical relation which poverty, misery and depravity bear to regular earnings and comparative comfort, and to describe the general conditions under which each class lives.'[5] He began in the East End in 1886 and later extended his inquiry to the rest of London, publishing his findings in seventeen volumes, the first in 1891 and the last just after the end of the nineteenth century. He classified the London population into an ascending series of social and economic grades, A to H, and presented a graphic representation of their distribution by streets, in a series of coloured maps. He revealed in staggering detail the deprivation, squalor and isolation of the East End poor. Thirty-five per cent of the population of his East End survey area, containing some 900,000 people, were in poverty and even want. 'My "poor" ', he explained, 'may be described as living under a struggle to obtain the necessaries of life and make both ends meet; while the "very poor" (12%) live in a state of chronic want.'[6] In the central part of East London the percentage of the 'poor' rose to 44 per cent and in the district from Whitechapel to Bethnal Green it was 49 per cent. Booth's lowest class of all, (A), comprised about 9000 persons in the whole of London; more than a quarter were concentrated in Whitechapel, in the very district in which Toynbee Hall was to be opened.

Booth's survey was limited to the County of London which, in 1891, had a population of rather less than 4¼million. In the years between Booth's survey and the new survey the increase in the population of London proper was only 250,000 and this in the first quarter of the period. From 1911 onwards there was an actual decline. But the population of the eastern ring of outer London had more than doubled since 1891. The average density of the county of London as a whole had undergone little change, being sixty persons per acre in 1928 compared with fifty-seven in 1891, the most congested parts being in the centre. In 1881, in the seven poorest boroughs, 254 in each 1000 were born in other parts of the country; in 1921 the figure was 122. The age distribution of the London population had been very powerfully affected in the period between the two surveys by two factors: the Great War of 1914–18 which had destroyed many men in the prime of life and greatly reduced the number of births; and the progressive fall of the birth rate with a decline in the rate of mortality. For every 1000 women between the ages of fifteen and forty-five, 121 children were born in London in 1821 and only eighty-three in 1921. The accrued birth rate, that is, without allowing for differences in age and sex distribution, was greater in 1891 – 31.9 per 1000 compared with 16.2 per 1000 in 1928. The accrued death rate in 1891 was 21.1 per 1000 and in 1928 12.1. Another result of the 1914–18 War was to increase the existing excess of females over males, an excess which rose from 11 per cent in 1891 to 16 per cent in 1921.

The *New Survey* established that the poverty line as 'fixed either by Charles Booth 40 years' ago or by independent estimates of the cost of satisfying primary necessities, is now much further below the level of current wages for unskilled labour than it was in Charles Booth's day'.[7] Charles Booth's income of twenty-one shillings which, for a moderate-sized family, marked the poverty line, had now been raised to forty shillings or, say, 90 per cent above the level of that in 1890. The 'real' rates of weekly wages in London, measured in purchasing power of essential objects of expenditure, had risen on average by about 20 per cent, that is, 14 per cent for skilled and 28 per cent for unskilled occupations. Moreover, this real remuneration was for a shorter working week, 15 per cent shorter since the war. Thus the average real remuneration had increased by over a third. For unskilled labour it was greater, one hour of such labour being worth about half as much again as in 1890, measured in terms of the necessary commodities which it commanded. 'The fact that the average workman in London can now buy a third more of articles of consumption in return for labour of an hour's less duration per day affords conclusive proof that the material conditions under which the mass of London workers live have considerably improved.'[8]

Certainly, if average earnings could be assumed to apply to each individual worker Charles Booth's proportion of poverty would have been reduced from over 30 per cent to less than 8 per cent. This, however, would have been an over-simplification. Nevertheless, the percentage of poverty (according to Booth's standard) must have diminished considerably. Moreover, real privation by those still living in poverty had been largely reduced by the various forms of public social service. Pensions for old age, widows and orphans; national health and unemployment insurance, industrial legislation and educational progress had made life easier and more secure for a large number of people. Indeed, the striking characteristic of the forty years between Charles Booth's survey and the new survey was the initiation and development of organized social-health services ranging from the medical inspection of school children to such services as health-insurance pensions, school clinics, maternity-and-infant welfare centres and schemes for the treatment of special diseases.

The new survey gave great credit to the education service for the improved state of London's health and its part in the growing sense of individual, parental and communal responsibility for public health. Nevertheless there was much still to be done. 'There is strikingly apparent at the present time a need of levelling up, and securing for the poorer members of the community still better educational facilities than those they now possess.'[9]

The London County Medical Officer supported the findings of the survey when he reported:

A reading and discriminating public has been substituted for an illiterate and ignorant public, and though intelligence may not have kept pace with knowledge, a public opinion has grown up which now supports instead of thwarting the effects of the sanitary reformer. The progress of public health has benefited immeasurably both from the direct and from the indirect effects of the development of the London Education Service. A single example is afforded by the striking fall of infant mortality, and by the saving of child life, which came about as soon as a generation which had passed through the primary school had become parents of a new generation. [10]

In the 1870s nearly a third of the children of elementary-school age were entirely without schooling and another third were in schools not counted by the School Board for London as 'efficient'; this left less than 40 per cent on rolls of efficient schools. In 1891 the proportion of children in efficient schools had risen to 80 per cent, i.e. double the 1871 percentage. The percentage of children of compulsory school age (five to fourteen) on roll in 1891 was 92 per cent; in the new survey it was between 98 – 9 per cent.

The transformation of the adult population of London into a literate community was more gradual. It was established that, in 1891, nearly half of the parents of school children in London had probably received no school education. By 1921 this proportion had fallen to one tenth and by 1928 'the uneducated residue' was less than 5 per cent 'including all those who escaped education in their childhood whether through imperfect machinery for compulsion, or physical or mental defects or other causes. In effect this means that the problem of making the population of London a literate community has likewise been solved.' [11]

Striking evidence of the diminishing unpopularity of compulsory education was given by the statistics of summonses for non-attendance at school. In 1900 there were 445 summonses per 10,000 children on roll. Between 1900 and 1909 it averaged 273 and between 1920 and 1929, it was seventy-seven. In 1929 it was fifty-five and the unpopularity of compulsory education could be said to have disappeared.

The predominant influence of education, especially the growth of a generation of literate parents in the improvement of the general health in London, was cited by the *New Survey* as perhaps the most striking illustration of the intimate connection between the growth of education and social and economic welfare.

The transformation of an illiterate into a literate community means not only the growth of a public opinion which supports instead of obstructing the sanitary reformer or the disappearance of the early difficulties of enforcing school attendance. It also means a growing appreciation of the value of education, not merely as a foundation for the more intelligent pursuit of industrial and other occupations, but, what is still more important, as the master-key to all forms of self-culture. [12]

An indication of the expansion of cultural opportunities in London was the development of free libraries. In the thirty years preceding the survey the number of public libraries had more than doubled and the number of borrowers and of books borrowed had both more than trebled in proportion to the population. Nevertheless, the 660,000 borrowers were a small minority of the total population who had received a school education.[13]

Crimes of violence had diminished from ninety-four to sixty-one per million of population and, after making due allowance for the increased mobility of burglars with the advent of the motor car, it was clear that there had been a real decline in crimes against property in London. The increase in such offences as obtaining money by false pretences and other frauds (121 to 181) was connected with 'the facilities for such practices which result from improved education'![14] Offences against the Education Acts showed a great diminution — from 2820 to 594 per million of population and cases of drunkenness from 5824 to 3275 — a large reduction but less than that for the country as a whole where the fall was from 5681 to 1551. Begging had fallen from 349 to 197 and sleeping out from ninety-one to twenty-eight. On the other hand offences of betting and gaming had increased from 528 to 648. The advent of the motor car was shown by the increase in Highway Act offences in the metropolitan area from 266 to 9553.

Probably the most dramatic change that had taken place since the first survey was the vast extension of the transport system; The substitution of electricity for steam on the local railways beginning in 1900, the electrification of tramways in the first four years of the century and the displacement of the horsedrawn bus by the motor bus, practically completed by 1914. The unification of the London tramway system under the management of the LCC and the consolidation of most of the underground railways and the bulk of the omnibus system under a single control were important organizational changes which vastly increased the mobility of Londoners. Such developments in the transport system anticipated the public need for freer movement made 'more insistent by the increasing pressure upon the central and most congested areas for business and industrial purposes'.[15]

Since the beginning of the century the number of passengers carried by tramway or underground railway had trebled in each case and the number carried by omnibuses had increased sevenfold. These developments, by increasing the range of mobility of the London worker, had profound effects on the distribution of the London population, the conditions of housing, the access to open spaces, outdoor recreation and cultural opportunities as well as a levelling effect on prices, wages and conditions of life and labour throughout London. Improvements to transport, together with the shortening of the customary working hours, enabled many London workmen to live at a greater distance from their work. This in turn had its effect on new house building in the outer suburbs and the transfer of population from the centre to London's outer ring.

The benefit of increased mobility was offset by what the new survey called the 'disamenities' of increased traffic. Figures of traffic casualties show that, in 1891, the number killed and injured was 147 and 5637 respectively; by 1929 the figures were 1362 and 55,503. Traffic danger, noise and grime gave an added importance to open spaces, parks and gardens. The acreage of open spaces in the entire survey area had overtaken the population, the area of open spaces having risen from 137 to 168 acres per thousand inhabitants. The growth, however, had been greatest in the middle ring; in the fully built-up districts around the centre there had been little room for expansion whilst in the outer ring, outside the county boundary, the population had grown faster than the open spaces. Moreover, the remarkable growth in demand for playing fields had outgrown the possibilities of their supply.

The London worker in 1930 had a shorter working week, more time for leisure and more pleasure-purchasing power in his additional real earnings. The growth of the cinema since 1905 meant that there were between three and four times as many places of entertainment in London as when Charles Booth made his survey. At the time of the Booth survey theatres and music halls were the main types of entertainment. In 1891 forty-nine theatres and forty-two music halls provided seating accommodation of 65,550 and 50,000. But thirty theatres and ten music halls were in two boroughs, namely Westminster and Marylebone, and the remaining twenty-seven boroughs had nineteen theatres and thirty-two music halls. Between 1891 and 1911 the seating accommodation of London theatres increased by only 2½ per cent whilst that of music halls increased by nearly 50 per cent. By that time, too, a number were being converted into 'electric theatres' or pictures palaces. By 1911 there were already ninety-four cinemas in the county of London with over three quarters of the seating accommodation of music halls. In the next ten years they increased to 266; by 1929 the number of theatres and music halls had declined to eighty-seven with combined seating accommodation of 127,000 compared with 140,800 in 1911 and 115,500 in 1891.[16]

The cinema had become the 'poor-man's theatre' with seat prices at 4d. and 6d. compared with 1s. 6d. in the theatre gallery; it was a more formidable competitor with the public house and the streets rather than the 'legitimate' theatre. The extent to which the cinema filled a gap in the lives of the poorer classes was shown by the statistics of six typical working-class boroughs (Stepney, Shoreditch, Bethnal Green, Poplar, Southwark and Bermondsey). In 1891 this group of boroughs had eighteen theatres and music halls, that is, one such place of entertainment to 587,000 inhabitants. In 1929 there were fifty-nine cinemas, five theatres and music halls, that is one place of entertainment for 14,000 inhabitants, more than nine tenths of which consisted of picture palaces. The survey concluded that 'the local cinemas were practically the only form of indoor entertainment [for the working class] that was readily and continuously available, varied by an occasional boxing display, concert or some kind of pleasant evening organised by a local church or other cultural agency'.[17] The question of how the workman's extra hour of leisure was spent was therefore partially answered by the immense growth of the cinema.

A burst of popularity of the bicycle from 1895 to the early 1900s, with the advent of the pneumatic tyre, was followed by the short-lived development of roller skating. Up to 1905 there were five roller-skating rinks in London; by 1910 there were twenty-three and by 1920 they had fallen to four. In 1929 only three remained. Roller skating gave way to dancing. In Charles Booth's day public dancing was associated with saloons and public houses and was hardly 'respectable'; in the years immediately preceding the war, American dances made their appearance and, throughout the war and the years following, the popularity of dancing was at its height and public dancing was a frequent accompaniment of music in the London parks. The traditional games − cricket, football and tennis − maintained their attractiveness through the ebb and flow of these other sports. Great gatherings of Londoners were spectators at Highbury, White Hart Lane, Stamford Bridge; final cup-ties were attracting crowds of about 100,000 in the 1920s. Greyhound racing amounted to a craze in the late 1920s. The opportunity for gambling attracted total attendances at greyground races which rose from 3 million in 1927 to 6½ million in 1928 and 8 million in 1929.

One of the most important contributions to indoor entertainment since the time of Charles Booth's survey was the invention of wireless telephony and the organization of 'broadcasting'. The first regular programme of the British Broadcasting Corporation was performed in 1922 and between 1923 and 1929 the number of wireless licences issued in the London postal district rose from 201,000 to 541,000. The size of the increase indicated that the wireless had taken a hold on the working class as well as the middle class and its influence, cultural and recreational, was without doubt considerable.

Ramsay and Myers, in presenting the social background to their account of the LCC institutes in *London Men and Women*, point to 'the enormous production and consumption of safety razors and razor blades, the popularisation of collars − white and coloured, hard and soft − the supply for both sexes of underwear and overwear of a simpler and (for females) more easily washable type, the extensive sales of a wide variety of perfumed and unperfumed soaps, of face-powders and cheap manicure appliances, in working class districts,'[18] as indications of improved appearance and personal cleanliness. 'The streets are freer from the risk of personal violence: the old Ratcliff Highway, for example is absolutely safe for the pedestrian both by day and night, but, in addition, abuse of the stranger especially if respectably dressed, which was common at the opening of the century in certain districts and which was − where adults were concerned − generally associated with drunkenness has 'almost completely gone.'[19] They also observed other changes such as the almost complete disappearance of the barefooted child and more working men and women reading newspapers and books on the trains, trams and omnibuses in the mornings and evenings. 'Children are today more frank and polite with enquiring strangers in the streets. They behave better, go cleaner to school, and are less violent in their games, both in and out of the playground.'[20] Despite the increase of unemployment in the late 1920s and early 1930s 'what street corner loafing remains is of a less obstructive and objectionable kind.'[21] More people were going to places of entertainment notably picture theatres, music halls, boxing and wrestling shows.

On the whole the lot of the working-class housewife had improved.

> The 344,000 cinema seats in London – or at least a large proportion of them which are situated in or adjoining working class districts – are mainly occupied by working class women every afternoon and the queues outside the cinemas in the early evening include more women than men. Working class housewives go to 'mothers meetings', classes conducted by the London County Council, Labour (and other) Party women's section meetings, co-operative guilds, etc. held during the afternoon . . . they seem in greater measure than ever to have an afternoon to spare.

Attractive window displays in retail shops in the broad thoroughfares which ran through even the poorest districts, brought women out for longer periods than formerly and 'the sixpenny and other stores of the bazaar type are never without their idlers – mainly working class women – who may or may not buy, but who seem to have time to spare to wander through them.'[22] The average size of the working class and other families was smaller and was an important factor in increasing the leisure of the housewife from 'what was formerly endless toil'.

The New Survey of London Life and Labour indicated that the consumption of alcoholic drinks had decreased by half since the 1890s. Visits in 1933 to some 624 public houses, one in ten of all public houses in London, showed that the average frequenters of public houses were older and included fewer women than formerly. A sample count in eight public houses showed that three quarters of the men and women were over thirty-five. The statistics as to convictions for drunkenness showed that drink, especially excessive drinking, had lost much of its attraction for all sections of the community and especially for the working classes. The *New Survey* noted that 'the place which drunkenness occupied in the category of vices in the minds of moralists during the last century has today been largely surrendered to gambling.'[23] All of this pointed to the absence of drinking as part of the leisure-time pursuits of the younger adults.

Myers and Ramsay confirm the importance of broadcasting and the far-reaching effects it was having on working-class leisure. Listening in to the wireless was a home pursuit – a virtue in itself to some sections of the community.

The experience of people like Miss Ramsay and Mr Myers was that broad-cast matter was a prominent subject of conversation among working people. 'The talks are listened to and no doubt discussed in proportion to the other parts of the programme, but the organisation of discussion groups has not been found so necessary in London as in other parts of the country. The explanation is that facilities for adult education in all its forms are liberally provided in the Metropolis.'[24]

The Changed Educational Scene

The new survey included non-vocational adult education as one of the pursuits of leisure, estimating that some 55,000 men and women over eighteen were enrolled at LCC literary, men's and women's institutes and their affiliated club classes. It judged that, in addition, between 15,000 and 25,000 students 'according to the severity of the test applied' could be accounted for in classes organized by the university-extension and tutorial committees of London University, the Workers' Educational Association and social settlements such as Toynbee Hall, the Working Men's College, Morley College, co-operative societies and other less formal agencies.

Changes in non-statutory education from the time of the Booth survey in 1891 to the new survey in 1930 were as dramatic as those in the statutory sector. At the time Booth was conducting his first survey (1886–9) in the East End of London, the Working Men's College in Crowndale Road, St Pancras, founded by a group of Christian socialists headed by Frederick Denison Maurice, had already been operating for no less than thirty-two years. In 1930, with over 1000 students on the roll, it was supporting itself from endowments and a direct grant from the Board of Education. Most of its teachers were drawn from old students, the pro-fessions, the Civil Service and the universities and received no remuneration for their services. The work undertaken was akin to that of the more modern tutorial classes; music and gymnastics were the only recreational activities. Its sister college, the Francis Martin College for Working Women in Fitzroy Square, had about 150 students.

On 29 September 1889 the Morley Memorial College for working men and women opened in its new building, having graduated from the Royal Victoria Hall (Old Vic) and, by 1893–4, had an annual enrolment of 733 students. By 1924 it had moved into a new building in the Westminster Bridge Road opened by HRH. The Prince of Wales. An HMI's report on the college in 1928, when the total roll was about 2400, recorded:

> Subjects of every conceivable kind had been offered from the days when physical and natural science had the glamour of novelty to those in which psychology promised to reveal the secrets of every aspect of life. Classics and

theology, anthropology and archaeology, physiology and hygiene, political philosophy and metaphysics, economics and social history, biology and botany, all have been explored . . .

Out of 661 men and 1334 women at Morley College whose occupations were stated in 1926, the largest contingents were 1030 clerks (284 men and 746 women) and 321 in professional occupations and in public administration. To these should be added 100 engaged in 'commerce' as agents, brokers, or shop assistants, leaving about 544 or 26%, for such occupations as makers of textile goods, etc. (93); printers, bookbinders, photographers (57); transport workers (78); warehousemen (32); other artisans and manual workers (90); personal service (27); and undefined (133).

In the 1870s and the 1880s some university men had answered the call of Samuel Barnett, the Vicar of St Jude's, Whitechapel, to come and live among the poor of the East End to study and alleviate their conditions. Arnold Toynbee, the economic historian and reformer, with his distinguished circle of sympathizers, made opportunities for Barnett to talk at Oxford about the problems of the East End poor. His paper *Settlements of University Men in Great Towns*, was read before a distinguished gathering which included Cosmo Lang (late Archbishop of Canterbury) and representatives from Cambridge University. 'Young Oxford was becoming more and more conscious of deficiencies of the economic system and of the condition of the people and was sincerely anxious to help'.[25] A committee which included representatives of both Oxford and Cambridge University met at Balliol in January 1884 and resolved to found a university settlement in East London; it bought a disused industrial school behind Commercial Street, within a few yards of St Jude's Vicarage. The building was adapted to provide for six to eight resident university men and named Toynbee Hall in memory of Arnold Toynbee who had died the year before. An equally distinguished committee decided about the same time to establish the Oxford House Settlement.

Toynbee Hall was formally opened by a students' *conversazione* on 10 January 1885 with Samuel Barnett as its first warden. By 1930 there were no less than thirty settlements in the London area affiliated to their National Association. Toynbee Hall, Mary Ward and Bermondsey settlements were receiving financial aid from the London County Council for their educational work which was organized on lines similar to a literary institute, although the first two were strong centres for university extension and tutorial class activities. Toynbee differed from most of its fellow members of the British Association of Settlements in the extent of its educational work and its emphasis on investigation and research. The women's and mixed settlements were pioneers in the establishment of child-welfare clinics, play-centres and, in the early 1930s, nursery schools. In the majority, however, the emphasis was on club work, the clubs being a nucleus for all kinds of social activities. The Dockhead Settlement Clubs provided for club members of all ages and the Bernard Baron Settlement, a short distance from Toynbee, founded by B.L.Q. Henriques, a former Toynbee resident, had become a club centre for boys and girls of all ages.

In the forty or so years between the two surveys the London settlements had provided a very valuable infrastructure between the statutory services and the local community. By keeping a close informal contact as neighbourhood centres with the people in their area they were able to identify needs and initiate projects to meet them in advance of any overall provision which might be made in the statutory educational or social services. They were most effective when they worked in partnership with local representatives of those services. In this heyday of their development there was a tendency for some settlements to duplicate facilities provided by statutory services. The success of the settlements had been primarily due to their diversity and adaptability but, by 1930, the concept of the 'settlement' was changing. Many still had the important ancillary function of training social workers but the development of statutory social services had reduced the need for residential workers. Whilst a number still provided residence for prospective social workers, residence was no longer the primary consideration that it once was. They had become centres for social work by largely non-resident voluntary workers directed by paid settlement officials.

> It is no longer necessary, as in the 80s, for residents of Toynbee Hall to patrol the streets at night or act as voluntary sanitary inspectors. Some of its former educational work has been given up because adequate provision is now made by the local authorities, much of its present work is subsidised from public funds, and it is safe to predict that before long the state will take over, for example, the nursery schools at many settlements in respect of which grants are already received.'[26]

The London Society for the Extension of University Teaching (LSEUT) had been established on 13 March 1876 and, by the 1890s, was a thriving enterprise with sixty-three centres, thirty-five sessional and fifty-five terminal courses, 1463 lectures and 14,150 enrolments. In 1895 Dr C.W. Kimmins, an Inspector with the LCC Technical Education Board and later a Chief Inspector of the LCC (1904–23), succeeded R.D. Roberts as Secretary. In 1900 under a schedule to the University of London Act a Board to Promote the Extension of University Teaching (BPEUT) was appointed to take the place of the LSEUT. In 1906 the LCC made its first grant to the new body when it agreed to give £50 for each of nine sessional courses. In 1909, on the initiative of Albert Mansbridge who had founded the WEA in 1903, a Joint Committee for the Promotion of the Higher Education of Working People was set up, consisting of representatives of the University and the WEA. It was to play a notable role in the growth of the tutorial class movement in London. So successful was the first session's work that both the LCC and the Middlesex County Council made grants to enable seven additional classes to be arranged In the session 1910–11. In 1928–9 there were 115 university extension courses and fifty-three tutorial classes, the great majority of which were in the LCC area. A number of the classes were held in LCC institutes, usually literary institutes or establishments aided by the LCC such as Morley College, Toynbee or Mary Ward Settlement. In addition to residential settlements in the 1920s and early 1930s a number of non-residential settlements had come into being. Their primary activity was education, such formal classes as they ran being arranged through the WEA, although their activity was mainly informal – play-reading groups, debating societies and handicrafts.

The co-operative societies in London set aside funds for educational purposes and adult education classes were carried on through the WEA and the LCC institutes. Guilds for both sexes among members of the co-operative societies had opened up a new avenue for educational work which was co-ordinated by a Joint Educational Committee of the four London co-operative societies linked with the WEA. In 1926–7 there were 137 classes with about 3000 students in addition to classes organized by the WEA for the co-operative societies.

The 'Labour College' in West Kensington and its associated classes under the National Council for Labour Colleges, were financed and controlled by trade unions, branches of the Labour Party, workmen's clubs and trade councils and had 115 classes with 3725 students in the county of London at the time of the new survey. 'This movement makes the "class struggle" the foundation of its teaching and belongs therefore rather to the category of political and social propaganda than of adult education.'[27]

There were also a number of religious organizations who carried on adult educational work. Classes in Bible study and church history and institutions carried on by the Church Tutorial Classes Association were on the border line between adult education and religious instruction as were also the study circles organized by the Roman Catholic Social Guild to study social problems on Catholic lines. On the other hand schools belonging to the National Adult School Union, an old-established undenominational body, still did a good deal of general educational work of an informal kind. These schools generally met at weekly intervals throughout the year for the purpose of study, in addition to lectures, weekend and summer schools, wireless discussion groups and so on. The Young Men's and Young Women's Christian Associations also organized study circles and discussion groups on a wide range of subjects, in addition to popular lectures.

The newcomer in the field of adult education was undoubtedly the British Broadcasting Corporation. From the first the BBC had included educational talks in its programmes. It later took the step of instituting local area councils, under the supervision of a central council, which organized study circles which met regularly to listen to a course of lectures and discuss them under a trained group leader. This system, which met with considerable success in some parts of the country, made very little progress in the London area, doubtless because of the extensive facilities and variety of various types of institute and classes which existed in the LCC area.

The remarkable increase in the volume of voluntary educational activity was not only an important complementary provision to a statutory education service but was also a valuable stimulus to demand. Because of the extensive facilities already available in London the impact on the statutory provision was a good deal less than in the rest of the country. Outside London, the WEA, for instance, with its philosophy of student participation and of the students as the determinant of what should be studied, elicited needs and stimulated demand not only for academic subjects but also for creative arts, crafts and recreational pursuits which it passed on to the local education authority or campaigned for the authority to provide.

The overall result was that, although there was still a great disparity between one local education authority and another in the facilities offered for adult education, by 1930 there had been such a rapid growth in new and unexpected directions by local education authorities that the balance of adult education provision throughout the country had changed significantly. This change promoted the enquiry which resulted in the report, *The Scope and Practice of Adult Education*, published in 1930 by the Adult Education Committee. 'Adult Education can no longer be conceived as an experimental extension of university teaching, nor as a simple prolongation of school studies,'[28] said the report and went on to reveal that students of local education classes now far outnumbered those of universities and voluntary organizations. The Adult Education Committee felt therefore that there was a need to explain the aims and scope of adult education so as to make it intelligible to those concerned with other branches of education, public administrators and professionals whose work did not bring them into close touch with adult education.

Nowhere had the change been more rapid than in the LCC area and it was undoubtedly the initiatives taken by the authority throughout the 1920s that had encouraged other local authorities to make a greater provision for adult education. The report recognized the great contribution made by the London authority in identifying and providing for new categories of students. The Committee was obviously mindful of the doubts in some quarters about the educational validity of some of this work. Despite the weight given to student participation and determination in university tutorial classes, the extension of it to any other educational endeavour was not so readily appreciated. The pragmatic response to student needs was viewed uneasily by many in the university extra-mural departments and the WEA. The Committee, however, gave its *imprimatur*, to such work, in a passage which some of those working in the London institutes might have thought to be a little patronising.

We believe that good reasons are to be found for promoting simple hobbies and many forms of work which are recreational as well as educational: but they are not the same reasons as those urged on behalf of tutorial classes or university extension courses. Whether these tendencies towards greater and greater diversity are to be checked or carried still further, the policy must have some justification in educational or social theory. It may appear, at first sight, that the very absence of educational theory has helped forward the progress of adult education, by allowing room for diversity, and even novelty in its experiments.[29]

The Committee was very concerned that progress was likely to be hindered unless general lines of policy could be made intelligible. They cited the difficulties of voluntary bodies, largely dependent on public authorities, who could often obtain aid for established and recognized forms of effort but seldom for anything else. They even ascribed the disparity of local authority provision to the lack of an acceptable theory: 'the contrast between conspicuous enterprise and success of some public authorities and the apparent apathy of others is due, in part at least, to the absence of any generally accepted theory upon which a common policy might be based.'[30] More understandably they described the divergence of opinion on the form of any advance itself as an obstacle – which it most certainly was.

The Committee, however, was addressing itself to the confusion generated by many in university and WEA circles, who either did not accept much of the new provision by local education authorities (LEAs) as adult education, or at best regarded it as a dangerous lowering of standards. The charge then – and it lingers still – was that those working in men's or women's institutes had no educational philosophy. Indeed a previous report of the Adult Education Committee – *Pioneer Work and Other Developments in Adult Education* (HMSO 1927) – had expressed some of the fears in a reference to new developments in the London scene:

The growth of this type of work creates in a sense a new position in adult education: it is a source of great satisfaction to those whose chief desire is that adult education should be widespread: it is a source of some anxiety to those who see in it a danger of a confusion of aims between different kinds of adult education and of a decline in standard . . . Nothing could do more harm to the movement, or more quickly defeat the high aims which it has set before it, than the feeling that new developments involve the lowering of standards.[31]

Moves to adopt approaches that would attract men and women, hitherto untouched by adult education, were resisted by some on the grounds that standards were being lowered. The report of the Adult Education Committee reflected the continued uneasiness about the new work. Thus – 'A movement based solely upon the desire to meet any and every kind of demand, however superficial, however ill-informed, however transitory, could only result in a multiplication of classes without regard to quality and without discrimination of purpose. Such a movement could never call forth the enthusiasm or the spirit of self-sacrifice which have been evoked in the past.'[32]

One detects a certain ambivalence towards the new LEA work. On the one hand, there is wholehearted commendation of approaches which point the way to bringing a fuller life to many who previously were not to be seen in an educational institution; on the other, there was a dislike of any form of popularization which diluted the pure educational content. Understandably, the report was imprecise about the application of standards to the new work, since the measuring rods were so different. Indeed, the yardstick of standards had to be fashioned according to the different needs of individual students. To its great credit the Committee put considerable emphasis on the re-appraisal of what was meant by standards.

The report was an important recognition of the multifarious purposes of adult education and the changed nature of the demand. It was also an unequivocal commendation of the LCC non-vocational service. 'The strongest evidence of the change in the educational character of the "demand" comes from those districts in which the provision by the local authorities has been on a larger scale and more diversified in its forms than elsewhere. The question is complicated also by the fact that the most striking instance is that of London, which may be thought by some to be so exceptional in its circumstances, as to furnish no proper ground for comparison'.[33] It was a pity that, in paying tribute to the contribution London had made to the general development of adult education, it introduced the notion of London's exceptional circumstances. As a result the example of London tended to be much less effective. Too frequently for truth, the pre-eminence and exceptional circumstances of London were invoked as an excuse for not following an example which would have been equally applicable to many other areas.

In the early 1920s, after the Education Act of 1918 had charged authorities with the duty of providing for the progressive development and comprehensive organization of education, the majority of LEAs exercised their powers by assisting classes organized by the universities, the WEA and other voluntary bodies. An increasing number, however, began to provide classes for adults and, by the early 1930s, most LEAs, rural as well as urban, were providing classes of various kinds. The increasing role of LEAs prompted the Adult Education Committee, whose membership now included Mr G.D.H. Cole and Mrs (later Baroness) Barbara Wootton, to undertake a substantial enquiry into the provision for adults by LEAs and other bodies. The results of the enquiry were published in a report (Paper No. 11), *Adult Education and the Local Education Authorities* (HMSO 1933). The enquiry showed that as many as thirty-seven counties provided courses for adults and no less than sixty-three of the county boroughs made similar provision. Outside London there was 'an overwhelming preponderance of domestic instruction or what may be called vocational instruction for women'. This accounted for nearly two thirds of the practical group of courses and for over one third for the whole provision made by local education authorities. After that the most popular subjects were 'handicraft, languages, health subjects, science, physical training, literature and elocution in that order'.[34]

By comparison the LCC provided nearly as many classes for adults as all the other urban areas and '30% of the total provision made by all county and urban authorities together'. 'London', said the report, 'is especially strong in elocution, music, folk dancing and physical training: it also shows a far smaller preponderance of domestic instruction. Most of the appreciation of art classes are in London.'[35] Not only was the volume of work in London unusually large but the various groups of subjects were more evenly balanced than elsewhere.

The growth in the scope and variety of the curriculum in the London institutes is well illustrated by a comparison of the published programmes of the Walworth Men's Institute for 1927 and 1937. In 1927, forty-seven classes in fourteen subjects were offered and there were six clubs operated by the students. In 1937 there were 105 classes in thirty-six different subjects and there were no less than sixteen student-conducted clubs. Among the additional subjects were literature, fencing, public speaking, poster art and theory of music; the student-conducted clubs covered radio, camera club, cycling club, dramatic club, model-yacht club, gymnastic club, arts-and-crafts society, male choir, boxing club, sports club, camping club, swimming club, poultry-and-utility society, rabbit club, caged-bird society and a travel club.

Although from 1912 onwards it had been recognized by the LCC that there should be 'social' accommodation in both men's and women's institutes and that positive encouragement should be given to developing a 'club' atmosphere in those institutes – they were still evening institutes. The 1913 reorganization had marked them out as more than mere appendages of the day school but they were still regarded as solely evening institutes and there appears to have been no thought of day classes except those for the unemployed. The happy accident of redundant school accommodation enabled some of the men's institutes to build a club atmosphere, to give an adult ambience to their centres and so demonstrate the value of having their own accommodation. Nevertheless, since men's, women's and literary institutes were seen as evening institutes, their teaching was expected to be done in school accommodation since teaching accommodation for their sole use, it was thought, would stand empty during the day. There was clearly no conception that ordinary men and women would want, or have the time, to attend non-vocational classes during the day. In such circumstances a separate building for such institutes was an unjustifiable luxury.

One institute, however, broke through this barrier. The City Literary Institute was fast becoming the jewel in the adult education crown. Since 1924 it had had an advisory committee nominated by the LCC, but representative of local, as well as broader, interests of a metropolitan public; it included two members of the student body. By 1927 its strongly participative student body was reaching 5000 in total and many of its tutors were distinguished in their particular field. The institute operated in accommodation made available by the London Day Training College and the Bloomsbury Trade School and in no less than twenty-five other separate buildings. These circumstances lent considerable substance to the persistent claims of its redoubtable principal for a building which would enable the corporate spirit of the institute to be developed. T.G. Williams, its first principal, tells the story in *The City Literary Institute − a Memoir* of the decision in 1927 to recondition a derelict school in Goldsmith Street (now Stukeley Street), an alley off Drury Lane. Built in 1878 by the London School Board, it had been used 'for several generations by the disorderly and uncared-for youth of Seven Dials in the interests of discipline and hygiene . . . The LCC Further Education sub-committee decided that so doubtful a proposition needed careful looking into and a deputation led by Sir John Gilbert, the Chairman, and Mr (later Sir) George Gater, the Education Officer visited the building.'[36] The building and its surroundings would have daunted all but the most optimistic and determined. Williams and the students who examined the potentialities of the project had an abundance of these qualities, however, plus imagination, and presented such a confident report that the rehabilitation of the building for the institute was approved. It was ready for occupation in the autumn of 1928 and was ceremonially opened by the Lord Mayor of London, Sir Kynaston Studd, when lunch was served to 120 guests in the large lecture room on the third floor and speeches were afterwards delivered in the theatre below.

The acquisition of their own building was not only a landmark in the development of the City Literary Institute it was virtually the first recognition that non-vocational adult education provided by local education authorities had a day as well as an evening function and was worthy of some of the support and resources which hitherto had been reserved for vocational education. As Williams said,

> Enterprise in these conditions earns compound interest . . . The City Lit., by reason of its occupancy of its own premises, was, in consequence of that fact alone, saved an enormous expenditure of educationally unremunerative labour. It acquired many invisible assets. Its fixed allocation of clerical assistants could be more economically and efficiently used; progress could be made in integration and articulation of studies; information services could be better organised. The advantages were shared not only by the Principal and his staff, but by Class and Club secretaries who could acquire and store equipment.[37]

By 1930–31 the enrolment had reached 6000. The economic recession of 1931 brought a slight check but by 1935–6 enrolment had reached 6600. Behind this increase in student enrolment was the far more fundamental development of the curriculum. An analysis of student attendances during the session 1933–4 indicated that literature, languages (classical and modern), speech training and dramatic art accounted for 56 per cent; art appreciation, philosophy, psychology, religion and history accounted for another 29 per cent and physical culture and dancing, science, social and political science, topography and travel accounted for another 15 per cent. This expansion of the curriculum was accompanied by the prolific activities of numerous clubs and societies, most of which stemmed from one class or another. Lecture rooms were being used twice in an evening and pressure on accommodation was becoming intense.

During 1934–5 the momentous decision was taken to demolish the Goldsmith Street school and erect a purpose-built building for the institute. This was an event of national significance since it was the first building to be purpose-built by a LEA for non-vocational adult education. Since there was no blue-print for such a building the major responsibility for briefing the LCC architect fell largely to the principal. We have to remind ourselves that, apart from an accounting officer, seconded from the LCC's permanent staff in 1930, the principal was the only full-time member of staff. Between 1936 and 1939 when the new building was being erected the institute was dispersed in a variety of buildings. Most classes were accommodated in neighbouring schools, including Westminster City School, and in scattered buildings in the City and Holborn areas. The institute headquarters was set up in the 'Guild House' in Eccleston Square where, for many years, Dr Maud Roydon had ministered to large congregations. The institute office was in the vestry and the large hall beneath the church, with the aid of wooden partitions, provided for the canteen, library and theatre. Despite the disruption, the annual average enrolment during the 1936–9 period was over 5500. In the event the institute was not to have the full use of the new building, except for the summer term of 1939, until some years after the war and two principals had succeeded Mr Williams.

So far as other institutes were concerned the economic depression cut into enrolment figures. The fiery entry in the log-book of the Plumstead and Woolwich Literary Institute noted that 'session 1931–2 opened in a spirit of gloom and depression and uncertainty owing to the economic and political situation and the specific attack on education with the iniquitous May report (see page 133) as its poisoned spearhead'. Nevertheless, enrolment in men's institutes for that session increased to 19,879 compared with 18,879 the previous session, but dropped to 16,890 in the following session 1932–3. Enrolment at women's institutes dropped from 35,003 in 1930–31 to 31,991 in 1931–2 and to 28,194 in 1932–3. Literary institutes dropped from 14,805 in 1930–31 to 12,820 in 1931–2. In the session 1933–4 the LCC heeded appeals by the London Teachers' organisations and the London Council for Voluntary Occupation of the Unemployed and voted £5000 for day classes for unemployed men and women. Apart from those to be held at Morley College, Toynbee Hall and the Mary Ward Settlement the majority of such classes were to be in men's or women's institutes. The grant of £5000 was repeated in successive years and in 1934–5 there were 230 classes for men with an enrolment of about 3500 and eleven classes for women with an enrolment of 200. From then onwards enrolment began to improve and, for the session 1935–6, twenty-six senior and junior men's institutes recorded 26,696 students; forty-one women's institutes recorded 32,232 students; twelve literary institutes recorded 12,968 students.

Together with students in non-vocational classes in general institutes (7855), in club classes not affiliated to evening institutes (2940), the deaf institute (201) and in other institutes (27,093), the total number of such students was 109,985. This number represented 3.3 per cent of the total population over school-leaving age resident in the Council's area at that time.

Exhibitions and physical exercise displays had always been a feature of men's and women's institutes and the standard both of display and exhibits grew considerably in the 1930s. The number of visits by groups of women students to Paris, Rome and Holland, a feature of a number of institutes in the 1920s, fell off during the early 1930s but were beginning to appear again in 1937. Visits to exhibitions of paintings and music festivals, however, continued. In 1932 an entry in the Goodrich Road Women's Institute log-book records the visit by a party of thirty-two students to the Royal Academy. A note – 'I had catalogues typed of some of the most interesting pictures and their artists' indicated that they did not go unprepared. Appreciation of art and music had its place in some women's institutes as well as in the literary institutes. On the practical side, home decoration and upholstery appeared with greater frequency. The institutes responded to the needs of working-class mothers whose family duties kept them at home in the evenings, by offering afternoon classes. Heads of institutes were frequently approached by social workers, secretaries of co-operative guilds, YWCA and other women's organizations to provide instructors for afternoon classes. They were held sometimes in voluntary clubs, sometimes in a room not used by the day school – often with the enthusiastic support of the head of the school who saw in them an opportunity to make contact with mothers of children. Generally they were attended by working-class housewives

> . . . some of whom find it necessary to bring the baby (or the latest baby) . . . while most of these classes are in the needlework category (with renovation of clothing – an indication of successive, if not inherited, use of clothing in poorer homes – very prominent amongst them), subjects such as singing, dramatic literature and current events are taken. There is something remarkably stimulating in the knowledge that these women, in circumstances in which there is no lack of deterrent factors, will meet in the afternoons to sing, act, and discuss the topics of the day.[38]

Perhaps the most striking indication of curriculum development was to be seen in the presentation of physical exercises. The 'drill' of the School Board days had given way to physical training and then to gymnastics and physical exercises. Exercises to music – the service of a pianist was now permitted for part of the lesson – performed in a light blouse and shorts instead of the former skirted gymnastic costume, transformed the scene. It transformed it so much that the head of Cosway Street Women's Institute in 1935 records that 'the Rev. H.W. Conishee objected to the gymnastic dress of the club girls who used St Paul's Hall, so the class was transferred to the school buildings'. Physical exercises, or Keep Fit as it now increasingly came to be called, gave the opportunity to more and more London women to correct defects of posture and to enjoy a freedom and dignity of movement they had seldom experienced before. More important perhaps, it gave them a poise and confidence which hitherto they had lacked.

Vocal music, always a strong feature of women's institutes, was now supported by classes in the theory of music as well as instrumental and orchestral music. Mixed classes for vocal and orchestral music were permitted in women's, but not in men's institutes. Most music classes aimed to give a public performance either in the institute or often for some good cause in a local church or mission hall. Every year there were numerous productions of light opera, orchestral, choral or ballad concerts. All women's institutes had at least one dramatic class at which there would be some formal speech training and at which the reading and acting of plays of established reputation would be undertaken. Ramsay and Myers give an interesting indication of the literature in use in the 1930s:

> The appropriate section of the Council's loan collection, to which these classes have access, contains hundreds of sets of plays, Shakespeare, Shaw, Galsworthy and Barrie heading the list as regards the number of titles. There are many sets of one act, and collections of selective full length, plays. There are simple playlets (although of good quality) and all that is best of Tchekov. Sheridan still appears to hold his place. C.L. Anthony, Bennett and Knoblock, Clemence Dane, Decker (with the Shoemaker's Holiday), Drinkwater, Ashley Dukes, St. John G. Ervine, J.L. Fagan, W.S. Gilbert, Oliver Goldsmith, H. Granville Barker, Thomas Hardy, Stanley Houghton, Laurence Housman, Ibsen, J.K. Jerome, Maeterlinck, Masefield, Somerset Maugham, A.A. Milne, Milton (with Comus), E. and A. Philpott, Pinero, R.C. Sherriff, Wycherley (with Love-in-a-Wood, the Gentleman Dancing Master, The Country Wife, and the Plain Dealer) and Yeats are amongst others on the list whose works are obtainable and are read, studied, acted and often produced.[39]

The Rev. Stewart Headlam, that much revered member of the London School Board and the LCC Education Committee, had died in 1925 and the log-books of many institutes have entries recording concerts and performances to raise money for a memorial fund to the man who, possibly more than any other, had so consistently supported and fought for the work of London's institutes. One such memorial was the Stewart Headlam Shakespeare Association – the Rev. Stewart Headlam was a great lover of Shakespeare. Founded in the 1920s it held annual competitions which attracted the bulk of their entries from classes at the LCC women's institutes. A verse-speaking section introduced into the competition in the 1930s proved popular and encouraged good diction in classes. In its first year the competition in this section was won by a girl from a woman's free institute in one of the poorest parts of London. The Shakespeare section of the competition was devoted to the acting of a scene from Shakespeare (a selection of four or five being set). The entries were graded according to the standard of the class and there were junior and senior sections. The scene set had to have at least five speaking parts and not take more than twenty minutes to perform.

Since the women's institutes had first opened women had been given the vote. By the middle 1930s there had a been a marked growth in the interest shown by women and girls in social and political problems. One suspects it is Miss Ramsay who comments in *London Men and Women*:

> The tendency to leave such matters as the choice of political party and of candidates at elections to the men of the house, whether father, husband or brother, is gradually disappearing. The organisation of women's sections of political parties is one of the signs of this change. 'We don't have to take Dad's [the husbands] word for it now' said one working class mother when a proposal to open an afternoon class on current events was being discussed. 'We don't want to know about politics,' said another, 'but we want no more of these floods [referring to the danger of seasonal flooding on the riverside], and what about the price of milk and bacon, and when are they going to build a new school in – Street?'; these remarks and others like them show that the participation of women in public affairs, although by no means complete, may add new realism to our approach to social problems.[40]

The table of students' occupations for the session 1933 – 4, reprinted here (page 133) from *London Men and Women*, throws an interesting light on both the occupations of Londoners in the early 1930s and the different appeal to particular sections of the working community made by the three main types of non-vocational institute. Most students at literary institutes were drawn from the professions, the upper echelons of public and private office workers and 'retired or not gainfully employed', a category which includes housewives. Housewives, (5475), textile and dressworkers (5308), those in 'personal service' (2219) and clerical workers (4519) accounted for over 60 per cent of those in women's institutes. A substantial number of unemployed women were included in the 'undefined workers and unemployed' category (3473). In men's institutes the largest single group (over 30 per cent) included the unemployed (7770); of the remainder just over 50 per cent came from transport and communications (2333), commerce (excluding clerks) (1219), clerks (1131), metalwork trades (1120), and wood and furniture workers (1035).

It is significant that a large proportion of students in the men's institutes were unemployed; it is even more significant that non-vocational classes grew steadily during and following periods of acute economic depression. The institutes were a major means of keeping men (and women) sane by providing an outlet for the frustration and privations of unemployment.

By 1931 the country was in the grip of a severe world economic crisis. Unemployment, which in 1929 was about 1.5 million, rose to 2.6 million in 1931. Not until 1935 did it fall below 2 million. A Committee of National Expenditure (the May Committee) recommended savage economies in the public sector, one of which was a 5–10 per cent cut in the wages and salaries of public servants. One unforeseen side-effect of this was that a number of young teachers, whose salaries had been cut by 10 per cent as a result of the May Committee recommendations, were attracted to part-time teaching in adult institutes. In addition to supplementing income many of them found a new educational inspiration in the eagerness of adults to learn which stimulated their teaching and their inventiveness. From their ranks instructors in charge, deputy heads and future principals were drawn.

LCC Literary, Men's and Men's Junior, and Women's Evening Institutes
(Figures for the literary institutes have been included for purpose of comparison.)

Occupations of Students Session 1933–4

	Occupational group as per census returns 1931	Evening Institutes		
		Literary	Men's and Men's Junior	Women's
1	Land	19	43	—
2	Mining and Quarrying	—	1	—
3	Gas, coke, lime, cement, etc.	10	86	3
4	Bricks, pottery, glass, tiles	4	57	7
5	Chemical processes, oils, paints	32	90	171
6	Metalwork	55	1120	152
7	Precious metals and electro-plate	2	60	33
8	Electrical trades	64	358	160
9	Watches, clocks, scientific instruments	7	84	49
10	Skin, leather and leather-substitute goods	14	367	215
11	Textiles	—	21	4
12	Textile goods and articles of dress	84	761	5308
13	Foods, drinks and tobacco	63	587	840
14	Wood and furniture trades	11	1035	232

		Evening Institutes		
Occupational group as per census returns 1931		Literary	Men's and Men's Junior	Women's
15	Paper and cardboard trades, bookbinding	22	182	880
16	Printing trades	78	457	453
17	Building trade	18	767	7
18	Painters and decorators	8	144	4
19	General trades .	30	542	808
20	Transport and communication	130	2333	472
21	Commerce, finance, insurance and allied occupations (excluding clerks)	744	1219	898
22	Public administration and defence (excluding typists and professional men)	1800	192	606
23	Professional occupations (excluding clerical staff)	1141	116	807
24	Entertainments and sports	7	35	22
25	Personal service	139	439	2219
26	Clerks and draughtsmen	3825	1131	4519
27	Warehousemen, store-keepers and packers	25	969	1073
28	Stationary engine drivers	1	31	1
29	Undefined workers and unemployed persons (not otherwise described)	590	7770	3473
30	Retired or not gainfully occupied	3129	476	5475
	TOTALS	12,052	21,473	28,891

Men's and Women's Institutes Comparative Figures Since 1920

(The numbers shown for men's institutes include those recorded at both senior and junior men's institutes. The figures would otherwise not be comparable as between men's and women's institutes, the 14–18 age group being included in the numbers for women.)

	Men's (senior and junior)			Women's (free and fee-paying)		
Year	No. of institutes	Enrolment	Student hours	No. of institutes.	Enrolment	Student hours
1920–21	5	2128	99,410	37	35,573	1,423,882
1921–22	5	2906	156,090	37	27,936†	1,175,221
1922–23	5	3349	171,847	37	27,431	1,225,272
1923–24	5	4021	192,135	37	27,296	1,274,963
1924–25	6	4747	237,798	37	29,928	1,331,758
1925–26	11	7727	403,763	37	30,194	1,310,348
1926–27	13	10,096	531,274	36	32,113	1,438,152

	Men's (senior and junior)			Women's (free and fee-paying)		
Year	No. of institutes	Enrolment	Student hours	No. of institutes.	Enrolment	Student hours
1927–28	16	12,098	641,508	37	32,893	1,525,688
1928–29	17	14,325	816,181	38	33,195	1,565,803
1929–30	17	15,777	974,864	38	34,465	1,613,420
1930–31	21	18,879	1,197,458	39	35,203	1,700,062
1931–32*	23	19,187	1,253,384	39	31,991	1,530,450
1932–33*	23	16,890	1,222,646	37	28,194	1,412,767
1933–34	23	21,473	1,409,472	38	28,891	1,428,406
1934–35	26	23,000	1,499,749	41	31,449	1,539,588

* A year of educational economies and industrial depression.
† Decline probably due to opening of compulsory day-continuation schools, revision of fees and trade depression.

In the mid-1930s school rolls in London were falling and, despite London's central schools and its well-established scholarship scheme, there was mounting dissatisfaction with the exclusive elementary and secondary division of the educational system. Non-vocational institutes were enabling a large number of 'ex-elementary school' men and women to develop talents which they did not know they had. Nowhere was this more apparent than in the rapidly developing men's institutes. Those who witnessed it marvelled at the application, skill and depth of knowledge of labouring men in the pursuit of interests fostered by the institutes. There is little sign, however, that educationalists of the day sought to apply to the wider educational scene the approaches and teaching techniques which had brought about such a transformation. It is perhaps one of the remarkable aspects of London education that, despite the extensive use of schools, the primary and secondary sectors of education were scarcely conscious of adult education other than as occupiers of accommodation. Educational approaches in the post-school sector were not seen to be relevant to the primary and secondary schools of the day. In the mid-1930s the education of adults, particularly in men's institutes, was providing evidence that an education for all according to their aptitude and ability, could be found in a broad-based curriculum.

Those who doubted the lack of a philosophy behind the work of men's and women's institutes were misled by the fundamental simplicity of the approach. This approach started from some aspect in which the student had an interest and encouraged him or her to go on from there in an atmosphere of mutual learning. The success of this approach was nowhere better illustrated than in the classes and clubs for caged birds, pigeons, poultry, rabbits and the brass-and-silver bands of the men's institutes. The impact they made on the communities they served by the unobtrusive social education of students was considerable. A report of a full inspection undertaken by the Council's inspectorate of the Walworth Men's Institute in the session 1936–7 shows the quite remarkable progress made by one of the original five institutes established in 1920. The student roll of Walworth had grown steadily from 371 in 1920 to 1382 in 1935–6, excluding day classes for unemployed men which accounted for another 317. In the previous session the former junior section of the institute, with a roll of 414, had become a separate institute (the Robert Browning Men's (Junior) Institute), under a whole-time head. No less than 701 of the 1219 students enrolled at the time of the inspection attended for more than one evening; 207 attended for more than three evenings a week.

The report commented on the remarkable number of new students each session. Of the 1343 senior students who enrolled in 1934–5, no fewer than 774 did not return in the session 1935–6. According to the head of the institute this was fairly representative of the annual turnover of students at the institute. There was a solid core of some 500 students who could be relied upon to enrol year after year, the rest being new students. This meant that each session demanded a vigorous publicity campaign. As the report pointed out, if this pattern continued the institute would be attended by well over 8000 students over a period of ten years. The population in 1935 of the six parishes covered by the institute was 232,234, a drop, incidentally, of over 19,000 since 1931. At that time there were few firms in Walworth which employed more than 100 men. Camberwell had become a centre for laundries, Walworth had some small foundries, motor-engineering works and a considerable number of minor printing firms. The largest group of male workers were employed on road, rail and water transport.

Apart from the Council's institutes, few organizations in the district were associated with adult education. Cambridge House Settlement was concerned primarily in co-ordinating the work of boys' clubs; the 'Clubland' church was attended only by juveniles, while Morley College was just outside the area. In Camberwell, the Health Centre and Stafford Street Museum were doing pioneer work but without the co-operation of public bodies. The Catholic churches and the Jewish synagogue were beginning to form adult clubs of a recreative nature. Browning Hall, formerly a centre of considerable local influence, had become merely a meeting place for a few clubs. Avenue Road (SB) School was being rebuilt and it was hoped that, at the end of July 1937, the institute would move from the inadequate accommodation at John Ruskin (J) School to the more commodious, electrically-lit Avenue Road School with its large handicraft and metalwork rooms, three craft rooms, a gymnasium with spray and foot baths, changing room and storage for apparatus and woodwork models as well as an indoor lavatory. The Nelson School evening institute branch had the good fortune to have complete possession of the first floor.

Active corporate life had always been an outstanding feature of men's institutes. 'Jimmy' James, MC, MA, head of Walworth Men's since 1928, had steadily fostered the corporate life of the institute, encouraged students to regard it as a club (rather than an aggregation of classes) and make it a self-governing community. Every class had its own committee, chairman and secretary who co-operated with the instructor in keeping the class up to strength and in preserving a friendly atmosphere in it. Every committee sent one representative to the Institute Social Committee and this committee was the basis of the social organization. Meeting monthly it organized all the general activities of the institute such as the annual exhibition, the children's party, the annual institute dinner and the music festival. It allocated to the various clubs and societies dates for their social evenings. In the session 1935–6 there were forty-three social events.

The football, cricket and table-tennis clubs were controlled by the sports' club under the chairmanship of the schoolkeeper who was the club's first secretary and 'one of the most ardent and persistent propogandists on the institute's behalf'. The football club played in the Peckham and District League of which the institute was the headquarters. The cricket club was self-supporting with sufficient funds to purchase its own equipment and rent a ground at Eltham. One of the outstanding events of the summer term was the annual match against the staff, when the staff and their wives took tea with the club at Eltham. The cycling club, which had grown around an old local club of repute, 'the Rodney Cycling Club', arranged weekly runs, took part in track and road racing in which it had a distinguished record and held an annual dinner. The swimming club held its first gala at Manor Place Baths in 1935–6 session. The well-established boxing club had already won the championship of the Federation of Men's Institutes on three occasions and produced two Amateur Boxing Association champions. A 1936–7 student, R. Shrimpton, represented Great Britain at the 1936 Olympic Games and E. Ryan fought in the 'Golden Gloves' team in New York, winning his event. His brother, F. Ryan, was the Empire Bantam-Weight Champion in the Empire Games held at Wembley. The travel club organized frequent excursions to places of interest and had made five visits to the Continent. Two members of the last party had passed the elementary stage in French, one studying at Morley College and the other at the Southwark Commercial Institute.

Most of the other clubs were directly connected with the classes from which they had developed. The caged-birds society used to hold two very successful annual shows and a photograph of the club members taken at the time displays the many valuable competition trophys presented by friends of the institute. The poultry club, known locally as the 'The Walworth Poultry and Utility Society', had, at its 1935 open show, attracted entries from all parts of the United Kingdom and 253 birds were exhibited. The Horticultural Society held a spring show at which the eight cups in its possession were annually awarded. It won the Royal Horticultural Society's Banksian Medal for spring flowers and one of its members secured the Daffodil Championship of Great Britain in a competition sponsored by *Amateur Gardener*. The rabbit club which specialized in English breeds held two shows annually and helped a group of unemployed men in breeding rabbits for fur value. The John Ruskin Camera Club, affiliated to the Royal Photographic Society, organized an annual exhibition of work and the 1936 exhibition was held at the Southwark Public Library. In addition to club activities there were four major functions which were held annually. Foremost amongst these was the annual exhibition, opened on each occasion by a prominent educationalist or some other eminent person. The exhibition of 1936 was opened by Dr Albert Mansbridge. The annual children's party was organized by students assisted by the staff and the advisory committee, the necessary funds being subscribed by the students. The guests were the children of the students and at the party in 1935–6, 220 children were entertained to tea and a concert, 'every child leaving with cup, saucer and plate of Coronation ware, together with sweets and fruit'. All the musical classes, bands, orchestras and male-voice choirs united in organizing the annual music festival. The Southwark Borough Council gave free use of their hall at the Manor Place Baths and, at the 1936 concert, some 123 students took part. The annual institute dinner provided an opportunity to bring the advisory committee in closer contact with the staff and with those students whose devotion to the institute gave them some prominence.

To meet the popular demand for woodwork and home carpentry there were no less than twenty-three classes held in buildings which housed woodwork centres. Five physical exercise and boxing classes at the main institute were filled to capacity. Music, which had always been strong at Walworth, had five classes and the music group had recently 'received a fillip from the modern craze for accordion playing. To satisfy the insistent local demand two strong classes have recently been opened for those who aspire to master that instrument.' Classes in petrol engines and radio classes provided a small science group while five classes in leatherwork, photography (two), painting and poster art made up the arts and crafts section. Home decoration, boot repairing, caged birds, rabbit keeping, poultry keeping and horticulture classes provided for the large body of men whose interests were in practical hobbies. In addition there was a public-speaking and current-events class and two dramatic-literature classes, one of which was held at St John's Institute, Larcom Street. At the branch institute housed in the Nelson School and supervized by the deputy head some fifteen classes, roughly representative of all sections of the curriculum, were held. Three cookery classes were held at the Crampton Street Centre for the destitute men of the Embankment Fellowship 'who hoped to gain enough knowledge of the rudiments of cookery to fit themselves for vacancies for sea cooks and the like'. Day classes for the unemployed were an extra institute provision in that the LCC supplied neither the accommodation nor the equipment.

In its commentary on the teaching of the various subjects the inspector's report paid particular tribute to the strong general education classes which it said 'are all too rare in the men's institutes'. Walworth had two large elementary classes, one in reading and writing and the other in arithmetic. In the arithmetic lesson the instructor was compelled to give every student individual attention but in English he taught the class for the most part as a whole. 'A mass of written work willingly produced every week by his students was marked by him with care.' One section of the inspector's commentary is of particular interest in demonstrating the extent to which men were prepared to tackle unfamiliar subjects under the guidance of a teacher for whom they had a special regard.

Students of a slightly more advanced grade are to be found in an English and mathematics class under an instructor who formerly taught gymnastics only. His students were so devoted to him that the head decided to entrust him with classes in the far less popular subjects of English and mathematics both of which he is qualified to teach. It is pleasing to record that under his energetic leadership the classes have made far more than enough progress to justify his appointment. A large volume of written work is undertaken by his students, some of whom, more than middle aged, are proud to display for inspection their exercise books in which accurate work of high quality has been accomplished. His English class produces an institute magazine, 'The Gateway' which is distributed without charge throughout the institute. Well kept records of the progress achieved in both classes are preserved by the instructor, who is to be congratulated both on the standard attained by his students and on the relationship he has established with them.

The physical education inspector does not share the approbation of his colleague about the 'capturing' of this promising instructor; under 'gymnastics' he comments that 'four teachers share in this work, and while all achieve reasonably good results, one in particular has built up most effective classes. The organiser of physical education regrets this instructor has given up a certain amount of his gymnastic training in order to concentrate on other subjects. His services can ill be spared at the present time. The lessons seen were virile and the students showed a commendable standard of performance.' (The instructor concerned was A.E. Auerbach who later succeeded Mr James as principal).

Comments on violin classes, orchestral music, instrumental music (wind) and the silver band were all generally favourable but the piano-accordion band was evidently introduced against the wishes of the music inspector who commented:

The inclusion of this recently formed class in the timetable was permitted only on condition that it must be regarded as an experiment. On the occasion of the inspection, the class was found to consist of 16 instrumentalists, most of whom were of a type not easily attracted to institute activities. They were, however, enthusiastic and willing to learn. At present they played by ear music of a very cheap and sentimental kind.

Although it would be unfair to pass a final judgement at this stage, it has been pointed out that the continuance of the class will depend on
(a) their ability to read and play simple music;
(b) the acquisition of good fingering and general piano technique;
(c) a general raising of the standard of the music played in class.

A generally congratulatory comment on the two dramatic classes included a reference to the performance of *Journey's End* by the Walworth Men's Dramatic Club in 1936 which was rehearsed by the author, Mr R.C. Sheriff, who complimented the company on their high standard and gave them a donation of five guineas to meet the royalty costs. Apparently, previous productions of the second class (St John's Players) had included 'several Edgar Wallace melodramas and other plays of mediocre quality' although they had also been successful at one time in Shakespearian scenes in the Stewart Headlam Shakespeare Association competitions. But 'as no women can be admitted to the class and as men are invariably awkward in the attempts to portray female characters, the class has lost its eagerness to participate in these competitions'.

After warmly commending the instructor the note ends with the ungracious comment, 'with the material at his disposal, his task has not been easy'. Evidently dramatic art and music had to conform to certain accepted patterns – even in men's institutes.

The language and tone of the report were markedly different from that of today. The occasional ungracious, sometimes rude and arrogant and often patronizing comments which would not be tolerated today were evidently accepted in 1937. We have to remind ourselves that inspectors commented from a loftier height than now and often reflected their culture or that of higher education rather than that of the men and women of the institutes. Although the class structure of society may not have altered fundamentally since 1937 it is certainly less sharply overt.

By 1937 the severity of the unemployment problem had been substantially lessened, but there were still day classes for unemployed men. The classes were affiliated to men's institutes but were housed in non-Council premises and such equipment as they had was not supplied by the Council. Because of this the inspection report indicated that 'a standard of achievement comparable to that of institute classes is not therefore to be expected of them. Many of them, indeed, are conducted in circumstances which would not be found in classes under the complete control of institute heads.' The main difficulties, apparently, were that the most satisfactory instructors were already fully employed in the day time and that the accommodation did not always separate games rooms, where darts and ping-pong were allowed, from the actual instruction. As the unemployment situation eased, the personnel of the classes became more stable and inspectors classified students under three headings:

'(i)   the over ''40s'' whose hope of securing employment is negligible;

(ii)   the ''ins and outs'' men who are either casual workers or in seasonal employment;

(iii) young unemployables.'

The starkness of these categories is continued by the comment on the third class which presented the most acute social problem. 'It consists in the main of the confirmed street lounger, but is not confined to men of low intelligence.' It went on to make a suggestion which one suspects was well ahead of its time. 'A solution of the general problem might be found in the establishment, in various parts of London, of attractive, well equipped and thoroughly supervised centres, ''institutes of leisure,'' where everyone who had day time leisure, whether unemployed or not, should be encouraged to attend, the term ''unemployed'' being completely tabooed.'

Classes in handicrafts were held on three mornings a week and boot repairing on two mornings each week together with an afternoon travel-talks class at the Embankment Fellowship; boot repairing in the Mayor of Lambeth's Hut on two afternoons weekly; an orchestral music class composed almost entirely of unemployed musicians, many of whom had had a long experience of orchestral playing, was held at Christ Church, Westminster Bridge Road. A woodwork class operated in premises at the Camberwell Fellowship which had been partially renovated by the students; there were two afternoon classes in boot repairing and petrol engines in an old house in Camberwell with an outhouse on the premises being used for practical work. Despite the general comments on difficulties of obtaining staff the comments on the individual classes indicated that very competent instructors had been obtained and that the low expectations of the inspectorate were not confirmed.

The full inspection report provides a valuable insight into the development of the curriculum of the Walworth Institute which, although one of the earliest and one of the largest, was also broadly representative of the general progress made by men's institutes. It also gives an indication of the success of these institutes and the fact that, by the late 1930s, the Council, encouraged by the remarkable standards achieved and the public recognition given to its initiative, realized the potential for the ordinary men and women of London in its non-vocational institutes. There was recognition, too, that although the best means of recruitment was through the students themselves, throughout the institutes there was a considerable turnover of students, largely for all the reasons which adults have for varying their commitment to such regular activities as evening classes. This meant that each session required a publicity campaign on the part of principals which could be helped and sustained by a more general publicity campaign conducted from the centre.

In 1937 *Floodlight*, a guide to LCC evening classes, was first produced. This alphabetical list of all the subjects in which instruction was offered and the establishments (vocational and non-vocational) at which it could be obtained, gave striking testimony to the unrivalled scope and opportunities offered by London evening institutes. In the same year a competition in London's art schools was held for a poster which would provide the general publicity to support the annual local effort. Although it attracted a satisfactory number of entries it did not produce a generally acceptable poster and the Education Officer was given authority to ask several professional artists to submit designs for a suitable poster for the session 1938–9. The result was posters from two brilliant cartoonists, Bert Thomas and Grimes; Bert Thomas for the session 1938–9 and Grimes for the session 1939–40. Their cartoons, which appeared on London's buses and in the Underground and elsewhere, amused thousands of Londoners who had never been to evening classes and attracted national and overseas interest. The Bert Thomas cartoons, depicting the proud display of some accomplishment over the caption 'I owe it all to LCC evening classes'; and Grimes with his cartoons of the empty chair or place and the caption 'Gone to evening classes' brilliantly exploited the variety of LCC evening institute provision. There is no doubt that the centrally organized publicity such as *Floodlight* and posters made a major impact, not only in London but elsewhere. Whether the Bert Thomas or Grimes cartoons brought more students to men's and women's institutes will never be known since before the session 1939–40 was due to open the Second World War had begun. In retrospect principals doubted whether this kind of publicity brought more students into the institutes. Certainly, after the War the pressure was for any money to be spent on local, rather than central, publicity. It is, however, quite remarkable how many people still remember the Bert Thomas and Grimes cartoons and there is reason to believe that this kind of publicity made attendance at evening institutes rather more 'respectable' for middle class and professional people.

For the next five sessions London was at war. Before turning to the London institutes in wartime, it is necessary to refer to the Physical Training and Recreation Act of 1937 which was to have far-reaching implications for the adult education institutes, not immediately discernible at the time.

The Act was the result of growing concern over the years, particularly following the economic depression, for the physical health and well-being, primarily, of young people. Admin. Memorandum 172 (1938), which followed the passing of the Act, was the subject of a report to the Education Committee by the Higher Education sub-committee. The Memorandum dealt with the authority given by the Act to local authorities, who need not be local education authorities, to establish or support community centres and recreational institutes and urged the general extension and improvement of opportunities for physical training and recreation for older and younger students. The Education Committee decided that there should be representation of the LCC on management committees of community centres and that grants should be made towards the salary of the warden and towards the cost of caretaking, redecoration and repair of premises. As far as recreational institutes were concerned, non-vocational institutes had already gone a long way in providing physical, social and recreational activities. It was proposed to seek recognition of these institutes as recreational institutes under Section 86 of the Education Act 1921 as amended by the Physical Training and Recreation Act of 1937. The Committee agreed that the new character which these institutes would assume made it desirable that they should be accommodated, where this was practicable, in premises wholly devoted to their purpose. Memorandum 172 suggested that facilities could be improved by making a more comprehensive provision for physical training and recreation for students already in classes of a technical, commercial and academic character and that separate courses of physical activities, should be available for those who did not wish to take other subjects. The Education Committee proposed to give special attention to increased facilities in the 1938–9 sessional arrangements in all evening institutes and to include separate courses in physical activities.

The general anxiety about the physical health of the nation at this time is to be seen in the eagerness with which the LCC, which already had done more than most authorities, responded to the Physical Training and Recreation Act by increasing the facilities for physical recreation in London. The provision of separate courses for physical exercise, for those who did not wish to take other subjects, was a complete reversal of the previous policy which had insisted that students of such courses must take other subjects. The Education Committee went even further: 'It may be possible in due course, to organise an evening institute devoted solely to physical training and health subjects.'[41] A survey of evening institute voluntary activities showed that there was a most significant and admirable volume of such activities on the part of the various societies, clubs and associations of the institutes. The Committee felt, therefore, that consideration should be given to the establishment of a Central Social Activities Fund on similar lines to the Games Fund of Secondary Schools and called for a further report on facilities for field games, camping sites, the inclusion of shower-baths, and rest-and-recreation rooms in evening institutes. The Central Social Activities Fund was authorized on 28 April 1938. Physical training was already available for full-time students in technical colleges and commercial institutes. The Committee proposed that the restriction on enrolment for physical exercises as a single subject, already removed in all but junior technical and commercial institutes, should apply in technical institutes as long as no vocational-course student was displaced from a physical exercise class.

Memorandum 172 also promised 75 per cent instead of 50 per cent grant on the salary of approved physical training straff for work with those who had left school. It was hoped that the National College of Physical Training would ensure a sufficient supply of suitable candidates for employment. As far as London was concerned the LCC College of Physical Education provided short courses of training as qualification for entry to the LCC panel; a grant for a new building and a maintenance grant had already been promised to the Lucas Tooth Gymnasium which trained male club leaders.

The LCC lost no time in implementing some of these decisions. Such was the speed that one has the impression that plans were well laid in anticipation of the legislation. A report of 4 May 1938 to the Education Committee, less than a month after the Committee decision, set out plans for the development of the Honor Oak Community Centre on the isolated Honor Oak Estate in Lewisham. The documents of the time give no hint of a major change of policy and, indeed, give strong support for the existing pattern of institutes. Throughout the years there had been suggestions for additional accommodation at both men's and women's institutes to provide recreational and social facilities and, where accommodation was available in schools, such adaptations had taken place. There had, however, been no proposals, other than the rehousing of the City Literary Institute in its own premises in 1939, for the building of specific premises for men's and women's institutes. The Physical Training and Recreation Act gave authority to local authorities other than education authorities to provide community centres and the LCC, under its housing powers, could have done so. It may well be that the Housing Committee was concerned at the lack of facilities for recreation on the isolated Honor Oak Estate and had communicated this concern to members of the Education Committee.

The plans for the community centre provided for an assembly hall with stage, dressing rooms, lavatories, kitchen and canteen and, on the first floor, rehearsal and lecture room with warden's office, classrooms and lavatories. On the second floor there was a gymnasium (with a flat roof for open-air exercises), dressing-rooms, shower-baths, stores, club and craft rooms, lavatories and cloakrooms; on the third floor there were hobbies rooms. A school treatment centre was accommodated on the ground floor together with a maternity and child welfare centre which would be leased to Lewisham Borough Council. The estimated cost of the centre was £22,000 (£15,895 for the community centre, £3,349 for the treatment centre and £2,756 for accommodation to be leased to Lewisham Borough Council).

The London Parochial Charities promised to contribute £2000 towards the erection of the buildings. The LCC was to be responsible for the direct payment of the warden's salary, the caretaker's wages, the rates and the repair and redecoration of the premises. The Community Centre Committee was to provide for any expenses over and above these items. Although the building was not likely to be completed until the summer of 1939 a warden was appointed from

1 September 1938 by means of a secondment offered to any interested person in the LCC's evening institute service. The head of Poplar Men's Institute, Mr F.C. Giles, was seconded to be the warden of the centre and head of the Ivydale General Evening Institute which would provide evening classes for Honor Oak Estate tenants at the Turnham School. In November 1938 it was decided that, pending the erection of the premises, Turnham School should be regarded as the community centre premises.

Evidently a survey was undertaken to identify those areas in London in which it would be desirable to establish community centres. On 5 July 1939 a report to the Education Committee indicated that there was already a community association on the Cowley Housing Estate in Lambeth 'which is one of 21 areas where we propose to consider in due course the establishment of community centres'. Recognizing that it would be some time before premises could be made available it was decided that evening institute facilities in this area 'should be so framed as to provide a basis on which the organisation of a community centre, at which the facilities would be of greater volume and more suitably housed' could ultimately be built.[42] The institute was to be a recreational institute at Cowley School under the direction of a full-time head who should be a man but have a staff which would include women. The salary and conditions of service were to be similar to those of a head of a junior evening institute. The institute, for both sexes, was to be like the existing free mixed type of institute but with extended facilities for physical, social and recreational activities. The registration fee was to be one shilling a session for those over eighteen and sixpence for those under eighteen. The decision that the head should be a man was subsequently changed and the post was advertised as man or woman (1939). In addition a site was sought for a community centre by the London Council for Social Service on the Dog Kennel Hill Estate and a site was reserved for a community centre on the Tulse Hill Estate. The general object appears to have been for these centres to operate under a voluntary committee with substantial aid by the LCC towards the salary and maintenance of the building and for instruction to be under the aegis of the local non-vocational evening institute.

The growing concern for the general well-being of young people led to a Board of Education Circular 1486 – 'Service of Youth' – which dealt with the social and physical development of the fourteen to twenty age group and set up a National Youth Committee. On 19 July 1938 it was decided that, from 1 October 1938, the work of the Joint Council of London Juvenile Organisations, a joint committee of representatives of voluntary youth associations, should be undertaken by the Council and the London Advisory Council of Juvenile Organisations Committee was established with orders of reference which set up Borough Juvenile Organisations Committees, later called Youth Organisations Committees, as part of its constitution. As a result of its consideration of Circular 1486 the LACJOC suggested that these later committees should be Borough youth committees and that they should be closely associated with the Higher Education sub-committee rather than with special services.

Despite the welcome that had been given to the LCC's initiative in establishing junior men's institutes, the numbers enrolled in the fourteen institutes so established by 1938 were a clear indication that there was a large section of this age group for which these institutes and the junior commercial and technical institutes had no appeal. The concern for the development of physical training and social and recreative facilities, which had promoted the Physical Training and Recreation Act 1937, prompted the search for some alternative provision. Community centres such as the ones proposed at the Honor Oak Estate, Cowley Estate, Tulse Hill, Robert Browning and elsewhere were clearly moves in the direction of welding the various education and community services together so that a physical and recreational provision could be integrated with the education services. Perhaps more important they could be the means of providing purpose-built premises which, for so long, had been denied to institutes. Such an approach also provided an opportunity for co-operative action between the voluntary and statutory sectors. London abounded in voluntary youth groups, usually attached to some wider voluntary organization such as a settlement.

The outbreak of war stopped building work on projects such as community centres but in 1940 the LCC returned to the question of recreational institutes for young people.

Men had been admitted to women's institutes for such classes as orchestral music and dramatic literature for some years but it was not until July 1939 that formal permission was given for women to be admitted to classes in vocal music, instrumental and orchestral music, dramatic literature and elocution in men's institutes, although some men's institutes had previously admitted women unofficially. In 1939 it was judged that about 1 per cent of the student roll in men's institutes was women and some 2 per cent were men in women's institutes. This rigid segregation of the sexes in men's and women's institutes was another aspect which, as far as young people were concerned, needed to be reconsidered.

8. The 1939 – 45 War

Although war was declared against Nazi Germany on 3 September 1939 the evil forces leading towards war had been apparent in the East End of London since the early 1930s. Sir Oswald Mosley and his British Union of Fascists preached racial and religious hatred at meetings held in the East End. Communists and Jews attended to oppose the views or break up the meeting; despite a substantial police presence fighting was frequent and many arrests were made. From Germany in 1935 came stories of the merciless persecution of the Jews and terrible atrocities by Nazi storm-troopers. The Jewish community, with their memories of age-long persecution, from which they had been free in England, were naturally terrified. Dr Mallon, warden of Toynbee Hall, organized a small group of people to consider what could be done. It was not until December 1936, however, that their efforts resulted in the passing of the Public Order Bill which forebade the wearing of uniform by political parties. Without their uniform, black shirts were shown to be the thugs and social misfits that they were and their influence diminished.

Miss Ramsay, principal of the Raleigh Women's Institute, records the climate of the times in Stepney: 'Three memories are to me vivid. One is the little Jewish boy who was tied up on an improvised wooden cross in White Horse Lane, another, the only Jewish family living in Duckett Street who were afraid to go home at night till they could creep in unnoticed and the last, the old wigged Jewess, wailing on a stool outside Rothschild Buildings who said to me "Oh lady, lady. I have seen it in Poland, it is coming here." ' Miss Ramsay, herself, had her own troubles from the Fascists at the Ben Jonson branch of her institute:

> I had letters (ironically) pressing me 'Be British! Ban Jews'. One evening the schoolkeeper came and said there was a crowd outside the main entrance demanding to see me. He opened a gate that I did not know existed, away from the main entrance and the girls and women in our classes – about 200 of them – left quietly. Then Jean Thompson and I walked out through the mob howling before we appeared, but completely silent as soon as they saw us.

War seemed imminent in September 1938 and log-books of institutes record that trenches were being hurriedly dug at night by the light of flares on the various neighbourhood open spaces. On 28 September 1938 Neville Chamberlain, then Prime Minister, flew to Munich to meet Hitler. He returned waving a piece of paper which he claimed was an indication of peace with honour. The country sighed with relief and set about preparing for a war which was inevitable. Surface shelters were built and an Air Raid Precautions Organisation and

147

Auxilliary Fire Service set up with an intensive programme of training in which the women's and men's institutes played a substantial part by providing many first-aid courses. Mr G.A.N. Lowndes, the Assistant Education Officer in charge of the General Purposes Branch of the Education Officer's Department, was seconded to the Home Office to assist in drawing up plans for the evacuation of women and children from London.

When war was declared on 3 September 1939 teaching staff in all sectors of education were involved in the evacuation plans. The majority volunteered for escort duties with parties of children and mothers, pregnant women and the disabled. On 14 August key staff were recalled from holiday and, on 25 August, schools reassembled and plans were checked in the succeeding days. On 31 August the evacuation order was received to be put into operation the following day. London had assumed responsibility for evacuation planning for the whole of the Greater London area and the Education Department was also responsible for the evacuation of old people and pregnant women. Separate arrangements had been made for special schools and nursery schools with transport to take them to holiday camps, country houses and seaside hotels which had been requisitioned for the purpose. By the morning of the fourth day some 600,000 persons had been moved out of the Greater London area. The first aid-raid warning came at 11 a.m. on 3 September when the Prime Minister was making his broadcast to the nation. Miss Ramsay wrote:

> I was in the playground of a large local school responsible for a party of 500 including most of the categories . . . (the aged, chronic sick, infants, children and mothers, the disabled) to be taken to Paddington on route for the City of Bath. Similar parties met throughout Stepney and throughout all London. As the siren sounded we moved into the school and a number of evacuees uncertain till then whether to go or not, appeared to join us. But in 10 minutes the all clear sounded, there had been a false alarm.

Some 49 per cent of the London school population – about 200,000 – was dispersed in the first ten days of September. Their escort duties completed, those principals of London institutes who had taken part as volunteers in the evacuation plans – and most of them had – returned to London in the following week. Initially, many of the principals of men's and women's institutes were either allocated, or attached themselves, to rest centres set up in schools to deal with those rendered homeless as a result of enemy bombing.

1938–9 had been a peak year for enrolments in institutes. The steady growth from 1932 onwards, together with the additional demands, following the Munich crisis of September 1938, for first-aid, home nursing and physical-training classes for civil-defence organizations, had made it so.

High expectations for session 1939–40 were dashed. The opening of evening classes was postponed and heads of institutes were asked to survey their areas and get advice from the Chief Aid-Raid Warden on suitable buildings in which to hold classes. Many buildings used by institutes had been taken over as rest centres or civil defence depots. Large windows were a 'blast' hazard and a blackout problem and many buildings had no shelter protection. From the scanty notes in log-books it is clear that aid-raid wardens were not anxious to have more safety and security hazards in the shape of students in evening classes.

The practical problems facing the LCC and principals before evening classes could be opened were immense. Some of the most difficult practical problems arose from 'the blackout' which came with the declaration of war and consequent air-raid precautions. This meant no street lights; car lights masked to a small rectangle of light; traffic lights shaded and masked; and entrances to ARP posts and other authorized places marked by a faint blue light.

One look at a School Board for London school – those 'lighthouses of learning' which shone out in peacetime like beacons – will give some idea of the practical problem of ensuring that, if used after one hour before sunset or on a dark November day, no evidence of that use could be seen from the air. Most of the schools had no provision for curtains and fitting light-proof blackout was a major task. Moreover the preparations before and after the Munich crisis of 1938 had included the identification of those educational buildings which would be used by the civil defence services, and other specialist accommodation such as that in polytechnics and technical colleges which would be needed for training service personnel or for other 'war work'. Blackout material, sandbags and other necessary materials had been supplied and protective work had either been carried out or provision made for it, in buildings classified as essential to the war effort. Literary institutes, men's institutes and women's institutes were not so regarded and, except for strips of adhesive brown paper across windows, the accommodation they normally used, unless taken over in whole or in part for civil defence purposes, were without blackout or protective shelter.

The absence of air-raid 'alerts' after the first 'alert' on 3 September encouraged former students of institutes to enquire whether classes were available; a good deal of pressure began to be exerted for classes to resume. Women whose children had been evacuated and many whose men folk were in the Forces, wanted things to do 'to take their minds off the War' by which they usually meant to fill the gap left by the absence of family demands on their time. Equally, the men at home felt the need 'to do something'. For others, the sudden cessation of the companionship they had had from evening classes increased the sense of an uneasy void. There grew up a general and almost feverish demand for a resumption of classes from all types of people. The most insistent clamour, for example, at Norwood Technical Institute came from former students of the vocal-music classes. In addition, session 1938–9 had shown principals the sizeable demand which could arise from the personnel of the civil defence organizations alone.

As soon as it was known that the opening of classes depended upon an effective blackout of buildings and shelter protection, principals with volunteer parties of part-time staff and students set to work. They filled thousands of sandbags and stacked them against ground-floor walls and windows to make an improvized shelter in a particular part of the building. They covered acres of windows with blackout material. Principals of men's and women's institutes had long been masters of improvization and had never been at a loss to acquire necessary materials. They had contacts among the faithful students whose acquisitive skill and ramifications of supply were never revealed. They quickly found a way round difficulties.

On 30 September the Education Officer suggested to heads of institutes that they take particulars of students' requirements but not accept fees. In October those institutes occupying buildings with reasonable blackout and shelter facilities were authorized to open and, by 9 November 1939, eighty-six institutes, which included a substantial number of men's and women's institutes and the City Literary Institute, had opened. By 1 December there were 114 evening establishments open of which more than half were men's, women's and literary institutes.

From then on classes began to build up gradually. Numbers were naturally lower than before the outbreak of war but the response of institutes to wartime conditions and needs was immediate. Principals of men's and women's institutes not only responded to express requests; they anticipated wartime community needs. Wartime London allowed their initiative and innate innovatory talents free rein. The Principal of Tower Bridge Women's Institute lived in Bloomsbury. At the outbreak of war she went along to a Bloomsbury warehouse and bought large quantities of materials of all kinds and a substantial stock of wool. This same warehouse was subsequently destroyed by enemy action. Her foresight enabled students of her institute to have wool throughout the war at a stable price. This and the other materials kept her institute supplied throughout and ensured a steady income to the institute fund, as a result of which there were always good subsidized meals for students before classes. Like so many other heads of institutes she also took responsibility for a junior institute temporarily without a head. By so doing facilities for the local community were made available which otherwise would have had to be suspended.

On 21 February 1940 a report to the Education Committee by the General Committee[1] which had replaced all sub-committees of the Education Committee, stated that although the resumption of evening institutes had been delayed about 140 were now open. During the next financial year, it continued, the number of students would be about 100,000, that is to say, about 50 per cent of the normal volume. On this basis the number of non-vocational students was between 30,000 and 40,000. The varying dates of opening made it difficult to apply the

1907, millinery class, Choumert Road Evening Continuation School, Peckham, and *below*, 1913, cookery class, Montem Street, Islington

1914, health class, Cosway Street Evening Institute, Marylebone, and *below*, 1914, millinery class, Laxon Street Evening Institute, Bermondsey

1914, singing class, Laxon Street Evening Institute, Bermondsey, and *below*, 1914, cobbling class, Redriffe Institute, Rotherhithe

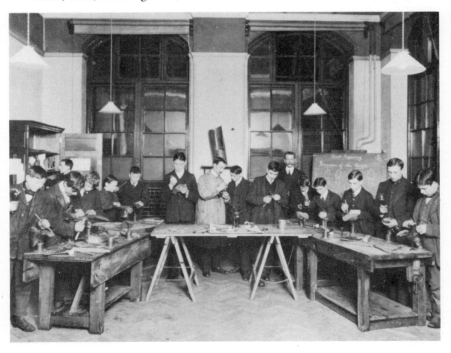

Wartime, ladies cobbling class, Battersea Evening Institute, and *below*, 1915, club swinging, Glyn Road Evening Institute, Hackney

1930, home decorating class, St Giles Women's Institute, Holborn, and *below*, 1931, physical training, Bow Creek Evening Institute, Poplar

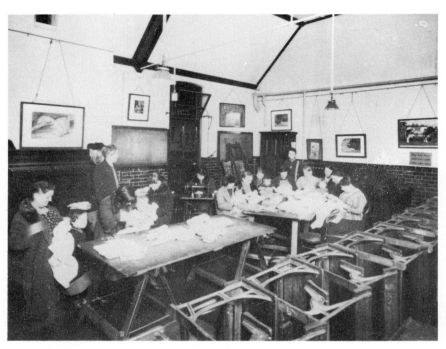

1931, sewing class, Bow Creek Women's Institute, Poplar, and *below*, 1937, class with broody hen, Bethnal Green Men's Institute

1939, City Literary Institute, lecture room, Holborn, and *below*, 1939, woodwork class, Gopsall Street Women's Institute, Haggerston

1940, singing class, crypt, Shoreditch Church, and *below*, sewing class, Penn Street shelter, Shoreditch

1941, boot repairing, Pitfield Street Library shelter, Shoreditch, and *below*, 1941, dressmaking, Kennard's shelter, Hoxton

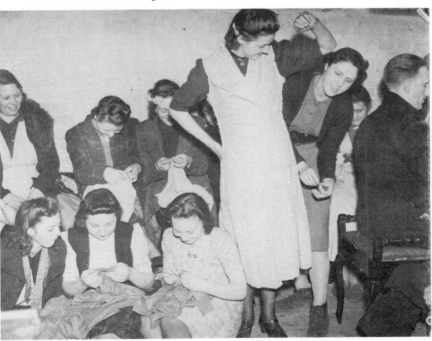

1940, make-do and mend class, Hoxton, and *below*, 1951, model parliament, Battersea Evening Institute

1951, motor-cycle maintenance class, and *below*, 1956, woodwork class, Finsbury Women's Institute

1960, piano class, City Literary Institute, Holborn, and *below*, 1961, women's keep fit class, Marylebone Institute

1961, pottery class, Putney and Roehampton Institute, and *below*, 1961, affiliated society class, Marylebone Institute

1963, poise and personality class, Fulham and South Kensington Institute, and *below*, 1965, Mr James Young and Mrs (later Dame) Margaret Cole admiring a student's work, Chaucer Institute, Southwark

1973, painting class, Camden Adult Education Institute, and *below*, 1973, creche, Highway Manor Adult Education Institute

Above, 1973, karate
class, Bethnal Green
Evening Institute,
and *below*, 1981, new
Stanhope Street
building, now
Central Institute, off
Euston Road

normal scales of fees and, in view of wartime conditions and the restricted facilities, it was decided that students who would normally be admitted to a free branch of an institute would be admitted on the same conditions to a men's or women's institute. Auxiliary Fire Service and civil defence personnel would be charged 1s. 3d. a term for all subjects.

The service that the institutes gave to young people, particularly in 1940, was extremely important. In addition to the substantial number of children who had not gone to reception areas in the country, the absence of bombing had led many mothers and children to return to London. The LCC began opening 'emergency schools' from December 1939. Since many of them had inadequate protection against air raids, attendance at them was voluntary with the consent and know-ledge of parents and at the parents' risk. In December 1939 it was estimated that there were 192,000 children of school age and about 71,000, mainly under five, who were not on the school rolls. A frightening number of children of school age, as well those between fourteen and eighteen, were running wild. Many of the schools had been requisitioned by the military or the civil defence authorities and unoccupied school buildings were only sufficient to provide schooling on a double-shift basis for children aged eleven or over. H.C. Dent in *Education in Transition* gives a lively account of the impact of evacuation on education generally with a number of references to the London scene. On the London situa-tion in 1939–40 he makes the point 'that in many districts parents were singu-larly unhelpful.'[2] In other words there were still parents who were only too pleased to have children out of school in order to help at home or to add to the family income from early employment.

In October 1939 a National Youth Committee had been set up to advise the Government on problems of juvenile welfare in wartime. A special Juvenile Welfare Branch to deal with the organization, development and administration of grants was also set up in the Board of Education. See page 145.

In a report to the Education Committee on 21 February 1940[3] the General Committee said that, although evening institutes in association with voluntary clubs were doing a valuable service, they were concerned about that group of young people to whom these facilities did not appeal. They therefore proposed recreational institutes of a distinct type and as a definite experiment: one for boys, one for girls and one mixed, in carefully selected areas where the need appeared to be clear. The institutes would offer facilities mainly of a physical, social and recreational character but it was suggested that a syllabus of attractive classes should be provided in each institute and that a condition of joining would be a willingness to take part in some educational activity. The Committee also decided that grants for youth work should be made to voluntary organizations and not to individual clubs. The institutes proposed were very similar to the institutes that were developing for young people under the aegis of both women's and men's institutes and their separation from the adult institutes was strongly resented by principals, particularly those who had been most successful in covering the activities of young people. It is interesting to note, too, that the recreational institutes when formed were put in the charge of these same principals. But for the extraordinary post-evacuation conditions in London it is doubtful if the reaction would have been quite the same.

One indication of the extent to which men's and women's institutes had provided for young people was their absorption of most of the forty youth-advice centres, which had been set up in central schools and neighbouring elementary schools at the outbreak of war to give advice to young people in difficulties of any kind. As evening institutes opened the youth-advice centres gradually ceased to exist in their original form; some developed on recreational lines and extended their accommodation, becoming junior sections of evening institutes. Others went to outside centres. By the spring of 1940 only seven existed in their original form and operated under the control of the Borough Youth Committee. It was decided that these should continue with the approval of the Borough Youth Committee and be affiliated to the appropriate evening institute.

The Government had at last given a lead on provision for the fourteen to twenty age group by establishing a National Youth Service. Despite the steps that the LCC had already taken to establish recreational facilities for young people in its area, the national lead, the appalling situation in London following evacuation and the return of many young people to London from the reception areas, impelled the LCC to provide more recreational institutes. It is significant that, initially, each recreational institute replaced a junior men's institute.

An increasing number of classes, arranged for women refugees, were sponsored by the Central Refugees Committee (Domestic Bureau) and the fees charged were on the basis of average attendance at classes. In March 1940 the General sub-committee authorized the reopening of the LCC College of Physical Education so that courses could be provided for women training for evening institute work and for club trainees for the keep-fit panel of instructors and keep-fit courses for adults.

In July 1940 Mr E.G. Savage succeeded Mr E.M. Rich as Education Officer. Mr Rich had been one of Mr Blair's young assistants and had been very much involved in the reorganization of 1913. Like his first chief, Blair, his primary interest had been the development of technical and commercial education and those opportunities for higher education presented by an extensive scholarship scheme. When he took over from G.H. (later Sir George) Gater in 1934, the education service was climbing out of the depression of the early 1930s only to become battered by the major conflict of the Second World War as he retired.

To make up for lost time at the beginning of the session the 1939–40 session was extended to September. Since January 1940 a considerable number of elementary school buildings had been brought into use for emergency schools and air-raid protection provided for children in attendance. This made their use for evening institutes practicable. Another eleven institutes were opened in districts in which there was no evening class provision and a number of institutes who had been forced to use unsuitable buildings were able to return to their normal location. Twenty-three branches were reopened in districts formerly served by sessional institutes or well attended branch institutes or in which, under present conditions, additional facilities appeared to be needed. The remaining institutes with sessional or half-time heads were not reopened. Nevertheless, there was a class for stammerers which was authorized at Kingsway Institute and altogether 197 buildings were occupied by evening institutes and branches as compared with the 258 before the war. A food education campaign was launched, organized by local borough committees to promote the right use of food and prevent waste in its preparation and consumption during wartime. Cookery classes and demonstrations took place in Council schools and in evening institutes. Classes in gardening for allotment holders were opened at a number of evening institutes and an instructor at Kentish Town Men's Institute attended at the allotments on Primrose Hill for a two sessions a week to give practical advice and demonstration. No fee was charged, there was no formal registration and the cost was recognized by the Ministry of Agriculture for a 60 per cent grant. 'First aid in brief', consisting of three one-hour lectures, was given by qualified assistants in evening institutes; again no fee was charged.

The expected air raids did not begin until towards the end of August 1940. During the first half of September 1940 over 2000 civilians were killed by bombs in Britain and nearly 10,000 were badly wounded. Four fifths of these were in London, the majority in the East End. Miss Ramsay records: 'Nightly, people took refuge – in local halls and shelters, in underground railways and provision of food and sanitation was arranged with lightning speed. Many of the aged and infirm lived underground. "Moaning Minny" wailed, the drone of planes was heard, the crash of bombs and rumble of falling masonry and broken glass. The barrage of guns sounded and search lights lit the sky. In the mornings tired humanity trailed home, often to find their homes in ruins, broken glass to be cleared and any possessions remaining, to be collected. "But before long, an immense weariness in the relentless regularity of the attack", wrote one journalist, "had found its match in the dogged determination of the people to go on, no matter what the cost."

'On Monday, 23 September 1940, King George VI and the Queen (the present Queen Mother) visited Stepney and talked to raid victims in the wards of the London Hospital. The large building had already suffered from bombing when their Majestys visited. 'The King ain't run away – 'e's like us, still in London', was a popular remark.' After 7 September 1940 East London was bombed by an average of 200 planes nightly for fifty-seven nights in succession. On 7 September 1940 the Education Officer wrote to institutes saying that holiday classes must close sufficiently early to allow students to reach home before blackout and, on 16 September, the opening of institutes was postponed owing to air raids.

Miss J.C. Blackman, appointed as the half-time head of Goodrich and Ivydale Women's Institutes from September 1940, records in her log-book that, on 14 October, enrolment was still postponed but heads were invited to meet Mr. E.G. (later Sir Graham) Savage, the new Education Officer, at County Hall to discuss conditions of life in London. Apparently at that meeting the advice was given by heads that institutes should reopen and, on 19 October, both institutes of which Miss Blackman was in charge were open for enrolment. On 22 October classes met. She records that response was poor but hopeful. On 24 October, when the Education Officer apparently asked for a return of the position, she records that six classes were open, that attendance was not good but encouraging. Other principals, in the few available records, note the opening of afternoon classes and opening for enrolment in mid-October.

But even before classes were open much had been happening. Miss Plastow, the Principal of the Women's Institute in Bermondsey, in response to a call for help from Bede House Settlement which was coping with bombed-out families, went to help with the washing-up and stayed for three weeks. With others she was allocated a space in which she could just put her case containing a few necessaries. They slept in the basement and hoped, if they ever thought about it, that nothing would cause a flood since it was well below the flood level. They set about feeding the victims of air raids. At that time the Council rest homes had very little except 'bully-beef' and tea and no cooking facilities; they had plenty of coffins but no hot meals. She, with many other voluntary workers, fed the people until the rest centres could establish cooking facilities.

Bermondsey Borough Council, formed a shelter council consisting of representatives of churches, statutory and voluntary bodies in the area. The shelter council not only helped to settle people in shelters and deal with many of the problems that arose as a result of casualties and houses being bombed, it also gradually began to organize activities in the shelters themselves. Members of the shelter council arranged entertainments and the Borough Council saw to it that pianos were available in the shelters by arranging for them to be taken round in the Council's dust-carts. Artists, sent by the Council for the Encouragement of Music and the Arts, (CEMA) were frequent performers.

CEMA came into being in January 1940 as a result of an initiative taken by the President of the Board of Education, Earl de la Warr. He approached the Pilgrim Trust to see whether it would make a grant towards the maintenance and encouragement of music and the arts in war time. The Trust awarded a grant of £25,000, to which the Treasury added another £25,000 and a committee of four

– Sir Kenneth Clark, Director of the National Gallery; Sir Walford Davies, Master of the King's Music; Dr Thomas Jones, Secretary of the Pilgrims Trust; and Mr W.E. Williams, Secretary of the British Institute of Adult Education – was appointed to advise the Board of Education on how the money should be spent. The purpose of CEMA was defined as the encouragement of musical, artistic and other cultural activities outside the larger more prosperous organizations. CEMA got to work quickly and made an impact on the arts throughout the country during the war years.

Principals of institutes and others who worked with Londoners in the air-raid shelters and emergency rest centres during the terrible days of the blitz are warm in their praise for the artists of CEMA.

> Night after night – I believe many did it five nights a week for months – CEMA artists travelled by taxi, in buses and on foot, often while the bombs were falling to play and sing to audiences of people who had just lost homes and belongings or who might lose them at any moment. I saw CEMA artists come into rest centres full of men and women stunned into apathy by their experiences (they had all been bombed out scarcely 12 hours previously), and, by the sheer grace and sympathy of their art, warm them first to clapping, then to singing and – within an hour and a half – to joyous cheers and radiant laughter. If ever a body of men and women helped to revive and sustain the morale of English people, during a time when this was most needed, those CEMA artists did.[4]

The Bermondsey shelter council attracted the attention of the Education Officer and Mrs Helen Bentwich (later to be Chairman of the Education Committee) and in December 1940, at a meeting with Miss Plastow, it was Savage himself who said, 'Why not start classes in the shelters?' From that meeting Miss Plastow went back and, with the help of the shelter council, began classes in the shelters. As happened so easily in London, no sooner had one institute started shelter classes than others followed suit. Indeed, it is more than likely that the same idea occurred to a number of principals at the same time, particularly in those areas where bombing had been most intense and where whole communities virtually lived in shelters. In Bermondsey there were dressmaking classes and, at first, when sewing-machines were in short supply, they were taken from centre to centre by Bermondsey Borough Council transport or by members of the staff pushing them from place to place on trolleys. More machines were made available after Savage, on one of his visits to the institute in the blackout, saw a member of the staff struggling with sewing-machines on a trolley. There was ballroom dancing in Atkinson's factory, current events, in which everybody joined, in the tinplate factory. Under the Stainer Street arch of London Bridge there was painting and current events. This arch later had a direct hit and there were many casualties. Arch 61, the big arch under London Bridge Station, where at one time they used to have a circus and circus horses, was a popular shelter which housed a very large number of people and was the scene of many activities, including large-scale concerts. Indeed, for many this particular shelter and others became home from home; old people were often reluctant to leave it because of the comfort and security it gave them.

Principals and their willing teams of helpers spent the day taking round bales of material – some of which, as has already been told, acquired with great foresight at the beginning of the war – in order to keep the various classes supplied for their work in the evening. After a time it was necessary for students to give up coupons for the material used and this meant the collection of coupons and the keeping of records. Usually the principals had loyal friends who kept the records and accounted for the material and the coupons. No registers were kept for classes in shelters since it would have been completely impracticable to do so. A family would be sitting together and according to who happened to be there, father or any other member of the family would join in whatever was going on. Current events, painting and art work, art classes, physical exercises, ballroom dancing, needlework and handwork and even boot-repairing classes were held in shelters. One principal recalls that handwork and leather work involved the purchase of skins from a store at the LCC depot, established at Furzedown Training College. Apparently it was a requirement that for every purchase of two skins X-pounds of pieces also had to be bought. These pieces were used to make patchwork coverings for cushions, tea cosies and purses and if, by good fortune, the pieces were large enough, even a pair of gloves. Distribution of hundreds of pieces of leather to students meant that they had to be parcelled up and sold by weight. The memory of this operation still rankles in the mind of one principal who brought the operation to an end when she discovered one sack of pieces grossly over-weighted by the inclusion of an old army boot!

H.C. Dent in *Education in Transition* refers to the opening of LCC institutes in October 1939 as one of the minor epics of the war. The work of the institutes from August 1940 to the end of night bombing was more than this. It was a major epic. Unfortunately, records are scanty and what little is recorded is so matter-of-fact and the recall of those who lived through those days, so modest and self-effacing that the narrative is robbed of any account of the undoubted heroism of those who kept the institutes going during the war years. When the blitz on London began, before there was any suggestion of classes being opened, most principals were at their posts working alongside the people in their institute areas. Many were working in rest centres when they returned from evacuation duties. They had no full-time staff and a great many of their former part-time staff were doing war work or had moved out of London. Yet every principal seemed to find a small band of part-time staff who gave him or her loyal support and, night after night with public transport disrupted and wearing tin hats, made their way through raids and falling shrapnel to shelters and other places to run an amazing variety of communal and group activities.

Throughout the war years the City Literary Institute handsomely repaid the hospitality it had enjoyed whilst its new building was being built. The National Fire Service established a depot in the basement and so superior was the accommodation that it expanded its depot to include the canteen and several other rooms. The City of London College, an early fire-bomb casualty, occupied the third floor for three years; the LCC Primary Education Department, from damaged County Hall, occupied the first floor; and later, the Poplar School of Engineering and Navigation and RADA were given shelter in the Stukeley Street premises. The Institute also became a centre for Army Bureau of Current Affairs discussion group leaders' training courses. Nevertheless, classes were held throughout the war and the City Lit. played its part in shelters and underground stations.

It was not difficult in the underground railway subways and tunnels to find recesses where groups could gather, and wall space on which lantern slides could be projected. It happened that there were available several projectors of a simple type which could be plugged in to lamp sockets. They were light enough in weight to be carried about easily. I had the use of about half a dozen and these I made available to shelters in my area on a rota system for illustrated lectures on London's history, travel, art and current affairs. Discussion and dramatic groups were also formed and wherever pianos or gramophones were available, recitals of music were arranged. I remember in particular the series given by Miss Eiluned Davies on one of the main platforms of Holborn Station.

. . . and so, evening after evening during the period of shelter life, I led a troglodyte existence groping along in the blackout from place to place in the subterrene, beneath great office blocks of warehouses or railway arches, along tunnels and subways, establishing contact with this strange new society, and being everywhere received with something approaching enthusiasm.[5]

For safety reasons national art collections had been removed from London. The City Literary Institute made a significant contribution to filling the resulting cultural gaps. In 1939, in co-operation with the British Institute of Adult Education, it staged an exhibition to which no less than 7000 visitors came to view the work of over sixty foremost British artists. At an exhibition in 1940 leading artists talked, as they worked, about their respective arts and in 1942, with the help of CEMA, nearly 3000 visitors came to see the work of three contemporary artists: Henry Moore, John Piper and Graham Sutherland.

Enrolment for classes in the reduced accommodation available in the new building at Stukeley Street reached 2671 in 1941–2, 3947 in 1942–3 and 4201 in 1943–4 – a testimony in itself to the resilience both of Londoners and the City Lit.

There is a tendency to think that, since we were at war and men were being conscripted into the Armed Forces, there were very few men about. In fact, apart from the considerable number who were in the Civil Defence Services (ARP and AFS), there were substantial numbers in reserved occupations as well as those who were waiting to be called up and those who were above conscription-age limits.

At the height of the blitz, at the end of 1940 and beginning of 1941, men's institutes, like their women's counterparts, ran classes on Saturdays and Sundays and, where practicable, on other days in daylight hours. During the remainder of the war years the institutes were open every evening as usual. In those places where there were no shelters, staff and students were sometimes unable to leave the building until the early morning when the all-clear had sounded. Classes at the Walworth Men's Institute in Avenue Road School were interrupted for five weeks when a bomb fell on the building. Fortunately it did not explode and was removed by a Bomb Disposal Unit. During that time classes were organized in shelters, church crypts and in office and factory basements. Tin-hatted principals visited their scattered flock in its odd assortment of meeting places, often during an air-raid alert. As one principal put it, 'You had the choice of walking in the centre of the road exposed to shrapnel or close to the wall exposed to falling masonry.'

For some of the older principals wartime conditions were too much. One log-book of an institute in north-east London records the return of Miss Eyden, the principal, after evacuation duties and the opening of the institute in October 1939 for enrolment and advice. But as there were no air-raid shelters within reasonable distance, no classes were allowed. Later, in December 1939 some afternoon and early-evening classes were opened and enrolment, 'considering the circumstances, is quite satisfactory although the students find the earlier hours distinctly difficult'. In February 1940 classes in English for foreigners were recorded as particularly successful, over eighty foreign refugees (mainly Jewish) having enrolled: 'They are people of exceptional intelligence and are making rapid progress. In addition the women (these are mixed classes) are being slowly persuaded into other classes – dressmaking, millinery, etc. They all, men and women, appreciate tremendously the social activities of the institute.' The institute took part in the food economy campaign in June, students being canvassed for help and to attend the demonstrations at three centres. Then came the bombardment of London and, when it abated, classes reopened in November on Sunday mornings and Tuesday and Thursday afternoons. Church Street School became a rest centre for bombed-out people and the log-book records: 'Although it is good for the head to be on the premises (many of the bombed out folk being students or students' parents) the question of evening institute accommodation is becoming very difficult.' Afternoon classes, depending on the general public, were not a success according to the principal and the knitting and arts and crafts were closed. There were shelter classes running at the Albion Parade, Defoe Road and at Sumner House Road. With the light evenings at the end of April there was a satisfactory response to evening classes from 6.30 p.m. to 8.30 p.m. In the meantime, however, the successful classes for English for foreigners had been moved to the supervision of 'another type of institute', presumably a vocational institute — and the principal records her discouragement at this and doubtless other frustrations and wartime conditions on 30 August 1941 by the one-word entry 'Resigned'. Here the continuous record of the log-book ends.

Happily Miss Malcolm-Forth who succeeded Miss Eyden in November 1941 added, a few years later, a summary of events since the date of the last entry. From it we learn that in the autumn of 1941 there were a negligible number of students at that institute meeting at weekends, most of whom were middle-aged or elderly. In the beginning of session 1942—3 Miss Malcolm-Forth founded the Stoke Newington unit of the Girls' Training Corps. The company, 100 or more strong, paraded every Sunday at the institute, which was its headquarters, and met there for instructional classes during the week. The principal as its command-ing officer took part in all the borough's wartime activities and paraded with her brother officers of the pre-service units on all special occasions. In this way the institute became linked with current activities and was 'generally brought into the public eye'.

After Easter 1941, with the introduction of summer time, classes could con-tinue until 9 p.m. Institutes reopened on 21 April 1941 with much enlarged pro-grammes of afternoon and evening classes. Evening classes could now continue until 8.30 p.m. by which time the building had to be cleared to comply with the LCC blackout rules. In May the alteration of clocks to one hour in advance of summer time meant that work could be extended and classes could continue until 9.30 p.m. Additional classes in a variety of subjects were now being offered for members of the Armed Forces and by the end of the session, 15 August 1941, there had been a major increase in the number of classes formed and in the number of students enrolled. Goodrich Road Institute in Dulwich which, at Easter 1941, had an enrolment of 159, closed the session with an enrolment of 455 and a pro-gramme of forty classes. Mrs Evelyn Lowe, an LCC member and former Chairman of the Education Committee, presided at what must have been a celebration open night at which the band of the Royal Army Service Corps from the local Highwood Barracks played for dancing by 'kind permission of the Officer Commanding'.

The comment above by Miss Malcolm-Forth that, in taking over the High Street Newington and Dalston Women's Institutes, she found the students to be mainly middle-aged or elderly, probably applied to many institutes at the time. Her action in forming a girls' training corps in order to bring a younger element into the institute's activities was illustrative of a general development in the latter part of 1941 and throughout 1942.

In January 1941 the Secretary of State for Air, Sir Archibald Sinclair, announced a new and nationwide air training corps scheme to provide facilities for general education and service training for boys between sixteen and eighteen. The object was to prepare entrants of the right standard for air-crew and technical trades in the Royal Air Force. The qualification for entry was a desire to serve in the RAF or Fleet Air Arm. The corps was to be modelled on the RAF and cadets would wear RAF uniform which would be issued to them free. There was an immediate and mighty response to this appeal and within six months 200,000 had enrolled. The Army decided to expand the Army Cadet Force in December 1941 for boys between fourteen and eighteen and, by the end of 1942, 170,000 had enrolled. When the Admiralty decided, early in 1942, to expand the Sea Cadet Corps from 120 units to 400 units, with 50,000 cadets, the response was equally enthusiastic. No similar organizations were proposed by the service departments for girls but, by the middle of 1941, the Women's Junior Air Corps with a number of units throughout the country was in existence as a voluntary body unaided by public funds. Meantime there had sprung up, without any service initiative, a variety of voluntary units under the general name of the Girls Training Corps. To avoid the development of a number of voluntary 'pre-service units' for girls the Board of Education, after consultation with the various voluntary organizations announced the formation of a National Association of Girls Training Corps. The corps was to prepare girls for entry to HM Forces, civil defence and other forms of national service. The minimum age of entry was fourteen and conditions of entry were physical fitness and the written consent of parent or guardian. Units of the corps could be formed by LEAs, schools, voluntary societies or other bodies and the uniform (not provided) consisted of navy blue beret, white blouse, blue tie, navy blue skirt and the GTC badge. The course of training included, as compulsory subjects, first-aid, hygiene, despatch carrying, a handywoman course, squad drill and physical training. By September 1942 the corps had enrolled 100,000 members and, by the spring of 1943, 130,000. In June 1942 the National Association of Girls Training Corps and the Women's Junior Air Corps were amalgamated into one single movement, later called the National Association of Training Corps for Girls.

From 1938 onwards women's and men's institutes had provided first-aid courses for civil defence personnel, for borough council staff and other local organizations. Increasingly they were called in by the borough to train personnel in first-aid and physical exercises and to cater for leisure periods of civil defence and other staff. Close liaison was established generally between boroughs and institutes. Men's institutes were asked to undertake the training of Army and Air Force units, stationed in their locality, in car maintenance and other subjects.

Similarly, women's institutes would provide first-aid and recreational subjects for any service unit stationed near any of their branches. It followed naturally that the men's institutes took under their wing the educational training of pre-service units such as the Air Training Corps and the Army Cadet Force and women's institutes provided training courses for the Girls Training Corps. A number of women principals became commandants of Girls Training Corps and men principals Commanding Officers of Air Training Corps squadrons.

Session 1941–2 opened on 1 September 1941 after only two weeks' closure. According to a note in Goodrich Road Women's Institute log-book evening classes could only continue for a further two weeks as the civil defence authorities were not prepared to allow people to assemble in the blackout. It seems likely that this was a local order since there is no indication in other log-books or records of any general decision to this effect. Certainly classes in shelters, which had been prohibited with the advent of summer time, were now generally resumed. Goodrich Road needlework classes were transferred to Cornflower Terrace ARP shelter with the permission of the Borough Chief Warden. These classes were popular because they catered for renovations and adaptations, thereby saving clothing coupons being spent on new garments. It may have been this fact and the desire to reduce the demand on the ARP shelter accommodation that resulted in permission being given for classes to be reopened in the evening where blackout was available. The decision was evidently welcomed by the Principal of Goodrich Road who obtained fifty yards of material from the District Officer and carried out the necessary blackout work herself. Afternoon classes were not well attended because most of the women were working throughout the day. With the resumption of evening classes people needed to get accustomed to coming away from home in the blackout and progress was therefore initially slow. But classes gathered momentum and enrolment and attendance improved quite dramatically. By the end of the 1941–2 session Goodrich Road Institute, for example, had an enrolment of 776 at the main branch, 557 at the Morden Terrace Branch, 188 at the Creek Road Branch and seventy-nine at the Ivydale Road Branch, a total of 1600 which included 261 girls from the Women's Junior Air Corps with which Miss Blackman was closely associated. It was a very different picture from the 159 enrolment of 9 April 1941.

Session 1942–3 began on 31 August 1942 after a month's break. During the autumn of 1942 and spring of 1943 there appear to have been a number of severe air raids. Raids on 17, 18 and 20 January appeared to have hit south-east London badly and 173 people were homeless in the vicinity of Goodrich Road; on 20 January Catford Central School was hit by a bomb. Despite the interruption caused by air raids Goodrich Road Institute, from which the Morden Terrace and Creek Road Branches had now been separated to form a separate institute, recorded ninety-one classes open on 30 February 1943 with an enrolment of 954.

It was clear that Londoners had once again adjusted to the conditions of the black-out and, undeterred by the possibility of raids, were making good use of institute facilities.

It was clear, too, that institutes were making a valuable contribution to the social life of London. From April 1941 onwards keep fit and dancing displays, musical and dramatic art performances, exhibitions, open evenings and other social events abounded. In March 1941 a gym display and sale of work for an adopted prisoner-of-war attracted an audience of 100 at a time of frequent air raids; in the same month 200 attended an open meeting at which students of dressmaking and craftwork displayed their goods. In 1942 and 1943 there were frequent regional and national gatherings in which students of institutes took part.

Men's institutes, in particular, in 1942 and 1943 staged most remarkable competitions and shows. The Brixton and District Rabbit Club which was formed by students of the rabbit-keeping class of the Walworth Men's Institute had a membership of 250 in February 1942. In the same year it mounted a rabbit show of Belgium hares and Chinchilla rabbits at which there were no less than 1400 entries drawn from all over the country, including Scotland, and at which some of the animals were priced as high as £100. Poultry-keeping classes, which had always had the utilitarian purpose of helping London's back-yard keepers of poultry, now had a direct war effort of food-campaign appeal. The need for a maximum production of eggs led to a study of those strains of hens which could be kept in greater numbers in the small accommodation available and yet produce as good a yield of eggs. A show organized by men's institute clubs was entirely devoted to the rearing of bantam hens as the war-time 'utility' chicken.

A fur-and-feather show at the Walworth Men's Institute in February 1942 comprised some 700 exhibits of poultry, rabbits, pigeons and caged birds. Entries had come from Scotland as well as from the north and west Country. There were 117 classes of caged birds, five classes of pigeons, twenty-five classes of rabbits, five classes of poultry and three classes of eggs. The *South London Observer* reported, 'Crowds of people were constantly to be seen along all the passageways, the whole of the two days, and a splendid crowd was present for the official opening on Saturday.' The show was opened by a Russian lady, Mrs F. Moxom and was held 'primarily to raise money to assist Mrs Churchill's Aid to Russia Fund'. The highlight of the show were ten pigeons which had seen service in the Battle of Britain and which, despite severe wounds, had carried on through bursts of shell fire and machine gunning to deliver their message. A second show of caged birds in 1942, opened by David Seth-Smith, 'radio's famous zoo man of children's hour', attracted exhibits of over 400 birds including 350 budgerigars – the largest number in any one show since the last national show at Crystal Palace before the war. A similar exhibition in December 1943, run under the patronage of the Budgerigar Society, the Yorkshire Budgerigar Society, the Midland Society and the London and Southern Counties Society, attracted no less than 1000 entries from Scotland, Lancashire and the north of England as well as London and the south.

Dig-for-Victory exhibitions organized by students of allotment classes, make-and-mend demonstrations by students of dressmaking and needlework classes and household repairs, homecraft classes and exhibitions of the work of London's backyard farmers all illustrated the part played by men and women's institutes in the life of wartime London. Not only were they of immense practical help in the constraints imposed by rationing, they built communities and comradeship which sustained morale. In the 1942–3 session there were the greatest number of classes and greatest enrolment of students since 1938–9, the total for all institutes, vocational and non-vocational, being 129,642, compared with 201,605 in 1938–9, – a quite remarkable achievement. Of these, 60,000 were estimated to have enrolled at non-vocational institutes. When the new session 1943–4 opened on 30 August 1943 enrolment for classes was brisk and there was every indication of an increased demand. Moreover, after four years of war, attention was being more and more focused on what would happen after the War; there seemed to be a new confidence that the tide had turned in favour of the Allies.

In January 1944, however, London was again the target. This time a new type of bomb was carried in a pilotless aircraft. No bigger than a small trainer aircraft, jet-propelled with the reddish-yellow glow from the jet at its tail, they travelled very fast and came by day and by night. They were known as Vls, 'buzz bombs' or 'doodle bugs'. In the first twenty-four hours, 144 buzz bombs had crossed the channel and seventy-three exploded in London. They could be seen and heard quite clearly. When the motor stopped and the light went out their rapid descent and explosion were imminent. Those chilling seconds between the engine stopping and the explosion stretched the nerves of many a Londoner to breaking point. Whilst it was essential to take shelter when the imminent warning was given, work could be quickly resumed. Many people found the buzz bombs more trying than the early bombs and large numbers of people left London to escape them. Such was the resilience, however, that many carried on regardless of this new hazard, confident that sooner or later the RAF would bomb the launching sites out of existence. As one principal records,

The classes endured successfully throughout the successive bombings, the students becoming comparatively indifferent to explosions. The principal has seen the GCT on parades standing to attention, heard a sudden explosion quite near and observed that no one batted an eye lid. The other students preferred to remain in their classrooms at work even when flying bombs approached and passed like express trains. The principal sitting in her office in day time would hear an explosion, rush up to the roof to see where in her area it had fallen and at night had the shock of a sudden deafening crash, which blew in the curtains and burst open all the doors. She often wondered if a rocket would fall beside her as she waited outside the institute for the last 73 bus or while she was running about in the blackout from outside class to outside class. But none did.

Session 1944 – 5 was heralded by the re-publication of *Floodlight* which had been suspended on the outbreak of war. In his foreword the Education Officer, Mr E.G. Savage, said:

As, at the time of going to press it is not possible to foresee the European situation in September next (when the institutes will reopen for the new session) the compilation of this edition has presented some difficulty. Most of the classes and courses mentioned in the following pages have continued without interruption throughout the War period, and, unless unforeseen circumstances should arise in the meantime, it may be assumed that they will continue to function next session . . .

The Council can regard with some pride the War time record of London's evening institutes. They have continued to work almost without interruption. When during the height of the 'blitz' it became impossible for students to attend the institutes during blackout hours, day time classes were arranged on Saturdays and Sundays. In addition, thousands of special classes were organised in public air raid shelters. Many of the shelterers had, previously, only a vague idea of evening classes or what they meant. They developed new interests. They listened intently to lectures on current events, international affairs, music and art. Grandmothers, mothers and children were taught dressmaking and needlework – in many cases their first lessons in 'Make-do and Mend.' Portable cinemas projected topical films. The hours until bed-time were spent in an atmosphere of industry and enthusiasm. Those men, women and children were able to forget, for a while, the grim happenings so near at hand.

With the typical understatement and gentle cynicism of the public official, he went on:

It is difficult to estimate the value and importance of these activities, but it is permissible modestly to believe that they played a certain part in the maintenance of public morale and the will to endure. Whether, when the official War diary is compiled, the historian will record the part played by those men and women teachers, mostly past middle-age, who braved the raids night after night to conduct shelter classes is, in the light of experience doubtful, but I shall always be full of grateful appreciation for what I know to have been strenuous, difficult and often hazardous work.

It would be unwise to look too far ahead, we do not know what the future may hold for London and its citizens. Perhaps peace is round the corner, or it may be that there are many more trials to endure before the end.

When that foreword was written London was adjusting itself to the new horror of 'flying bombs' and, for the first time during the war, the institute session ended early on 15 July 1944. The re-publication of *Floodlight*, however, was itself an indication of the growing feeling that the end of the War was in sight. This growing confidence was reflected in the curriculum and classes devoted to post-war reconstruction and other forward-looking subjects, particularly in literary institutes. The publication of *Floodlight* placed on record for the first time the true extent and scope of evening institute provision during the war. Indeed it appears to be the only public statement which gives a record of the number of institutes functioning in 1943–4 and the subjects and activities they covered.

Recreational institutes, of which three had been opened experimentally for young people between the ages of fourteen and eighteen in 1941 and a further five in 1942–3, now numbered fourteen. It is also apparent that a number of them, Huntingfield, Woolwich and Senior Street to mention only three, were not exclusively concerned with young people. The number of junior men's institutes which, in 1939, was fourteen had now dropped to nine, largely as a result of the opening of recreational institutes. All twelve of the men's institutes were open as were the forty-five women's institutes. All nine literary institutes, together with the Bermondsey Settlement, Goldsmith's College Literary Department, Mary Ward Settlement, Morley College, Norwood Technical Institute Literary Department and Toynbee Hall, had kept going throughout the war. The scope of the provision made by literary, men's and women's institutes is illustrated by the fact that, of the 380 subject headings listed in *Floodlight*, 120 were covered by these non-vocational institutes. In addition, women's departments of polytechnics and technical colleges (with the exception of those at Northampton Polytechnic, North Western Polytechnic and Paddington Technical Institute which were temporarily suspended during the war), general institutes and those recreational institutes which catered for adults as well as young people, also provided a range of non-vocational classes. As we have seen some of the women's institutes had an enrolment of 1000 or more and this was equalled by the largest of the men's institutes. The City Literary Institute, despite its central position and difficulties of travel in wartime London, had upwards of 5000 students. Flying bombs had reduced the overall enrolment and attendance in the session 1943–4 to a little below that of 1942–3. The number of institutes offering facilities was the greatest since 1939 and demand promised to outstrip anything so far experienced throughout the war.

E.G. Savage's cautionary words in the foreword to the 1944–5 *Floodlight* were to prove prophetic. Peace *was* just around the corner as were more trials in the shape of Hitler's most devastating weapon, the V2 rocket bomb. V2s travelled at such speed that their interception by aircraft or defence batteries was impossible.

They were soundless and no warning of their approach could be given. On impact the devastation they caused was greater than that of the landmines in the blitz of 1940. Only the confidence that 'it would not be long now' sustained the war-weary. On 8 and 9 May the institutes, in common with all other educational establishments, celebrated victory in Europe (VE) Day and on 30 June 1945 the 1944–5 session came to an end. Unknown to staff and students at the time, it was to be the last of the six wartime sessions. In June the war with Japan still had to be won. The atom bombs were dropped on Nagasaki and Hiroshima and Japan surrendered on 14 August 1945 (VJ) Day. The Second World War had ended.

From their earliest days men's and women's institutes had been discovering and developing, usually through their everyday interests, the hidden talents of the ordinary men and women of London. The constraints of wartime rationing and the general need to make do and mend were aspects which the principals of these institutes were well geared to exploit. Through six long testing years the literary, women's and men's institutes of London had provided a magnificent service which had sustained many thousands of Londoners. Principals had displayed their innate gifts of initiative, innovation and intuitive understanding in responding to the needs of ordinary men and women in the most difficult and hazardous conditions. More than this, they had inspired hands of part-time teachers, for the most part well past middle age, to face physical dangers with a quiet heroism to keep that service going. Scanty records and the self-effacing recall of those with whom one has talked, make it difficult to do justice to them. There is no doubt, however, that the devotion of the men and women of these institutes was a major factor in maintaining morale and sustaining Londoners in some of their most dark and desolate days.

9. The Post-War Period: 1946 – 57

London now faced the awesome task of reconstructing its education system for the returning evacuees. Only fifty of London's 1200 schools had escaped damage; about 290 had been demolished or seriously damaged and another 310 had been extensively but less seriously damaged. A new Education Act was now on the statute book, reaffirming the raising of the school-leaving age to fifteen (enacted in the 1936 Act) and giving effect to a 'secondary education for each child according to his or her age, ability and aptitude'. In addition to a scheme of secondary education the LCC, in common with other local education authorities, was required to submit a Scheme of Further Education under the Act. Under Section 41 of the Act it was the duty of every LEA to provide adequate facilities for further education, that is to say:

1. full-time and part-time education for persons over compulsory school age; and

2. leisure-time occupation in such organized cultural training and recreative activities as are suited to their requirements, for any persons over compulsory school age who are able and willing to profit by the facilities provided for that purposes. The proposals for such provision were required to be secured in accordance with schemes of further education approved by the Minister.

The Green Paper and general discussion clearly attached considerable importance to the provision of non-vocational adult education. Developments during the war, typified by the Army Bureau of Current Affairs, the extent to which civil defence personnel had taken part in adult education and the activities of the Committee for the Encouragement of Music and the Arts, had clearly extended the appreciation of the importance of this sector. It was envisaged that local authorities, in association with voluntary bodies such as the Workers Educational Association and the universities would play a greater part than hitherto in the provision of facilities for non-vocational classes for adults. The role of non-vocational adult education in maintaining morale throughout the war, and the growing recognition that it stimulated adults to greater thought and consideration of day-to-day social problems, were aspects which gave increased importance to adult education in this reconstruction period.

Session 1945–6, the first peace-time session since 1938–9, was a time when men and women were demobilized from the Armed Forces, the Auxiliary Fire Service and other civil defence services. Children and families evacuated from wartime London flooded back, many to quite different districts from those in which they had been born or lived for generations. Bombing had destroyed not only the houses they left and laid waste areas around them, it had also destroyed whole communities and their way of life for all time. The large LCC estates on the periphery of London, such as Downham and Bellingham in the south-east and St Helier, Morden in the south-west, built between the wars, rehoused whole sections of London's pre-war population from Bermondsey and the East End. Many of the East Enders never returned to their old haunts.

From autumn 1944 many schools, previously required by civil defence or the Armed Forces were made available for educational purposes. Many needed to be reinstated and repaired before they could be used as schools again.

From 1945 every child over the age of eleven was entitled to receive a secondary education free of charge. The school-leaving age was to be raised to fifteen as soon as possible but, because of war damage and the consequent pressure on accommodation, the Minister of Education was permitted to make an order keeping the school-leaving age to fourteen for not more than two years. After consulting LEAs the Government decided not to postpone raising the age after 1 April 1947. The Education Act 1944 required every LEA to submit a secondary-school development plan. The London school plan was started in 1944 but the onset of flying bombs and rockets made it necessary to divert staff to more urgent tasks. The plan, therefore, could not be submitted by the due date, 31 March 1946, and the LCC was granted a one year's extension. The plan was eventually approved by the Council on 25 March 1947 and, with comparatively minor amendments, accepted by the Minister. Two more years were to elapse before the London Scheme of Further Education was submitted to the Minister in 1949.

Floodlight for 1945–6 was again a best-seller and all 30,000 copies were sold. In the year before, despite flying bombs and V2 rockets, literary, women's, men's and recreational institutes had enrolled, just under 41,000 students by 11 November 1944. In the new 1945–6 session some 60,000 students had enrolled by 10 November 1945, nearly a 50 per cent increase. By the end of the session the total enrolment was just under 99,000. The new recreational institutes numbered twenty and had replaced all but eight of the men's junior institutes.

More than 18,000 of the 47,000 students in women's institutes and 4000 of the 13,000 in men's institutes were under eighteen; in the new recreational institutes well over 5000 of the 13,000 students were over eighteen whereas, in the men's junior institutes, only 487 out of the 6800 students were over eighteen. In 1945–6 there were forty-four women's institutes, fourteen men's institutes, eight junior men's institutes, twenty recreational institutes and nine literary institutes, plus the literary departments at the Bermondsey Settlement, Goldsmiths College, Mary Ward Settlement, Norwood Technical Institute, Morley College and Toynbee Hall.

Restrictions on the admission of men and women to each others institutes had been relaxed during the war and, although there are no precise statistics available, there were now substantial numbers of men in women's institutes and women in men's institutes. A report of the Higher Education sub-committee to the Education Committee on 26 June 1945 noted this and decided that there should be a return to single-sex classes, although mixed classes should be permitted for approved subjects. Despite the difficult post-war accommodation conditions non-vocational institutes were recovering lost ground and some of them had already had a record number of students. The City Literary Institute Advisory Committee, in its annual report for 1945–6, noted that the Institute had not only recovered lost ground but, with an aggregate enrolment of 6831, had made an advance of 61 per cent on the 1944–5 enrolment.

From a report by the Higher Education sub-committee to the Education Committee of 29 May 1946 it is evident that, in preparation for the 1946–7 session, there had been a general survey of evening institutes in order to regularize their organization and concentrate non-vocational work still further in non-vocational institutes. Only one of the three literary institutes in north-east London in 1939 (Dalston, Highbury and Holloway) was operating in 1946 and that was supervised by a principal of a commercial institute. It was decided to open Holloway and Dalston under a principal to be appointed and to continue the arrangement made in 1945 for the Putney and Hammersmith Literary Institutes to be supervised by principals of neighbouring literary institutes.

Men's institutes which had perhaps been more adversely affected by war conditions than other institutes were now beginning to recover. Woolwich Men's Institute had been closed during the war and Woolwich Recreational Institute had been given permission to offer men's classes. It was now thought that a separate men's institute should be opened in Woolwich and that the principal who had been seconded to be warden of the Honor Oak Community Centre should be given charge of it. Two more men's junior institutes were reorganized as recreational institutes, another was replaced by a recreational institute and two others merged with men's institutes. The future of the remaining junior men's institutes was to be reviewed after the raising of the school-leaving age on 1 April 1947.

There was evidently consultation about the current organization of women's institutes and it is interesting to note that the Association of Women's Heads suggested that the area of institutes should be co-terminus with metropolitan boroughs. Apparently this suggestion was examined but found 'to be not always practical'. Women's departments at junior commercial and junior technical institutes (known as dual institutes) were transferred to women's institutes and the areas of women's institutes were redrawn to effect a better distribution of work, although no increase in the number of heads was proposed. Morden Terrace Institute, which covered most of the Borough of Lewisham, had been supervised since the retirement of its head in 1944 by the head of Fossdene Road Institute. Since Fossdene covered the whole of Greenwich this arrangement could not continue and a new head for Morden Terrace was proposed. Morden Terrace School had been destroyed and the institute met in Lewisham Bridge School; the institute was therefore renamed the Lewisham Women's Institute and, with the transfer of the supervision of women's classes from Plassy Road Junior Commercial and Junior Technical Institute, a full-time head was appointed.

The head of Tower Bridge Women's Institute (Miss Plastow) also supervised Tower Bridge Recreational Institute. The latter proved to be a very successful institute so the Tower Bridge Women's Institute was redistributed between Waterloo and Keatons Road and the recreational institute took over recreational classes and the work in youth clubs in Southwark, Bermondsey and Rotherhithe which formerly had been attached to one or other of the women's institutes. Miss Plastow was reappointed as head of the Tower Bridge Recreational Institute.

Although, in general, the Education Committee was anxious to move in the direction of providing for young people under eighteen in recreational institutes and for adults in men's and women's institutes they clearly wished to do this gradually and not inflexibly. They also had an eye to those principals who were successful with young people and they were prepared to adjust organization and general policy to enable such principals to continue to work with young people. Miss Plastow's appointment as the principal of Tower Bridge Recreational Institute was an example of this, as was the reversion of Cephas Street Recreational Institute to the Raleigh Women's Institute, of which the head was Miss Ramsay. The latter was also given authority to continue to provide recreational classes for young people at Senrab Street and Cayley Street.

The question of registration of students in classes had evidently been the subject of some discussion and no doubt the freedom from the necessity to register students in shelter classes during the war led principals to seek some easing of the registration requirements. They seem to have met with some success. As recreational institutes they were relieved of the requirement to call the register ten minutes after the opening of the second hour. The Committee therefore decided to implement the decision of 10 May 1938 by which all men's, men's junior, women's and free mixed institutes be deemed recreational institutes under Section 86 of the Education Act 1921.

The age limits of the various institutes had been blurred by wartime conditions. For the time being the Education Committee did not wish to lay down precise age limits but called for a further report on this in due course. By a decision of the Committee on 29 May 1946 'heads' of men's and women's institutes, as well as recreational institutes, were to become 'principals'. Yet another milestone on the road to comparability with vocational institutes. Two whole-time deputies free of teaching duties were appointed to Fairclough Street and Sayer Street Women's

Institutes in place of the previously sessional appointments. On 6 March 1946 the Committee approved the following scale of salaries of principals determined from, and including, 1 April 1945. This scale covered all types of further education establishments from Regent Street Polytechnic to Women's Institutes:

1a.	Regent Street Polytechnic	£1450 – 50 – £1750
b.	Other polytechnics	£1300 – 50 – £1600
2	Other polytechnics and senior technical colleges	£1150 – 50 – £1350
3	Other senior technical colleges	£1050 – 50 – £1250
4	City Literary Institute	£950 – 50 – £1100
5	Norwood Technical Institute	£850 – 50 – £1000
6	Other technical and senior commercial institutes (including four day-continuation-school men principals)	£775 – 25 – £925
7	Commercial institutes and four literary-institute men heads	£700 – 25 – £850
8	Morley College: thirty-nine evening institutes with men heads	£650 – 25 – £800
9	Three technical schools for women, one women's institute and Eltham Literary Institute	£600 – 20 – £720
10	Thirty evening institutes with women heads and day-continuation-schools with women heads	£550 – 20 – £670

Pride of place in the salary scale for non-vocational institutes went to the City Literary Institute. Four literary institutes with men heads qualified for group 7; Morley College and all the institutes with men heads qualified for group 8; one women's institute only and three principals of technical schools for women qualified for group 9. Group 10 the lowest scale of all, covered thirty evening institutes with women heads. A woman principal, because she was a woman, had a starting salary of £100 less than her male counterpart, £5 less on each increment and £130 less at the maximum. Equal pay for equal work was still some years ahead.

In June 1947 the Education Committee re-defined the age limits of the various institutes. In general, students of evening institutes must have left school or, if over fourteen and still at school, have permission from their day-school head to attend. Admission to literary institutes was no longer to be restricted to students over seventeen or to those under seventeen who has passed a recognized first-school examination. In future they were to be open to students who had reached sixteen years and were capable of profiting by the tuition, subject to the head of the day school's consent if they were still at school. Students of men's institutes must be over eighteen, although, by agreement with the principals concerned, they could be admitted under that age. For men's junior institutes students had to be under eighteen but, again by arrangement with the principals concerned, students over that age could be admitted and students over the age of eighteen who did not wish to transfer to the senior institute might continue at junior institute until they were twenty-one. Recreational institutes were for students under eighteen but they could continue until they were twenty-one. Where the Education Officer was satisfied that suitable provision could not otherwise be made, classes for adults might also be organized in recreational institutes in isolated districts.

There were a number of developments during the war which were to have a profound effect on both the immediate and long-term future of the non-vocational institutes. The first of these was the coming into being of the youth service as a separate service. Three recreational institutes, one for boys, one for girls and one mixed were opened in 1940 and followed two years later by another five. All these institutes were put under the general supervision of heads of men's or women's institutes. The peculiar circumstances of wartime London, with its large numbers of young people at a loose end awaiting 'call-up', ensured the success of these institutes. They were virtually junior counterparts of men's and women's institutes, with the important distinction that young people need not register but could join any group at the institute they wished. Principals like Miss Plastow of the Tower Bridge Women's Institute operated the recreational institute part of the institute in a separate building; young people were encouraged to join, and did join, classes with adults in other branches. In 1941 a flood of pre-service training units operated from the newly formed recreational institutes, although they were based mainly at men's or women's institutes. Many principals saw the separation of young people and adults as a retrograde step which robbed them of the opportunity of serving all sections of the adult community. The appeal of pre-service units to young men and women of sixteen was that they were being treated as adults. Those principals who had successfully provided for young people had also treated them as adults but recognized that there must be recreational facilities and a social life compatible with their youth. Recreational institutes set out to service the large number of voluntary youth clubs, that already existed in London, by providing specialist accommodation. This led to accusations of 'poaching' from youth clubs. On the other hand, recreational institutes operated in day schools which created difficulties both with the heads of day schools and in building up a youth-club atmosphere.

A second consequence of the war was the breaking down of the rigid rules on the segregation of sexes. This increased mixing of the sexes in men's and women's institutes enlarged the scope of dramatic art and music, particularly choral and operatic. There was a boom in ballroom dancing classes even though there was a general requirement, not strictly enforced, that ballroom dancing classes were open only to *bona fide* students of other classes. In 1950–51 Stanhope Institute, for example, had seventeen ballroom dancing classes, including old-time dancing, Latin American and ballroom dancing in various stages, and one ballroom dancing class for the blind. The LCC viewed with some alarm the rapid growth in the number of dancing classes in evening institutes and reiterated the requirement that students of such classes must be *bona fide* students of other classes. Since there seemed to be some difficulty in ensuring uniformity of practice, it was emphasized that continued active membership of a class in another subject was a definite requirement for admission to a class in ballroom dancing; attendance in a dancing class was restricted to two hours.

On 23 February 1938 the Education Committee had decided that the opening and continuance of evening classes generally should be regulated on the principle of the attainment by the end of each session of fifteen student hours to one teacher. In March 1948 it was decided that, irrespective of the ratio of student hours to teaching hours for any particular institute, an enrolment of not fewer than twenty should be required for the opening of a class in ballroom dancing and not fewer than eighteen for other types of dancing. An accompanist could be employed only if attendance during any two consecutive weeks did not fall below fourteen students for physical exercise classes or eighteen for classes in dancing other than ballet and advanced national dancing. Moreover, the practice of employing a pianist for informal recreation periods (which had been allowed during the war) was only to continue if the Education Officer was satisfied that no other suitable means was available for dance music.

Before the war men's and women's institutes had not been permitted to offer subjects which were deemed to be 'literary' and such subjects as the appreciation of music and the teaching of foreign languages had been denied them. During the war there were so few literary institutes that both men's and women's institutes had begun to offer subjects, hitherto only available in literary institutes. In 1945 authority had been given for them to offer modern languages and this authority was renewed in October 1948.

The Education Act of 1944, for the first time, brought all stages of education under one statutory system. Section 7 of the Act stated: 'The statutory system of public education shall be organised in three progressive stages to be known as primary, secondary and further education: and it shall be the duty of the local education authority for every area, so far as their powers extend, to contribute towards the spiritual, moral, mental and physical development of the community by ensuring that efficient education throughout these stages shall be available to meet the needs of the population of their area.'

In June 1947 the LCC, under Section 11 of the Act, issued its development plan for primary and secondary schools; in June 1949, under Section 42 of the Act, it produced its *Scheme of Further Education*. Mr I.J. (later Sir Isaac) Hayward, Leader of the Council, in his foreword to the *Scheme of Further Education*, reflected the keynote of the debate which had preceded the Education Act of 1944: 'In these days of increasing population, of scientific and industrial development and of international complexities, there is no greater need for our nation than a highly educated people, and in this scheme generous provision is made for every form of educational advancement. . .' Mrs Helen Bentwich, Chairman of the Education Committee, in the preface to the scheme said: 'The aim in this scheme of further education is to develop in the future, along the lines laid down in the past, a system of education broad enough to meet the needs of Londoners in the whole range of vocational, cultural, social and recreational activities.'[1]

Before the 1944 Act the provision of higher and technical education was a permissive power of LEAs. The LCC could point to more than three quarters of a century of development and generous provision in this field. From the earliest years of the School Board for London great importance had been attached to evening schools; the LCC's Technical Education Board, working closely with the Charity Commissioners, had developed polytechnics and technical institutes. The LCC, as education authority from 1904, had built from these beginnings a network of further education, colleges and institutes – both vocational and non-vocational – directly and by grants, which covered the whole range of higher and further education. Because of this, the review of all the existing institutions and their projected development was a major undertaking. Moreover, it was undertaken at a time of immediate post-war problems, intensified by a shortage of materials. Nevertheless, a review was overdue and the requirement of the Act for a Scheme of Further Education presented an opportunity for officers and elected members to do, what otherwise they would have had every excuse for not doing, namely, take stock of the present situation and formulate a broad framework for future development.

The policy and thinking which led to the *Scheme of Further Education* are set out in the introduction. It argued that the Council's system of further education had been able to adapt itself progressively to meet the changing needs of the community it served but that it had reached a stage when it was now severely handicapped by restricted sites and a general shortage of buildings – much aggravated by the war and the acute difficulties in obtaining equipment and materials. Despite the richness of its provision those colleges which had their own buildings were housed in premises which were now too small and out of date. The rest of further education had to share premises. The major problems were sites, buildings and equipment. Conscious, no doubt, that to the outsider London had a great variety of establishments with different functions which, outside London, would have been gathered together in multi-purpose establishments, the introduction examines the argument for more diversified institutions.

The argument that polytechnics concerned with the exact sciences would be better educational institutions if, say, they offered a range of studies such as was available at the City Literary Institute, reflected the dilemma which seemed to lie 'between intensity of effort and high quality on the one hand against wideness of spread on the other; between distinction and breadth – or to put the matter another way, to determine whether the synthesis to wider education should be made in an institution or in a person'.[2] The argument for not diversifying is confined to the pursuit of excellence in a specialized institution which will give the student the full opportunity to proceed to the limits of his capacity in a student body large enough to provide for progressive stages to advanced levels. A densely populated area like London enabled such a variety of specialized establishments to be supported. The resultant size of a diversified vocational and non-vocational establishment, and its demands on site areas and buildings, were not mentioned.

The *Scheme of Further Education* took account of a number of developments in the late 1930s and during the war years in relation to men's and women's institutes. Also the case was made for a variety of opportunities and facilities in non-vocational institutes in which 'students find the greatest happiness in environments which are suitably differentiated'.[3] Community associations based on neighbourhood units, WEA, university tutorial courses, literary, men's and women's institutes, all contributed to this variety of provision.

One particular paragraph in the introduction throws an interesting light on the interpretation of developments in institutes and their implications for the future.

> The creation of the men's institutes and the development of the women's and recreational institutes revealed an educational consideration which was missed at the time these steps were taken; a consideration which is of the utmost importance in future planning. The men's institutes and the recreational institutes in particular were thought of at the time of their inception as primarily remedial measures to cure social evils. They were sited in densely populated areas to make a contribution towards the solution of a social problem. Experience has shown that the appeal of such institutes is not limited to a particular social stratum. The men's institutes attract numbers of the so called 'black coated' workers just as surely as the literary institutes attract a widely varied range of social groups. In fact, the institutes are rapidly becoming representative cross sections of the whole social community, but having the characteristic that some particular activity is well catered for and that those who practise it, from whatever social stratum they come, can find the satisfaction of adequate standards. It is also heartening to find that in increasing numbers students attend institutes of two kinds concurrently – a literary institute and a men's or women's institute, a technical college and a literary institute and of course, a community association or club and an institute. This consideration demands action of two kinds. In the first place admission conditions should be made adequately flexible and secondly the students should find at each place he attends something worthwhile – something really well done. It is believed that in achieving this end better premises are a first urgency.

Evidently, the educational consideration which was thought to have been missed was the attraction that many of the original activities at men's, women's and recreational institutes (but particularly at men's institutes) had for a wider social grouping. In fact it was not missed since, in areas where manual workers did not predominate and in which additional men's institutes were later established, black-coated workers and men from other social groups attended in substantial numbers. As more men's institutes were established and as the curriculum was widened, the social groupings certainly became more varied. The same was true of women's institutes. There was, however, another important consideration which was perhaps not so readily discernible, that as institutes changed they were not so attractive to some of their original clientele. There is in the paragraph quoted above an unfortunate implication that availability to the wider social strata demanded better accommodation whereas the real case for it stood on the surer ground of increased demand for a whole range of interests. Whether the practice, to which attention was drawn, of students attending more than one kind of establishment was sufficiently extensive to justify the expectation that it would become a general feature, is open to doubt. It was mentioned as another aspect which demanded a general raising of the standard of accommodation for adults and more flexible admission conditions. Other than in the suggestion to provide 'mixed' rather than 'single-sex' establishments more flexible admission was not pursued further. If the compilers of the *Scheme of Further Education* had in mind the possibility of some general ticket of admission to all types of institutions they did not say so. One would have thought that any great development in this direction would have been extremely unlikely since, as the Scheme itself suggested, vocational establishments would have sufficient social and recreational facilities to meet the needs of most of their students. Also the statement that men's institutes and recreational institutes in particular were thought of as primarily remedial measures to cure social evils, itself missed an important educational consideration. Those concerned with the inception of both men's institutes and recreational institutes saw an educational need which could only be tackled if those concerned could be encouraged to take part in activities which would expose them to an educational influence. Recreation was seen as an important means to education and interest in recreational activities as the stimulus to educational advancement.

The fact that some people used more than one educational establishment was taken to be further evidence justifying a variety of further education establishments with differing functions, each of which would have a degree of excellence in some particular area for which the conditions of entry would be flexible. Women, particularly, needed adequate provision of day classes in centres with comfortably furnished libraries, clubrooms and canteens. For all this the main difficulty was lack of accommodation. There had been no building during the war and much accommodation had been destroyed. The Education Act of 1944 had increased the numbers at secondary schools due to the higher leaving age and new schools were needed for the reorganization of secondary education. Moreover, the Minister of Education had indicated that, in view of the importance of technical education, the building programme would be increased from £1 million a year to £15–22 million by 1952. The *Scheme of Further Education* was based on the assumption that London could expect to claim a substantial proportion of this.

Whilst the Scheme of Further Education provided for some new specialist technical colleges, colleges of commerce and extensions to others the major innovation in the scheme was the implementation of the Education Act's requirement for county colleges. They were defined as 'centres approved by the Minister for providing for young persons who are not in full-time attendance at any school or other educational institution such as further education, including physical, practical and vocational training, and will enable them to develop their various aptitudes and capacities and will prepare them for the responsibilities of citizenship.'[4] A young person was one who was over compulsory school age but had not attained the age of eighteen years. Those liable for attendance at county colleges were to attend for one whole day, or two half-days, a week in each of forty-four weeks a year or, alternatively, for one continuous period of eight weeks or two continuous periods of four weeks, a year. This last provision was judged to be more appropriate to rural areas and the scheme foresaw that there would be no great demand for this alternative in London. The Council's plan provided for student attendance on one whole day a week at one of thirty-four colleges, each providing about 500 places with a weekly attendance at each of some 2500 students. Their evening departments would gradually absorb the recreational institutes except for a few which would serve areas from which it would be difficult to travel to the county college. These colleges, working closely with the youth service with its grants to voluntary organizations, would provide the cultural, social and recreational activities for persons under eighteen years.

The aim of the Council's system of non-vocational education was set out as

. . . the provision of the widest possible range of cultural, social and recreational activities to enable men and women of varying aptitudes to achieve the fullest personal development of which they are capable. It is concerned, therefore, not with an average curriculum for an average person, but with the individual needs and interest of the potential student body. Generally those attending the non-vocational institutes are a representative cross section of the whole social community. Experience has shown, however, that there must be some differentiation of function between the institutes if adequate standards of work are to be secured, but that the functions must embrace broad fields of related activities. The resultant differing programmes of work are well expressed in the present titles – literary, men's and women's and recreational institutes – and are well understood by the student body.[5]

The importance still attached to the Local Joint Standing Conference of principals and the Central Joint Standing Conference, established at the time of the 1913 reorganization of evening institutes, is indicated by the statement, 'the principals of the institutes are full-time officers charged with the duty not only of recruiting students for their own institutes but also of advising them of the other provision in London for further education. These functions of the principals are co-ordinated by local and central conferences at which residual student problems are solved.'[6] Whilst there is no doubt that the Local Joint Standing Conference and the Central Conference were valuable forums for the interchange of information between principals and the delineation of spheres of influence they were not as successful as the statement implies in solving residual problems. Despite an increasing demand the most serious handicap for many years had been the lack of suitable accommodation for non-vocational work. 'With few exceptions the institutes have no buildings or rooms for their sole use.'[7]

Non-vocational education in 1949 was offered at nine literary institutes and the literary department of Norwood Technical College; four aided establishments, namely, Goldsmiths' College, Morley College, Toynbee Hall and Mary Ward Settlement; thirty women's evening institutes and fifteen men's evening institutes.

In addition, there were twenty-one recreational evening institutes for juniors of both sexes and two 'general' evening institutes which combined the functions of several types of institute and were situated in areas where transport facilities were too limited for normal planning.

As has already been indicated the recreational institutes were primarily for young people under eighteen although their enrolment of 36,400 in the session 1947–8 contained a sizeable number of adults over twenty-one as well as between eighteen and twenty-one. The Council's policy, however, was to reduce the number of adults in these institutes and to regard the institutes as an integral part of the youth service. (In 1946–7 over-eighteens numbered 6477.) In addition, the Council for many years had paid the fees of instructors for approved courses sponsored by the WEA as well as maintaining close co-operation with the extra-mural department of the University of London. Statistics had shown that it had been possible with increased facilities and larger student bodies to build up a wider range of liberal studies at centrally situated literary institutes. At the smaller suburban institutes which used day-school premises the range was more limited and music and drama dominated. Literary subjects in men's and women's institutes, increasingly offered of late, were welcomed as opportunities for exploring new interests which could be continued at higher levels in literary institutes and elsewhere. The total enrolment in literary institutes and the four aided institutes was as follows:

1945–6   18,000
1946–7   23,000
1947–8   25,000

Of the total in 1947–8,6000 students were from outside London but 4000 of the 6000 worked in London. The City Literary Institute, designed for 6000 students, now had an enrolment of 10,000, was overcrowded and turning away many applicants. Morley College was in a similar position until its war-damaged wing could be restored. The success of these two centrally placed colleges illustrated the demand from students employed in central London for early classes and for premises for their sole use with special facilities. The Scheme of Further Education proposed that there should be a new literary institute for 6000 on a site in or near central London; the roll of the City Literary Institute should be reduced to 6000; Morley College should be rebuilt for 4000; the Adult Education Department at Goldsmiths' should accommodate 3000 students; and four institutes should be provided in appropriate outlying districts in specially adapted redundant schools or other suitable buildings. Supplementary use of accommodation should be available in neighbouring comprehensive schools, in each of which there should be two special rooms for administration and storage. Classes at Mary Ward and Toynbee Hall were to continue to be recognized for as long as the governing bodies of those two establishments desired to include classes and courses similar to literary institutes.

Men's Institutes

Men's institutes, originally opened for working men in densely populated areas, were now judged to have an appeal which transcended variations in social circumstances and previous education. Their 'club' atmosphere had a particular appeal and standards were stimulated by federations of clubs and by inter-club and inter-institute competitions and exhibitions. Women were being admitted in growing numbers and in 1947–8 represented about one tenth of the total enrolment: 1945–6, 13086 (1608); 1946–7, 15574 (1460); 1947–8, 18463 (1891). The most important factor in any development of the men's institutes was accommodation for the sole use of that institute. 'The joint user of primary or secondary school premises is antagonistic to the creation of the adult club atmosphere which is fundamental to the success of a men's institute. The members must be able to regard the building as equipped and furnished for their use – a place where they can work or relax in comfort. Ideally there should be special buildings with equipped workshops, lecture rooms, common rooms, clubrooms, library, gymnasia and boxing rings, shower baths, changing rooms and canteens.'[8]

Women's Institutes

In addition to practical subjects such as domestic cookery, dressmaking, millinery and decoration these institutes now covered a wide group of activities concerned with full citizenship and enjoyment of leisure, for example, current affairs, discussion groups, music, art, drama and physical training and dancing. Family relationships, hygiene and health also had a place in the curriculum. This extended curriculum reflected the growing number of men in the student body and the introduction of subjects which both husbands and wives could attend together. Statistics for the first three sessions after the war showed that some 14 per cent of the student body were men: 1945–6, 46831 (7602); 1946–7, 49135 (6982); 1947–8, 56014 (7431). Considerable improvement was necessary in the provision of social amenities in the cramped condition of shared accommodation. The increased provision for secondary education, the raising of the school compulsory-leaving age and the introduction of county colleges would, it was thought, increase the interest in subjects outside the traditional range. There was great interest in the non-vocational craft classes provided in women's institutes and, despite the severe handicap of unsuitable and inadequate accommodation arising from the use of school premises, the pre-war enrolment figure (55,000) had already been overtaken.

In those institutes where it had been possible to allocate accommodation for their sole use the increased liveliness which resulted bore testimony to the benefits this could bring. There was a pressing need for daytime classes but there had been little progress in providing these due to the lack of free space in schools or in neighbouring church halls or clubrooms. Work in the institutes was further hampered by the fact that furniture used by the day school was often unsuitable and had to be changed over for the evening and make-shift arrangements made for office accommodation, staff and students' rooms and for canteens. Lavatory accommodation was rarely suitable for adult students of both sexes. Lack of storage space was another severe obstacle to expansion. 'The importance of providing some ad hoc accommodation both for day and evening use can hardly be overstated'.[9] Taking all the various factors into account it was considered that, on a long-term basis, provision was required for a considerable increase over the present roll. The statement of the general policy for the development of both men's and women's institutes reflected the current anxiety at the great demand on sites and additional accommodation in London – and was a compromise between the ideal and the practicable. The conception of men's and women's institutes as primarily evening establishments made it difficult, despite the recognition of the need for accommodation for their sole use, to realize the great potential demand that existed for day classes. The expectation of considerable additional evening accommodation in the new comprehensive high schools was understandably seen as an important contribution to the institutes.

While the ideal would be special buildings, this would be uneconomical and unnecessary duplication and result in a large measure of accommodation standing empty in the day time and a much larger measure of perfectly suitable accommodation (particularly as regards halls with equipped stages, class-rooms, gymnasia, classrooms and domestic subject centres in the new compre-hensive high schools) standing empty in the evenings. The programme of building is such that, in these circumstances, recourse must be had to an alter-native scheme which will provide an adequate measure of separate accommo-dation with a ready means of securing supplementary accommodation.[10]

Nevertheless, the proposals in the *Scheme of Further Education* were notable steps forward in the development of men's and women's institutes; proposals which recognized the substantial progress made before and during the war.

To meet the estimated demand it was proposed that, ultimately, there should be sixty institutes organized on the basis of the communities in the County of London plan. Their development was to be arranged so as eventually to abolish the distinction between men's and women's institutes 'in accordance with the modern social trend'.[11] The exclusive use of a redundant day school (or other suit-able premises) was to be acquired for each institute. 'They would need some new equipment, and a relatively small sum per place would enable them to develop satisfactorily.'[12] Additional accommodation would be found in nearby com-prehensive schools to which a few special rooms for the sole use of the institutes would need to be added – one room for the principal and office staff, one general-purposes room, one general store-room and storage accommodation attached to the six practical work-rooms in greatest demand for evening classes. This latter proposal was an invaluable practical one which, if implemented, would ensure accepted use of specialist accommodation which hitherto had often been denied because of the lack of storage.

Community Centres

The development of community centre facilities, after the passing of the Physical Training and Recreation Act 1937, had been interrupted by the war. The Council, however, had considered the question in 1938 and determined the main lines of its financial assistance on the basis of a few experimental projects, for example, the Honor Oak Community Centre. Sites for community centres had been earmarked on seven other Council housing estates; on two – White City and Woodberry Down – accommodation was being planned in conjunction with the building of two new schools. The Scheme of Further Education proposed that aid was to be as decided from time to time and would include the supply and payment of instructors through affiliation to local evening institutes. Indeed the role of evening institutes loomed large in relation to any consideration that the Council gave to community centres; the Scheme laid down that, in the short term, the pressure on accommodation and building programmes made it unlikely that separate premises would be possible for a long time. It suggested that hired accommodation in privately owned buildings and in school premises, and attendance at evening institutes, might provide the alternative. The hiring of Council premises by community centres was to be at a special rate which covered the cost of heating, lighting and caretaking. In the long term the Scheme proposed that, as a matter of principle, community centres should be provided primarily as a result of local initiative, co-ordination of effort being secured by the Council to avoid wasteful duplication. It recognized that new proposals, arising as a result of the extensive reconstruction scheme, might well be complicated or give rise to a demand for small units or community clubs as distinct from centres. For the latter, consideration would be given to the appropriation of a few rooms to serve as club premises or, where space permitted, to the erection of suitable club houses. In the long and short term the Scheme emphasized that the contribution made by the Council's evening institutes would be a major consideration. 'Community centres are only one form of adult education and not all students desire to be tied to the neighbourhood; indeed many prefer the evening institutes and the WEA activities.'[13]

The total estimated cost of the proposals in the Scheme of Further Education was £28,973,000; £14 million of this was for the provision of county colleges. As far as non-vocational education was concerned one new building in central London for a literary institute, the reconditioning of the Stanhope Women's Institute, the rebuilding of Morley College and evening institute suites in new comprehensive schools, amounted to an estimated total of £934,800. In the event no county colleges were built, no additional literary institute in central London was provided and a number of the sixty comprehensive schools were built without further education accommodation. Successive financial squeezes limited the cost per place and caused their exclusion from plans on the grounds of economy. Indeed, the emphasis in further education building programmes for the next thirty years was to be on technological and technical education. London's share in such building programmes was to be severely restricted in favour of more pressing needs elsewhere. In addition, the high cost of sites and building in the metropolis was drastically to reduce the number of projects that could be tackled in any building programme year, thus slowing down the building programme to a pace which could not keep up with the accommodation demands of technological development and changed teaching techniques. In such circumstances non-vocational education, never a high priority to Government in post-war years, did not figure in further education building programmes. The first non-vocational project to do so, to the great credit of the ILEA was the new extension to Morley College in 1972. This only came about through the insistent opportunism of an ILEA senior officer when it was put in the further education building programme as a last-minute replacement for a technical college project which was unable to start.

Despite the separate provision for young people under eighteen now offered by the twenty recreational institutes and their absorption of the men's junior institutes the post-war recovery of the non-vocational institutes – literary, men's and women's – continued apace. In 1949 – 50 the nine maintained literary institutes, fourteen men's institutes and twenty-eight women's institutes enrolled 113,030 students and at least another 10,000 had been enrolled in aided establishments offering literary courses and subjects. This compared with 111,994 in 1939, excluding students at aided colleges and settlements. They had therefore more than overtaken the best pre-war year. Recreational institutes in 1949 – 50 had a total enrolment of 44,335. The major advances were made in literary and women's institutes, 17,806 and 71,133, compared with 13,715 and 54,975 respectively in 1938 – 9. Men's institutes were never to recover their pre-war strength and total enrolment in them was never to exceed the 24,091 of 1949 – 50. The total enrolment in literary institutes and women's institutes was also to decrease and not until 1959 – 60, two sessions after the reorganization of 1957, were the non-vocational institutes to reach a total enrolment equal to that of 1949 – 50. There were a variety of reasons for this, some of which affected men's institutes particularly, and other reasons which affected literary institutes rather more than women's institutes. The immediate cause affected all types of institutes, namely, the raising of fees.

Revision of Fees

The last review of fees had taken place in February 1932 and July 1934. In July 1942 a simplified scale of fees had been adopted for evening institutes other than literary institutes. Since the last review the cost of further education had risen considerably. Moreover the Minister of Education in Circular 210 suggested that fees at evening classes might well be raised, without causing hardship, by an amount which would increase the aggregate income to the LCC by 10 per cent. The Education Committee on 7 March 1950 reviewed the fees for all establishments of further education and determined the scale for non-vocational establishments as set out overleaf.

The increased fees had a marked effect on enrolment, particularly in men's institutes which suffered a drop of 17 per cent. Women's and literary institutes each had a drop of 8 per cent but recreational institutes fared worst of all with a drop of 30 per cent. (See Appendix A(ii)). Further increases of fees in 1952, 1953 and 1956 were reflected in decreased enrolments. By 1956 – 7 a total enrolment of 91,441 for literary, men's and women's institutes represented the lowest enrolment since 1947 – 8. It was not until 1959 – 60 that the total enrolment recovered to that of 1949 – 50. (See Appendix A(iii)(a).)

Revised Fees

Type	Present	New
Literary Institutes	7s. 6d.	10s. a session
Each additional class	4s. 6d.	5s. a session
All classes	15s.	Subject to a maximum of 30s. a session
Men's institutes	All classes 1s. a term (3s. a session)	Over 18: 6s. a session Under 18: 3s. a session
Women's institutes	Over 18: 1s. a term Under 18: 6d. a term	Over 18: 6s. a session Under 18: 3s. a session
Recreational and Junior Men's	Over 18: 1s. a term Under 18: 6d. a term	Over 18: 6s. a session Under 18: 3s. a session

Although there was a general fall in the number of enrolments the effect of increased fees varied from institute to institute. Institutes like the Walworth Men's Institute which catered for a generally more working-class area suffered most. The drop in enrolment at those institutes in 1950–51 was as high as 25 per cent and it was several years before the position was regained. In some institutes the former total enrolment was never reached. Fulham Men's Institute, however, with a wider and more varied catchment area, dropped from a total enrolment of 1910 to 1674 (12 per cent) and, in the following session, to 1658 but, despite the further increase in fees in 1952–3, rose to 1810 in 1952–3 and 1964 in 1953–4. The Marylebone Women's Institute served a very mixed area which covered the Borough of Marylebone (with the exception of a small area east of Great Portland Street) and the whole of the Borough of Paddington and its total enrolment increased steadily throughout the 1950s, except for a drop of 10,000 student hours in 1952–3. Walworth Men's Institute was one of the original five institutes opened in 1920 whereas Fulham Men's Institute was not established until 1938 and was less of a traditional men's institute than Walworth. Also many of the institutes were serving areas which, as a result of war damage and rebuilding, were very different from the old close-knit pre-war communities.

The increased fees were a disincentive to those whom, in the 1920s and 1930s, the LCC had been at such pains to encourage. The institutes were offering a wider programme: practical subjects in both men's and women's institutes still held pride of place but there were more of the creative arts such as pottery and a greater range of painting classes. Art appreciation, music appreciation and modern languages catered for a wider public than hitherto. In the women's crafts the influence of 'haute couture' on women's dress and skilled instructors giving greater attention to design were attracting students from broader social groupings than before. General exhibitions and those presented by individual institutes demonstrated the new range and the high standard achieved. Moreover, the pressure on secondary-school accommodation and the programme of war damage repairs tended to hamper large concentrations of classes in any one centre and principals were opening more centres throughout their areas. This was particularly true of women's institutes, although some of the later men's institutes, such as Fulham, tended not to be centres for the wide range of backyard hobbies to quite the same extent as some of the more traditional men's institutes. The increased number of women admitted to men's institutes extended the range of classes at men's institutes. These new classes catered for a different type of student from those working men who had been attracted to interest and hobby classes.

Although there are no detailed statistics to confirm or deny any such change, there is reason to believe that the social structure of the student body began to change in the early 1950s. Certainly the increased fees in 1950–51 inhibited many of the former traditional students of men's institutes from joining. Some returned, only to find that the institutes themselves were changing and that the old camaraderie had disappeared. On the other hand 'the silent social revolution' was changing society itself. It could be that higher standards of living were inducing different expectations and needs and widening interests to which the institutes were responding. One principal wrote of an institute that it was becoming 'less a social meeting place and more a specialist centre where students came to study a particular subject or further a special interest'. Doubtless such a comment reflected the piecemeal scattered growth which was taking place in some institutes, as principals sought accommodation for small groups of classes over a very wide and often ill-defined area.

After eleven years of crowded activity Sir Graham Savage retired in 1951. He had seen the London education service through the trauma of the war years; set on foot the repair of its war-ravaged plant; supervised the LCC's response to the Education Act 1944 and played a major role in the introduction of comprehensive schools. His successor, John Brown, had joined the LCC in 1919; he was a man of phenomenal memory who knew the service thoroughly and a quite remarkable number of people in it. To take his place as Deputy Education Officer, W.F. Houghton, then Deputy Education Officer for Birmingham, was appointed. John Brown was a consolidator rather than an innovator and, throughout his service, culminating in five years as Education Officer, probably did more than any other man to personalize the service which, by reason of its size, was in danger of becoming remote. Houghton, as Deputy Education Officer, set about getting to know the service – its strengths and weaknesses. He was a man of prodigious intellect, industry and integrity – but with a disconcerting attention to detail and an equally disconcerting humility and shyness. Although to Sir Robert Blair and stalwarts like Stewart Headlam must go the honour of laying the foundation of the London evening institute service, it is to W.F. (later Sir

William) Houghton and Mrs Margaret (later Dame Margaret) Cole, the Chairman of the Further Education sub-committee from 1949 to 1965, that the non-vocational adult education service owes its important post-war development. It was Houghton, when Deputy Education Officer, who pushed forward the review of adult education provision. With characteristic thoroughness he had visited many of the institutes to see for himself the problems that principals were encountering. After he became Education Officer in 1956 he regularly visited non-vocational institutes, attended many of their social functions and generally made clear to principals his own firm conviction of the important role that adult education had in the London education service.

Throughout the London Scheme of Further Education the importance of adequate and suitable accommodation and the need for literary, men's and women's institutes to have accommodation for their sole use had been strongly emphasized. The increased child population of the 1950s and the heavier demand on school buildings by the enlarged scope of secondary education for all, meant that virtually every available school building was pressed into service and redundant schools for adult education were not to be available for some time to come. In addition new services since the war – the school meals service and the youth service – with their need for accommodation in schools, intensified the problem of dual use in schools. Developments in the evening institutes themselves in scope, standards and volume, meant that they needed more room and better facilities.

10.   The Reorganization of 1957 – 9

The London Scheme of Further Education had expressed the intention to abolish the distinction between men's and women's institutes. The Minister of Education, in approving the Scheme, had stated that, before rigidly applying such a policy, it would be desirable to observe carefully the effect of the mergers already undertaken. On the face of it, this was a routine cautionary comment on the part of the Ministry. Certainly the Minister made no further detailed comment to suggest otherwise. In retrospect, however, it could be that, mindful of the enthusiasm with which the Board of Education had applauded in the 1920s and 1930s the initiative of the LCC in breaking new ground by setting up men's institutes, he was expressing some anxiety lest their particular contribution in attracting working men might be lost. In any case the social trend of men's and women's institutes was already dictating the way forward. Since the easing of restrictions on single-sex admission of students, 14.6 per cent of the students in women's institutes were men and roughly the same percentage (14.2 per cent) of students in men's institutes were women. Except for a limited number of men's institutes there was little distinction between men's and women's institutes. Both men's and women's institutes were also offering an increasing range of subjects which hitherto had been restricted to literary institutes. With the encouragement given in the Scheme of Further Education this practice had grown. Added to this, the 'catch-as-catch-can' efforts of principals to secure accommodation for classes wherever they could had led to a conglomeration of small centres spread over the area of each institute. There was considerable overlapping.

These factors, together with wartime devastation, rehousing and consequent shifts of population, made some reorganization inevitable. Reorganizations are seldom welcomed by those whom they most directly affect, and the morale of principals of non-vocational institutes in 1955 was generally at a low ebb. High expectations after the war had come to nothing. Dual use of school buildings, always a trial, had become exceptionally difficult. Having built up enrolment by 1949–50 to its pre-war strength, increased fees in 1950–51 and 1952–3 caused substantial reductions in the number enrolled and many potential students turned away. In many areas people were being rehoused and attracting students from new housing estates and flats was proving difficult and unrewarding. Even though the increased fees were still comparatively low they were still sufficiently high to deter those to whom education was not a high priority. To people settling into a new house or flat with more often than not hire-purchase payments to be

187

met on furniture, additional charges of any kind were a real disincentive. There was also another peculiarly post-war factor. After the disruption of wartime a new flat or a new house was itself a valued amenity to be enjoyed for the first time for many years, and which, once home from work, people were loth to leave.

The Further Education sub-committee on 30 November 1955 instructed the Education Officer to report, after consultation with the Chairman, on the most practicable means of surveying the provision of evening institutes throughout the county of London. The aim of the survey was to ascertain the adequacy of evening institute provision, having regard to the movement of population and the large masses of population in areas newly developed as a result of housing operations. It was evident that the additional burden of a survey and the consequent upheaval it would cause, was approached cautiously by George Mavor, the Senior Assistant Education Officer in charge of Further and Higher Education Branch and by Margaret Cole the Chairman of the Further Education sub-committee. Mrs Cole, as she was then, kept her ear to the ground. In 1950 she had arranged for a Consultative Committee for Non-Vocational Institutes, consisting of members of the Further Education sub-committee, principals and representatives of the part-time staff of non-vocational institutes, to be set up so as to give principals, who had no advisory committees to whom they could turn, the opportunity to raise matters of concern with members of the committee. It was a valuable safety valve for a section of the education service which felt very much on the periphery of a large higher and further education service. Mrs Cole's association with the survey was therefore important and it was in consultation with her that it was decided that the best way of conducting the survey would be to work through the Further Education Local Joint Standing Conferences. There were nine of these, one for each of the education divisions; each conference included the principals of all evening education establishments and day colleges in the division. One of the duties of the conferences, as prescribed by Rule 14 of the Education Committee, was 'to arrange for adequate provision for any particular branch of education in the division concerned', and, for this purpose, to forward proposals to the Education Officer and 'to consider any questions which are common to the evening institutes in the district'. It was felt that if the survey was made in full consultation and with the help of the local conferences it would make for the greatest possible measure of agreement between the principals and members of the institutes affected. The Education Officer was instructed to proceed on these lines on 30 August 1956.

The survey which followed showed that the overlapping between literary institutes, on the one hand, and men's and women's institutes on the other, was more extensive than had been appreciated. Whilst they did not offer courses in such subjects as sociology, philosophy, history, religion and archaeology, a number of men's and women's institutes already offered courses in art, drama and music to a very high standard. Similarly, although the overall percentage of men in women's institutions in 1955–6 was 14.6 per cent, in one women's institute the percentage was as high as 33 per cent, the number of men in that institute being more than the total number of men in the smallest men's institute. In one men's institute the percentage of women was as high as 32 per cent and in another 25 per cent. At the other end of the scale there were no women in Stepney Men's Institute and only 6 per cent of the students in Deptford Men's Institute were women. The institutes which had admitted substantial numbers of men and women had not experienced any consequential difficulties either in organization or recruitment. Huntingfield Recreational Institute and the two general institutes which had been established as mixed institutes were found to be both acceptable and convenient to run. The existing single-sex organization, however, presented difficulties in the unequal distribution of men's and women's institutes. There were wide variations, too, in the size of institutes. Women's institutes ranged from a little over 1000 students to over 5000 and the resident population in the areas served varied from under 70,000 to over 250,000. At one extreme the proportion of students to resident population was less than 1 per cent and, at the other, more than 4 per cent. In men's institutes the student roll ranged from 800 to over 3000 and, as far as could be judged having regard to the uneven distribution, the resident population varied from 68,000 to over 300,000.[1] The City Literary Institute, with a student roll of 8005, had 2363 male students, that is, 29.5 per cent, compared with the average for the four literary institutes of 37.5 per cent. Huntingfield, which had been developed as a mixed institute, had a men's student roll of 37.6 per cent.

The branches also varied considerably without any definite correlation between the number and size of branches and the size of the institute as a whole.

With the exception of central London institutes the service provided was very local and almost all students, in women's institutes particularly, were drawn from within a mile of the branch attended. Most came from a much more localized district, measured in most cases in hundreds of yards. Secondary factors were proximity to a relevant bus or rail route. Even well-appointed institutes had difficulty in attracting students living more than a quarter of a mile away; between a half mile and one mile from the building, the number of students could become less than a tenth of that in the immediate vicinity of the institute. Only a very small number of specialized courses ran contrary to this. The survey also emphasized that the metropolis remained a continuing patchwork of communities, with patterns of travel behaviour limited by physical boundaries such as canals, the river Thames, railway lines and large open spaces such as parks and commons. In addition, there were the less definable, but equally real, social boundaries. There were areas or districts at that time – for the same reason but perhaps to a more limited extent they still exist – in which the general pattern of movement was, say, from east to west and very seldom north to south and others where the normal route was north to south and rarely east to west.

Of 330 school buildings used by institutes, 65 per cent were primary schools. Some institutes depended wholly on accommodation in primary schools. Of the fifty largest branches, 75 per cent were dependent upon primary schools. Although understandable this situation could not be regarded as satisfactory.

The preparation of a satisfactory scheme depended on the allocation of adequate and suitable accommodation. The Scheme of Further Education had dealt with this question at some length and emphasized its importance. The provisional scheme drawn up as a result of the survey was based on the following assumptions:

1. that the minimum accommodation which should be exclusively available for evening institute use, in default of completely self-contained buildings, was as follows:

   principal's office; general office; common-room or general-purposes room (which could be used also as a library); adequate storage space not less than 600 sq. ft.

2. that adequate accommodation should be available for the preparation and serving of refreshments and for all activities requiring space and special equipment, for example, woodwork and physical education.

3. that it would be necessary to use school buildings, in addition to such self-contained premises, as become available.

4. that, as far as possible, the use of primary school accommodation should be discontinued and the maximum use made of secondary school premises.

5. that the fewer the number of school buildings required for dual use the more probable it was that adequate facilities could be provided for exclusive evening institute use.

Other key points that arose from the survey were:

a. the very localized recruitment of students which suggested a pattern of institutes recruiting students mainly from a half-mile radius.

b. the provision for cultural subjects was likely to succeed if available locally and both men's and women's institutes had shown that they could successfully promote such studies.

c. that a more effective organization could be achieved by establishing mixed institutes to replace the existing separate men's and women's institutes. Such an organization would be in line with present trends, would not adversely affect the provision of courses required solely by men or by women and could increase the demand for those which were common to both.[2]

With all these considerations in mind a provisional scheme was prepared which provided for:

i. the establishment of thirty-three general (mixed) and two central London literary institutes to replace the existing thirty-seven men's and women's institutes, the South-East and South-West Literary Institutes, the three general institutes and Honor Oak;

ii. a reorganization of districts to be served by the general institutes which would vary in area from one and a quarter to five square miles and in size of resident population from about 80,000 to about 170,000.[3]

The scheme envisaged a substantial reduction in the number of schools used, particularly in the number of primary schools. The number of students at each institute, judged on the existing potential, seemed likely to vary between 2000 and 4000 as compared with the present variation of between 800 to 5300. The scheme expected the reduction of the current number of institutes to the proposed general institutes to be achieved in ten years. The intention was to base the changeover on retirements as far as possible, together with one or two transfers of principals. No major difficulties were expected to arise and it was hoped to carry out the major part of the plan by 1960. Any financial disincentives for principals to transfer were, to a major extent, removed by the proposal that principals' existing salaries should remain personal to them.

The results of the survey and the scheme were submitted to the Further Education sub-committee on 20 June 1957.[4] The sub-committee's agreement was sought, in principle, to the development of general institutes in place of the current men's, women and suburban literary institutes and to the working out of a detailed organization, in consultation with principals, together with an estimated cost of the new system. The sub-committee agreed.

On 3 July 1957 the Education Officer personally outlined the scheme to a meeting of all the principals and it was followed by detailed consultation with every principal involved, both individually and in groups, in each of the nine administrative divisions. Prior to the divisional meetings the divisional officers and officers of the Schools and Development Branches had been consulted on which schools should be allocated to which institutes, bearing in mind the particular accommodation needs. Schools for each institute's use were selected on accessibility and the extent to which they offered not only immediate accommodation but also the prospect of some accommodation for the sole use of the institute. Individually, and in the divisional meetings in the presence of colleagues, principals were given opportunities to seek an alternative for additional schools, variations in area boundaries and so on. It was a very thorough consultation aimed at securing the greatest possible measure of agreement and security of tenure in a small number of schools. There was no doubt that it was a very successful undertaking which reflected great credit on all concerned, but particularly on Dr L.G. Wooder, the officer-in-charge of the survey, who had so painstakingly researched the ground and amassed such a wealth of information that points raised by principals and others could be accepted or rejected on the basis of unassailable facts.

On 30 October 1957 the Education Officer was able to report[5] the general acceptance of the proposals. With one exception those principals, whom it was proposed to move to another area, were happy to accept the transfer. The one exception accepted the transfer but with some disappointment. In their written observations the principals had accepted the basis of mixed institutes as reasonable and their comments ranged from enthusiastic agreement to acceptance. At the divisional meetings with principals no adverse comment was offered on this aspect of the proposals. Principals' observations were confined to requests for minor (except in one instance) adjustments of proposed boundaries and requests for the use of either more or different schools from those proposed. The meetings had been marked by a frank but co-operative discussion and such variations on boundaries or lists of schools as were proposed by principals were accepted or rejected by mutual agreement.

The reorganization removed the wide variations in size, population or potential number of students. The schools provisionally agreed with principals represented a compromise between schools offering sole use of accommodation (either immediately or in the future), those already established as successful branches of existing institutes, and the schools attractive to principals and students (mainly by reason of their situation), although offering little prospect of accommodation for sole use. Principals were reluctant to exchange schools, known as well-established centres, for others which, although they offered better possibilities of accommodation for sole use, were not so well established and well positioned.

The number of schools designated for use by non-vocational institutes numbered 183 as compared with the former number of 363. Some thirty-one of the 183 schools were used by recreational institutes and thirty-five were used by vocational colleges or institutes. It was hoped that the review of recreational institutes which was then proceeding, and later of vocational institutes, would remove as far as possible the existing dual and treble use of schools by various further education establishments. As a result of the survey 110 schools had been completely vacated by further education users and no less than 150 primary schools had been vacated by men's, women's and general institutes. It was hoped that this would ensure not only a better service but also greater security of tenure and better facilities.

The merging of men's and women's institutes and the suburban literary institutes into the proposed general institutes gave an opportunity for the new institutes to offer courses hitherto regarded as exclusively in the field of literary institutes. The new institutes were enabled to become centres of adult education, catering for a complete cross-section of the adult community in their area. The heavy demand for liberal studies was to be served by the City Literary Institute, the North-London (now Marylebone) Literary Institute, Morley College in the centre and Goldsmiths College in the south-east.

For the time being it was decided that principals, hitherto responsible for education classes in HM prisons, should continue to supervise such classes even though the prisons themselves might be immediately outside their institute's area. For a similar reason Mr Huddart, the principal of the Walworth General Institute (previously Principal of Greenwich Men's Institute), continued to supervise the classes in the Cutty Sark, even though the Cutty Sark at Greenwich was outside his institute's area.

In considering the staffing of the institutes, in particular the supervisory staff, regard had to be had to the fact that all institutes would now have men and women students. It was therefore proposed that there should be a deputy principal of the opposite sex to the principal at each institute. The development of day classes at some institutes and the general extension of activity which the new institutes might be expected to undertake called for consideration of the need for a full-time vice-principal at each institute. The cost of such a proposal would have amounted to £47,000 and would not obviate the need for instructors-in-charge at some of the branches. Mindful that the reorganization, like most reorganizations, was expected to save money, the Education Officer felt unable to justify a full-time vice-principal at that stage but proposed a deputy principal, a part-time fifteen-hours-a-week appointment, at each institute. There were, at the time, fifteen deputy principals, eleven of whom were in women's institutes. Not surprisingly the Association of Women Principals made it known that deputy principals should be filled by the best candidate – man or woman – and if this could not be done they would be prepared to have instructors-in-charge as their deputies. Clearly, they were anxious not to lose some of the valuable women supervisory staff who had in many cases been with them for a number of years. The Education Officer, with the agreement of the Committee, however, remained firm on the appointment of a deputy of the opposite sex. In the event, one or two exceptions were permitted where a woman deputy had a short time to go before retirement. A major difficulty was the allocation of supervisory assistance in the shape of hours for instructors-in-charge. The report to the Committee proposed a maximum total of supervisory time of thirty-nine hours a week (deputy principal fifteen hours, instructors-in-charge twenty-four hours). In spite of the fact that, at the former forty-five institutes, with their larger areas and a greater number of schools, only eighteen had more than thirty-nine-hours supervisory assistance, a number of principals indicated in no uncertain terms that the supervisory hours proposed were too low. Suggestions varied from acceptance of the proposed thirty-nine hours to a request for one hundred hours a week. Since there seemed to be some confusion between the duties of instructor-in-charge and those of clerical assistant, it was decided that the thirty-nine-hours supervisory assistance should stand, pending an examination of the relationship between clerical assistants and instructors-in-charge.

The total expenditure on non-vocational institutes estimated, in 1957–8, at £800,000, had three main elements; supervisory costs, accommodation costs and tuition costs, all of which would be affected by the reorganization. Since the scheme would not be fully implemented until 1961 the full financial effect would not be realized until then but the ultimate saving on the basis of existing costs was estimated as follows:

1. *supervisory costs* – the employment of ten less principals produced an annual ultimate saving of £15,000. The proposed total of thirty-nine hours-a-week supervisory staff for each institute would give an ultimate annual saving of £9000 but, since this was likely to be in dispute and must await the investigation in relation to clerical assistants, no firm savings under this heading were given other than the £15,000 for the ten less principals.

2. *accommodation costs* – the proposed use of half the buildings, including the complete vacation of 110 schools, was estimated to produce economies in electricity and staffing (schoolkeeping and cleaning) costs of at least £30,000 a year.

3. *tuition costs* – the grouping of classes in fewer buildings should, it was thought, bring economies in fewer instructors as would the reduction in overlapping classes. From a total expenditure of £390,000 (under this heading) it was thought to be not unduly optimistic to look for a saving of £5,000.

It was expected that £50,000 would be saved from the reorganization. The grading of the institutes was to be reviewed after three years operation in the new form. The Education Committee approved the report of the Further Education sub-committee, recommending the new scheme on 20 November 1957.[6]

Although at one time it was thought that the complete implementation of the reorganization would need to be spread over a much longer period (the report on the preliminary scheme had, very cautiously, mentioned ten years), it was completed by the end of the 1960–61 session. No less than twenty-nine of the thirty-three new institutes (excluding the two central literary institutes) were established by September 1958. The remaining four institutes were re-established within the next two or three years.

An important aim of the reorganization was to concentrate institute use into fewer schools – on average about five schools per institute – to give the new institutes a greater security of tenure in designated headquarters and branches. Apart from the consultations that had already taken place with the Further Education Local Joint Standing Conferences it had been necessary to try to secure the co-operation of individual heads of designated schools. Dual use of schools was, and is, always difficult. In London, it had, at least, the merit of having been the recognized policy of the School Board and the LCC. It was also established practice for schools to be used for further education evening classes. But policy and established practice are only acceptable to all concerned, including policy makers, as long as they operate reasonably smoothly. The reduction in the number of schools to be used by institutes, particularly primary schools, was generally welcomed by committees, management branches and bodies such as the Consultative Committee for Headmasters and Headmistresses, representing heads generally. Such a reduction, however, carried with it the not so welcome corollary that the school selected would be used more intensively. Not only was this likely to be looked at rather more doubtfully by heads of the schools concerned but also by other evening users such as principals of junior commercial and technical institutes, the evening departments of some vocational colleges, the play-centre service and the increasingly heavy user of schools – the youth service. Schools designated for the new adult institutes had been carefully selected in consultation with divisional officers who, in London, have the responsibility for the day-to-day management of schools. Regard had been had to avoiding, as far as possible, designating schools used in the evening by other services. Nevertheless, in advance of a similar survey of the other services, like the youth service, adjustments were inevitable. The Education Committee took the view that a start had to be made somewhere but it was not always easy to counter the argument from services, such as the youth service, that the adult institutes had had first pick.

The first task, however, was to secure the co-operation and support of the heads of designated schools. For what appears to have been the first time, lists of schools designated for use by adult non-vocational institutes was widely circulated in the education service together with a summary of the aims of the reorganization. Divisional officers were asked to use their best endeavours to see that heads of the schools concerned were made fully aware of the reorganization and what it was designed to achieve and to ensure that every practicable facility was made available during the difficult transitional period. This they did and, apart from the difficulties at those schools where for the time being at any rate there were more than one evening user, there was general acceptance of the new arrangements.

Steps were also taken to lay down a more systematic procedure for extending or varying the designated accommodation for each institute. Previously it had been the responsibility of each principal to meet the local demand for classes and to develop his or her programme in the best practicable way. Where this had meant bringing more school accommodation into use the principal had informed the divisional officer of the need and it had been left to the divisional officer to complete the arrangements between the principal and the head of the school concerned. Now that the new institutes were to work within a planned grouping of school accommodation unrelated local development was no longer appropriate.

The new procedure required that if a principal considered that another school should be used in place of the one already designated for the institute or that some additional school premises should be brought into use by the institute, he should put the case in writing to the management section of Further Education Branch. The management section would consider the proposal in relation to the overall scheme, taking into account the views of the Development and Equipment Branch (the branch concerned with the building of schools, minor works programme and equipment) and the divisional officer who would consult the day school head before submitting his comments. If the proposal was finally agreed, the divisional officer and the principal would be so informed and asked to take the necessary action in consultation with the day school head. As regards the further education use of new, large, secondary school premises the existing procedure was retained.

The Local Joint Standing Conference gave its recommendation on which local institute should use the accommodation and, if agreed in principle by the Education Officer, the divisional officer was then asked to arrange a meeting at the school with the head, the principal or principals concerned and the appropriate officers from County Hall, in order that details of the evening use could be arranged and agreed. When the school had been designated for use by an adult non-vocational institute, however, the Local Standing Joint Conference would be so informed and would be concerned only with the consideration of whether some additional use should be made of the premises by another institute, or possibly two or more other institutes, without prejudice to the use by the adult institute.

This central control of the allocation of accommodation was an important step forward. The steps taken to make known to all concerned the aims of the reorganization; the designation of schools for the new adult institute's use; and the determination of a formal procedure for varying those arrangements, all gave emphasis to the importance the LCC attached to this particular part of the service. If credibility was to be given to the designation of schools a procedure for varying it was inevitable. For too long, perhaps, the sole basis of dual use had been the good sense of the respective users and the head of the day school. Where that important ingredient had been lacking in one or other a point of friction developed which was difficult to contain. The adoption of a formal procedure, requiring consultation before approval was given, added weight to the decision. While some grumbled at the red-tape and loss of local freedom the majority of principals recognized it as an indication that services other than schools had a claim on the use of school premises. As one principal put it: 'At last we have established a place in the sun!'

The Education Committee and the Education Officer stated publicly that the object of 'designation' was to give adult institutes some priority of consideration in buildings in which they could expect to have greater security of tenure and increased chances of more and better accommodation for their sole use. An important corollary of this was that other users of designated buildings would need to be encouraged to move to other premises if the new institutes were to be given their promised opportunity to expand and develop. The exodus of men's and women's institutes from a large number of primary schools provided some relief accommodation, particularly in the shape of halls, to which such services could transfer. Evening users of schools such as recreational institutes, however, needed those same facilities, gymnasia and practical rooms, found only in secondary schools. Principals rightly set great store by the undertaking to 'designate' schools for their use and were not slow to point out the limitations on possible expansion when other services also used those schools. The general publicising of the reorganization throughout the education service, together with the new procedure for varying accommodation requirements of institutes in schools, helped to set new standards of consultation. Patient investigation at senior-officer level of specific cases and consultation with all concerned gradually did a great deal to remove many real difficulties.

Once the turmoil of anxiety, inevitable perhaps in any major reorganisation had ceased, principals were quick to see the potential of the new institutes. The Senior Assistant Education Officer, in conveying to principals the formal approval of the Education Committee to the reorganization, in a letter dated 21 November 1957, suggested that they should aim first at consolidating existing work rather than attempt to introduce any spectacular developments. 'There is little doubt that once students settle down to the new conditions and realise the wider scope of activities to be made available, numbers will increase, but to establish a new organization and at the same time attempt to cater for increased numbers appears inadvisable.'

The advice was timely since, even at that early stage, it was clear that, with their customary opportunism, principals had recognized the possibilities of reorganized institutes and were losing no time in preparing expanded programmes. Also, the Ministry of Education had just informed LEAs, in Circular 331, that there would be a substantial reduction in expenditure on minor works in the next financial year. It was to this programme that the LCC looked for adaptations which would provide specialist services, additional storage and so on for adult institutes. Principals were therefore asked to make every effort in selecting rooms for specialist classes and to select those having the necessary services — water, gas and electricity — in order to reduce minor works to a minimum. The question of supervisory assistance had still to be determined on the basis of the revised organization and, for the time being, each institute was given thirty-nine hours, fifteen of which were for a deputy principal. The thirty-nine hours supervisory assistance per institute was a simple redistribution of the previous total of supervisory hours used by former men's and women's institutes. Savings on supervisory assistance had been limited to that derived from principals' salaries caused by the ultimate reduction in the total number of institutes from forty-five to thirty-five.

The impact of the reorganization was quite dramatic. The merging of men's and women's institutes brought together the best of the staff of both and, with it, a greatly extended range of specialized knowledge and experience. The institutes had a new vigour and a new look. It gave to most principals a new impetus – the opportunity to look afresh at their organization and presentation of programmes. Women deputy principals in no time at all brought a gentling influence to bear on men principals – cups and saucers replaced mugs overnight! Men deputy principals brought a welcome support, not always admitted, to the majority of women principals. The total enrolment for the session 1959–60 jumped to 124,394 compared with 92,015 in 1957–8 and, by the end of the 1960–61 session, had reached an all-time high of 140,979.

The reorganization of 1957–9 did not directly affect the City Literary Institute. The capacity of the Stukeley Street premises had been assessed at 6000 students but, by the time the Scheme of Further Education, with its provision for a second City Lit. had been published, the Institute had an enrolment of 10,000 students. Col. Archie White, VC who succeeded TG Williams as principal, was therefore instructed to reduce its size. By 1957, however, it was clear that the likelihood of any adult education project being included in an overcrowded further education building programme was virtually non-existent. Under its new principal, H.A. Jones, despite the continued use of some of the accommodation by Westminster College of Commerce and Kingsway Day College until the early 1960's, it was soon proved that, by double and treble banking classes many more than 6000 students could be housed. Some indication of the expansion is given by the number of classes on offer in the prospectuses for various years. In 1930, there were 199 evening classes and twenty-one day classes; in 1947–8 day classes remained about the same but evening classes had risen to 331; by 1962–3 the number of classes had risen to about 560 of which 140 were in the day, and the number of students was well over 10,000.

Curriculum Changes – 1950–61

The ten years between the session 1950–51 and the session 1960–61 saw significant changes in the curricula of the adult non-vocational institutes. Some changes, though not all, were due to the changed circumstances of the institute after the reorganization· (see Appendix B). The most notable change, perhaps, was the decrease and, in some cases disappearance, of those subjects which were the distinctive feature of the early men's institutes. Nineteen classes in caged birds had been reduced to two by 1960–61, poultry keeping from twenty-seven to four; twenty-five rabbit-keeping classes had disappeared and fourteen aquaria classes had been reduced to six. Shoe and boot repairing and boxing classes had been more than halved, and speech training classes were reduced from 116 to eighty-nine. There were still, however, the same number of classes (twelve) in the care and training of pigeons and a sizeable number of classes in bands and orchestras, although the number had dropped from 104 to seventy-nine classes a week.

Some of these changes, such as the disappearance of rabbit-keeping classes and the reduction in the number of poultry-keeping classes, were doubtless the result of the changed living conditions in many areas – flats instead of houses – and to the changed interests and hobbies of the post-war years.

Debating societies and public speaking classes, so popular in the 1930s, were no longer in such demand and elocution and speech training became a part of dramatic-art classes. Boxing remained a feature at one or two institutes, for example Battersea, where special facilities could be offered to affiliated amateur clubs. Boxing was the only physical education activity in the adult institutes which declined during the period 1950–61. The total number of physical education classes almost doubled and in 1960–61 represented some 19 per cent of the 8500 classes a week offered in London's non-vocational institutes. Apart from keep fit and circuit training no less than twenty-one physical activities, compared with fifteen in 1950–51, were now catered for. Archery (three), cycling (two), golf (fifty), lacrosse (one), sailing and rowing (three), trampoline (three) had been added to the list. Badminton classes (four) had leaped to 218, football, rugby and soccer (twelve) to 118, judo (forty-two) to 134, table tennis (seven) to 121 and weight-lifting (forty-four) to ninety-three.

The fall in the demand for those traditional 'hobbies' of the former men's institutes was being overtaken by new demands for motor-car and motor-cycle maintenance (fifty-two to 258), amateur radio (fifty-three to eighty-four) and home furnishing and soft furnishing, etc. (forty-two to 149). Individual instruction in such musical instruments as guitar, banjo, violin or piano increased (120 to 157). The number of seamanship and navigation classes doubled (nine to twenty).

The approach to other old-established subjects was changing too. The most notable, perhaps, was in women's craft classes. The 'make do and mend' approach of the war years gave way to fashion as a whole, to a great interest in the many different kinds of fabric available, the choosing of styles and methods of making up and the linking of the various crafts involved in creating a whole ensemble. Older methods were replaced by new techniques for students who wanted stylish and exciting clothes which did not take too long to make. A minor boom (five to seventy-seven) in poise, dress and personality and good grooming classes was illustrative of the demand from both mature and young women to be helped to make the best of themselves and wear their clothes with distinction.

The increase in physical education classes reflected the growing interest in individual sports and, to some extent, the new accommodation (gymnasia) which was becoming available in the new secondary schools. Even so this new accommodation could not keep pace with the avalanche of demand for tuition in all kinds of sport; the fact that school halls were often the only available accommodation in which badminton could be played, of itself created a major accommodation problem. Courses at the LCC's college of physical education prepared instructors for evening institute classes. The strict insistence on appropriate standards for such instructors and the provision of refresher courses was leading to much more purposeful work in the various skills which enabled students to reach high standards of ability. Clubs found it of great assistance to affiliate to institutes in order to secure accommodation and qualified instructors. On the other hand students of classes were themselves forming clubs affiliated to the institutes and so increasing the pressure on the available sports accommodation.

The most notable development, however, was in the field of modern languages. The number of classes a week trebled (219 to 680) between 1950–61 and language classes represented about 10 per cent of the total provision. Whilst the major increases were in the more common European languages – French, German, Italian and Spanish – the seventeen languages taught in 1960–61 now included Russian (twenty-four), Swedish (four), Hebrew (two), Arabic (one), Anglo-Saxon (one) and Esperanto (one). The large number of people taking holidays abroad not only gave a stimulus to language classes but undoubtedly had a general effect on the creative arts, music and other cultural subjects.

The surge of interest in the creative arts – drawing and painting (119 to 258), modelling and pottery (thirty-eight to 199), photography (sixty-nine to 121) – was an indication of the desire of many to record their new experiences and develop interests and hitherto undiscovered talents. Again, new accommodation and equipment and allocation of storage space for the sole use of institutes also offered an encouraging incentive.

A comparison of the prospectus of the Stanhope Institute for 1950–51 and for the session 1960–61 gives a very good illustration of the changes which had taken place in the institutes during that period. Whereas in the 1950–51 prospectus there were long lists of cooking, dressmaking and lingerie, art and crafts, millinery and physical exercises, in the 1960–61 edition the programme of classes was prefaced by subject notes on the aim and content of tuition and an explanation of the various gradings in the subjects. In 1950–51, in a programme of 235 classes, there was one class in painting and drawing and another in drawing and design and only two pottery classes; in 1960–61 there were fifteen painting and drawing and eleven pottery and clay-model classes. Twelve language – ten in French and two in German – had expanded to thirty-seven classes in French, German,

Italian and Spanish. Physical exercises had become physical education which covered keep fit, gymnastics and games; the latter included tuition in fencing, judo for both men and women, golf and badminton. The total number of classes on offer had risen to 355.

The most striking development, however, was in the provision of day classes. A direct comparison is possible since the Stanhope Institute used the same premises for its main institute both in 1950–51 and, after the reorganization, in 1960–61. In 1950–51 twenty-five day classes were offered in a week; in 1960–61 eighty-four classes were offered at the main institute and another twenty-eight at its Bloomsbury branch. Many institutes did not have accommodation for their sole use but, wherever there was accommodation available during the day and classes were offered, the response was such as to indicate that there was a real demand for day classes. Institute prospectuses show only those classes on offer to the general public but a note in the Stanhope Institute prospectus for 1960–61, indicating that classes would be arranged by the institute at various clubs, firms and other organizations if application were made to the principal, gave a clue to a hidden sphere of activity which was growing apace.

The Marylebone Institute prospectus for the same year included a note: 'The following societies meet at the institute – Royal Amateur Orchestral Society, Strolling Players Amateur Orchestral Society, London Medical Orchestra, Erard Orchestra, Hampstead Choral Society, BELRA Light Opera Group, HFA Light Opera Group, Royal Scottish Country Dance Society, The Mountaineering Association, Hampstead Townswomen's Guild, Amateur Orchestra of London.' In addition to such affiliated groups institutes were developing a substantial number of what came to be called ''welfare'' classes. Men's and women's institutes had always worked with local clubs providing instructors for classes on club premises and instruction for classes in places of detention and H.M. prisons as well as for the handicapped in hospitals and other institutions. In the ten years after the war this work was extended considerably. The close relationships developed between institutes and borough council staff during the war was maintained and principals, in consultation with the local welfare departments, were providing an increasing number of classes in welfare centres, rehabilitation centres and day centres for the blind and physically handicapped. More often than not the request for such instruction came from welfare officers who were in touch with principals but principals were also taking the initiative in devising projects which would have a stimulating and educational, rather than therapeutic, approach. Although craft classes aimed at the acquisition of repetitive skills still predominated in residential homes, here and there attempts to stimulate mental activity by more creative activities were being accepted and sometimes encouraged. Darby and Joan Clubs affiliated to institutes were provided with a range of classes and other activities.

As early as 1945 a Ministry of Health Circular (Circular 15) had suggested that, when patients were in hospital for any length of time, there was 'ample evidence that in addition to its educational value, a course of study on craftwork, whether general or educational, in which the patient is interested, can help recovery'. LEAs were recommended to provide classes in hospitals. A further circular in 1956 distinguished clearly between classes of a therapeutic or diversionary nature, for which the LEA could provide a tutor but the hospital would reimburse the cost, and classes which were educational where the LEA paid for and provided a tutor and charged student fees. Institutes were extending the provision of therapeutic classes at the hospitals in their areas – classes for which the hospital reimbursed the LEA. Similarly, the cost of classes provided at welfare centres was met by the local borough council. The 1960s were to see an extension of this part of the institutes' work and a quite remarkable response to the new needs which changing social and educational influences in society brought. In 1960 it was clear that if institutes were to fulfil the role that was opening up for them as both day and evening centres of adult education they would require more than one full-time member of staff. Up to this time principals had had no full-time assistants, teaching or clerical, and yet had built up establishments with a high standard of work in a remarkable number of educational fields and were supervising the work of hundreds of part-time teachers in a programme of classes which in some institutes exceeded 400 a week. Their remarkable achievements had earned greater support.

Teaching Staff

The use of some of the new facilities for the creative arts and for physical exercises in newly built secondary schools were sometimes eased by the appointment of a teacher from the school as an instructor for a particular evening institute class. Although many art teachers in London secondary schools proved to be first-class teachers of adults the majority of part-time teachers of art and other subjects in the non-vocational institutes were not full-time teachers in day schools. London has always had the good fortune of being able to draw upon a remarkable pool of talent outside the full-time teaching profession for its part-time tutors. This was particularly true of the needlecrafts; from the earliest days of women's institutes instructors were recruited from the clothing trade.

Throughout the 1930s day-school teachers were increasingly employed as part-time teachers in vocational institutes, particularly junior commercial and technical institutes, whereas the men's, women's and literary institutes looked more and more to men and women recruited to subject panels outside the day-school teaching force. With the growth of language classes, for example, many part-time teachers were drawn from the large number of native speakers of the particular foreign language who were living in London. As the curriculum widened part-time tutors were recruited from practising artists and craftsmen who taught for the love of encouraging adults to appreciate and practise their art or craft; and from skilled professionals in industry or commerce with an infectious enthusiasm for their art and craft or specialist interest which they were only too anxious to communicate to adults in evening institute classes. An aid to the recruitment of part-time instructors (later called tutors) and an important contribution to maintaining standards was the panel of approved instructors kept by the Further Education Branch of the Education Officer's Department at County Hall. Whilst instructors were often 'discovered' locally by principals they had to be approved by the appropriate inspector or consultant employed by the Council for appointment to the appropriate subject panel. The principals applied for lists of possible tutors from this panel from which to select a suitable teacher for their particular vacancy. The panel of approved instructors for a particular subject was built up and maintained by individual applications, often initiated by principals, and, from time to time as the need arose, the Council issued a public advertisement inviting applications for admission to a subject panel.

Part-time supervisory posts, such as deputy principals and instructors-in-charge, were the subject of advertisement and selection by a panel of inspectors and the principal concerned. Although recruited from men and women with experience of the work of non-vocational institutes, a substantial number of instructors-in-charge tended to be full-time teachers, usually in primary schools. Deputy principals, on the other hand, were usually tried and trusted instructors-in-charge who could be available for fifteen hours a week. Since most institutes either had, or were in the process of, developing day classes, usually for women, women deputy principals were needed to supervise such day classes. There were no male deputy principals in the reorganized institutes who were available during the day. Whereas a number of women deputy principals could combine their supervisory duties with a teaching programme or some other work, there were few men who were prepared to give up a full-time post for such a speculative prospect. Until full-time vice-principal posts were established, this was a serious handicap to the recruitment of potential principals. It must also be said that most deputy principals worked devotedly for more than the fifteen hours a week for which they were paid.

1960 also saw a change in the basis on which classes in institutes were organized. From 1938 to 1960 an average attendance of fifteen student hours to one teacher hour by the end of the session was a necessary requirement for evening institutes as a whole (vocational and non-vocational). In addition, opening numbers for individual classes were strictly prescribed, the numbers varying for different subjects. A mid-term return of attendance in individual classes was required to be submitted to the Education Officer. Principals had the option of making a case to retain a class which was below the prescribed closing number.

Not only did this procedure cause a good deal of clerical and administrative work, it also created a difficulty for those principals who wanted to foster new classes or a new approach to meet a latent demand. An experimental class would obviously take some time to get off the ground.

In 1960 the system was changed in order to place the responsibility for opening or closing classes firmly with the principal and, at the same time, remove a good deal of meaningless administrative work. Separate staff/student ratios, based on the actual ratios achieved in preceding years, were set for different types of institutes. The ratio for literary institutes was set at 1:16, later reduced to 1:14 and eventually to 1:13, and 1:13 for the new adult institutes where more craft work requiring individual help and instruction was provided. Opening numbers and closing numbers for classes were abolished, although the former was kept as a guide until 1964. This meant that, as long as an institute achieved an overall ratio of one-teacher hour to thirteen student hours, the distribution of staff and classes was entirely at the discretion of the principal with, where necessary, advice and help from the inspectorate. Popular classes in music or dancing, with a regular attendance of thirty-forty students, could provide a significant margin in the overall staff/student ratio which could enable the more advanced classes in, say, languages or an exploratory class, to be sustained. This was a major step forward which was generally welcomed by principals, some of whom took a little time to appreciate its full significance. They had to learn, for example, that protests from students about the closure of a class could no longer be blamed on 'the regulations from County Hall'. They, and not the Education Officer, had to explain to students why their class had to close. Some principals, too, had to learn that to achieve an overall ratio of 1:13 required more careful planning of classes and a more balanced distribution among subject areas since it was not acceptable to achieve the required ratio by sudden closures of classes in the last term of the session.

Review of Supervisory Assistance

For many years the backbone of the non-vocational institutes had been the instructors-in-charge, usually responsible to the principal for the day-to-day running of a branch. Before the organization of 1957–9 the approximate basis for their appointment was one instructor-in-charge for each group of five or more classes held on a site. Generally, no supervisory assistance had been given for groups of up to four classes on a site, on the assumption that the principal would be responsible for these, although some additional assistance was allowed when the number of small groups was exceptionally large. One of the aims of the 1957–9 reorganization was to reduce the number of small groups and, by 1960, it was apparent that this aim was being achieved. The number of small groups had decreased but the total number of classes had increased and the number of classes in groups of five or more had increased by 46.2 per cent. The absence of any increased allocation meant that instructors-in-charge were supervising, on average, groups of over eight classes. An investigation into the duties of instructors-in-charge and clerical assistants had shown that, while the duties of instructors-in-charge varied over the whole range of institutes, no general duties were undertaken by supervisory staff which should have been done by clerical staff. Therefore, after consultation with principals, it was agreed that, for the session 1960–61, the allocation of supervisory assistance should be as follows:

1. fifteen hours – deputy principal
2. for two-hourly evening classes in groups of five or more on one night, instructor-in-charge time would be given on the following basis:

   Up to 50 classes   – one hour a week to each two classes
   51 to 100 classes   – one hour a week to each four classes
   101 to 150 classes   – one hour a week to each six classes
   151 or more   – one hour a week to each eight classes

3. for all two-hourly day-time classes and for two-hourly classes in groups of four or less at one time – one hour a week to each eight classes.

This allocation gave a greater weighting to small institutes and, in order to encourage the bringing together of classes in both time and place, a lesser weighting was given for groups of up to four classes.

At three institutes, namely, Clapham and Balham, Central London and Stanhope, where the number of classes exceeded 300 a week, and morning and afternoon classes were offered as well as evening classes, from the 1 September 1960 a full-time vice-principal in place of the present deputy principal was established. Approval was also given (Education Committee 11.5.60) for the Education Officer to consider establishing similar positions at other institutes with a large number of classes (240–300) where the spread of classes throughout the day justified such an appointment in place of the fifteen hours deputy and fifteen hours instructor-in-charge.

This was of course a major development which reflects great credit on the LCC. For so many years principals of institutes had been the one full-time member of staff with responsibility for responding to the needs of those in the community; directing a staff of hundreds of part-time teachers, assisted only by part-time supervisory staff; the enrolment of several thousands of students and accounting for substantial sums of money received in fees as well as from the sale of a considerable stock of materials used by them in classes. The establishment of posts of vice-principal at three of the largest institutes and the approval of similar posts at institutes with over 240 classes a week and a wide spread of subjects, was welcome recognition of the new status of non-vocational adult institutes. By 1965 vice-principal posts had been authorized in a further twenty-three institutes making a total of twenty-six in the thirty-three general institutes. In addition, in fourteen general institutes the appointment of a third full-time member of staff had also been authorized. Since the creation of the first of the vice-principal posts the work of general institutes had increased very considerably, student hours showing an increase of 44 per cent from 1959–64. Increases in the provision of sole-use accommodation had made possible a considerable increase in the number of day-time classes held and, by 1965, all general institutes were offering both day and evening classes in a wide variety of subjects.

Not all principals who were entitled to a vice-principal were anxious for an appointment to be made. The appointment of a vice-principal meant the replacement of a part-time deputy principal and giving up fifteen hours of instructor-in-charge time. Since vice-principals were appointed by public advertisement there could be no guarantee that part-time deputy principals would necessarily be appointed to the institute at which they had given such devoted service. Principals had managed alone for so long that the prospect of sharing the management of an institute with another, perhaps unknown, full-time vice-principal filled many with considerable apprehension. To some it was almost equivalent to choosing a marriage partner and in some respects more hazardous since the choice very often was made on the basis of a short acquaintance or on other people's recommendation. It was a very difficult business which had to be handled with tact and patience. Wherever possible the vice-principal post was not authorized until a valued part-time deputy principal retired or moved. At least one or more deputy principals, recognizing the need for a full-time post, took selfless action to bring it about, with no other incentive than the welfare of the principal they had worked with and respected. It is to the credit of all concerned that, with one or two exceptions, satisfactory appointments were made and good relationships maintained. The fact that it took five years to appoint vice-principals to twenty-three institutes entitled to them indicates the very personal administration which such institutes demanded.

By 1965 a new factor had entered into the need for vice-principal appointments. Between 1965 and 1970, ten principals of general institutes were due to retire and a further eight principals would be eligible to retire, having reached the age of sixty years. The size and scope of the London system of adult non-vocational education was exceptional. Although vacancies for both principal and vice-principal posts were advertised publicly, candidates with the requisite experience for appointment direct to principalships were not normally found outside the service. Vice-principal posts were a valuable recruitment field for future principals. It was therefore important for the health of the service that there should be a good field of experienced vice-principals available for consideration for appointment to principal in the next five years. With this in mind the Further Education sub-committee authorized the appointment of vice-principals in the remaining seven general institutes, three of which had more than the required 240 classes a week but the remaining four – Bow and Poplar, Clapton and Kingsland, Greenwich and Walworth – were in areas where it had been shown that development of the work was more difficult and progress slower. With no other full-time member of staff there was clearly a limit to the time the principal could devote to the painstaking work which the development of new classes required. The principals at these institutes needed a vice-principal to help them with development work. A vice-principal post was also authorized at Morley College.

11.   The Years of Fruition: the 1960s

The 1960s were years of unprecedented growth. The 8524 classes a week in 1960–61 had grown to 14,366 in 1968–9; physical education classes were now part of a large section of games and sports numbering 2300 classes a week; the explosion in the creative arts had doubled the classes in art and crafts to a total of 2327; the number of language classes had trebled (680 to 1911) classes a week in no less than twenty-eight different languages; and the number of classes in literary, cultural and historical studies had doubled. Total student enrolments increased from 139,894 (7,345,462 student hours) in 1960–61 to 187,987 (12,027,019 student hours) in 1968–9. No less than fifty-eight 'new' subjects were added to the list of subjects offered between 1960–69, the total number of different subjects offered each week being 189. Japanese and Polish were offered for the first time in 1964–5 and Dutch and Portuguese in 1966–7. The introduction of Japanese came about as a result of a party of judo students from an institute in south London visiting Japan to study judo. They became so interested in the Japanese scene that they asked to learn Japanese. Despite some inspectorate doubts on the propriety of this language being offered at an adult education institute, it was approved experimentally. The class flourished and there have been classes in Japanese in adult education institutes in each year since 1964–5. Yoga was offered for the first time in 1968–9. Classes for the first time in enamelling, lithography, mosaic and porcelain illustrated developments in the creative arts; and the growth of interest in antiques was signalled by twenty-three classes in the study of antiques in 1964–5 and subsequently.

There is little doubt that this expansion and development was due to two main factors, the appointment of additional staff and the increasing availability of additional accommodation. As we have already seen adult education provision in London had been developed on the basis of the dual use of school premises. Most maintained county secondary schools in the ILEA's area were, by 1969, now used for adult education, youth service or both. Full use had been made of the Department of Education and Science's Further Education Circular Letter 2/55 which allowed a limited amount of sole use accommodation for adult education to be provided as part of the capital project of a new school building. Each new county secondary school designed since the mid-50s had included some accommodation solely for adult education institutes, youth centres or both. This normally consisted of an administrative suite, a general-purpose room of 960 sq. ft., particularly important for the development of day classes and social activities requiring a common-room, and both a central store and institute storage adjoining specialist rooms (art, housecraft, handicraft). By the end of 1969 there were thirty-nine secondary schools in use where institutes had this full provision. Moreover, as new schools replaced the old it had been possible to adapt some redundant buildings to provide headquarters for an institute and/or a centre for its sole use which, suitably adapted, could make possible not only an expansion of evening classes but a wide variety of day classes. The fluctuating fortunes of minor-works building programmes throughout the 1950s and the virtual exclusion of adult education projects from major capital-building programmes had seriously limited the development of accommodation and therefore of day classes and provision of accommodation for wider activities. Nevertheless, by 1964, sixteen institutes had one building for their exclusive use and two had two such buildings. Only the City Literary Institute had purpose-built premises, built by the LCC in 1936–9. By 1969 more than half of the institutes, twenty-one in all, had at least one building of which they were either the sole user or joint user on equal terms with a teachers' centre. Two, Eltham and Putney, had art centres equipped for a full range of art and craft activities. Each acquisition of accommodation for their sole use enabled the principal and staff of an institute to stimulate a latent demand which made good use of accommodation day and evening all week. The majority of institutes by this time had sole use of some specialist accommodation, even if it was a detached housecraft or handicraft centre on a site shared with the school, and no longer needed by the school because of rebuilding or remodelling.

The headquarters of each institute was generally based on a secondary school where specialist accommodation had been provided or in a building of which it had sole use. Each institute had, in addition, from five to seven branches based wherever possible at secondary schools but also using some primary schools. Children born in the post-war baby-boom had now passed through primary schools and primary-school rolls had fallen, releasing accommodation for some institutes in primary schools. By 1969, ninety-nine secondary schools and 109 primary schools were in use by adult education institutes. The use of primary schools was limited mainly to halls for such activities as judo or folk dancing. Even so it was necessary to hire accommodation for other physical education activities. The provision of storage accommodation adjacent to specialist rooms had removed a good deal of friction in the dual use of secondary schools and there was a growing recognition of the need for increased use of schools for community purposes. The adoption of procedures drawn up after the 1957–9 reorganization for the use of additional accommodation, together with the use of concordats between principals and head teachers' organizations, as well as local agreements providing for the use on some evenings by the school for extra-school activities, had gone a long way to removing or easing some of the more obdurate problems of dual use of buildings. The continuing demand for physical education, together with that for day classes including lunch-time classes, led to the hiring of accommodation. By

1969 over 150 halls, more than 130 rooms and twenty-four swimming baths were hired by the ILEA for the use of institutes.

On the other hand the extension of welfare classes, that is, classes in hospitals, welfare centres, welfare homes and clinics had been given a new impetus in that they were excluded from the classes to be taken into account in determining the institute's teacher/student ratio. A survey by the Association of Principals of Adult Education Institutes in 1968–9 revealed that, in twenty-nine of the thirty-three institutes surveyed, classes were held in 1968–9 in the following outside accommodation to meet special demands.

Accommodation at	*Number of hours weekly in use*
community centres	280
hospitals	191
prisons	436
clubs	465
commercial and industrial premises	55
welfare centres	555
welfare homes	337
clinics	90
others	321

Eight institutes had, in addition, creches in use for a total of fifty-seven hours weekly on average.

Staffing

The second major influence on the development in the adult education service in the 1960s was undoubtedly the improved staffing of the institutes. In 1961 a review was undertaken of the grading of the twenty-nine principals appointed to the reorganized general institutes in September 1958 and the five reorganized in 1959 and 1960 – the latter's grading was subject to further review when the institutes had been operating in the reorganized form for three years. Progress since the reorganization had been rapid despite the difficulties which accompany any major reorganization. The total enrolment had risen from 96,000 in 1957–8 (5,300,000 student hours) to 124,390 (6,700,000 student hours) in 1959–60 and 139,894 (7,345,462 student hours) in 1960–61. The growth was reflected in the regrading of principals on the ILEA's own scale as follows:

Grade B   £1550 × £50 to £1750 plus London allowance – nineteen institutes of which four were formerly on Grade A

Grade C   £1750 × £50 to £1900 plus London allowance – fourteen institutes of which eleven were formerly on Grade B and one on Grade A

The upgrading of sixteen principals and the concentration of all thirty-three principals in two grades indicated that the disparity in the size of the institutes had been substantially diminished by the reorganization. By 1965 full-time vice-principals' posts were established in all the thirty-three institutes. By 1969, sixteen institutes with over 400 classes a week, had a full-time lecturer Grade 1 with £185 allowance with special responsibility for a particular group of subjects; seven were responsible for art, four for modern languages, three for dress, one for music, dance and drama and one for men's technical studies and practical subjects. One large institute had a second full-time member of staff employed as a head of department in charge of a branch of the main institute.

Following the reorganization a good deal more attention was paid to training. Hitherto it had been left to individuals to avail themselves of general courses that might be appropriate. Sporadic courses were also run by individual inspectors and principals did what they could in the limited amount of time at their disposal. In the early 1960s conferences were arranged for principals, deputy principals and instructors-in-charge at weekends and a programme of courses devised for new part-time tutors as well as courses in specialized subject areas. Principals and later vice-principals were encouraged to attend courses and conferences including, for example, the Diploma of Adult Education offered by the University of Nottingham. The increasing use of audio-visual equipment in institutes led to more part-time tutors attending the ILEA's Wandsworth Technical College course in visual aids. By the end of the 1960s institutes were themselves arranging courses for part-time staff; specialist full-time staff were also giving instruction. Between 600 and 700 part-time teachers attended courses organized by the ILEA's inspectorate or the staff of non-vocational adult institutes in each of the three years 1966–9. These courses were held at residential weekends or during the day and evening at the ILEA's residential centre at Stoke D'Abernon, Surrey or the other centres in London. Courses for teachers of dress and the crafts were particularly well supported and there is little doubt that the high standard achieved was largely due to the readiness of part-time teachers to undertake training courses. Considering that part-time tutors attended these courses at their own expense, the response was encouraging.

Changing Social Needs

In the early 1960s the growing need for, and interest in, voluntary play groups resulted in a number of requests to the LCC for help, advice and resources. Some institutes made arrangements for pre-school play groups to meet on institute premises and to run associated courses of training for prospective play-group leaders. The original suggestion was for a six-week refresher course and induction courses. Principals soon recognized that, if they ran their own play groups in conjunction with the training courses, it would be possible for more young mothers to attend ordinary day classes. This would help the recruitment of prospective play-group leaders who were themselves usually mothers of young children. Play groups were therefore started to provide demonstration groups in conjunction with the adult course to complement theoretical discussions with practical experience. The response was so lively that it soon became necessary to organize introductory and graded courses for leaders and helpers, planned jointly by the LCC, the Save the Children Fund and the Pre-School Play Groups Association. The courses included practical guidance in story-telling, music and movement and organization; observation of children and training in record-keeping; health and hygiene; and the psychology and emotional background of how children learn and develop. In some areas the courses were requested by voluntary organizations and in others they were offered in response to demands from parents. In 1968–9 there were courses at eleven institutes as well as at Morley College and Goldsmiths' College Department of Adult Studies. Some of them were financially assisted under the Home Office Urban Development Programme.

In 1964 the BBC produced a television programme 'Growth and Play' aimed at helping parents to understand the development of young children. The BBC approached LEAs and adult education centres with a view to setting up discussion groups whose members would watch the programme together and then, led by an experienced tutor, discuss its contents. This was seen by the Assistant Education Officer of the time as an opportunity to involve heads of primary schools and principals of adult education institutes in the education of parents. Approval was given for some twenty-four centres in London with primary-school head teachers, or teachers nominated by them, to be appointed as tutors to each group; some twenty-four groups were eventually established. One interesting incentive was that those primary schools who had no serviceable television set were able, by taking part in the programme, to secure one! The series was quite successful and established an interesting and fruitful contact between a number of heads of primary schools and principals of adult education institutes which led to classes for parents in primary school mathematics, the new approach to science, child-centred learning and child psychology. They proved to be very popular and established a valuable connection between a sector of the population who, by reason of being parents of young children, had not felt able to take advantage of the usual facilities for adult education.

This increased contact with young parents marked an important change in the approach of adult education in London. Hitherto the provision for young married men or women had been through a range of classes geared to their personal needs as adults rather than as parents of young children. Certainly craft classes had given the opportunity for many a young man or woman to help furnish a home and many a young woman to make clothes for herself and her children. The new approach, however, was specifically to them as parents of very young children, often of pre-school age. It was significant because it involved institutes meeting the social needs of a section of the community for whom they had previously not been able to cater. With the increased facilities for day classes, the staff of institutes were quick to see the need for arrangements for caring for young children if young mothers were to be able to attend a class. Institutes found themselves involved in organizing self-help caring for children among the mothers who wished to attend classes and becoming better acquainted with the difficulties of house-bound mothers and their day-to-day problems.

In 1965 the 'general' institutes were renamed adult education institutes – on the face of it not an event of any great importance. Nevertheless, they were the first local education authority institutes providing non-vocational education to be so called. It is necessary to remind ourselves that, even in the mid-1960s, the work of non-vocational institutes was still not regarded by some as *bona fide* adult education. For the London service it was the culmination of the process begun by the 1957–9 reorganization to establish non-vocational education institutes as educational establishments in their own right. The renaming set the seal of their improved status on the institutes; principals and their staff for the first time had a clearer sense of direction. Certainly the renaming coincided with a more overt community consciousness.

The review of men's, women's and literary institutes in 1957–9 had been immediately followed by a review of the social and recreational facilities for young people under eighteen. As a result of that review the constitution and orders of reference of the London Youth Committee and the Borough Youth Committees were revised in order that those bodies should have specific executive as well as advisory functions; a principal county youth-officer post was established and Mr R.W.J. Keeble appointed as the first principal county youth officer for London with effect from 1 August 1960. He was responsible to the Assistant Education Officer (Further Education) for the youth service in London and was directly responsible for the work of the borough youth officers who formerly had worked to the divisional officers. Four senior youth officers were appointed to assist him. It was also decided that recreational institutes should be transformed into sixty youth centres but that this change should be made gradually as principalships of recreational institutes became vacant.

Special provision for youth in the shape of a clubroom, coffee bar, leader's office and some storage space was to be made in four new schools (Daneford, Blakesley, Lollard Street, Whitehouse Lane) at which youth centres would be established; similar provision was to be made as practicable in other large new secondary schools. Where the youth centre and an adult institute operated in the same building the two services were to act as separate entities and not as a combined institution. 'General institutes would not be asked to admit unduly large numbers of young people into their classes.' Youth centres would be controlled by youth officers and part-time wardens who would service the needs of voluntary and statutory clubs in the area for activities which required accommodation in the secondary school. The report to the Education Committee in November 1960 stated that the development of the general institute should not be inhibited by the growth of youth centres. There must be close association, said the report, between youth centres and general institutes which should continue to provide facilities for at least some young people between sixteen and twenty-one where this was clearly the most appropriate arrangement either for the individual member or for a group from the youth organization. The arrangement should be flexible and designed to meet the needs of the individual rather than conform to the requirements of an administrative pattern.

In addition to youth centres it was proposed that there should be a general extension of recreational facilities including a purpose-built indoor-sports centre (5000–6000 sq. ft.), two of which were already planned at Westhorne Manor (Woolwich) and Albion Square (Hackney).

The overall effect of this survey of the social and recreational facilities for young people was to delineate clearly the function of the youth service and to emphasize the partnership between the statutory and voluntary sector throughout London. Whilst principals of adult general institutes gave a tempered welcome to the delineation of the function of youth centres which would remove some of the difficulties caused by the recruitment of adults into recreational institutes, they viewed with some concern the expansion of the provision for young people in separately organized youth centres housed in secondary schools at which branches of general institutes had been established. At the time of the review some 13,000–14,000 young people under twenty-one and about 5000 under the age of eighteen were attending general institutes.

Throughout the 1960s there is no doubt that demands on school accommodation from the school itself, general institutes and youth centres, particularly for large spaces in schools for physical activities, grew alarmingly. Where there was good co-operation not only between the principal and youth officer concerned but more particularly by the tutor-in-charge of the general institute branch and the part-time warden of the youth centre there was a sensible allocation of space. Activities of young people most likely to disrupt the activities of adults were separately provided for, to the mutual benefit of both sectors. On the other hand there were many instances of classes provided by the general institute and almost identical classes by the youth centre which could, with advantage, have been amalgamated.

Up to 1962 one assistant education officer had direct responsibility for further and higher education which covered all non-vocational and vocational further and higher education establishments. In 1962 the administrative structure of the further education service in London was reviewed and the work of the former further education branch was divided between two new branches concerned with further and higher education respectively. The assistant education officer (further education) was made responsible for those services primarily concerned with young people in the transition from school to work and/or further education; with non-vocational adult education, with the colleges for further education which, in London, were primarily concerned with day-release students in the fifteen to nineteen age group but which also provided full-time courses and evening classes, some of which were concerned with non-vocational activities for young people; with the youth service and the youth employment service. Not only did this reorganization group the services that were concerned with young people during the transition from school to work and/or further education it also grouped the non-vocational services of adult education and youth work – a most important consideration in the light of the review of the two services then recently undertaken. Although the review of the youth service had emphasized the separateness of the youth service and its lower-age range was below the age of admission to an adult education institute, the two services were obviously very closely related and many young people over the age of sixteen could use the facilities of either or both services. By the end of the 1960s this relationship was to become a major issue.

One particular aspect of this relationship was brought into renewed prominence by the emphasis given in the youth review to the partnership between the statutory and voluntary agencies. As we have seen, on the purely adult education side the LCC had, for many years, aided the non-statutory section of the work which was complementary to the Council's direct provision. From the inception of the University of London's extra-mural classes the LCC had provided accommodation and given both them and the WEA grant-aid. Morley College, Toynbee Hall, the Mary Ward Settlement and Goldsmiths' College Department of Adult Studies had received regular grant-aid from the Council for their significant contribution to adult education in London. In 1968–9 grant-aid to these establishments, together with the Royal School of Needlework and the College of the Sea, totalled £210,000. In addition, assistance was given to the Working Men's College (£3000 in 1968–9) and a grant of thirty shillings a class was given to the WEA and the University of London for extra-mural classes, the grants totalling £540 to the WEA and £10,000 to the University of London in that year.

By 1961 community centres and settlements were receiving grant aid varying from £140 per annum to £705 per annum (a total of £4588 for 1961–2). In 1964 it was decided to allow grant towards assistant-warden salaries; grant was also paid at the rate of 75 per cent of salary for youth-leadership work at four centres. The scheme for aiding community centres approved by the LCC and continued by the

ILEA provided for a grant towards salaries, the amount to be decided having regard to the financial needs of the centre, the amount of educational work conducted at the centre and the salary scales prescribed by the Joint Negotiating Committee for youth leaders and community centre wardens. The centres aided by the ILEA were mostly settlements involved in general supportive community work which varied from centre to centre. One centre, for example, aided by the ILEA for the first time in 1966–7, was engaged in work with educationally subnormal adults, delinquent boys, a club for ex-mental-hospital patients and a holiday play-group for children.

The ILEA also regarded the training of voluntary workers as educational work qualifying for aid. Grants in 1968–9, made to thirteen voluntary centres, totalled £15,000 and individual grants ranged from £800 to £880. Applications from settlements and other organizations for grants for their youth work often spilled over into applications for the other community work in which they were engaged. In many instances it was difficult to separate *bona fide* claims for youth work from the other work of a settlement which appeared to them to qualify equally for a grant. Such applications required some fine judgement as to whether the work being done was educational or social.

Two aspects of community work by voluntary agencies with an undoubted educational content emerged during the 1960s, both of which were to lead to a substantial commitment by the adult education service; they were illiteracy among adults and the education of immigrants. Cambridge House Settlement in Camberwell, in the course of its general work in the community, came across a number of adult men and women who were unable to read or write adequately and so began a service to help them by recruiting volunteer men and women who were prepared to teach an individual man or woman on a one-to-one basis. By the middle 1960s the settlement was offering an extensive service to adults with reading and writing difficulties, over the greater part of the London area, by recruiting and training volunteers and matching them with an adult in need in their area. A grant towards the salary of the organizer of this service was paid by the LCC for the first time in 1965 and was later increased to provide the salary of full-time workers and clerical assistants.

A similar service was being undertaken at the same settlement for newly arrived immigrants who needed help in language, both to cope with the social demands of working, shopping and mixing in their neighbourhoods and with their children's school development. These immigrants were not at a stage, or lacked the confidence, to join a class in an adult education institute. The LCC aided this, too, by contributing towards the salary of the organizer of the service to immigrants.

Both these schemes were an illustration of the kind of educational work which could be undertaken by a voluntary organization, such as a settlement, in helping individual men and women to reach a stage when they could be taught in a group in an adult education institute. Most adult institutes had what they called a general education class for men and women who felt that their basic education was insufficient. In many institutes this was a mixture of native speakers of English and immigrants whose native language was not English. In general the latter were predominant. Their inability to write English was understood and when they came to enrol, such writing as was necessary was done for them. With the English-speaking adult the situation was very different; he or she had to admit to someone, who might or might not understand, that he was illiterate. The genuinely illiterate adult was therefore not very likely to enrol at an adult education institute. Even those who had been sufficiently prepared by the Cambridge House Literacy Scheme to take their place in a general education class at an insti-tute, very rarely felt confident enough to leave the security of their one-to-one instruction by a volunteer. It was to be some years before this situation was to be tackled.

The question of helping immigrants was rather different. For many hundreds of years the population of London, particularly in the East End, had been used to absorbing immigrants from non-English-speaking countries. Voluntary organizations and statutory evening continuation schools and evening institutes had made special provision for them to learn English and be helped with their general education. In the 1930s many non-English-speaking Jews had found a haven in the Yiddish communities in London and many learned English in London's evening institutes. When large numbers of non-English-speaking immigrants began to arrive in the 1950s many came to the institutes seeking help with their educational problems and, above all, in learning the language. Rather than separate them into special classes principals at that time thought it best to give them basic educational help in the existing framework of the general education class. Immigrants who were educationally more advanced often found the tuition they required, in language and other subjects, in the various vocational educational establishments maintained by the LCC. Institutes therefore tended to attract those immigrants who needed a wide range of educational and social help in addition to language. By contact with voluntary and other local organizations, including community relations offices, by leaflets printed in many languages, by approaches through children in schools, principals tried to make the facilities in institutes known to the immigrants.

In some areas concentrations of immigrants meant that large numbers of students enrolled in one branch and here it was possible to organize a variety and progression of classes to meet the needs of different groups of students. Classes were graded into beginners, intermediate and advanced; special classes were provided for students who needed help with speech, with reading and writing, with English manners and customs or some other particular aspect. The needs of students were diagnosed by tests on enrolment. Some branches experimented with alternative classes in which the methods of teaching reading were based on the methods to which the immigrants had been accustomed in their countries of origin – grammar-based or situational or look-and-say.

In some branches, as a result of a less concentrated immigrant settlement, a few immigrant students were enrolled in general education classes. Here tutors could not be given well-graded classes and they had to cope, by group methods, with classes in which there was a wide range of abilities and attainments. The picture changed from year to year in every institute. A flood of immigrants from a part of the world which had hitherto not sent many immigrants to this country would present the tutor with students with a different linguistic reference. There was a tremendous variety of students. West Indians spoke and wrote English and had some schooling but used different structures and vocabulary, accepted in their own island but not in England; having been taught to read by a phonic method, they had a peculiar and typical difficulty in comprehension. Nigerians read and wrote English fairly well but their accent was not comprehensible in England. Arabic writers had eyes and hands accustomed to move acrosss the page from right to left. There were men, and more especially women, of all nationalities who were illiterate in their own languages and had never been to school. In some cases they had never held a writing implement.

Of all the problems the most intractable was to attract and teach in class women from the countries where women are still segregated. The story is told in one report of a successful effort to bring in and teach the section of the immigrant population which had been most difficult to reach, the Muslim women. The principal of Central Wandsworth Institute, attending by invitation the local consultative committees of head teachers, learned that the progress in English of Pakistani children in their schools was being held up because the mothers knew no English, so that, as soon as the children arrived home, they spoke and heard no more English. It was agreed to start to tackle the problem in one school where the proportion of children from Pakistan was high. Notes were sent to mothers through the children in the school informing them that a class was being formed for them in a room in the school during the day. No Pakistani mothers presented themselves, though two Japanese women did enrol.

Wandsworth Council for Community Relations was now in being and the principal was a member of its education committee, on which members of both native and immigrant origin served. A social evening was arranged at the school at which there was to be a cookery demonstration – making an apple pie. Members of the committee made personal calls, inviting the women and persuading the husbands to give their co-operation. The party was held and twenty Pakistani women attended. Great care was exercised to avoid offending any susceptibilities. The women were invited to enrol in the class and they were also introduced to the tutor. This party took place in April 1968 and, by July 1969, the original enrollment had grown to four classes.

By far the greatest number of tutors of these classes were day school teachers with an ordinary background of training in general teaching. Particularly useful were primary school teachers and teachers of remedial classes who were familiar with problems of teaching writing and reading. Short, inservice training courses were held once or twice every year to give them some further knowledge of the special techniques of teaching English as a second language, and of the special problems of adult illiterates. In general, however, it was found that what they needed in their work was sympathy, conviction and sound general-teaching ability, rather than special skills in the teaching of English as a foreign language. There were also a small number of teachers of these classes who themselves originated in the West Indies, in India or Pakistan or in Africa. Tutors found that teaching of English and other basic subjects had to be accompanied by their personal support. This might involve simply a sympathetic attention while the student talked about his own life, or excursions of many kinds in evenings or weekends, or help with letter-writing, form-filling, and even job and room hunting. Lessons were usually based on the interests of the students, discovered in this way. At the time of the Motor Show, for example, car manufacturers' brochures were common 'text books' in general education classes; mail-order catalogues of dresses or furniture were frequent sources of material. The Highway Code was a group reader in many a class where some students had ambitions to work as lorry drivers.

The immigrant student was not always confined to the general education class. The immigrant student who joined the badminton class learned English from other students; the women who joined a cookery or dressmaking class often made faster progress with their command of English than in the general-English class. Institutes organized special short courses in cookery and dressmaking for immigrants who perhaps had not been familiar with the working of a gas stove or with buying cloth in England to make their children's dresses.

There was one sector of the adult education service – namely that operating in HM prisons – which had been dealing with the problem of illiteracy among adults for a number of years and was aware of its increasing prevalence. Education in the five major prisons in London had been provided by men's institutes and one women's institute and, after the 1957–9 reorganization, by general institutes and later adult education institutes: in Brixton Prison by Clapham and Balham Institute, in Holloway by North Hackney Institute, in Pentonville by Holloway Institute, in Wandsworth by Battersea Institute and in Wormwood Scrubs by Addison Institute. Before 1 April 1953 expenses incurred by local authorities in connection with education in prisons and borstals had been treated as a rate-borne service attracting the usual grant from the Ministry of Education. After 1 April

1953 local authorities were reimbursed by the Home Office the full net cost of the education services.

Basic education ranked high among the classes provided as well as courses aimed at assisting the illiterate or semi-literate to master the arts of reading and writing. It is interesting to note that, in the 1960s, there was strong evidence to link illiteracy with recidivism and that, at Pentonville, a scheme had been developed whereby some literate students were given brief training to enable them to assist their less able colleagues with these basic skills. Since most students at that prison had short sentences the training of those student helpers had become a permanent feature of the tutor/organizer's work. By the end of the 1960s each prison except Brixton had a full-time tutor/organizer and, in addition, there were four full-time lecturers at Wormwood Scrubs and one full-time lecturer at Wandsworth. A part-time tutor/organizer was employed at Brixton. Tutor/organizers were supported by a large body of part-time teachers; for example, some sixty at Wormwood Scrubs and forty at Wandsworth.

The problem of education in prisons was, as now, that it had to accept the overriding claims of the prison administration for security, for the need to see prisoners as convicted offenders and not, as the education service needs to see them, as students. The pressures on London prisons had made it virtually impossible to provide accommodation that, by any educational standards, could be regarded as adequate. There were indications, however, that the Home Office was beginning to remedy this situation but that it would be some time before improvements could begin to make themselves felt. Classes were being held in open halls, in inadequately heated rooms, in adapted cells, in chapels, libraries, vaults, in rooms adjoining noisy machinery and wherever else space could be found. There had, however, been a welcome increase to a total of nine in the number of full-time teaching staff during 1968. A policy statement issued by the Home Office in 1969 gave some hope that the place of education in prisons was being seen as an increasingly significant factor in the rehabilitation of prisoners. The appointment of a Chief Education Officer in the prison department was an indication of the increased concern.

The growth of the number of welfare classes is to be seen in the record of student/teacher hours which were exempt from the calculation of the institutes thirteen to one ratio. In 1961–2 the number of student hours exempted from the ratio calculation was, for literary institutes, 14,043 and, for general institutes, 475,117; the number of teacher hours was, for literary institutes, 1855 and, for general institutes, 37,349. For 1969–70 the figure for literary institutes was 28,260 and for general institutes 1,151,811 student hours; teacher hours for literary institutes were 4211 and for general institutes 96,049. The figures for literary institutes were those for the education of deaf students at the City Literary Institute. The figures indicate that the provision for the deaf doubled in the eight years concerned and provision of welfare classes in general (adult education) institutes almost trebled. This increase, together with the increased concern for the social needs of members of their local community, give a very clear indication of the changing community role of the adult education institutes in the London scene.

The London Government Act 1963

The London Government Act of 1963 abolished the London County Council; the Greater London Council which took over most of the LCC's former functions did not become the education authority. 'Attempts, reminiscent of those in 1902 and 1903, were made to divide responsibility for education between the London boroughs and the GLC (as recommended by the Herbert Commission), but the combined resistance of the London Education Service and the Ministry of Education prevented the break-up of London as an education area, and with a few minor, tidying, adjustments the education service for London continued to be provided over the area originally drawn up for the Metropolitan Board of Works in the middle of the last century.'[2]

The Inner London Education Authority became the new education authority for London and the former LCC education service remained virtually intact. Technically the ILEA was a special committee of the GLC but with autonomous financial powers to raise finance by precepts on the inner London boroughs and the City of London. The members of the authority comprised forty GLC councillors representing the twelve inner London boroughs and the City and thirteen members appointed by the Inner London Borough Councils and the City. The ILEA operates through an Education Committee to which up to nine additional members are appointed and four main sub-committees, one of which, the Further and Higher Education sub-committee, has the responsibility for adult education.

No service would have suffered more than the adult education service had the education functions of the LCC been distributed to the boroughs. It had always been a close-knit service and the 1957–59 reorganization, with its removal of the barriers between men's and women's institutes and the literary institutes, concentrated and consolidated it still more. Moreover, it had always been directly controlled from County Hall – a control which had left principals free to develop and respond to local needs. The steps taken as a result of the 1957–9 reorganization strengthened the support from the centre and increased the responsibility and local autonomy of principals.

Too frequently central control is thought of as an impersonal, anonymous bureaucracy. The management section exclusively concerned with London's adult education institutes in the 1960s consisted of no more than three to four people. The relations between them and principals were friendly and personal.

There were no long chains of command and principals came direct to the Assistant Education Officer and he to them, either individually or at regular meetings and conferences. More important perhaps was (and is) the support principals received from each other. There are no more assiduous attenders of each others' exhibitions and social events than London adult education principals; no group more concerned for each others' personal welfare in times of sickness or bereavement. The communication network has to be experienced to be believed. One senior officer used to reckon it took about thirty minutes for news to get round to London principals. If it was very good news it took a little longer because it was examined more closely during its passage from principal to principal in order to uncover any 'snags'. The close collaboration and mutual support given by principals to each other is an important factor in a service which, if it is to respond quickly to people's needs, must be innovatory and flexible.

The ILEA came into being in 1965 with Mr (later Sir) Ashley Bramall as its first Chairman.* Mr James Young was Chairman of the Education Committee and Mrs B (later Baroness) Serota, Vice-Chairman. Sir Harold Shearman was appointed Chairman of the Further and Higher Education/sub-committee and Mrs (later Dame) Margaret Cole Vice-Chairman. It was particularly appropriate that these two distinguished educationalists, both with their roots in adult education, who had contributed so much to the London education service, should be Chairman and Vice-Chairman of the first Further and Higher Education sub-committee. The record of office of Sir Harold Shearman and Dame Margaret Cole illustrates a feature of London's education administration which is not always adequately recognized, namely, the remarkable continuity of partnerships among its leaders which gave them an unrivalled depth of knowledge and experience of London and its education service. Both had held early office in the sub-committee concerned with further and higher education. Sir Harold, after two years as Vice-Chairman, succeeded Mrs Helen Bentwich as Chairman of the Higher Education sub-committee when, in 1947, that great champion of women's institutes became Chairman of the Education Committee. Dame Margaret, after a year as Vice-Chairman to Mr Ronald McKinnon Wood, another strong supporter of adult institutes, became Chairman of the Further Education sub-committee when Mr McKinnon Wood became Chairman of the Education Committee in 1949. She remained Chairman of the Further Education sub-committee, apart from two years as Vice-Chairman, until 1965 – a quite remarkable record. Meanwhile Sir Harold had, from 1950, been Vice-Chairman and, from 1954 to 1961, Chairman of the Education Committee. The Chairman and Vice-Chairman of the ILEA Further and Higher Education sub-committee were therefore continuing a

---

* The designation Leader of the ILEA was first used in 1967. Sir Ashley Bramall was Leader from 1970–81.

collaboration begun some twenty-two years before when both had been co-opted to the LCC Education Committee as people with special educational experience.

In 1967, for the first time since 1934, the education service came under the control of a Conservative Party administration. Mr Christopher Chataway was brought in from outside the ranks of elected members as the Leader of the ILEA. Mr Frank Abbott was Chairman of the ILEA and the Education Committee. Dr Gerard Vaughan was appointed Chairman of the Further and Higher Education sub-committee but was succeeded by Mr Michael Grylls in 1968; Lady Walton, for many years Chairman of the Governing Council of Morley College, who had led for the opposition on the Further Education Sub-Committee, became Vice-Chairman. Serving a Conservative administration was a unique experience for even long-serving officers. After years of being attuned to the policies of a Labour administration and serving LCC members with a long and deep experience of London's government, they found themselves advising and informing a group of mainly young men with demanding careers outside local government. Most of them became MPs in the next Conservative government.

12. The Years of Enquiry and Review: 1969-73

The Crowther Committee on the further education of the fifteen to eighteens (1959); the Robbins Report on Higher Education (1963); the Newsom Committee on the education of schoolchildren aged thirteen to sixteen of average and less than average ability (1963) and the Plowden Committee on the education of the primary-school child (1967) had accorded the accolade and stimulus of a national enquiry to these fields. The Youth Development Council in two committees chaired by Mr Andrew Fairbairn and Dr F.W. Milson were examining the role of the youth service in the late 1960s. Throughout the 1960s the demand for adult education, despite successive prunings in periodic economic crises, had far outstripped that of pre-war years. With it had grown a demand for greater central government recognition of the role of adult education as an integral part of the education service. Moreover, there had been no major review of the whole field of adult education since the final report of the adult education committee of the Ministry of Reconstruction in 1919.

In February 1969 a committee of enquiry was set up by the Secretary of State for Education and Science (Edward Short) under the chairmanship of Sir Lionel Russell, CBE, the former Chief Education Officer for Birmingham, 'to assess the need for and to review the provision of non-vocational adult education in England and Wales; to consider the appropriateness of existing educational, administrative and financial policies; and to make recommendations with a view to obtaining the most effective and economical deployment of available resources to enable adult education to make its proper contribution to the national system of education conceived of as a process continuing through life'.

Although the ILEA was consulted on the advisability and need for such an enquiry, no one from the authority was invited to serve on the Russell Committee. The authority decided to present written evidence to the Committee and a small working group of officers and inspectors under the chairmanship of the Assistant Education Officer (Further Education) was set up to prepare it. The preparation of evidence provided a welcome opportunity for the ILEA to review the progress of adult education in inner London since the reorganization of the service in 1957-9. In the event, this review was to prove to be the first of a number of enquiries undertaken by the ILEA in this field over the next four years. They were to have a profound effect on the development of the adult education service.

224

The ILEA's evidence to the Russell Committee and the reports of the various working groups – *A Chance to Choose*, *The Social Structure of the Student Body of Adult Education Institutes* and *An Education Service for the Whole Community* – have all been published. Nevertheless, their inter-relationship and contribution to the development of the adult education service at this watershed in its history are such as to demand rather more than a reference to the published text. This chapter, therefore, is an account of how they came about and the salient issues which they covered, in the belief that they are essential to an appreciation of the subsequent shaping of the inner London adult education service.

The Review of the Youth and Adult Services

It soon became apparent to the working party preparing evidence for the Russell Committee that there were issues emerging which could affect the future development of adult education and, therefore, the evidence which the ILEA might wish to present to the Russell Committee. We have seen how the adult institutes themselves were developing a heightened community consciousness. The ILEA, through its youth service, was giving strong financial support to voluntary organizations, such as settlement and community associations, for youth work with which the ILEA's youth officers were in close touch. Many of the voluntary organizations so aided, also provided social and educational facilities for adults complementary to that offered in adult education institutes. Unlike the youth work there was no formalized grant structure or yardstick by which to measure the adult education work of these organizations and, whilst it was relatively easy for them to secure grant for youth work, a great deal of haggling and subjective appraisal went on before grant was given to their work with adults. To the voluntary organizations any division of this overall community work into youth and adult appeared, to say the least, arbitrary.

On the statutory side there was growing concern at the failure of the youth service to attract school leavers or members of the sixteen – twenty-one age group generally. Adult education institutes were attracting a substantial number of under-eighteens. Although there were notable exceptions, the hopes that youth centres and adult institutes operating in the same large secondary-school premises would avoid duplicating classes, were generally unfulfilled. In consequence a divisive and overlapping provision too often resulted. In the mid-1960s, in order to build a closer relationship between youth centres at large secondary schools and the school itself, the ILEA introduced full-time posts of tutor wardens who would have a commitment to a particular aspect of the school curriculum and be in charge of the youth centre. Such appointments were made only when the head of the secondary school had requested such an appointment, usually after a good deal of consultation with senior officers of the Further Education Branch. The

London Youth Committee had registered the need for a review of the 1960 youth-service provision and this had been approved by the Further and Higher Education sub-committee. Nationally the results of a review of youth work by two committees under the chairmanship of Mr Andrew Fairbairn and Dr F. Milson were awaiting publication although their contents were already widely known.

This piecemeal patchwork of provision seemed at odds with the developing sense of community in both the youth and adult services and the Education Officer (Sir William Houghton) set up, in addition to that preparing evidence to the Russell Committee, another working group of senior officers from the youth service and the inspectorate under the chairmanship of the Assistant Education Officer (Further Education). This working group was briefed to examine the possibility of a more coherent and co-ordinated pattern and policy for the education of the community (youth and adult), which might be projected in the evidence to the Russell Committee. Apart from all the other considerations the planning of the new Thamesmead Estate, virtually a new town, presented an opportunity for community provision *ab initio* which was unlikely ever to be repeated, and officers were very conscious of the need for some clarification of policy. The working group produced a report which was approved by the Education Officer on 7 June 1969 and presented as document ILEA 388 to the Further and Higher Education sub-committee on 10 July 1969.[1]

The report set out the various factors, indicated above, leading to the need for a review and referred to the growing tendency to view community services as a whole. It noted that, 'The provision for young people on the one hand and for adults on the other can no longer be looked at separately and any review of the one must include the review of the other.' It examined the present position as far as the organization of adult education was concerned, making the point that from as early as 1913 the appointment of full-time principals had given recognition to their social role in which the successful principal became an important figure in the local community and 'an interpreter of the community's recreational and cultural needs'.

Some 21,000 young people under twenty-one had enrolled in adult institutes in 1967–8. In the youth service the number of recreational institutes had now been reduced to six and there were twenty-six youth centres. *Bona fide* members of youth clubs were admitted free to both. In 1967–8 the number of young people enrolled in recreational institutes and youth centres was 39,000. At the time of the report there were nine tutor-warden posts, graded as Burnham Lecturer 1 with a responsibility allowance. About 25 percent of the warden's time was spent as a member of the staff of the school and 75 per cent as youth centre warden based on school premises. The report drew attention also to the provision for non-vocational activities for young people being made in colleges for further education; it noted that some colleges were now beginning to offer recreational opportunities in the evening and students and their friends in the locality were starting to make wider use of them.

The report argued that adult institutes were already bringing a cross-section of the community together in a range of practical and cultural pursuits but that the opportunity presented for joint action with the youth service by the location of youth centres and institutes in the same school premises was not being used. There was growing concern about the seeming inability of the youth service to satisfy the needs of more than a small minority of young people and a growing realization that it could not continue to operate in isolation from the community and society at large. The need was, therefore, to provide for continuity of growth and development to bridge the gulf which so often separated young people from the older generation. Many voluntary organizations, aided by the ILEA, catered for both youth and adults. Whereas the ILEA youth officers were in close contact with the youth work of these agencies, there was no comparable relationship with the important community field-work for adults. Although this work did not necessarily lead to a demand for formal classes, it was an important preliminary activity for an adult education service.

The report therefore proposed the merging of the youth and adult services in an education community service. The ILEA's separate youth and adult education establishments would be brought together in single establishments which, under one principal, would cater for the full range of education and community needs. This would include separate provision, where appropriate, for some youth activities.

To implement the proposed reorganization there would be an extension of the existing tutor-warden joint school/further education appointments. Instead of being in charge of youth centres they would be responsible to the principal of the adult education institute for the continuing development of an informal programme for young adults stemming from their outward-looking programme of informal education in the field of liberal studies in the school.

A closer partnership with voluntary organizations was proposed in which an outreach approach both to young people and adults would be predominant. Youth officers would increasingly be relieved of the direct supervision of youth centres and the formal class aspect, as the number of tutor-wardens grew. Youth officers would become advisers to the voluntary sector for fieldwork for both youth and adults and would be restyled, it was suggested, as education community officers. The principal youth officer would become the principal education community officer responsible for the team of fieldworkers to the Assistant Education Officer for Further Education and would also be responsible for advising and directing a training and retraining programme. Borough youth committees would become ILEA education community committees and would advise the

ILEA on youth and community provision and development with a broader representation basis than just youth. The Inner London Committee of the Greater
London Standing Conference of Voluntary Organizations would be invited to
act as an advisory body to the ILEA on matters relating to voluntary organizations and would be asked to set up, in conjunction with the London Council
of Social Service, a panel to advise the ILEA on the training needs of voluntary
organizations in youth and community work. It was expected that the transformation would be effected gradually and would involve a retraining programme for youth officers. The Further and Higher Education sub-committee
reported these proposals to the Education Committee on 16 July 1969 and authorized the Education Officer to discuss them with all interested parties; when their
views were known the Committee would give detailed consideration to the
suggestions.

The report met with strong opposition from the minority party (Labour) in the
Education Committee. A leader in *The Times Educational Supplement*, doubtless
inspired by some of the reactions against any merging of the youth service,
accused the report of paying no more than lip-service to the current thought of
attracting the unattached and advised 'London, which has done so much in the
past to make a success of the partnership between statutory and voluntary work in
both the youth service and adult education field, would do well to think hard
before burying its youth service in an ill-defined community service.' The opposition to the report was concentrated on the suggested merger of the youth service
and paid little or no attention to the need to support the work with adults in
voluntary organizations also engaged in youth work. Outside London the report
attracted considerable interest and support, reflecting as it did many of the views
which were later to be published in the Milson and Fairbairn reports.

The timetable for the submission of evidence to the Russell Committee had
already been overrun and it was decided to submit that evidence without waiting
for the outcome of the youth and adult services review. If need be the ILEA could
either submit an addendum to the evidence or introduce it in the oral evidence
that they were to give later in 1970. The evidence to the Russell Committee was
submitted to the Further and Higher Education sub-committee on 11 February
1970 and approved by the Education Committee for submission to the Russell
Committee on 18 February 1970. It is notable that the statement of evidence was
commended by both the majority Conservative group and the Labour group
except for one point to which reference will be made later.

The ILEA Evidence to the Russell Committee[2]

The necessity to present evidence to the Russell Committee gave the ILEA a
unique opportunity to review the adult education service, to state or restate what

it believed to be the aims of adult education and to set out the present and future means of achieving these aims.

The evidence made two specially important contributions to the national scene:

1. the survey of students undertaken by the ILEA's Research and Statistics Division put the spotlight on those who were not being served by the ILEA – which had done more than most to make facilities widely available;
2. its detailed consideration of the effect on student enrolment of the level of fees charged.

A survey of students, included in the evidence to the Russell Committee, was of particular concern to the ILEA and the London service but, because of the size and scope of the London provision, it was also of general interest. The four questions which the Further Education Branch, the Branch responsible for the administration of the adult education institutes, decided it would like to be able to answer were:

1. who are the students?
2. what age group do they represent?
3. do they live or work locally, and by extension does the institute provide for the locality?
4. how far are we providing for all classes and types?

The detailed survey and report was attached as an appendix to the ILEA's evidence.[3] From a sample of just under 10,000 students the survey showed that two thirds of the students were women as compared with just over half in the adult population in inner London as a whole. The average age of students was comparatively low, thirty-five years; two fifths were aged between twenty-one and thirty-five years. The average age of 'adult' students (that is, those aged twenty-one and over) was about thirty-eight years as compared with forty-six for the London population. Seven per cent of the students were over sixty-five. The most striking factor revealed by the survey was, however, the dominance of non-manual work in the occupations of students. In the London employed population just under half were in non-manual jobs and only one in ten in professional or managerial; in the survey, four fifths were in non-manual jobs and one quarter in professional/managerial occupations. The other interesting point was that one fifth were housewives, a further 5 per cent retired or unemployed while 2½ per cent were students; that is, between one quarter and one third were not employed.

The survey was of great interest and value to the ILEA, its officers and those engaged in the adult education service. Those involved with the service were well aware that adult education institutes reflected the improved education in schools and that the majority of students were below the age of thirty-five. They also knew that the majority of students came from the locality of a branch or a head-quarters' building, except in the central London institutes. But − most principals would have claimed that they were serving the whole community and that there was a good spread of students from each social class. The survey showed just how atypical the student population was as compared with the London population as a whole, and confirmed the views of those who had been critical of the service for meeting only a middle-class need. The differences at the other end of the scale were even more striking − only 4 per cent of students were in semi-skilled and unskilled jobs compared with 31 per cent in the London-employed population as a whole. To those who had thought of the service as providing for the whole range of social class, this was a shattering statistic. It has to be noted that 4 per cent represented the proportion of students in the overall student body; the percentage varied considerably from one institute to another. The overall average for manual occupations was 14 per cent, ranging from Central London with 5.6 per cent to Lansbury with 36.6 per cent; ten institutes had more than 21.7 per cent. The proportion of students in semi-skilled and unskilled occupations ranged from 0 per cent at Eltham Institute to 10 per cent at the Walworth Institute; thirteen institutes had more than 4 per cent. Also there was no evidence to show how many of the substantial number of housewives were the wives of semi-skilled or unskilled workers. The statistics for housewives in themselves were interesting. The overall average percentage of housewives was 21.7 per cent which ranged between 6.1 per cent at Kensington to 42.8 per cent at Church-down. Fifteen institutes had more than 21.7 per cent.

The virtual absence of any significant number of students in semi-skilled or unskilled occupations indicated that either there had been a significant shift in the emphasis of the work of adult education institutes since the war or that a substantial section of the working population of London (30 per cent) felt that facilities offered by the institutes had no particular relevance to them. Whatever the cause, for so significant a proportion of the working population to be absent from the student body of these institutes was clearly a matter of major concern. This concern was registered by the London principals and officers and members of the inspectorate before the evidence was approved by the Further Education sub-committee. Indeed, at the sub-committee at which the evidence was considered for approval, the Assistant Education Officer was able to report the receipt from the Association of Principals of a request for a working party to examine further the social structure of the student body.

Another aspect of the evidence − the effect of fees on enrolments − was not irrelevant to this social structure. From time to time, throughout the country, particularly at times of economic difficulty, local education authorities increased fees for adult education classes; they had been encouraged in this by successive

Conservative Governments. The ILEA's evidence to the Russell Committee examined the effect of fees on enrolment. Starting from the three major principles set out in the introduction to the evidence, namely, that adult education was necessary, integral to the education system and the duty of all education authorities to provide; that it should be readily available to all who want it; and that quality and variety were of paramount importance, the statement argued that all activities and subjects of study should be dealt with on the same basis. 'As the underlying aim is the same irrespective of the form of pursuit it is accordingly inappropriate to regard any activity as being more important than or as having greater ascendancy over another.'[4] Against this background it set out guiding principles, observed by the ILEA and formerly by the LCC, in determining the level of fees to be charged to students taking non-vocational classes:

(i) That non-vocational adult education is an integral and proper part of the educational provision.
(ii) That it should be readily available to all who wish to take advantage of it.
(iii) That a fee should be charged to act as some guarantee of the seriousness of intent on the part of the student.
(iv) That the fee should not be set at such a level as to prevent any significant number of people from making use of the provision.
(v) That no person should be deprived of the opportunity for attending classes because of his inability to pay the fee.
(vi) That fees should not vary for different levels of work or subjects of study. Implicit in this is that minority and specialist interest and advanced studies should be provided for without additional charge.[5]

The evidence presented clearly indicated that the level of fees charged for non-vocational classes was a matter of considerable importance, since too large a fee or too sharp an increase could be damaging to the fabric of the service and detrimental to the provision that was available to the community. It was apparent, too, that increases in fees affected first those who most needed the adult education service. The modest increases in fees made over the previous three years had decreased the enrolments of mothers with young children and of young people working in London and living away from home. Nearly 11,000 (approximately 6 per cent) of all students enrolled qualified for reduction of fees on grounds of hardship or because they were retired citizens.

The latest available figures showed that the average cost per student hour at adult education and literary institutes in the area of the ILEA was approximately 5s. Each student attended, on average, for sixty-four hours a session which meant that the cost per student amounted to approximately £16. The fee of 42s. 6d. which the student paid for one class per session was equivalent therefore to about 13 per cent of the actual cost. To charge the economic cost of a two-hour class would clearly exclude a large number of people. To charge no fee at all would remove a considerable amount of administrative cost but would tend to encourage frivolous enrolment. The evidence rejected any suggestion that there should be different fees for different subjects on the grounds of the difficulty of saying that one subject was more educationally relevant than another.

In London the fee charged both under the LCC and the ILEA had been a registration fee which had roughly represented 10 per cent of the cost. The evidence had adduced that fees do affect enrolment and that some types of students were decidedly discouraged from joining classes if higher fees were charged.

> Since the object of the Adult Education Service is to encourage all sections of the community to follow an interest together and since in the very doing of it there is a valuable social education, it is difficult to consider charging a fee which will exclude various sections of the population. The evidence of the students survey already suggests that some sections do not use the facilities and there is a strong feeling among officers who have known the institutes for a long time that this is a new situation and that the present student body no longer presents the cross-section that at one time it did. If this is so, and the object of the adult education provision by the Authority remains as it has always been to provide an opportunity for any man or woman to develop his individual talents or interests, then it is difficult to consider fees which represent more than a modest percentage of the actual cost.[6]

The suggestion that certain areas in London might be charged a higher fee than others was dealt with by a reminder that, like other large cities, London had its deprived areas but they were not so delineated that a specially reduced scale of fees could be applied to them; similarly, more affluent areas had their poor inhabitants. The statement of evidence went on to say that the ILEA felt that it might well be necessary, if more resources were to be provided, to move gradually towards a contribution from users of about 20 per cent, with continuing safeguards for those who would otherwise be prevented through hardship from taking part. As has been indicated above the evidence was approved by a Conservative administration. When the time came for the ILEA to give oral evidence to the Russell Committee the political complexion had changed and a Labour administration was in power. It is significant that the only difference of opinion between the two parties was on this question of fees. In its oral evidence Labour made it clear that for 20 per cent in the written evidence they would wish to substitute 10 per cent.

It is clear from the final section of the written evidence that due note had been taken of the result of the survey of students. The evidence showed that, despite the tremendous development that had taken place over the years in the number of classes, the wider variety of subjects, the continuing increase in the number of students and the special provision which the service made for the disabled and the handicapped, the number of men and women covered each year in the youth and adult service was only about 10 per cent of the population. The survey of students had shown that about 40 per cent of students were first enrolments and that most students had been attending classes for two years. In other words there was a substantial annual turnover of students. Over a period of ten years it was likely that one in three of the people in London had attended non-vocational classes. 'Nevertheless it is clear that there are still large sections of the population which are not sufficiently represented in the student body.'[7]

A passage in the concluding statement indicated the extent to which the ILEA was looking towards a greater community role for the adult education service and greater attention to that section of the population which apparently, since the war, had not seen the relevance of the service.

> The service exists to educate and not just to continue the education of the educated. It is doubtful if the role of adult education in educational priority areas, for example, has been properly thought out, but it must surely have a part to play in these areas. The approach is likely to be very different – a community fieldworker approach with individuals and small groups being helped to determine and satisfy their needs. Such a fieldworker might well be attached to the staff of an adult education institute or employed by a voluntary organization substantially aided by the Authority. There is need for ad hoc accommodation in such areas, where a creche, pre-school playgroup or nursery class can be held and classes or group work at specially reduced rates can be provided for mothers.[8]

The ILEA recognized the need for a much greater emphasis on work with educationally disadvantaged adults and for joint action with voluntary agencies. 'Similarly there are many disadvantaged and/or illiterate men and women who are not at a stage when they can be effectively catered for in a group or class. There is room for the development of more schemes such as that aided by the Authority at Cambridge House Settlement in which volunteers undertake to teach men and women to read and write until they have reached a stage when they can join a general education class.'[9] There was evidence that this approach could be extended to those ethnic minorities who were now very much a part of the London community.

With this increased concern for the disadvantaged and those for whom so far the adult education service had not catered came the conception of adult-education institutes as resource centres 'for a whole range of self programming activities, whether they be for clubs and societies stemming from classes or voluntary organisations or families or individuals. Places where people can work on their own – paint, weave or practise a craft that they have learned in a class or just simply study in congenial adult surroundings. More consideration needs to be given by the community generally to how such provision can be made.'[10]

Throughout the evidence there had been frequent reference to the need for additional accommodation and for central government help by way of a building programme to allow this accommodation to be made available. If a response was to be made to the substantial growth in day classes in the inner London institutes, additional accommodation was essential. In London there were large numbers of people who were on shift work, for example, nurses and transport workers who, together with housewives with young children, could not be adequately catered for until accommodation was available during the day. 'Such accommodation needs to offer amenities and provision for creches. It is significant that the Authority has not felt able to launch an all-out publicity campaign on its provision for adult education in the last ten years, since the natural growth prior to the economy limitation two years' ago has been such that it could very well have been embarrassed by the resultant demand for classes, particularly, but not exclusively, during the day.'[11]

The ILEA's willingness to consider joint schemes with voluntary organizations and others had made little headway in the joint provision of facilities. The hope was nevertheless expressed that approaches to inner London boroughs about the possibility of providing shared facilities, used for adult education and the general public on the sites of new schools, would bear fruit. 'Currently the officers are discussing such a scheme in four Inner London Boroughs, by which accommodation for various sports and school physical education accommodation, together with amenities such as creches and restaurants, can be provided by the borough and the Authority on a school site.'[12] The ILEA saw this joint provision of accommodation, for educational/recreational use by students and the general public, as the means of making a broader community provision (not only creches) for a larger range of activities for a much wider cross-section of the community. Such schemes, however, were dependent on a close partnership in the running of communal facilities by borough councils and the ILEA and the satisfactory working out of joint forms of management and financial contribution – which was not easy. 'There is also the ever present difficulty of acquiring suitable sites in the dense urban situation of London.'[13]

Although no direct reference was made to the review of youth and adult services there was a significant reference to the need for a more integrated approach of the educational non-vocational services to a broader community.

> The development of such schemes (referred to above) is an alternative to what has come to be known as the Egremont pattern,[14] by which communal facilities for the general public are provided as part of the education complex and where the overall supervision of school and adult education provision is undertaken by the headmaster. In Inner London adult education institutes with full-time principals have been developed for a long period. They have become sizeable educational establishments with a specialised professional approach and staff, providing an extensive programme for a densely populated catch-

ment area. The concentration of non-vocational work in such institutes has been possible not only because of the dense population they serve but also because of the extensive provision of vocational further education in the many establishments of further education maintained by the Authority. The London alternative to the Egremont pattern would therefore seem to be the linking of youth and adult service in one institute with a tutor/warden acting as the link between school and the institute and the provision by either a joint scheme for shared facilities or the provision by the Authority itself of additional recreational and communal facilities for students' clubs and societies and the general public. [15]

In the concluding paragraphs of its written evidence the ILEA expressed its concern to protect the fabric of the adult education service in times of financial difficulty and its awareness that, in raising fees, it was in danger of excluding many whom it would most like to see benefit by the service. It reaffirmed its belief that discriminatory fees against particular subjects should be avoided since it was inappropriate to say that one subject was educationally more relevant than another. Whilst welcoming the growth in adult education and the likelihood that it would continue as more and more young people enjoyed a fuller education, it recognized the danger that some sections of the population could become isolated and felt it important 'that real attempts should be made to ensure that the educational development of the community continued outside the classroom as well as in it'. [16] The strength of the London service for more than fifty years had been the employment of full-time principals and, in the last ten years, the appointment of full-time vice-principals and other full-time specialist staff. In the ILEA's view the development and maintenance of good teaching standards through supervision, training and sensitivity to the needs of a dense urban community would be 'virtually impossible' without 'a substantial cadre of full-time professional staff'. Recognizing that the arguments for the importance of adult education, and therefore for its expansion, had to be considered and evaluated in relation to the other stages in the educational process, it hoped that in 'any debate on priorities in education the case for adult education would not go by default . . . we think it proper to state that in consideration of these matters, in any debate, the claims, relevance and contribution of adult education towards the creation and consolidation of a civilised society should be given full weight'. [17]

No one listening to the debate in the Education Committee on 18 February 1970 could doubt that the statement of evidence by the ILEA was meant to be a powerful statement by both the majority and the minority party of the importance attached by the ILEA to its adult education service and of the increasing role that that service would need to play in the education of the whole community in London.

The Review of the Youth and Adult Education Service Continues

The Education Officer's report (Ed. 839)[18], on the result of the consultations on a proposed new education community service, was submitted to the Further and Higher Education sub-committee on 25 February 1970. The report dealt with the consultations and sought approval for a revised scheme, revised terms of reference for relevant staff and revised constitutions for relevant committees. An appendix (A) gave a brief analysis of the views on six major aspects of the proposed scheme, together with other matters raised. Another appendix (B) gave the full text of the observations sent in by those formally consulted, together with individual submissions. Attached also to the report was the draft scheme for the education community service together with papers on the duty of the tutor-warden and the principal education community officer, the senior education community officer and education community officers generally and the terms and reference of the central advisory committee for education community service and the borough education community committees.

The report commented on the six major points which were fundamental to the new scheme, namely, the unification of the youth and adult non-vocational services; a new extended role for youth officers; the role of the tutor-warden; an extended role for borough youth committees as local education community committees; a revised central committee structure; and training.

The Education Officer's report indicated that almost all organizations and committees consulted accepted the proposed integration of the two services with, in some cases, reservations of which the new draft scheme took account. Reference to the text of written comments, given in the appendix to the report, shows that, of the twelve borough youth committees, Camden, Islington, Lambeth and Wandsworth were opposed to unified institutes; Greenwich, Hammersmith, Kensington and Chelsea, and Lewisham were generally in favour of the scheme. Hackney, Tower Hamlets and Westminster, although not wholly opposed to the scheme, had reservations on whether the merging of youth and adult institutes would encourage more young people to use the service. The London Youth Committee was opposed to the scheme but community organizations such as the National Federation of Community Associations and the London Council of Social Service saw it as a step in the right direction. Comments on the substitution of a Standing Conference in place of the London Youth Committee were distinctly unfavourable. The discussions had indicated the need for a closer link between the local committees and the Further and Higher Education sub-committee and for representation of the voluntary sector at policy-making level.

The Education Officer, therefore, suggested a revised central committee structure to that presented in the former document ILEA 388. He suggested that a new section of the Further and Higher Education sub-committee, with some delegated responsibility for the education community service, should in future deal with policy issues and the scheme of grant-aid. The section would consist of four members of the Further and Higher Education sub-committee, one of whom would be Chairman, together with the Chairman and two other representatives of a Central Committee which would replace the London Youth Committee and represent the voluntary sector and the Borough Education Community Committees.

The Further and Higher Education sub-committee (25 February 1970) approved the setting up of the new education community service as outlined in the draft scheme attached to the report, the designation of the principal youth officer, senior youth officers and youth officers as principals, senior and education community officers; the gradual integration of adult education institutes, recreational institutes and youth centres; the replacement of borough youth committees by borough education community committees, with the constitution and orders of reference indicated, and the revised central committee structure. Approval in principle was given to the establishment of an advisory committee on training for the education community service and the Education Officer was authorized to draw up schemes to implement proposals for the establishment of joint institutes and to report back.

The minority party (Labour) reserved their position at the sub-committee and maintained their strong opposition when the report of the Further and Higher Education sub-committee, recommending the scheme, came to the Education Committee on 4 March 1970. This was the last meeting of the Education Committee before the elections; any matter of major policy, such as the proposed new scheme, required the approval of the full meeting of the ILEA. The scheme for an education community service was approved by a majority vote in the Education Committee. The next meeting of the ILEA was scheduled for 29 April 1970, after the GLC elections. The Labour Party made it very clear in the debate in the Education Committee that they were opposed to the proposals.

At the elections in March 1970 the Labour Party swept the board and, at the meeting of the reconstituted ILEA on 29 April 1970, the Education Committee's report recommending approval to the introduction of an education community service was referred back to the Further and Higher Education sub-committee. The new chairman of that committee, Mr Alec Grant, made it clear to the Education Officer and other senior officers concerned that Labour felt that merging the youth service with the adult education service would diminish the facilities available to young people. It was considered that this fundamental objection had not been adequately met and that the scheme was therefore not acceptable.

This decision left issues raised by the reports and the consultations unresolved. A further report from officers, without prior consultation with the bodies previously consulted, could have led to considerable difficulties in view of the strongly expressed wish by voluntary organizations, during the consultations on

ILEA 839, for closer involvement in policy-making. This apparent *impasse* was eventually overcome by a suggestion by one of the senior officers that a working-party representative of the appropriate voluntary and statutory organizations should be set up under an independent chairman, from outside the ILEA, to examine (a) the proposals set out in the Education Officer's report ILEA 839; (b) the National Youth Development Council's report *Youth and Community in the 70s*; (c) the London Youth Committee's Study Group report 1967, and to make recommendations to the Further and Higher Education sub-committee on the ILEA's provision of youth and adult services. This proposal was warmly commended by the Chairman of the Further and Higher Education sub-committee. On 3 July 1970 he invited Lord Longford to be the independent Chairman of a working party, the membership of which was set out in a report to the sub-committee on 15 July 1970[19] as follows:

Committee Membership

London Youth Committee, Borough Youth Committees (Inner London)	4
Standing Joint Committee	2
Central Consultative Committee of Headmasters and Headmistresses	1
Conference of Youth Officers	1
London Training Group	1
Inner London Committee of the Greater London Standing Conference of Voluntary Youth Organizations	2
London Boroughs' Association	1
London Council of Social Service	1
Association of Principals of Adult Education Institutes	1
Association of Principals of Recreational Institutes	1
Principal Youth Officer or representative	1
Assistant Education Officer (Further Education) or representative	1
Inspector for Further Education	1
TOTAL	18

Lord Longford agreed to chair the working group and the first meeting was held on 21 October 1970. The working party met on thirty-one occasions of which nine were whole-day meetings; two further days constituted a short residential conference. The results of the working party's deliberations over two years were set out in *A Chance to Choose*,[20] published by the ILEA in January 1973. The main task was the examination of the relationship between the three documents (outlined above) to see how far they were in sympathy with each other or how far they conflicted and, as a result of the working party's examination, to advise the ILEA concerning the recommendations contained in them.

The working party felt that the major concern was for young people and it was that concern which was predominant in their report.

> During our discussions a number of weaknesses and deficiences in the existing provision became apparent but in many instances we considered that improvements could be implemented either within a unified or a separately structured service and unification itself was not a sufficiently decisive factor. In our view the most serious single feature to emerge was that the Authority's provision is no longer attracting a representative cross section of the whole community and we were concerned to increase and widen its appeal. We were aware that a separate working party [see page xx] was already studying this problem as it affects adult education institutes and this knowledge strengthened our concern to ensure similar consideration for the needs of young people.[21]

They concluded that much needed to be done for young people, particularly for the younger age-range of the youth service, and that since much of this could be undertaken in the existing statutory and voluntary partnership of the youth service the unification of the two services was an additional complication which should be left for the time being.

> The combination of these main factors finally weighted the scale against a unified service. It was not an easy decision to make. The scheme was bold and forward looking and held promise of advantages, but we concluded that the desirability of a downward extension of the age range coupled with increased social provision for young people in the statutory sectors demanded the preservation of the separate youth service identity and overruled all other considerations.[22]

The working party did not, however, reject the philosophy of an education community service. 'We therefore wish to make clear that in rejecting unified institutes we do not reject the general concept of an education community service. We accept the definition of the function of community based education as set out in ILEA 839 . . . but we would prefer to make the approach to our objective by a different and perhaps slower route.'[23]

The working party's report, approved by the sub-committee, as was to be expected represented a compromise. Since a majority of the members of the working party felt that unified institutes, providing for both youth and adults, would be either harmful to the interests of young people or would not improve the service to them, those who thought otherwise were not prepared to press their view. The working party concentrated on the needs of young people and how the youth service, with its separate identity preserved, could be improved to meet them. Only one of the sixty-seven recommendations made by the working party was concerned specifically with adult education institutes. It recommended that adult education institutes admit students below compulsory school-leaving age, either as individuals or as groups, at the discretion of the principal and of the head of the schools attended. Three recommendations covered the youth service and adult education institutes and recommended more social provision as an integral part of non-vocational education; closer relations with community relations councils and consideration of possible ways of further extending ILEA's education services into the community.

One of the major aspects of documents Ed.388 and Ed.839, namely, the need to develop a closer partnership with voluntary organizations working with adults and to encourage initiatives with those members of the community who did not use the facilities of adult institutes, appears to have been virtually ignored in the consideration of these documents. There seems to have been an assumption that the adult provision in the unified institutes would remain unchanged whereas both Ed.388 and Ed.839 sought to relate their work very much more closely with the voluntary sector and innovatory work in the community. However, this aspect became a major preoccupation of another working group set up as a result of the findings of the survey of students enrolled in adult education institutes since September 1969, undertaken as part of the process of compiling the ILEA's evidence to the Russell Committee.

The Social Structure of the Student Body of Adult Education Institutes

In March 1970 the Association of Principals of Adult Education Institutes wrote to the Education Officer expressing concern about the low proportion of manual workers in the institutes and asking him to consider setting up a working party to investigate the matter. A working party of principals from the Association of Principals of Adult Education Institutes and members of the Further Education Inspectorate, under the chairmanship of the Assistant Education Officer (Further Education), was set up to consider and report to the Education Officer on the reasons for the low numbers of unskilled and manual workers enrolling for classes at adult education institutes and on ways in which their interests might be stimulated. The working party held its first meeting on 9 September 1970 and met on a total of twenty-nine occasions, the final meeting being on 30 January 1973. Its report, *The Social Structure of the Student Body in Adult Education Institutes* (March 1973)[24] was published by the ILEA later that year.

The working party first satisfied itself as to the accuracy of the survey. Allowing for all the factors that might have distorted the results, they concluded that the discrepancy with regard to manual workers was probably not as large as 4 per cent to the 31 per cent overall and, in some institutes, the percentage of manual workers in the student body was probably between 10–20 per cent. They were, nevertheless, generally satisfied that the overall student population of adult institutes was not typical of inner London's population as a whole and, in particular, that the number of manual workers in the student body was low. Moreover, the pattern revealed by the survey was not peculiar to inner London. A survey published in March 1970 by the National Institute of Adult Education showed that of those students in LEA classes 77 per cent were female, 48 per cent were between the ages of eighteen and thirty-four, 57 per cent left school at sixteen or over and 75 per cent were in the social-economic groups AB/C1, that is, upper-middle class or top-level administrative and managerial classes to lower-middle class or supervisory non-manual. The general population figures corresponding to these characteristics were, respectively, 52 per cent, 27 per cent, 25 per cent and 36 per cent.

Although the student body of adult institutes was reported at the time of the 1957 organization to have become a cross-section of the whole social community no statistical investigation had been undertaken to support this. Principals and others with long experience in the London service had no doubt that a change in the composition of the student body had taken place. A detailed sociological survey was beyond the resources of the working party and they had therefore to seek an explanation of this through the more obvious changes which were matters of common knowledge and observation in the inner London scene and which were particularly relevant to the education service. One important factor was the declining population in the area covered by the ILEA. The 1951 census gave the population as 3.3 million. At the 1971 census the figure had fallen to approximately 2.7 million and the Greater London Development Plan Statement Revisions (1 February 1972) forecast population figures varying from 2.38–2.48 million in 1981. At a conservative estimate, a fall in the population of over 500,000 in the twenty years after 1961 seemed probable. This would be in line with the 622,000 decline recorded for the period 1951–71.

The greater part of the exodus could be attributed to the influence of housing and employment prospects and was voluntary and unplanned. People moved out in order to buy homes and in search of more attractive environments in which to raise their families. While some found work locally many retained their jobs in London and commuted each day. Traditional industries, notably in the Dockland areas, were declining and changing and the movement of manufacturing industries out of London contributed to the exodus of the more skilled. Prices for houses outside London were generally lower. Conditions such as these were more likely to attract the higher-paid skilled worker than the lower-paid unskilled worker. There was evidence that people tended to move gradually further out by easy stages while possibly retaining links with London through their work. The establishment of new towns, for example, had a ripple effect rather than a major direct impact.

Whilst the decline in the population had the advantage that pressure on schools and housing was relieved, extensive developments such as slum clearance and major road-building projects created new problems in the process of solving the old ones. The working party commented:

> The displacement of many families means years of disruption, the disturbance of local communities and of a settled way of life. The replacement of terraced houses by tower blocks, for example, may greatly improve the standard of living accommodation but it also presents serious problems of adjustment for the rehoused families. The children are often unable to play outdoors within sight and sound of their parents. The mothers feel personally isolated and anxious for their children. The fathers are deprived of the interest and creative outlets which they previously found in their gardens and backyard sheds. [25]

Inner-city problems were beginning to show themselves. The cost of living in London was high but the average earnings of Londoners compared unfavourably with those in other parts of the country. The abstract of regional statistics produced by the Central Statistical Office for 1972 showed that Londoners with a 'medium' wage of £1220 were poorer than people in the Home Counties and many parts of the Midlands. Dr Eversley of the Central Council for Environmental Studies was quoted in the working-party report[26] as saying that the wage of 25 per cent of London workers was only £805 – less than £16 a week – compared with £885 in Hertfordshire. He pointed also to the movement out of London of employers who paid the highest wages and to the 25–30 per cent decline in manufacturing jobs in London in the last six years. 'This movement of the manufacturers inevitably leaves the unskilled Londoners who cannot afford to follow with fewer and fewer employment opportunities.'[27] The report also referred to a recent survey undertaken by the ILEA Careers Service Officers which had expressed concern at the increasing scarcity of employment prospects for the young unskilled person.

> In many cases adequate incomes may be achieved only by means of overtime, inconvenient but more highly paid shift work, second jobs, etc. As the stress of urban living steadily mounts so the demands on the social services increase . . .
> If the more able and prosperous members of the population move to the suburbs and beyond, leaving behind the less successful members of the population, social dangers may arise, such have been experienced in major American cities, where central areas have become depopulated or turned into ghettos. [28]

At the time of the preparation of the report only the preliminary report of the 1971 full census had been published and the working party drew comfort from the figures quoted in the 1966 sample census which showed a diverse population of London with semi-skilled and unskilled manual work taking 31.1 per cent of the total employment population.

The working party noted the changes in the institutes themselves and the greatly broadened scope of their activities. There had been a dramatic increase in the popularity of arts subjects and languages although domestic crafts remained the most popular group overall. Expenditure on publicity at the time of the report was £30,000, roughly 15p per capita. They noted that the occupational pattern of employed women in the survey sample was even less representative than that of employed men: 2.5 per cent of the women students were in manual jobs as against nearly 36 per cent in the general population. Among men the divergence was 5.8 per cent as compared with 27.7 per cent. As far as the manual-worker students were concerned four fifths of them left school at fifteen or younger; three fifths were over thirty-five and they studied fewer subjects than non-manual workers or those who were not employed. The 1969 survey, however, had not indicated whether particular subjects attracted any one category of students more than another or whether normal manual-worker students were strongly represented in a narrower range.

Adult education was only part of the total education system – a part of the area of voluntary leisure-time 'in which deep and subtle problems of motivation abound' and 'which caters for many different tastes, some of which are inborn and some of which are conditioned by opportunity and experience.'[29] The working party, therefore, looked at the education service as a whole and recognized that the first parting of the ways began on leaving school. Those who stay on 'are usually those who are vocationally motivated . . . whose natural inclination is fostered by the experience of school life and who have the necessary parental support, environment and encouragement to continue'.[30] The evidence suggested that these were the people who later formed the bulk of non-vocational adult education students.

> Those who leave school at the earliest opportunity often feel obliged to do so because of the complex variety of economic and social pressures unconnected with their feeling towards the school itself. Some may need to earn immediately, some may lack ambition or doubt their own capacity for higher educational achievement and the improved employment prospects which might be expected to result. Some may lack encouragement from parents or the home environment to remain at school and some identify early leaving with an assertion of independence. Whatever the reason, or combination of reasons, these are mainly the people who tend to take up unskilled manual work, at any rate as a first step.[31]

The working party was critical of the existing system of voluntary training and release from work to further education since it made little or no provision for early school-leavers who lacked skills and who were not natural seekers after continued education. They cited the Training Opportunity Scheme which made no provision for young people and so denied the education service a valuable opportunity to stimulate and develop the interests of the great majority of young workers.

The working party were in no doubt that the institutes currently presented a

middle-class image. There was strong evidence that socio-economic status corre-
lated strongly with interest in education. They noted that the evidence of the
TUC to the Russell Committee had commented on the need for education to be
seen to be more relevant to the working class. 'It is also as essential to secure the
confidence of potential working class students as to stimulate their interest. There
is inevitably some suspicion of public education authorities (which are often associated with unsatisfactory experiences of school) and of educational institutes
whose main activities are remote from the lives of most working people.'[32]
Equally stringent comments came from Tom Lovett, a WEA tutor working with
the Liverpool Education Priority Areas Project, with which the working party
made contact. The working party was not, however, disposed to apply the Liverpool experience to London or to attribute the ills of modern society too readily to
the influence of schools.

In 1972 nearly 70 per cent of school-leaving age youngsters chose to stay on in
London schools. Since non-manual workers represented only 45 per cent of the
employed population of London it seemed likely that the children of manual
workers were also remaining at school in substantial numbers and that a significant change might be taking place to upset the theory of the difference between
middle and working-class attitudes towards education. The 1969 survey had
shown that two-fifths of the manual workers who enrolled in the institutes were
under thirty-five years of age, that is, they had had a full secondary education with
all the benefits and advantages introduced into the post-1944 Education Act. This
did not appear to indicate any dramatic change in attitude attributable to failure
by schools. It could be that the younger manual workers were more ready to join
the exodus from inner London than their parents; or that the younger ones,
during their early married life, had heavier domestic commitments and needed to
work long hours to supplement their incomes, whereas the older generation had
more leisure once their families had grown up and left home.

It could be that the institutes might be continuing to attract roughly the same
proportion of manual workers from the general population as they had always
done but that they now constituted a smaller proportion of the greatly enlarged
student body of the institutes. It was equally conceivable that the 1957 reorganization of institutes might have been responsible to some extent for any decline
in enrolment by manual workers. The enhanced educational atmosphere brought
about by the improved standards of achievement and professionalism in the
institutes may have become too rarified for 'men who are usually indifferent to
formal instruction or specialised study'[33] for whom the men's institutes were first
opened.

Since the war there had been great social changes. Manual workers were no
longer necessarily the lowest-paid members of society and many more activities
were available to them than in the past. Cars were no longer the prerogative of the

middle and upper classes, television was in most homes and material aspirations had taken on a new aspect of importance. Also many people were forced to work long hours of overtime or on the shift system to achieve a good standard of living or even a modestly comfortable one. The absence from institutes of women employed in manual occupations might well be accounted for by the combined demands of employment, care of the children and general household responsibilities.

Many people who do not come to institutes may, quite simply, be too busy. Irregular working hours, two jobs, voluntary work of one sort or another, the problems of bringing up a family, pursuing hobbies without feeling any need for additional instruction other than that obtained from books, magazines or fellow enthusiasts – all are time consuming . . . To assume that all people who do not enrol in the institutes are leading impoverished lives would clearly be wrong.[34]

Whether the problem had been over-magnified or whether the institutes, consciously or unconsciously, had concentrated too heavily on the articulate sector of the community whose needs were more easily made known and therefore more easily met, the working party thought that there was a need for the institutes to move closer to the whole community. Very early in their discussions they realized that there were no easy answers to the problem of attracting more manual workers.

The reasons for their not attending were too complex and quick generalisations were not to be trusted. We were troubled by the thought that many people appear to be divorced from the educational system, that negative attitudes may develop early in life and need to be overcome and that although the institutes have always seen themselves as an important and integral part of organised community life this claim can no longer be made with the same degree of confidence as before.[35]

The working party came to the conclusion that a new impetus was needed and that even greater efforts should be made to reach those who did not participate fully in community life for whatever reason. Once having come to that conclusion it was clearly necessary to explore ways of assessing the needs of those who did not use adult institutes or other educational services and of ways in which responses could be made to them.

As a result of an interim report by the working party the Education Officer sought the approval of the Further and Higher Education sub-committee (11 May 1971) to the appointment of an action-research worker, to be attached to the Walworth Institute which operated in an area in which there was considerable housing development going on and where there were known to be a considerable employment force of manual workers. The worker was given some responsibility for day-to-day work in the institute itself but was largely left free to make contact with local people and organizations, find their interests and needs and organize or suggest ways in which they could be made. He was in fact the first out-reach worker to be appointed to the London service.

One of the great merits of the London adult education service is its swift reaction to any new idea. The out-reach worker appointed to Walworth Institute took up his duties in the autumn of 1971 and, by the middle of 1972, a number of institutes had used staff vacancies to make similar appointments. Such appointments provided the working party with valuable evidence of the kind of developments that might be possible with such workers. This, together with a number of other projects, gave the working party a basis for their cogent demand for closer links between the various sectors of the education service in its general approach to the education of the community.

In the controversy over the proposals in Ed.388 and Ed.839 much had been made of the lack of definition of the word 'community'. The working party pointed out that many communities existed within and beyond a particular geographical community:

> One useful definition is the richness (or paucity) of content and inter-relationships current in the particular areas in which an individual and his family live, work and play. In addition to geographical communities, the individual may belong at one and the same time to many sub-communities or groups of people. At work, he may have feelings of loyalty to the firm as a whole, or to particular groups of colleagues. He may be a member of a trade union, a political party, a church, a voluntary organisation, a social club, a residents' or tenants' association, a parent-teachers' association, he may be a student, he may have a particular hobby, support a particular football team. He may have a strong allegiance to his national or ethnic group particularly if this is a minority group. Some of these allegiances may be very real to the individual, yet never translated into explicit action – the number of people who support a particular organisation far exceed the numbers who are prepared to accept responsibility for its management. Many of these interest groups overlap. People active in one sphere are often active in others. Active people are more easily defined as members of a community. But apparent inactivity does not automatically mean that no interest or feeling of identification exists.[36]

With such a complex web of individual or group loyalties the working party made a strong demand for a variety of approach which would try to reach those prevented from joining in any community activities by a combination of circumstances or lack of personal confidence.

> Young mothers are often lonely, particularly in new estates and high rise blocks of flats. The chance to mix with other adults, undertake some creative and mentally stimulating activity and be free of the constant need to keep an eye on the children for a few hours has a tonic effect. This is most marked

where the woman has been used to interesting work with lively company, and the feeling of independence and self-confidence this generates. The need may not be recognised by the person concerned as a need for adult education but as a general need and is not confined to the manual worker families that are the specific concern of this report. Neither is it right to assume that the depth of need is greatest for those who have previously led interesting lives. Indeed it is all the more important to find ways of involving those for whom life and society in the past have offered little.[37]

Such passages of the report reflected the working party's down-to-earth appreciation of the needs of many who, for one reason or another, did not use adult education facilities. Perhaps more importantly they indicated a recognition, too, that educational needs were often disguised in the yearning for some practical alleviation of day-to-day frustration or isolation which personal circumstances or way of life imposed. Once the conception of 'out-reach' work had been grasped, the working party set about identifying initiatives which illustrated the flexible and imaginative contribution they believed the adult education service could make to the local community.

The report called for closer links between the different sectors of the education service and the removal of artificial barriers between them. The late 1960s and early 1970s provided a number of exciting initiatives to illustrate the point. Reference has already been made to the part played by adult institutes in training pre-school play-group leaders (pages 211–12). By 1972–3, sixty-six classes a week for play-group leaders were being provided by ten institutes. Originally the demand had come from middle-class mothers but there were signs that this was no longer so. Moreover, the involvement of mothers and, to a lesser degree, fathers, with the play and development of their children, was beginning to provide a foundation for the personal development of the parents themselves. Nowhere was this better illustrated than in Battersea. Mothers there who had been attending pre-school play group classes wished, when the course ended, to continue their association with fellow members of the classes and a number of them began meeting in accommodation made available to them by the Wandsworth Pre-School Play Group Association. The Association, which had already been working closely with the ILEA, turned to the Authority for help for the mothers in programming their activities. The ILEA responded by appointing a worker, in consultation with the Association, to work with the five adult institutes operating in various parts of Wandsworth. The worker's task was not to organize groups but to keep contact and to be available to respond to the immediate needs of the groups by using the resources of the appropriate adult institute. The worker appointed was a very good illustration of one type of out-reach worker appointed by the ILEA. She herself was a Battersea 'mum' who had attended one of the ILEA's pre-school leaders' training courses and had become very much involved with the Wandsworth Pre-School Play Group Association. She had no academic or teaching qualifications but she had a lively and intelligent personality and, most important of all, an appreciation and understanding of the problems of working-class mothers in Battersea.

The working party, commenting on the growth of creches where day-time students could leave their children for a small extra charge, pressed the need for accommodation for the exclusive use of the institute throughout the day. By the time the working party reported the ILEA had approved a financial contribution amounting to half the cost of staffing the creches; in some instances heads of schools had co-operated in the running of the creche by allowing girls to help, as part of their housecraft course, to the mutual benefit of all concerned.

The working party report noted how the concept of using the primary school as a basis for the wider involvement of the community had been gaining ground. This was a reference to the proposals being considered by the managers of Brackenbury Primary School to provide accommodation for adults; some of this accommodation, for example, a gymnasium would be available for use by the school during the day. The philosophy behind this proposal was summed up in an extract from a report to the managers:

> It is now generally accepted that a child's education is affected by his environmental circumstances. In this conception the association and involvement of the parents with the child's education and the general acceptance that the school and the teachers in it are an essential part of the local community it serves are very important. There is need for greater effort to relate the education service in London to the community at large and remove the impression by many young people and adults that schools and colleges are establishments provided by 'them' and having little or nothing to do with 'us'.[38]

In addition to Brackenbury one of the Thamesmead primary schools was also being planned on the same pattern. Prior Weston School in the Barbican development of the City of London was already associated with the Hole-in-the-Ground Youth Club and the Central London Institute and a number of primary schools were associating themselves very much more closely with adult education institutes than in the past. This closer relationship between primary schools and the adult education service contrasted sharply with the general attitude in the 1950s. One of the principal merits claimed for the 1957–9 reorganization of men's and women's institutes was that it removed adult institutes from 180 primary schools.

At the old Robert Montefiore School in Spitalfields four different agencies, a school, an adult education institute, a youth service and a voluntary body with a joint management committee of users was an encouraging step forward in a joint operation to meet the needs of the local community. A warden had been appointed to implement the management committee's decisions and it had already been agreed that the building would accommodate a club for mentally handicapped young people and provide an office for a community relations officer for the Council of Citizens of Tower Hamlets. The working party emphasized the importance of schools as focal points of the community in which parents and others in that community should feel involved.

> If parents and other adults are really to see schools as important focal points of their community, it is essential that there should be activities for them as adults. If such activities are not to be viewed by heads and staffs of schools as a threat to or an intrusion into the life of the school, it is equally important that additional accommodation for these activities should be provided in the complex which houses the school and that it should be seen to be available for the use of the school as well as for adults and young people.[39]

The working party's concern to establish schools as focal points in the community not only reflected the general concern of the ILEA for a close working relationship between schools and the youth and adult services but also a growing demand from various bodies, including borough councils, for their increased availability for recreational and sporting facilities. There had been many discussions between elected members of the ILEA, borough councils and officers of these respective bodies to explore ways in which gymnasia, playgrounds and playing facilities generally could be made more available. It was very difficult for representatives of borough councils to appreciate the extent to which London schools were fully used during the evening and to accept the fact that the ILEA had no authority to spend money on the supervision of general community activities by individuals and groups at weekends and holidays when the facilities might be available. In any case, during the holidays extensive cleaning operations, minor improvements or repainting took place in many schools; in addition, many were used as holiday play-centres. Where facilities were available, borough councils showed a notable reluctance to foot the bill for the payment of staff in the supervision of any communal activities.

A number of borough councils were involved in the provision of recreational and sports facilities; one way in which these facilities could be provided in partnership with the borough councils was by the provision of shared facilities in a new school. The provision of such facilities in a new school was governed by the Department of Education and Science limits on expenditure. Given a suitable site, however, the facilities could be extended if the borough agreed to pay for the additional building. The borough then had use of the facilities on an agreed basis proportionate to its investment. Running costs would be apportioned according to use and both partners would have the benefit of more extensive accommodation than could be provided separately. A number of such projects had been jointly financed by different local authorities in various parts of the country, notably in Nottinghamshire. The problem in London, as always, was the availability of sufficiently large sites.

At the time of the working party's report, negotiations were proceeding on the first of such projects in London, namely, Manwood School in Lewisham and also in Thamesmead, Greenwich and George Green School, Tower Hamlets. The schemes at these schools envisaged the provision of sports accommodation, namely, games hall, gymnasia, squash courts and a swimming pool. Such schemes were extremely difficult to bring to fruition. The first major obstacle was the synchronizing of building programme dates within the vagaries of the DES school-building programme. This was difficult enough in normal times but in times of economic crisis, when building programmes were cut and starting dates delayed, there were very real financial problems; borough councils had to make forward estimates which, due to rising costs, required later supplementation. Nevertheless, when such projects were successfully carried through, they brought closer co-operation between those concerned within the local community in meeting jointly the needs of that community.

In its conclusion the working party had no doubt about the general validity of the students' survey conclusions and reaffirmed that the student body in London was atypical of the adult population in other ways besides the proportion of manual workers. For example, the average age of students was lower than the average age of the London adult and there were more women than men. In considering the future, therefore, they had gone beyond their terms of reference in order to look at ways in which the interest of the wider community might be stimulated. 'We believe that if the basic approach is right then adult education should naturally attract and serve a complete cross-section of the community without any need for special discriminatory measures between arbitrary defined sectors.'[40] There were many reasons why some people did not use the facilities available, 'not the least being that the business of earning a living may well leave no time for anything else. In truth we do not yet know enough about their absence or their needs; although we suspect that much of what is already on offer would not be inappropriate if only they knew about it and it could be made available in circumstances which demonstrated that it was for them.'[41] There was no easy or quick way to bring about a situation in which the educaion service was recognized by everybody to be a means of helping each individual to a full personal development as involved members of society. It was significant that a greater majority of adult education students left school well after the statutory school-leaving age.

In other words education begets education and interest begets further interest. Many of those who leave school at the earliest possible time do so because they have become disenchanted with education or do not see its relevance to their personal or environmental circumstances. Their subsequent circumstances often do not encourage them to change this view . . . The education service will be used according to the extent that it can demonstrate its relevance to the circumstances of the people it tries to serve. We believe this process begins early.[42]

Contact had to be made on the broadest possible front and adult education had to start from where the individual was in ability, attainment and environment; opportunities for continuing education had to be made available at every possible point of contact. The various projects that the working party had reviewed indicated that prejudice against educational establishments could be changed to interest and involvement with them, if those educational establishments were seen as places of pleasurable experience, both for children and adults. 'This means that every educational establishment has to be related in some way or another to the community in which it is situated. It means too that attitudes of many heads and teachers of schools as well as principals of further education establishments have to change.'[43] If more was to be known about the needs of people who hitherto were unknown to the education service then there must be 'out-reach staff' and 'out-reach' activities from schools and adult institutes or as a partnership of the two. The working party called for an extended programme of in-service training to promote an understanding of the role of all staff in relating the education service to the community and the part that adult education institutes could play in this process.

In any new school project consideration should be given to planning it with youth and adult facilities as a community education complex and where this was not possible additional accommodation for adults should be provided in all new primary and secondary schools and, where appropriate, accommodation for the youth service also. There should be a programme of improvements to existing school buildings used by adult groups to provide better standards of social provision, lighting, furniture and equipment.

Other recommmendations called for the ILEA to encourage the development of community education complexes and represent to the Secretary of State the impact that such provision must inevitably make on school and adult education building and minor-works programmes. They asked for every opportunity to be taken to provide shared facilities in partnership with borough councils and voluntary organizations and for consideration to be given wherever appropriate to the management structure proposed in the Brackenbury and Robert Montefiore projects, whereby a 'collective' consisting of representatives of the school, the youth service, the adult education institute and the community, working through a warden, used to the full the total resources of the complex.

The report of the working party was warmly received by the Further and Higher Education sub-committee which authorized its publication for wider distribution. The report was a particularly significant document. It represented the

prompt response of the ILEA, including the principals of the institutes themselves, to the disturbing results of the survey of students undertaken in 1969. It
brought together in one document a record of a number of particularly interesting projects which were taking place at that time and which were all seeking ways
in which resources could be pooled for the greater benefit of the community.
This, together with the working party's comments and recommendations, provided a basis for a new approach (not only by adult education institutes but by the
education service as a whole) by which the mesh of the educational net could be
more closely drawn and the needs of the wider community more adequately met.

Wisely the working party had not waited until the completion of its report
before making its views known on various aspects of its deliberations. The early
action it took on out-reach workers resulted in a number of institutes appointing
such staff from their own staff resources. The first out-reach worker appointed as
a result of the working party's interim report started in October 1971; in January
1972 Bethnal Green Institute made a similar appointment. When in April 1974
the Education Officer invited principals of adult education institutes to apply for
one of eleven new out-reach worker posts which had been authorized it was
found that no less than seven institutes had made appointments from their existing staff resources and two institutes were seeking additional support staff in this
kind of work. Such workers at Bethnal Green and Holloway were soon involved
with adult illiteracy. By October 1975 there were twenty-one 'out-reach'
workers employed in adult education institutes.

In December 1971 full-time administrative officers had been authorized at each
adult education institute.

In June 1972 the working party's recommendation, as a result of close consultation with the Association of Principals, was a factor in securing the approval
in principle for the establishment of governing bodies at adult education institutes. This was a major step forward. As we have seen, although governing
bodies of vocational establishments had been in operation for many years, such
bodies had not been thought to be appropriate for adult education institutes since
few of them had their own building or full-time staff. By 1972, however, all institutes had some accommodation for their sole use, all institutes were providing
both day and evening classes and all institutes had full-time staff other than the
principal and vice-principal. Four institutes, including the City Literary Institute,
had between 9000 and 11,000 students and another twenty had a student roll of
over 5000 students. In size and scope of work, therefore, they were now comparable to many vocational establishments which had governing bodies. But it was
not this factor which had prompted the working party on the social structure
of the student body to suggest that the time had now come for adult institutes
to have governing bodies. There were still a number of principals who were
distinctly lukewarm to the idea. Their representatives on the working party,

however, had come to the view that governing bodies would provide an important means of securing the direct involvement and interest of local organizations in the community in the work of the institutes; it was this factor which persuaded the Association of Principals to welcome the setting up of governing bodies. There was another important advantage which was not perhaps generally recognized at the time. Whereas elected members, particularly members of the Further and Higher Education sub-committee, took pride in the work of the adult education service and, from time to time, responded to invitations to attend functions, there was not the same personal interest in particular institutes as there was, say, in a particular school or college on whose management committee or governing body the elected member represented the ILEA. Not only, therefore, was there the need for members of the ILEA to know more about the work of the institutes but, in representing the Authority on a governing body which was broadly representative of the community they served, there was the added advantage of the Authority coming into closer contact with the local community.

The membership of governing bodies of adult education institutes was prescribed as follows:

Three governors appointed directly by the ILEA including, where practicable, one member of the Authority or its Education Committee;
Five governors appointed by organizations and bodies representative of community, educational and cultural interests in the area. Such persons do not have to be members of the body concerned. If no appointment is made the ILEA can fill the vacancy by a direct appointment;
The principal of the institute ex-officio (the vice-principal may attend and if the principal is absent may vote);
One member of the Academic Board;
Three members of the teaching staff (one full-time, two part-time);
Three students appointed by the student body;
Three governors to be co-opted by the governing body.

In July 1973 the Further and Higher Education sub-committee (ILEA 718)[44] approved individual institute proposals for organizations which would be approached to nominate the five governors representing community, educational and cultural interests. The organizations included social and welfare associations, community relations councils, councils of social services, arts councils and so on. The sub-committee also approved the appointment of the governor or superintendent of the penal establishments to the governing bodies of the five institutes responsible for the education service in penal establishments. The governing bodies were given power to make recommendations for the appointment of full-time staff including the principal and vice-principal. Governors were also required to give annual estimates under some ten headings of expenditure and were given power of virement (spending money allocated under one heading for another purpose).

By September 1973 all the governing bodies of adult education institutes had been formed and began their first cycle of meetings. As was customary in London governing bodies were free to select their chairmen from any of their members, with the exception of teaching staff and students who were not eligible for such an appointment. Most of the governing bodies elected chairman from one or other of the ILEA-nominated members of the body although not all were from the majority party; some governing bodies elected a representative of a voluntary organization as their chairman.

Tragically, on 16 November 1971, Sir William Houghton died suddenly from a cerebal haemorrhage. For more than fourteen years, longer than any since Sir Robert Blair, he had been London's Education Officer. His integrity, courtesy, wise counsel and resolute professional stance had steered the education service through the stormy waters which followed the Herbert Commission's Report on London Government. His balanced judgement and fairmindedness had won the respect of elected members of whatever party, and colleagues in education both in and outside the ILEA. Adult education institute principals and staff knew him as a regular visitor, with Lady Houghton, to their institutes and as one who had a deep appreciation of their work.

He was succeeded by Dr Eric Briault who had been Deputy Education Officer from the time of Sir William Houghton's appointment as Education Officer and who had spent all his working life in the London education service as teacher, district inspector and staff inspector. Quick-thinking and brilliantly articulate his style was quite different to Houghton's. A born innovator and ideas man he had spearheaded many advances which had had to pass the test of Houghton's caution. The ILEA's education-television service and house magazine *Contact*, which Briault had inspired and brought into operation, were perhaps apt illustrations of his urge to improve communications throughout the ILEA service.

Mr Peter Newsam, former Deputy Education Officer to the West Riding of Yorkshire, who was to succeed Dr Briault as Education Officer in 1977, was appointed as Deputy Education Officer.

An Education Service for the Whole Community

As Deputy Education Officer, Dr Briault had chaired the working party on the review of the further education and higher education colleges. The review was undertaken to resolve the growing demand for a further and higher education service which would provide courses at all levels below the advanced work undertaken by the polytechnics. With the concentration of advanced work in London's

five polytechnics, technical colleges and colleges of commerce found themselves
with a diminished role covering the upper part of the Ordinary National Certificate and the later years of City and Guilds Certificates to Higher National Certificate and, possibly, some Higher National Diploma work. In London the sixteen
colleges for further education were concerned with lower-level work up to
Ordinary General Certificate level and the first years of Ordinary National Certificate and City and Guilds. Three general and commercial colleges provided for
adults; thirteen colleges for further education were concerned with the average
and less-than-average student, the majority of whom were between sixteen and
nineteen. Academic ceilings had been placed on these colleges quite deliberately
in order to ensure that there was a concentration on the average and less-than-
average student. Amendments to examination regulations for Ordinary National
Certificate and the City and Guilds, by which the former natural division midway
between those examinations was removed, made the former natural progression
from a college for further education to a senior college more difficult.

As a result of the review, colleges for further education were amalgamated with
one or more senior colleges under a principal and associate principal. Special provision to ensure the continuance of lower-level work, particularly of a general
education character, was made by the appointment of a vice-principal with special
responsibility for this aspect of the work. With the decision to merge the colleges
the Assistant Education Officer (Higher Education) became responsible for all
vocational colleges and the former Assistant Education Officer (Further Education) became responsible for the junior clubs and play-centre service, formerly the
responsibility of the Assistant Education Officer (Schools). The old Further
Education Branch was renamed Community Education and Careers (CEC). The
Assistant Education Officer (CEC) remained responsible for the youth service,
adult education and the careers service together with the developing work of
community relations councils and community projects generally.

This organizational change brought together those services concerned with the
recreational, social and informal education or personal development of the child,
young person or adult in one administrative branch under one Assistant Education Officer. Together with the general responsibility for community relations
this arrangement gave an organizational focus to education for the community.
At the same time, the retention of responsibility for the careers service in that
branch gave the Assistant Education Officer and other senior officers in the
branch a valuable contact with the world of work, the schools and vocational
education. By this organizational change and the name given to the new branch,
the ILEA marked its commitment to a policy of providing an education service
which would reach out into the community and involve all sections of that
community in its operation.

A policy, however, is only as good and effective as the means taken to ensure its implementation. Administrative and financial incentives to encourage work in particular fields can do a great deal but there must also be an awareness at all levels of the need and an understanding of the policy if a sustained response is to be evoked. This means changing attitudes and changing attitudes is a slow and patient business.

A Chance to Choose, with its prescription for a community-orientated, flexible and varied youth service and the report on the *Social Structure of the Student Body in Adult Education Institutes*, had charted the way. Administrative incentives such as exempting classes for the disadvantaged from the one to thirteen ratio calculation, the retention of a pool of teaching hours for distribution to particular developments and, since 1971, the appointment of out-reach workers, had certainly encouraged adult education institutes to increase the provision for a wide variety of disadvantaged groups. Nevertheless, despite the advances made, there was plenty of evidence that there were many barriers between different sectors of education which inhibited joint projects and prevented one part of the service learning from another.

Dr Briault's personal concern to improve communications, not only throughout the service but between the service and the community it served, led him as soon as he became Education Officer to tackle this problem. He initiated an operation which was to be a unique experience for the education service. Intensive discussions at senior officer level discussed papers by the Education Officer, the Chief Inspector, Assistant Education Officers and Staff Inspectors. A joint seminar with leading elected members of the ILEA and senior officers, followed by five short residential conferences each of twenty and thirty inspectors and officers, discussed the theme of an education service for the whole community. The membership of each conference consisted of representatives of all branches of the service – school and further education inspectors, educational psychologists, administrators, officers from the youth service, the careers service and the education welfare service. ESWC (Education Service for the Whole Community) became a watch-word and, at times, an expletive! – but there was no doubt, as the resultant report said, 'The inter mixture has itself facilitated increased understanding and thus forwarded the concept of a more integrated service for the whole community.'

The report (ILEA 607), *An Education Service for the Whole Community*,[45] written by Dr Briault himself, drawing upon contributions made by colleagues as a result of the intensive discussions, was submitted to each of the sub-committees, including the community education section of the Further and Higher Education sub-committee, in the autumn of 1973.

The purpose of the report was 'to look at the education service in inner London as a whole and to propose developments, designed to enable it to serve more fully the needs of the whole community'.[46] It drew attention to important aspects of the community in inner London and its problems and described 'some of the exciting new developments which have recently taken place'. It examined the way in which change occurs and proposed a strategy of innovation which relied upon the 'the creativity of the educational institutions in responding to the needs of the community and the individuals who comprise it'.[47]

The report described some of the basic factors, such as the fall in population, which affected the community in inner London. Nevertheless, there was a comparatively high density in some inner London boroughs, particularly those north of the river, with some forty persons per acre compared with nineteen in Greater London as a whole. The age structure of the ILEA population was markedly different from the rest of England and Wales with a lower proportion of children under fifteen years and a higher proportion of those of working age sixteen — sixty-five years. London had always been an attraction for those of working age and the high proportion of the resident working population was given a daily boost by some 1.25 million daily commuters. Overall, the resident population included some 20 per cent whose place of birth was outside the United Kingdom; 8 per cent of these were from the new Commonwealth. The number of overseas-born residents varied greatly from one borough to another — 8 per cent in Greenwich and almost 35 per cent in Kensington and Chelsea and in Westminster. Similarly, the overall average of 8 per cent of those from the new Commonwealth masked differences of from 3.59 per cent in Greenwich to 11 per cent and over in Lambeth, Islington and Hackney. Predicted school rolls, September 1972 to September 1981, showed that there would be a rapid fall in the primary rolls with an accelerating decline in secondary rolls delayed until the last years of the 1970s.

The economic and social conditions behind falling rolls produced problems such as high teacher turnover and high pupil mobility. The exodus of middle and skilled working class from the inner city, referred to in the *Social Structure of the Student Body in Adult Education Institutes*, was an important feature of migration. Urban deprivation and stress were no doubt reflected in the verbal-reasoning scores of pupils about to transfer from primary to secondary schools. This had fallen throughout the 1960s and in 1973 had settled at a level well below the national average of 100. 'Furthermore the groups which moved out of the inner city are not only those who tend to give the most support to schools, but are those who tend to take the most active part in community affairs and further, higher and adult education.'

The report identified 'too many parents', the sixteen — nineteen year old and manual workers as examples of neglected groups. 'For some, the cycle of deprivation may come round in 17 to 20 years; the deprived infant becoming the backward and difficult primary school child, the reluctant and truanting secondary school pupil and, within a year or two, the unwilling and neglectful parent. Educational and social disadvantages are inextricably associated. The education we offer at all stages must recognise that the young people of today are the parents, work-mates and nextdoor neighbours of tomorrow.'[48]

There were many discontinuities in the service: between primary and secondary schools; between secondary schools and further and higher education; between primary schools and the play-centre service; between secondary schools and youth service; between youth service and adult education. 'Too many schools regard the adult education institutes as of no concern to them, yet the quarter of a million students who attend them each year, are the parents, the aunts and uncles and the voters who are the potential supporters of their schools, and perhaps more important, the essential ingredients of the social environment in which the pupils live.'[49]

It was necessary for the education service to recognize that inner London had a disproportionate degree of deprivation among its people compared with the country as a whole. Therefore, more of its children came to school with social handicaps than was the case elsewhere. There were areas where incomes were very low and unemployment very high and there were areas of gross overcrowding and very bad housing. There was also heavy pressure on existing property, particularly where rented, as developers moved in to convert. As a result of these difficulties there was a mobile population and the children of mobile families were difficult to settle in schools. 'Rehousing necessarily breaks up traditional social groups and improvement carries the penalty of insecurity. Recent immigrants present difficulties of language, of insufficient education before arrival, and problems of settling in to a strange urban way of life.'[50]

The high cost of housing, transport and living costs generally in London made it difficult for teachers to stay; teacher turnover, difficulties in recruiting and retaining experienced teachers added to the problems of the schools. 'Violence and disregard for the general good in society generally are reflected in problems of discipline in and truancy from the schools. For many, and especially for children, the urban environment is itself hostile; play spaces are too few, high flats too remote, the streets a harsh adventure. On a hot summer's day, with Mum at work, the exhaust smoke hits the five year old right in the face.'[51]

Set against the difficulties there were, however, many opportunities for progress. Supply of teachers was improving as was the pupil-teacher ratio. Falling rolls held out the prospect of improved accommodation and smaller classes. It also offered opportunity for more extensive provision for parents and other adult groups, for play centres and youth groups and for the school to become a more effective place for community education. The recognition that 'accommodation is a resource for the whole service and not just for a particular section of it' would go a long way to remove some of the separateness which existed between the various sectors of education. Projects which had already taken place had shown that, with co-operation across the 'divides' between these various sectors together with positive discrimination in the allocation of resources, progress could be made. Further and more widespread developments towards a more fully integrated service were needed. The ILEA had already laid down clear lines of policy on participation, support and positive discrimination which formed a basis for considering strategies of innovation.

> The essential strategy of innovation is to secure the creativity of the school, the college, the institute, so that it becomes capable of innovation which is essentially of its own making: of dealing positively with research and development projects; of taking advantage of social interaction; or recognising problems and new needs. Such a creative institution will organize participation on the part of its members; will call readily on appropriate support resources; and will be capable of using its own resources in ways which best meet the particular needs for which additional help is given. It will seek to understand its role in relation to the whole community and its right relations both to the individuals it serves and to the other institutions which serve them and the community.[52]

The report did not set out to do more than outline the need and the philosophy of an innovation strategy. Such a strategy called for pragmatic tactics which could not be laid down from the centre or uniformly imposed. 'In the simplest terms, we have to identify success, shout about it, encourage others to examine their own circumstances in the light of it and support growth as soon as it springs from the ground. Such tactics, however, can be and need to be supported by arrangements designed to increase awareness and understanding of the education service as a whole. This is the chief purpose of this report.'[53]

With the agreement of the other sub-committees, the Further and Higher Education sub-committee and the Schools sub-committee jointly submitted the report to the Education Committee over the signatures of their respective chairmen, Mr Jack Straw and Mr Harvey Hinds. The report was adopted as a major policy strategy statement by the ILEA and was authorized to be published and given the widest possible discussion within the service and with others concerned, such as borough councils and the Greater London Council. Sympathetic consideration was to be given to the responses and requests for growth which might arise from locally co-ordinated discussions and initiatives.

On the initiative of Mr (later Sir) Ashley Bramall, the Leader of the ILEA, the sum of £100,000 was included in the estimate for 1974–5 to enable officers to respond promptly to immediate needs in the field of community education. In addition, early notification was to be given to the inner London borough councils of projects likely to be in the ILEA's building programmes, to enable consideration to be given to the provision of community facilities by the borough councils.

The report was published by the ILEA in October 1973 and a copy sent to every teacher in the Authority and to many others inside and outside the service as well. As a follow-up to the report, in the spring of 1974 thirty-seven one-day conferences were held throughout the ILEA's area, each attended by representatives of teachers and support staff from every sector of education. Each conference was chaired by a member of the Education Committee and the report, *An Education Service for the Whole Community*, was introduced by a senior officer, each of whom gave a report later on the general tenor of the discussion, together with particular comments and recommendations on ways in which the general philosophy in the report could be advanced. The membership of each conference was limited to 100 and divided into four or five groups each broadly representative of the whole education service. At a number of conferences the absence of any recommendations, indicating specific action which could be taken, was the subject of critical comment indicative of a desire for more precise guidance. It took a little time to convince some that it was a policy-strategy document and not a prescription for precise action and that such action must stem from local initiatives aimed at developing co-operation with other sectors of the service and the local community. These criteria were essential to qualify for any grant from the £100,000 set aside for community projects. There was no doubt that it was an unprecedented exercise in communication within the service and to a lesser extent with the local borough councils. Since it was primarily undertaken to inform and bring representatives from the many different sectors together it was difficult to make any assessment of its success. There can be little doubt, however, that such gatherings were an essential step towards changing attitudes and developing a better sense of an integrated service. Equally there is little doubt that the availability of a fund to give some financial support to local initiatives encouraged many projects which otherwise would have not got beyond the design stage, to be fully implemented.

The report contained an analysis of the ILEA's net expenditure in 1973−4, showing the amount spent on different age groups and the unit cost for each age group. It also showed the amounts spent under six headings: teachers, non-teaching staff, premises, school allowances, furniture and equipment and support services and other expenses. Support services and other expenses included expenditure on school health, school meals, education-television service, aid to pupils, administration and inspection, in-service training of teachers, rural centres, games and swimming. The average unit cost was £410. The unit cost for the various age groups 0 − four years − £269; five − ten years − £252; eleven − sixteen years − £429; sixteen − eighteen years − £625; eighteen plus £935.

The analysis showed how labour-intensive was the education service. Teaching and non-teaching staff and support services accounted for 77 per cent of the cost overall and, in the eighteen plus group, it was 83 per cent. The number of students in adult education institutes was given as full-time equivalents, for example, 215,750 part-time students represented 12,880 full-time eighteen-plus students. The total expenditure on adult education in 1973–4 was £5,326,000 for a total of 13,700 full-time equivalent students. This was 2.55 per cent of the ILEA's total budget of £208,250,000. The unit cost, expressed in full-time equivalent adult education students, was therefore £389 (or, for each part-time student, £23), compared with £935 for the 18-plus age group as a whole.

13.   Reaching out to the Community

The quality and character of the thirty-seven conferences held in 1974 to consider the ILEA's report, *An Education Service for the Whole Community*, varied a great deal. Some were predominantly positive and forward-looking but in others more time was spent, both in plenary and group sessions, in considering current problems and difficulties than in charting a way forward. The stress and difficulties of teaching in London; the special challenge of the additional year as a result of the raising of the school-leaving age; and the widespread feelings of frustration among teachers because the London allowance had not been increased, tended to obscure any constructive consideration of a policy which appeared, to those concerned with schools, to be making increased demands upon them.

There was no doubt, however, that many came away from the conferences with a better understanding of the role of other parts of the service and the support which could be derived from closer links and co-operative action. Many contacts and arrangements to meet again were made. Many examples were revealed, too, of initiatives already taken along some of the lines of the report. A feature of many of the conferences was the contribution made by representatives of community groups and by people working in services administered by the boroughs.

As a result of the consideration of the Education Officer's report[1] on the consultations and conferences the Further and Higher Education sub-committee and the Schools sub-committee decided (September 1974) that the discussion should be widened. Managers and governors of schools, colleges and institutes were asked to discuss the report and to initiate discussions locally with a view to identifying local needs and action considered necessary to fulfil such needs. In order to promote a wide range of initiatives from outside the education service, consultations were extended to inner London borough councils, both members and officers; further meetings with local councils of social service or their equivalent were encouraged. The ILEA looked to its members representing boroughs to facilitate such arrangements.

£100,000 had been set aside in the 1974–5 estimates for community education. The committees indicated that they wished to consider the community education budget for 1975–6. As always, the problem was to ensure a right balance between a provision for general needs and that needed to raise standards in areas of special difficulty. Despite the gathering clouds of financial stringency the committees were firm in their resolve to respond to local initiatives. 'We shall wish to ensure that greater resources are given where they are more needed but at the same time hope that it will be possible to respond to initiatives which reach out towards the educational needs of the whole community wherever these may arise, but within the limits of whatever resources can be made available.'[2]

At this stage it was thought that, in order to take the discussions at the conferences and elsewhere further, individuals should be appointed to the following jobs: a convenor to bring groups together; a facilitator to carry initiatives forward; and outreach workers, such as had already been appointed at some adult education institutes and colleges, to make contact with, and interpret the needs of, the local community.

In June 1975 the Education Officer made his first report[3] on the expenditure from the £100,000 grant. In the same report he gave the results of the consideration of the main report by managing and governing bodies. The views of many of the latter were disappointing in that they 'tended to be negative and indicated that managers and governors were sometimes not fully aware of other educational services already in the area'. Others expressed the critical views apparent at the conferences held throughout London early in 1974 when the scheme was launched. They feared increasing demands on teaching staff without financial reward, assumed that the scheme could not succeed without massive injections of money and still resented the shared use of buildings. In many managing and governing bodies the report was merely 'received'.

There were, however, more hopeful signs of joint community action. There was no lack of applications for ESWC grants – 224 were received. The agreed criteria for the award of grants were:

1. that the project represents a new development arising from local consultation;
2. that it is not strictly within the competence of a single institution;
3. that it seeks to meet an identified educational need within the community not so far met or adequately met.

Projects costing less than £5000 in a full year were authorized under the Education Officer's delegated powers, subject to the concurrence of the Chief Financial Officer when expenditure exceeded £1500. Recommended projects in excess of £5000 were subject to the Further and Higher Education sub-committee's approval.

Despite the lack of enthusiasm of many managing and governing bodies of schools, no less than forty (totalling £25,145) of the 101 projects approved (£71,482) were from primary schools; five were from nursery schools. Most of the projects were for parents' rooms and parents and children's activities. Many were linked with local adult education institutes. For example, one nursery project was for an educational home-visiting pilot-scheme, based at Clyde Nursery School, to establish links with parents (mainly West Indian) prior to their children's admission to nursery school. The scheme was in order to help them with their children's development (particularly linguistic), in association with the Frobisher Institute. Another ten projects came from secondary schools. Fifteen grants totalling £20,995 were for adult education institutes which included Wandsworth Community Workshop for parents and children at the old Battersea Town Hall (£6255); the creation of a lecturer post to organize home tuition for language students, mainly from the Moroccan community; play group facilities for the children of mothers attending play-leadership courses at an adult education institute; a literacy post shared between Goldsmiths' College and the Eltham Institute for the Lee Centre, a study and recreational centre for young adults in the district, open day and evening for seven days a week.

In response to the concern expressed at the 1974 conferences at the overloading of school premises and the pressure on schoolkeeping staff, Users' Committees, consisting of representatives of services using a particular school building and the schoolkeeper, were increasingly being formed to plan the fullest and most effective use of the accommodation.

Whilst officers of the Community Education and Careers Branch, who administered the scheme, quickly became aware that the word 'community' was regarded by some as a magic password for additional funds, there was no doubt that the grant made available under the ESWC scheme had stimulated a very wide and interesting variety of projects. Often the contribution required to launch a project was modest, although by means of it a valuable link between a school and the community could be established.

The provision for the ESWC fund in the estimates for 1975–6 had to be reduced to £50,000 and the worsened financial situation emphasized the value of having a fund through which a response could be made to local initiatives if the impetus created by the launching of the scheme was not to be lost. It is to the great credit of the ILEA that, from 1973 to 1978 despite the pressures of increased financial stringency, it provided such a fund. Not only was the fund maintained but the continuing financial commitment in respect of staff appointed from grants, was provided for in revenue estimates and exempted from 'no growth' restrictions. Regretfully in 1980, as part of the ILEA's budget strategy, it was decided that no new community initiatives should be funded under the ESWC scheme. Throughout the seven years of its operation it had grant-aided 373 projects at a total cost of £328,806 which included £147,125 for staff, £100,575 for equipment and materials and £50,000 for building work. The continuing full-year cost of initial grants towards the salaries of additional staff amounted to £305,000.

Primary schools and adult education institutes, particularly, made good use of the fund and the progress made and level of sophistication of projects is well illustrated by two projects funded in 1979. A grant of £5850 was made to the Tower Hamlets Education Advice Centre towards the cost of a full-time co-ordinator

(Lecturer 2) and part-time secretarial hours (ten per week) plus materials, equipment and expenses for each project which aimed to give adults accurate information and advice about available educational opportunities at all levels. The guidance service was to help individuals to find their educational needs and relate them to what continuing education had to offer; the resulting 'feedback' would enable the education system to meet these needs more fully and effectively. The co-ordinator and part-time secretarial hours were attached to a local adult education institute; projects were monitored by the ILEA's Inspectorate.

Another grant was given to the Central London Adult Education Institute (£575 in 1979–80 plus £3000 in 1978–9) to enable the setting-up of a community learning-resources centre in south Islington in part of the former Chequer School premises used by the Institute. The centre would be available to primary schools, youth centres, local voluntary educational and community groups, the Central London Institute and the borough council's Play and Recreation Training Unit. The centre offered the use of the reprographic and audio-visual equipment, together with advice and information services on software and materials and training courses on the use of equipment. A wide cross-section of the community was thus involved and local groups enabled to improve and extend their services and facilities. Capital costs included equipment, building works and security measures. On-going costs were for secretarial assistants. The Institute's media-resources officer co-ordinated the project with assistance from the Centre for Learning Resources who provided a trainee audio-visual-aids technician. The London Borough of Islington provided a full-time worker and £2000 for additional equipment.

It is difficult to judge how successful the education service for the whole community operation was in changing attitudes and relating the education service as a whole to the community. Certainly, three years after the launching of the scheme divisional officers were aware of many more instances of links between one section of the service and another and a good deal more crossing of inter-service boundaries between primary schools, secondary schools, further education colleges, youth service establishments and adult education institutes. Certainly, too, there was evidence of a good deal more involvement of parents. Three hundred and seventy-three projects, many of which continue, were growth points for a more integrated service to the whole community. At a time when, up and down the country, there was a good deal of attention being given to the community use of education service resources and joint schemes of recreation and education were being developed and presented as community education and even community development, London attempted something quite distinct if not unique. A community grows from the ground up and an education service responsive to the social and educational needs of the community it attempts to serve, is more likely to grow from response to local initiatives, albeit more slowly, than if a preconceived system of community education is lowered on to it from above. Whatever may have been the effect of ESWC on the rest of the service there can be no doubt that it reinforced a growing attitude in the adult education service which stemmed from the report, *Social Structure of the Student Body in Adult Education Institutes*.

When the report of the Russell Committee, *Adult Education – A Plan for Development*, was published in 1973, the Further and Higher Education sub-committee[4] authorized the Education Officer to consult teacher's organizations and others on the recommendations in the report and also those made in the report on the *Social Structure of the Student Body in Adult Education Institutes*. The sub-committee, at the same time, approved in principle the setting up of a Local Development Council for Inner London, as recommended by the Russell Committee. The Education Officer was asked therefore to seek observations from those consulted on the constitution and orders of reference of such a body. The recommendations of the Russell Committee covered much of what was already established practice in the ILEA. Those concerned with 'areas of unmet need' endorsed the views expressed in the ILEA's own written evidence to the Committee and the general approach recommended in the social structure working party's report on attracting disadvantaged adults.

In general there was overall support[5] for the recommendations of the Russell Committee and the working party but there were some reservations. The London Head Teachers' Association (LHTA), for example, wondered 'if the Russell Report presents a need which does not exist in reality' and considered that any extra accommodation which could be provided 'should be made available for use by other sections – schools, youth, etc.'. The London branch of the Association of Headmistresses welcomed the proposed development in the field of adult education provided that additional resources could be made available: 'There would be little point in improving opportunities for disadvantaged adults at the expense of disadvantaged children.' Many references were made in the comments to consideration of the future of adult education in the context of the ILEA's report *An Education Service for the Whole Community*. On the whole the replies endorsed the reports rather than suggested new or different ideas and expressed anxiety concerning the possible adverse effect of the economic climate on the future rate of expansion.

The disparity in the grading (for salaries) of principals of adult education centres and institutes throughout the country had led the Russell Committee to recommend the national negotiating committee for further education teachers' salaries (Burnham FE Committee) to consider a separate scale of salaries for adult education with a view to establishing a reasonable career structure. In London, the Burnham Committee scales for vocational further education had been applied to adult education principals and other staff. The Association of Principals of ILEA Adult Education Institutes submitted a particularly interesting paper on this aspect to the ILEA's Consultative Committee for Non-Vocational Institutes (October 1974), in which they challenged the nationally established practice for grading teachers salaries, a practice, which it must be said, reflected the negotiating stance of all teachers' unions and which accepted that work with more advanced students should be rated more highly than that with the average or less than average. Only in special education for handicapped children was there additional weighting of salaries. The document strongly supported the ILEA's policy of increasing emphasis on work with the uncommitted and the disadvantaged and urged the need for channelling increased resources into this area. 'It seems to be endemic in our educational system that resources are more readily available to those who operate in what are generally known as the higher, or more advanced realms of study.' It went on to argue for 'a system of grading which will encourage us into areas of hard recruitment but which will, at the same time, enhance and protect our economic status and career potential.' It asked for positive discrimination to be given to those tutors who worked with the disadvantaged by grading classes for such students on a level with classes for advanced work. 'We are well aware that this will require a reversal of thinking which in terms of traditionally educational practice, is almost heretical.' Believing that the Burnham Committee would not 'at this stage' be brought to accept such a policy, they urged the ILEA to take independent action. The Consultative Committee agreed to recommend the Authority to set up a joint working party of ILEA officers and representatives of professional organizations, to examine the grading of classes in adult education institutes and the allocation of resources to them with particular reference to work in depressed areas for disadvantaged students.

As a result of the consultations on the Russell Committee report, the Social Structure Working Party, the discussions which arose out of the ILEA *Education Service for the Whole Community* report and the setting up of governing bodies for adult education institutes, it was decided to establish a Central Consultative Committee for Adult Education and twelve local consultative committees for adult education. Each local consultative committee covered the area of an inner London borough and was representative of a wide range of statutory and voluntary organizations in that area.

Adult Literacy

For many years adult institutes had provided for men and women who were unable to read and write adequately but it was almost a covert provision which reflected the embarrassment of an adult who had been through primary and secondary school and who was still unable to read. Such references as there were to general education classes in institute prospectuses indicated that help would be available to *improve* reading and writing and never to teaching adults to read and write. An adult unable to read and write, whose native language was English, was virtually smuggled into an institute, usually by a friend who completed the enrolment form for him or her and had a quiet word with the principal or other responsible member of staff. When he reached the class he would find that most of the other students in it were people whose first language was not English. Any group teaching in the class was for students of English as a second language and the tutor gave as much individual tuition as was practicable in a two-hour class of twelve-fourteen students. The number of illiterate adults, whose first language was English, who looked to the institutes for help with their reading and writing was therefore very small.

This absence of demand contributed to the general lack of awareness in educational circles of the existence of adults in need of help. Those institutes who were responsible for providing education in London's five prisons, however, were very well aware that a problem existed since tuition in reading and writing for adults had been a feature of the general education provision for a number of years. In some prisons, such as Wormwood Scrubs, a considerable expertise had been built up. In the 1960s voluntary organizations, dealing with the day-to-day problems of men and women in their area, found a disquieting number of adults who were unable to read and write adequately. A number of such organizations, notably Cambridge House Settlement, began to tackle the problem. Cambridge House began to recruit and train volunteers to help such adults on a one-to-one individual basis, usually in the adult's home. The ILEA gave a grant to the settlement from 1964 onwards for this work and Cambridge House became a centre to which adults with literacy problems from all over the London area were referred and matched with a volunteer, selected where possible from the area in which the adult student lived. By the early 1970s a trickle of students, given confidence by tuition in voluntary schemes, were coming to adult education institutes and Cambrige House was establishing links with institutes and youth centres with a view to encouraging students to use the adult institute facilities.

In January 1972, Bethnal Green Institute appointed an out-reach worker, previously a tutor in Wormwood Scrubs Prison. She quickly found the need for literacy tuition for people who lived in streets adjoining the Institute building. The one characteristic common to most adults unable to read and write was, and for many still is, an unwillingness to reveal this. They would only admit to not being able to read and write to someone whom they trusted and who was giving some practical help in a particular difficulty they faced. In general they were not prepared to join a class or even enter an educational establishment since by definition that required a standard which they did not have. Bethnal Green Institute and others who, through their out-reach workers had contact with individuals and organizations in the local community, recruited volunteers from friends and relations of staff and students and built up a referral system by which they could match volunteers with a student for tuition. The out-reach worker began to recruit and train volunteers and act as the co-ordinator for a literacy scheme which had marked similarities to that of Cambridge House. Once it became known that you did not need to join a class, that you could ask for an individual by name and could be helped, in confidence, the number of people willing to come forward grew. By 1973 it was necessary to make another full-time appointment at Bethnal Green Institute to assist the out-reach worker or community development worker as she was styled. By 1973 nine posts of out-reach workers, variously styled, and, in addition, twelve other full-time posts with responsibility for some form of welfare, literacy or immigrant classes, had been authorized. They reflected the closer working relationship which institutes were establishing with voluntary organizations whose workers could make known the day-to-day needs of the wide variety of minority and disadvantaged groups.

In the meantime the British Association of Settlements had mounted a campaign to tackle the problem of adult illiteracy and established a national literacy campaign committee under the chairmanship of Lady Plowden. The British Association of Settlements on 7 November 1973 staged a conference in London – Status: Illiterate – to which they invited representatives of voluntary organizations, local authorities and interested national bodies. At the conference the startling announcement was made that there were at least 2 million functionally illiterate adults in England and Wales. The campaign called upon the government to give a firm commitment to eradicate adult illiteracy and to use its powers to direct the course and content of adult education to help local education authorities improve facilities for illiterate adults. At the conference itself the representative from the BBC announced that the Corporation was working on a three-year television and radio adult literacy project which it hoped would begin in October 1975 and in which there would be a referral service by which people, in all parts of the country, would telephone the BBC to seek help and would be referred to the appropriate LEA. The national campaign gathered momentum and a private member's bill, introduced by Mr Christopher Price, MP for Lewisham, was withdrawn when the government announced that a sum of £1 million had been set aside to help tackle the problem of adult literacy.

It was decided to set up the Adult Literacy Resource Agency under the aegis of the National Institute of Adult Education to administer a grant of £1 million from the Education Department, in the financial year 1975–6, to help LEAs and voluntary organizations tackle the problem of adult literacy. In the autumn of 1974 a management committee for the Agency was set up, consisting of representatives of the local authority associations, the Education Department, the National Institute of Adult Education and voluntary organizations. The Assistant Education

Officer (Community Education and Careers) was invited to become the Director of the new Agency and was seconded by the ILEA with effect from 1 March 1975.

Meanwhile, the ILEA's provision for adult literacy had rapidly expanded. The activities of out-reach workers and a general stepping up of provision in the institutes themselves had encouraged many adults with reading and writing problems to come forward. Publicity given by the national campaign and through television gave an added impetus to their efforts. In April 1974 the ILEA appointed Miss Catherine Moorhouse as Director of Adult Literacy.

By the end of 1974 adult-literacy tuition was being given at all but one of the thirty adult education institutes. The exception was the Central London Institute which catered mainly for commuters and, at that time, there was no demand for literacy tuition at that institute. Well over 2000 literacy students were enrolled at adult education institutes, the majority receiving tuition in small groups and a few on a one-to-one basis within groups. In eight institutes a total of approximately fifty volunteer tutors assisted. There were four full-time appointments for literacy with an additional three posts approved. Some 147 part-time staff were employed in literacy tuition in the institutes, most of whom were qualified by virtue of their day-time employment as teachers; others had undertaken short courses on the teaching of literacy to adults. The development over the previous two years of informal adult education in the shape of 'workshops' had provided a means whereby students could come informally to specially equipped rooms for assessment and referral to the appropriate form of tuition. This initially might be on a one-to-one basis or by an individual programme of work with specially prepared materials, tapes or language equipment.

Bethnal Green Adult Education Institute had an extensive scheme catering for up to 100 students, offering sixty-three hours tuition weekly (morning, afternoon, evening and on Saturday mornings), using volunteers, full-time and part-time tutors. It also operated an in-service training scheme for its own tutors and the ILEA. The City Literary Adult Training Unit provided courses for teachers of literacy and it was estimated that 150–200 tutors and teachers of reading attended courses for teaching adult illiterates in 1974–75. Many institutes had, in association with media resources officers, developed a range of teaching materials suitable for adults with literacy problems, but it was felt that there was a need for resource centres to collect and select examples of such materials and to reproduce them for the use of all institutes offering literacy tuition.

Literacy tuition was not limited to adult education institutes, it was also being offered at some further education vocational colleges. Brixton College for Further Education had well-established link courses offering classes to eighty literacy students, full and part-time, including some referred from Cambridge House. In 1974 it had experimented with the use of some twenty-two volunteers and was developing an in-service training pattern for tutors and volunteers. Of the twenty-five higher and further education colleges special provision was being made for students with literacy problems in nine of them, the students being withdrawn from general-study classes, day-release groups, etc. It was estimated that some 400 students were receiving literacy tuition. A further eighty-five students were being catered for at six youth centres, some of which operated in conjunction with the local adult education institute.

The Cambridge House scheme had, by 1974, outgrown its resources and had recently been reorganized into two regions, north and south of the river. Cambridge House continued to cover the south and a new scheme was established at Beauchamp Lodge to cover the area north of the river. They established close links with adult education and youth centres with a view to arranging the transfer of students, when they had sufficient confidence, to the appropriate ILEA provision. In 1974 Cambridge House had 463 volunteer tutors and 505 students and Beauchamp Lodge, still in its infancy, had thirty-two tutors (fifteen of whom were in training) and fifteen students. The North Islington Literacy Scheme was closely linked with the Holloway Adult Education Institute and the Lambeth Rathbone Literacy Scheme was being established in association with the South Lambeth Institute. The Southwark Literacy Development Group (SLIDE), comprising representatives of Cambridge House, the youth service, adult education institutes, schools and community workers, was indicative of the increased concern in statutory and voluntary circles for a united approach to the problem in a particular borough. The Southwark Group had produced a directory giving comprehensive information about all the facilities available in the area.

The way in which the adult education service had changed gear and accelerated the provision for adult literacy throughout the ILEA area was a quite remarkable demonstration of its flexibility and response to newly revealed needs. It was also another illustration of the ILEA's anticipation of a national need. Along with other local education authorities it had been slow to realize the extent of the need; nevertheless, it was quicker than most to make the appropriate appointments and resources available as soon as the activities of its fieldworkers revealed the need. By the time the national need had been recognized and the Adult Literacy Resource Agency set up, the ILEA had already developed a substantial provision and an organization which could respond to the increased demand. The appointment of Miss Moorhouse as Director of Adult Literacy and, in the same year, the appointment of her assistant director were important steps by which the ILEA's varied provision could be co-ordinated and a large-scale training operation mounted.

In response to a preliminary notice in November 1974 by the National Institute of Adult Education on the setting up of the Adult Literacy Resource Agency and the general headings under which central government's £1 million would be allocated, the Education Officer reported to the Further and Higher Education sub-committee on the state of the existing provision in the ILEA's area, those aspects of it which needed strengthening and the headings under which financial help should be sought from the Agency. By this time it was known that the BBC's television and radio three-year project and its accompanying central referral scheme would operate from October 1975. The officers concerned with the central referral scheme and the principals of institutes had had an indication of the impact which a general invitation to people to phone-in for help could make when, as a result of a Thames Television programme some 400 potential students had been referred to the ILEA. They had little doubt that the BBC programme would make a considerable impact on the concentrated population of London. If this was to be met, training courses for tutors and volunteers, training of trainers and more materials and equipment would have to be increased. The ILEA had already instituted a pilot course for a Royal Society of Arts Certificate in the teaching of literacy skills to adults. Funds were sought from the Resource Agency for a second pilot course which could be mounted for teachers from the GLC area and the home counties. The ILEA also recommended to the Resource Agency that professional representatives from the various authorities should have the opportunity of meeting to design a work-pack for the use of volunteer tutors and that help should be given for setting up a Central Resource Agency in the ILEA which would house additional equipment and make facilities available to other institutions, both voluntary and statutory, within reasonable travelling distance. The Adult Literacy Resource Agency made an allocation of £20,000 to the ILEA in June 1975 – £6675 for training courses and £13,325 for teaching materials, audio-visual equipment and other technical aids. The allocation for training enabled the mounting of twelve special in-service training courses at various adult institutes for teachers and voluntary tutors; a one-week full-time seminar at the City Literary Institute for a literacy specialist to study training procedures and the establishment of a second Royal Society of Arts course in teaching of literacy skills to adults at Westminster College. The grant for teaching materials, etc. enabled a resource centre to be set up at the Frobisher Institute and a general supplementation of equipment and materials for literary tuition at adult institutes.

It is appropriate here to comment on the contribution that the ILEA made to the national literacy campaign. Mr Sidney Heaven, one of the ILEA's further-education inspectors with a specialist knowledge of the teaching of English to adult illiterates and as a second language, represented the Association of Metropolitan Authorities on the management committee of the Adult Literacy Resource Agency; the assistant education officer for Community Education and Careers (W. A. Devereux), on his appointment as Director of the Agency, was seconded by the ILEA. Miss Catherine Moorhouse, the ILEA Director of Adult Literacy, was a consultant to the BBC and a member of the team which produced

'On the Move' and other television and radio programmes; she was a member of the Agency Advisory Committee and of the group which produced the tutors' training pack, the volunteer tutors' pack and a number of booklets published by the Agency. She was also a member of the training team which ran national conferences throughout the country and was recognized as a national and international authority on adult literacy. Many of the adult literacy staff contributed to training sessions and conferences and a good deal of the practice and expertise available in the ILEA's literacy schemes were adopted nationally. By February 1976 the service was catering for about 4000 students and had recruited and trained some 600 volunteers. By February 1978, in the last year of the Agency's life and the publication of the national LEA literacy statistics, the ILEA was catering for 5600 students and using over 1100 volunteers.

The ILEA has continued its provision for adults with literacy problems and extended it as part of the broader approach to literacy and other basic education needs. Mr. Peter Clyne, the assistant education officer (Community Education and Careers), appointed when Mr Devereux retired from the ILEA in 1975, represented the Association of Metropolitan Authorities on the management committee of the Adult Literacy Unit which replaced the Resource Agency in 1978; he was appointed to the management committee of the Adult Literacy and Basic Skills Unit which was set up in 1980. There is national recognition of the valuable contribution made by the LCC and the ILEA in the extent to which they have always been prepared to share with others their experience and the expertise of their officers.

The ILEA's contribution to the national literacy campaign was indicative of a rather more fundamental contribution it had made to adult education generally. The literacy campaign itself was a remarkable illustration of a new approach to those who, hitherto, had been largely ignored or had felt that any form of continuing education was not for them. It had shown that those who had not set foot in an educational establishment since leaving school could, by the adoption of a sensitive approach and tuition relevant to their individual circumstances and needs, be encouraged to seek help. The philosophy of this approach was the philosophy of the out-reach worker and of an education service for the whole community which London had first expressed in its evidence to the Russell Committee and given practical recognition in the appointment of out-reach workers and its policy of positive discrimination.

The expansion of work with the disadvantaged was not limited to adult illiterates. In 1974–5 the number of classes a week offered by adult education institutes had reached an all-time record of 18,061 with increases in all sections other than drama and technical crafts which remained at about the same level. The most dramatic increase, however, was in classes under the general heading of 'basic education'. This jumped from 343 classes a week in 1972–3 to 879 in 1974–5.

They included 337 classes in English as a second language and 197 literacy schemes.

The service was now subject to the worsening financial climate and 1975–6 was a year of 'no growth'. As a report to the Further and Higher Education sub-committee in February 1976 indicated, most of the provision for adult illiterates as well as for those who were disadvantaged in other ways, for instance, immigrants needing language teaching, people in homes and hospitals, etc. had to be contained within the normal allocation of tutor hours. In 1975–6 a central pool of tutor hours helped to supply additional hours for institutes where the problems of meeting demands was particularly acute that, on the whole, the expansion of work with the disadvantaged took place at the expense of other provision. It is not surprising, therefore,to see that the total number of classes a week fell to 17,528. There was a general scaling down in all areas with particular decreases in the number of classes in languages and games and sports; those in basic education, however, rose to 1125. It is also interesting to note that the total student enrolment rose in 1975–6 to an all-time high of 294,478 as compared with 287,090 in 1974–5. By 1978–9 the numbers in most sections had remained much the same but the number of classes a week in basic education had risen to 1552 in a total of 17,451 classes a week.

The national literacy campaign was limited to adult native speakers of English and specifically excluded those for whom English was a second language. Whilst there are aspects of the teaching of both which are common and complementary, the important difference is that native speakers of English have had years of speaking the language whereas immigrants, or those for whom it is a second language, are learning to speak it. This exclusion of non-native speakers of English from literacy schemes emphasized the different methods necessary in teaching English as a second language and threw into sharp relief the need to provide specifically for adults from varied ethnic backgrounds now living in this country. Nowhere was this need greater than in London. It was not a new problem for London, particularly in the East End which, for centuries, had absorbed immigrants from overseas. The concentration of people from particular races in various parts of London, the natural tendency for them to look to their compatriots for support and the preservation of their native culture and way of life, sometimes made it difficult to discover their real needs or to respond to them in a manner which was acceptable to them. This was particularly true of Asian communities. What seemed to be an obvious need was for English classes but publicity – even leaflets in several languages – failed to evoke a response. It was not until close contact was made with the small nucleus of that community that members of it began to use the education facilities. Reference has already been made to the experience of the Central Wandsworth Institute (pages 218–19). The Bethnal Green Institute circulated leaflets in several languages advertising the availability of classes in

English. The response was very poor but, through contacts with Asians, they discovered a demand for classes in Asian cultural activities – poetry, dancing, music
and drama – taken by tutors of their own national background. John Brown, the
principal of the Institute, in an article in ILEA's *Contact* (issue 24), described the
Institute's response: 'We set up a loose structure to allow this to happen and then
discovered that they wanted to learn English, but with their own teachers again.
This caused us a lot of heart searching but in the end it was better to have contact
with 500 or 600 people on their terms than with 30 on ours. As a development of
this we are now beginning to double up tutors – an English native tutor with the
Asian.'

As with illiterates many immigrants lack the confidence to join a class and a
number of voluntary organizations and institutes operated schemes in which
volunteers gave tuition in English on an individual basis until the student felt
sufficiently confidence to join a class. In London these schemes were given additional impetus by the literacy campaign and the two programmes learned a great
deal from each other.

By 1976, five full-time development worker posts were established and
attached to the Chaucer (Walworth) and Holloway Institutes. They were from
Industrial Language Units and their job was to assist those with language-tuition
needs at their places of employment. In 1977 a deputy director was appointed to
the Adult Literacy Unit to co-ordinate language provision for adult immigrants.
The pattern of non-English speaking communities in inner London was a good
deal more complex than in any other area of high immigrant or migrant worker
settlement in the UK. The London provision had to cater for migrant workers
from the EEC, immigrants from the Commonwealth and Pakistan and the
successive waves of refugees, some, like the Poles, long-established, others more
recently arrived from South America, Cyprus, Ethiopia and Vietnam. Students of
English as a Second Language (ESL) classes came from a variety of educational as
well as ethnic and cultural backgrounds. It was, therefore, not unusual for a class
teacher, or group of teachers, to have to assess the language needs and provide a
syllabus for a Greek tailor, Pakistani book-keeper, Chilean radiologist, Portuguese chef and a Bangladeshi lathe-operator. Classes in main institutes were
unsuitable for many immigrant students for whom journeys of any distance were
impracticable or who lacked the confidence to join a class in an alien educational
system. For many, classes needed to be conveniently sited and timed in buildings
where they had already come into contact with other statutory services –
schools, clinics, job-centres or social meeting places such as mosques, temples,
community centres, Saturday-morning schools for first-language tuition or work
places. For all but the last – creches were necessary.

Provision for all potential students had to be extremely flexible; home tutors
had to be recruited and trained and small groups allowed to develop locally.

Networks of contacts and liaison with statutory services had to be developed in the area, as well as with local community groups, supported by publicity in minority languages and in English. By these means, individual referrals to language units could then be followed up by personal contacts, phone and home visits. National referral schemes such as the BBC Parosi project were notably less successful in attracting students and volunteers than had been the case in the adult literacy campaign.

In 1978 the ILEA Literacy Unit became the ILEA Literacy and Language Unit serving both literacy and English as a second language schemes. By this time the ILEA was providing some 700 ESL classes, off-site and on-site, for 7500 adults living and working in inner London. The pattern of provision reflected the different patterns of settlement of the ethnic minorities – for example, the greater demand for evening classes in north London was probably related directly to the large migrant-worker population to be found in the hotel and catering industry in the central and northern boroughs.

In eighteen months there had been a 79 per cent increase in the number of students receiving ESL tuition, due doubtless to the activities of the seven borough language organizers who researched needs, co-ordinated provision, organized home-tuition schemes and generally made contact with other agencies. There were also, in 1978, six full-time teachers at institutes with special responsibilities for ESL. The bulk of the teaching, however, was undertaken by part-time tutors. The increasing variety of demands made on teachers and organizers in this rapidly developing field called for a co-ordinated programme of in-service training in basic techniques, conversion courses for experienced English as a Foreign Language (EFL) tutors, a variety of short courses in specific skills, for example, role play and intensive courses for home tutors. Three courses were already running for the Royal Society of Arts Certificate in the Teaching of English to Immigrants which the ILEA had initiated. By 1980 there were over 800 on-site and off-site classes for more than 8500 adults and the number of full-time staff had risen to twenty-one.

John Brown's 'loose structure to allow this to happen' was illustrative of the approach adopted by many institutes to provide not only for people from ethnic minorities but for a whole range of 'community' projects. The institutes were becoming resource centres for a range of activities which allowed adults and organizations to develop informal contact which met an immediate need and led on to continuing education. Usually the projects arose directly as a result of the contacts made by out-reach workers. This was not always the case – sometimes it was the other way round, an out-reach worker being appointed in order to develop an activity which had arisen from a class. The appointment of Mrs Winstanley in Battersea and Central Wandsworth to work with women's clubs was such a case (see page 247). The Allfarthing workshop, which led to parents and children workshops, sprang from the initiative of the full-time art tutor and tutor of the pre-school play leadership course at the Central Wandsworth Institute. Mothers in Battersea were invited to come with their children to the Institute's accommodation at the Allfarthing School on Fridays. When they arrived they were given a cup of tea – prepared by one of the mothers – their children were usually swept (or enticed) away to play with toys or other children and 'Mum' could sit, untrammelled, to drink her tea and chat with other mothers. She would see around her simple exhibits of art and craft work and learned that Mrs X had made this or that and that she (Mrs X) had never done anything like that before. One or other of the two staff there would casually talk to her about the various activities going on and follow up any expressed or half-expressed interest by suggesting she might like to try to paint or make some object or garment. After one or two visits it was unusual if she was not to be found engaged in some art or craft work or in some musical activity.

Accommodation for their sole use was usually the essential ingredient of such projects and those institutes who were fortunate enough to have such accommodation were able to develop their institute as a resource centre for a range of classes and 'community' projects. Those who did not have their own accommodation sought the help of local voluntary organizations and settlements for the use of a hall or room.

These activities were in addition to the large number of welfare classes and groups provided in homes, old people's clubs, hospitals and the activities of the many students' clubs and associations which sprang from the classes themselves. An indication of the extent of the provision of welfare and community classes is given by the number of different establishments used by institutes for this purpose. In 1975–6 two institutes provided welfare and community classes at forty clubs, homes, hospitals, etc. Another two used between thirty and forty such establishments and another eight used between twenty and thirty.

Every review made of adult education throughout the years has referred to the need for more accommodation for adult education and, in particular, more accommodation for the sole use of institutes. Apart from the City Literary Institute premises in Stukeley Street opened in 1939, the extension of Morley College in 1972 and the new building for the Stanhope Institute in 1976, there has been no purpose-built accommodation for adult education in inner London. Stanhope's new building in 1976 was the result of ten years obstinacy in retaining an old building in the middle of a large-scale new development until the developers were prepared to make alternative provision on a nearby site. The demands on capital building programmes and expensive sites in inner London and persistent financial cut-backs on capital-building programmes have denied adult education a place in building programmes so far. A survey of the adult education service in 1976 showed that permanent teaching accommodation in adult education institutes varied considerably from institute to institute. Nine institutes had over 2000 sq. metres; eleven between 1250 – 2000 sq. metres; six between 750 – 1250 sq. metres and six had less than 750 sq. metres. Moreover, accommodation was often dispersed over several buildings. At one end of the scale four institutes had a building with over 2000 sq. metres for their own use; at the other seventeen had no building with over 750 sq. metres of teaching accommodation for their own use. Reporting to the Further and Higher Education sub-committee (27 September 1976) (ILEA 493) the Education Officer said:

> Day time classes are very valuable as a means of bringing the service to certain people such as the elderly, mothers of young children, and shift workers who might not otherwise be able to benefit. Day time classes are also extremely useful for literacy teaching and for attracting the unemployed and redundant into some interesting purposeful activity. However, the only substantial amount of accommodation likely to be made available to any institute for this purpose is in redundant school premises. These are usually old, perhaps unattractive, and probably located in areas of declining population. It therefore takes time to build up a day time programme, and it is also necessary to divert resources from the usually successful evening activities in order to foster these new developments. There are also certain other factors which limit the day time use of specialist accommodation. It is for example likely that classes which need to use a motor vehicle workshop or a sailing centre can only meet in the evenings or at weekends but the accommodation is not suitable for other use in the day. Again it is very desirable for institutes to have their own accommodation for certain craft subjects such as pottery, weaving, metalwork, sculpture, etc. for which technical equipment is needed and where it is difficult or impossible for students to take their work home between classes. It is obviously desirable for facilities to be used as much as possible, sometimes in conjunction with other education or related local services, but circumstances vary from institute to institute . . . Problems are indeed likely to occur from multiple occupation, particularly as the schools themselves develop evening activities frequently involving parents as well as pupils. Goodwill and forbearance are necessary on all sides, as well as an understanding of the burden on schoolkeeping staff.[6]

The survey showed that about a quarter of the resources of the adult education service were being devoted to special community needs although, of course, many more people with special needs enrolled in ordinary classes. The groups of people with special needs were defined as Commonwealth immigrants, hospital patients and residents of hostels and homes, the blind, the deaf, the mentally handicapped, the physically handicapped, those in prisons and penal establishments, residents of community homes, women at maternity and child-welfare centres, retirement pensioners' groups, pre-school play-group leaders' courses, parents of handicapped children, those undertaking literacy work, those undertaking basic education, other groups meeting specific community needs (for example, training volunteers for adult literacy work), parent/child workshops and speech therapy for 'stroke' patients. In the maintained adult education establishments alone, enrolments in courses provided for special community needs amounted to 18 per cent of the total enrolment (when classes at penal establishments were included) and 16 per cent when classes at penal establishments were excluded. Again, the proportion of enrolments in courses provided for special community needs varied greatly from one institute to another, ranging from 4–50 per cent. Excluding classes at penal establishments, two institutes had less than 5 per cent enrolments in the special category, nine institutes had between 5–9 per cent and five institutes had 30 per cent or more. Some of the reasons for such variation were the different characteristics of the catchment areas of some institutes and, in central London particularly, the influence of 'commuter' students.

In November 1975 there were about 185 authorized full-time lecturing posts in adult education institutes. Of these, twenty-seven were for literacy work and thirty-three for out-reach and community work (including parents and child classes). Thus, about 33 per cent of full-time staff were appointed directly in connection with classes for special community needs. In addition the Director of Adult Literacy and her assistant were clearly in this category, although not attached to any particular institute. Of the rest 39 per cent were appointed for work in art, craft, dress or fashion, 18 per cent for cultural and academic subjects, 7 per cent for mainly organization work (in charge of branches, short courses, etc.) and about 3 per cent (six posts) for physical education. There were twenty-four authorized full-time lecturing posts at the City Literary Institute of which twelve were in the centre for deaf studies, two with the adult education training unit and two with the Fresh Horizons course.

In the adult education institutes alone the number of students and student hours had increased from approximately 202,500 and 12,300,000 respectively in 1970–71 to approximately 260,500 and 15,250,000 in 1974–75. The proportion of the ILEA's expenditure on adult education during that period was about 2.7 per cent. (It was about 2.2 per cent at the time of the evidence to the Russell Committee.) There had been little direct publicity except for efforts made by out-reach and other staff to get in touch with the local population, institute exhibitions and local press reports. There was, of course, a spin-off from national campaign publicity such as that for adult literacy and, subsequently, for English as a second language. *Floodlight* and institute prospectuses sought to inform rather than persuade.

The aim of the 1957–9 reorganization had been to fashion an organization in which the adult education institutes would interpret individual and communal needs primarily in a local 'neighbourhood' area. The evidence to the Russell Committee envisaged that institutes would become educational and recreational resource centres increasingly reaching out to those who had hitherto not been served; institutes, it was thought, would also develop partnerships with other local statutory and voluntary organizations. By the end of the 1960s all but four had outgrown the 1959 modest conception of catering for about 3000 students, fourteen had an enrolment of more than 6000 and three, excluding the City Literary Institute had between 9000 and 11,000 students.

By 1976 the two smallest institutes had between 4000 and 6000 students; thirteen had 6000 to 8000 students; six had 8000 to 10,000 students; nine had over 10,000, including one over 14,000.

The ILEA's policy is nowhere more succinctly put than in the following passage which appears each year at the head of the Community Education Estimates:

> The Authority's policy for community education is to fulfil its obligations under the Education Act to provide for the cultural, recreational, informal and social education needs of young people and adults with the object of developing personality, satisfying creative and learning needs and fulfilling latent abilities. In so doing, the Authority recognises that this is an integral part of its education provision and no less important than other aspects of the service and that it should be readily available to all who wish to take advantage of it, irrespective of circumstances, but that in assessing priorities, the needs of those who are socially, physically or mentally deprived or who are disadvantaged in other ways, should receive particular attention.

The service has grown in the execution of this policy and has developed a high degree of expertise. It has evolved its own philosophy and ethos in which respect for the individual needs of students as adults, and high-quality tuition were cardinal aims. As the adult education service reached further into the community, new techniques directed towards enabling the individual to make informed choices in his personal life and society were being evolved. To this end there were courses designed to help adults to acquire the basic educational tools which, for a variety of reasons, they had failed to learn, for example, literacy, numeracy and English as a second language for immigrants; courses to help a man or woman understand and cope with the changing nature of society (such as 'second chance' courses for those who wished to extend their education so that they could study for a particular examination or qualification); and courses in civil rights and the nature and scope of the various services available to citizens, for examples, health, social services and education.

An analysis of the number of classes held each week in each subject at adult education institutes in 1970–71 and 1978–9 shows the remarkable and constant popularity of the traditional subject areas. In both years domestic craft heads the list with around 3300 classes a week; games and sports come second (2478 in 1970–71 and 2914 in 1978–9). Art and architecture (1758 and 2420 respectively) and languages (1848 and 2071) vie for third place. The overall numbers for the main divisions mask some changes in subjects. An additional eight languages – Bengali, Gujerati, Hindi, Czech, Finnish, Hungarian, Persian and Rumanian had been added in 1978–9 to the twenty-eight taught in 1970–71. Twelve additional sports – aikido, canoeing, circuit-training, fives, fly fishing and fly tying, kendo, karate, netball, rowing, rugby, sub-aqua, volley-ball – had been added to the twenty-six taught in 1970–71. Silk-screen printing had been added to the art subjects; learner driving to the technical crafts and deep freeze and Indian to cookery classes. Batik, crochet and macramé were additions to the domestic craft section and the number of classes in weaving, knitting and spinning were three times greater in 1978–9 (142 compared with forty-two in 1970–71). The notable exception to the overall similarity between the two years was in basic education. In 1970–71 there were 429 general education classes teaching arithmetic and English; in 1978–9 there were 287 such classes but, in addition, there were 724 classes a week in English as a foreign language and 541 literacy schemes which represented 8.9 per cent of the total as compared with 2.8 per cent in 1970–71.

In ILEA.493 (27 September 1976) the Education Officer emphasized the importance of high standards at all levels if interest was to be held. For many years it had been possible for a student in London to begin to study at the level at which interest first stirred and to pursue it as far as individual potential allowed. 'Adult students have high expectations of the institutes', said the Education Officer. Exhibitions of students' work at London institutes give eloquent testimony to the high standards demanded. These standards had been built up over the years by the quality of advice and training from further education inspectors, and by the careful recruitment and selection of full-time staff.

The appointment of full-time staff to be responsible for a particular subject area gave considerable impetus to the in-service training of part-time tutors. They enabled the influence of the small group of further education inspectors to be greatly extended and there is no doubt that the standard and quality of work in the classroom was raised noticeably in those subject areas where full-time staff had been appointed. As has been already said, London had the great advantage of being able to call on a galaxy of talent for part-time work. The range of provision and quality of tuition at the City Literary Institute, for instance, was in large measure due to the quality of part-time staff. It must of course be said, at once, that it also called for a pioneering initiative, opportunism and continued demand for high standards from a succession of principals to enable tutors of quality to be recruited and sustained. There is no question, too, that the availability of a purpose-built building for adult education in the central area, together with supporting services, was a distinct advantage. It is fair to say that the standard of work in London's institutes is acknowledged nationally as outstanding.

Inner London's major response to the adult literacy campaign would not have been possible had not the extensive organization in the institutes been available and had the ground not been prepared by developments in that field. Indeed, it was another illustration of how the vigorous ordinary provision of adult education can enable a service to grow to meet the needs of special groups. Good tutors demand of their students the best of which they are capable. Elderly people in residential homes, for example, responded to the challenge of progressive classes in art, creative writing or crafts in which they were taught new skills, rather than taught how to pass the time.

The impetus given to welfare classes and classes for disadvantaged groups made it necessary for the Education Committee and some principals to be reminded of the necessity of keeping a balanced provision. Many of the popular ordinary classes also made a valuable community provision not only for the disadvantaged adult but for ordinary citizens who had valid claims to benefit from a public education system for which they had paid. Moreover, students from special groups needed classes in other subjects and at other levels to which they could move when they either had sufficient confidence or had acquired some of the basic education they lacked. Literacy tutors were very conscious that literacy skills could quickly disappear unless opportunities to practise them were made available. Inner London pioneered courses in which literacy tuition was linked with fashion classes or with car maintenance – underlining the necessity for all tutors to be aware that some adults needed help to remedy basic education deficiencies. Although some were more conscious of it than others, London institutes generally had always been conscious of the valuable social education derived from attendance at an adult education class in which students from different backgrounds shared a common interest. The reaction of London principals to the student survey in 1969 and the resultant working party were a measure of this concern.

At a time of 'nil growth', when the development for community and special groups had to be provided at the expense of ordinary or traditional classes, it was clearly necessary for attention to be given to a balanced programme. The survey in 1975 had shown a wide variation in the different types of provision from one institute to another. The overall allocation of some 25 per cent of resources to special groups indicated that those institutes in which it was over 33 per cent were in danger of imbalance; equally so were those in which less than 10 per cent of their resources were devoted to special groups. Unless resources could be diverted from elsewhere specifically for work with the disadvantaged the Education Officer (2 January 1977)[7] felt it would be necessary 'to decide whether to limit this work to about or a little above the present level, say 25% to 30% overall, or to encourage its growth with the correlary that ''main stream'' provision is impoverished and a service suitable for the whole community can no longer be offered'. He pointed out that many of the students who joined ''main stream'' classes were themselves elderly or disadvantaged; these included increasing numbers who entered adult education by way of special classes.

ILEA.493 was a timely reminder of the continuing important role of the Authority's adult education service, its widespread beneficial influence to individuals from all sections of the community and its effect on the health of society generally. With 260,500 students in 1974–5 it made an impact on a large number of people and if, as in 1969, 40 per cent of students were first enrolments there was a considerable turnover rate and so an even wider influence on very many more people. Throughout 1975 and 1976 discussions were held with local and central consultative committees for adult education, governors of institutes, academic boards and principals and staff of institutes on how best to ensure the effective use of resources at a time of financial constraint and 'nil growth'. Every opportunity was taken to ensure that all were aware of the ILEA's policy and the balanced programmes which it required.

In January 1977 these discussions were reflected in a report (ILEA.770)[8] which discussed possible changes in criteria for the allocation of resources. Consideration was given to applying to adult education institutes an index of quantifiable criteria such as had been devised to determine resources for primary and secondary schools. In the operation of these latter it had been found that, if they were not to operate unfairly or harshly, a large amount of discretion was necessary. The Primary Schools Priority Index, because the catchment areas of primary schools were not compact or clearly defined, was based on information relating to the pupils of each school; the need for pupil-based information had been found to be even more necessary for secondary schools. Since adult students were self-selecting any index of need would have to be based on demographic factors relating to the area of each institute. There was no statistically comparable information generally available on certain factors, for example, the number of elderly or handicapped people in an institute's area. Such factors as the incidence of loneliness were unquantifiable. It was therefore concluded that it would not be feasible to devise an effective index for use in the central allocation of resources to all institutes. It was, however, considered that institutes could create a population profile of their area and a measure of relevant social-malaise factors which would help them to determine the content and balance of their programmes. Principals were asked to revise such profiles annually. These programmes have been found to be a valuable base for the determination of resources and a balanced programme of classes. (It is interesting to recall that in 1913 principals of institutes were issued with large tomes which required the completion of detailed information about the area they served. They were also required to submit an annual report which included a general profile of the area served by the institute. An examination of those volumes which are still extant suggest that they were completed for two years but, in the wartime conditions of 1914–18, they fell into disuse and were not generally used after that time. Annual reports, however, were submitted for some years afterwards.)

In addition it was agreed that, in order to increase the proportion of resources for special community needs and to even up the provision between one institute and another, 1 per cent of each institute's tutor hours and 1 per cent of the maintenance grant would be retained to form a central pool. This would produce a pool of about 11,000 tutor hours and about £6000 which could be used to meet requests for the development of new work for special community needs. The Education Officer was authorized to exempt from this scheme those institutes in which the development of special needs already took up so much of the available resources that the institute's capacity to provide an educational service for the ordinary adult citizen was in danger of becoming seriously impaired. This central pool was deliberately kept to modest proportions since the response overall by institutes to special needs had been considerable, particularly in respect of adult literacy. There were likely to be further demands, too, arising from the BBC's news service for Asians due to commence in October 1978.

A number of institutes had developed projects involving activities which did not demand continuing supervision by tutors but required facilities and equipment which was available in the institutes. This was a valuable means of stimulating the use of institutes as resource centres for the local community and of meeting needs and conserving tutor hours. It was necessary to ensure that the activities were not hazardous and liable to cause accidents. In consultation with the inspectorate, guidelines were produced about those activities which could reasonably be pursued without direct supervision. Physical activities such as weight-lifting, judo and archery clearly needed supervision but such games as table-tennis, dancing and team games, after a reasonable period of tuition, could be carried on in clubs, affiliated to the institute. As such, they could seek free lettings for training sessions, etc. Again, similar arrangements could be made for art and craft students whereby a tutor would visit the club from time to time to advise and help students.

In the prevailing financial circumstances it was clearly necessary for the ILEA to be satisfied that the maximum use was being made of the resources available and that its policy of positive discrimination was being maintained. The growth of day classes and special community projects had led, as the 1975 survey had shown, to a widespread use of accommodation wherever it could be found; institutes were now operating in many more than the five centres suggested in the reorganization of 1957–9. The Education Officer was therefore asked to examine the case for maintaining the various centres, taking as a broad guide that secondary schools rather than primary schools should be used and that compelling reasons would be needed to justify bids for additional accommodation for institutes which already possessed 1500 sq. metres of permanent teaching accommodation.

The ILEA recognized the value of a reasonable nucleus of permanent accommodation in which an adult ambience could be fostered for each institute and reaffirmed its long-term aim that adult education should be provided in attractive, welcoming buildings. The limitation on resources with a continued increase in the number of would-be students and the consequent more intensive use of tutors hours, accommodation and equipment raised questions of how far enrolment procedures enabled the use of facilities to be equitably available to potential students. To what extent were past students favoured and inner London residents excluded by those who lived outside the ILEA's area?

Enrolment procedures at institutes were not standardized. Some institutes had arrangements for postal enrolment before the standard-enrolment week. Some gave priority to existing students. Sometimes a limit was set to prior enrolments, sometimes not. Usually a limit was set on prior enrolments for popular classes. Some institutes operated a system in which all enrolments were required to be made personally and almost entirely on a first-come, first-served basis. No discrimination was made between students living in inner London and those living outside. Popular classes had waiting lists. In October 1976 members of the Further and Higher Education sub-committee had indicated that a standard enrolment procedure should be introduced for all institutes. The same working group associated with the survey presented in 1976, examined this proposition. They felt that postal enrolment tended to favour the better educated who might be more competent in filling forms, planning ahead and collecting prospectuses from which to select their class.

After considering a number of possibilities it was decided that the first two days of enrolment week should be reserved for inner London residents and those who work in London. The remainder of the enrolment period should be open equally to inner and outer London residents. Guidelines for enrolment, which would need to be extensively publicized, should be given for the session 1977–8.

Students' fees were increased for the session 1976–7 from £3.50 for a two-hour class for a session (or £1.20 a term) to £5.50 for a two-hour class (£2 a term). The net cost per student hour for 1976–7 was 67p; the cost to the ILEA of a student attending two hours a week for the thirty-five weeks of the session was therefore £46.90. For the first time for many years, therefore, the ILEA was charging more than 10 per cent of the cost which it had maintained was the appropriate proportion that students should be charged in its evidence to the Russell Committee. Even so the fees charged to students of adult education institutes in inner London were considerably lower than those of other authorities. *Floodlight* contained a statement that the ILEA did not wish to prevent anyone from attending classes because of financial hardship. 'Institute governors have discretion to remit up to 100% of the fees in such cases. A direct approach to the institute principal should be made.' A further increase in 1977 brought the fee to £7 for a two-hour class and in 1979–80 it had risen to £8.30 which having regard to inflation, represented about 10 per cent of the economic cost of a two-hour class a week for thirty-five weeks.

In 1979 the City Literary Institute celebrated its Diamond Jubilee. Whilst many of the existing adult education institutes can trace a thread of continuity, successive reorganizations have overlaid their early beginnings. The City Lit., of all the London institutes, has remained virtually unscathed. There have been times when the natural pride in the City Lit. by those who worked in the London adult education service has been tarnished at the edges by sheer envy at the special place it had always had. Everybody interested in adult education, at home or abroad, knew about the City Literary Institute. The fact that other adult education centres, some with total rolls equalling that of the City Lit., were not appreciated, was on occasions a source of irritation. Nevertheless, the City Lit. has always been an important barometer of the ILEA's commitment to adult education and to the standards which can be achieved.

The City Literary Institute was the first to have its own building, a full-time vice-principal, full-time staff, including administrative staff and a librarian, an advisory committee and then a governing body, and a students' association. In all these aspects it charted the way for an extension of these facilities to the rest of the service. Professor H.A. Jones, its principal from 1957 to 1968, writing in the City Lit's Diamond Jubilee publication *Matrix*, identified the creation of a departmental structure and the appointment of full-time staff as 'the most far-reaching in the whole history of the Lit., comparable at least with a purpose-built home in Stukeley Street . . . In every aspect of educational effectiveness there was an immediate surge forward, not just in number of students or of classes, but in quality – in the selection and briefing of part-time tutors, in the interviewing and advising of students, in the development of progressive courses that had extended over more than one year, and, above all, in the standards of excellence attained all round'.

Although the City Literary Institute, throughout its sixty years, has been concerned with the arts and the humanities, it has reflected in a quite remarkable way the general development of the London adult education service. Its central position, its own building and full-time staff with the support services which these demanded, have enabled it to be in the van of progressive change and to be a focus of London's adult education philosophy. Three aspects of its current provision (described below) are a particular demonstration of this and of the support which the City Lit. could provide for the rest of the service.

In the 1960s a part-time course called Fresh Horizons in Adult Education gave an opportunity for people – in the event, women – to reassess themselves and prepare for a new career or a different way of life. In the early 1970s there was a certain amount of pressure in some quarters for London to have its own residential adult education college. The experience of the part-time Fresh Horizons course had shown that, whilst there might be a demand for a full-time adult education course, a residential requirement would deter potential students. It would also, of course, have been much more expensive to provide and maintain. It was therefore decided to offer a full-time one-year course at the City Lit. for students who wished to prepare themselves for further study or improve their general education. The first course commenced in 1973 and, of the first twenty-five students, sixteen went on to study for degrees and three entered teacher training colleges. It is pleasing to record that both the full-time and part-time Fresh Horizons courses continue today. They are illustrative of that process which goes on in all London's adult institutes whereby the adult, taken at a particular point of interest, is encouraged to widen that interest and explore new fields. The men or women who discover latent talents, of which they were unaware, do not necessarily seek new careers but there is plenty of evidence of the revitalizing satisfaction which enriches their lives.

The City Lit.'s association with the deaf began in 1957 when it took over responsibility for a number of lip-reading classes held in various parts of London under the supervision of the principal of the Kingsway Day College. From the earliest days of the School Board for London there had been provision in evening classes for the deaf and partially deaf adults. The demand from adults so diminished, however, that by 1947–8 the few classes which existed were intended mainly for lip-reading instruction for deafened servicemen of the Second World War. The classes were widely dispersed and there were indications that they were not as strongly supported as they might have been because students had difficulty in reaching those offered in the suburbs. By concentrating classes for the deaf in a central London location it was hoped that difficult cross-London journeys would be avoided and a choice of a wider range of classes would be made available. A central London centre would serve a wider catchment area for both potential students and staff and would open up the possibility of recruiting a team of specialist teachers who could pool their ideas and experience. As is so often the case in London, accommodation was a major difficulty and the best that could be offered was a concentration of classes at St Clement Dane's School, Drury Lane under a part-time tutor-in-charge. Kingsway Day College had major accommodation problems and was using part of the Stukeley Street premises and it was felt that accommodation for the deaf was more likely to become available in the City Lit. premises when Kingsway Day College and Westminister College of Commerce moved out. In any case association with an adult education college seemed to offer the opportunity of a more varied approach and general widening of the opportunities for deaf people. In 1957, the principal of the City Lit. took over responsibility for classes for the deaf. The part-time tutor-in-charge at that time was Mr Kenneth Pegg, a dedicated headmaster of a secondary school for the deaf in

Essex. His informed and expert concern for the deaf, together with that of the part-time tutors he gathered around him, built up a practical service for deaf adults. A good service attracts customers and it became apparent that the provision was inadequate. The story of the development of this service deserves a history of its own. It was a remarkable illustration of triumphant progress over odds – mainly inadequate accommodation and facilities. The one advantage of a central London location was itself an embarrassment since it increased the demands on the inadequate facilities available in a primary school in the evening. There was no lack of recognition by the ILEA of the need for a deaf centre for adults in central London and the decision to allocate and specially adapt Keeley House, which adjoined the Institute, for a deaf centre was made as early as 1971. Despite this a complicated pattern of moves had to be worked through as well as considerable juggling with places in building programmes (which government economies threw into jeopardy), before Keeley House was finally available as The City Literary Centre for the Deaf in 1976.

Crucial to the development of an effective service for the deaf was the appointment of full-time staff. Apart from the obvious advantages which the pooled experience and ideas of a full-time staff team would give, it eased the persistent difficulty of recruiting part-time staff. The exacting demands on full-time teachers of deaf children during the day did not encourage them to take on evening work with adults and recruitment had usually been through the personal persuasion of the tutor-in-charge. Mr Pegg, now vice-principal in charge of the Centre for the Deaf, had been appointed full-time head of department in 1966 and a full-time assistant was appointed in 1971. In 1973 the Centre was given the brief to contact all London colleges with a view to setting up a service for hearing-impaired students who were following vocational courses. In 1974, four additional full-time appointments, including a peripatetic tutor for the deaf, were made and the Centre became a regional centre for hearing-impaired students covering nine counties in south-east England. It functioned as an assessment centre and clearing house for students who wished to continue their education. Not all hearing-impaired students could benefit from normal further education courses so two special courses were organized with North London College whereby students spent three days at the college and two days at the Centre and were supported throughout by Keeley House tutors. Today a wide range of link courses has been augmented by the Centre, in conjunction with central London colleges, in order to enable young people still at school to try new skills. From the small beginnings in lip-reading classes in a primary school, twenty-three day time and evening lip-reading classes now operate in Keeley House and nine classes are held in hospitals and homes for the elderly. Early in the 1970s the City Lit.'s Department for the Deaf initiated courses for the training of teachers of lip-reading and so made available lip-reading classes throughout the home counties.

In 1979 the Department for Health and Social Security financed a training programme for a new discipline known as hearing therapy. On completion of their
course, hearing therapists are based in hospitals and provide a local service to hard-
of-hearing people; this service includes a rehabilitation programme of lip-reading,
training with hearing aids, counselling on environmental aids and the training of
residual hearing.

Classes for stammerers were held at the evening continuation schools of the
School Board for London and, as with classes for the deaf, by the 1930s, were very
few and widely dispersed. Provision was made for speech therapy by Kingsway
College and responsibility for classes for stammerers was transferred to the City
Lit. at the same time as that for classes for the deaf. One of the full-time staff
appointed to the Department of the Deaf at the City Lit. in 1974 was a speech
therapist. Like the service for the deaf, the speech-therapy service offered by the
City Lit. has grown considerably. The speech-therapy unit attached to the City
Lit. Centre for the Deaf covers day intensive courses and evening classes for
stammerers, together with further training for qualified speech therapists. Group
work, with speech-impaired adults – mainly those who have suffered a stroke –
is also carried out.

From the small difficult beginnings in the 1950s the Centre for the Deaf now
offers a service from a well-equipped central London location of regional and
national importance. Throughout the first three years of the adult literacy campaign the City Lit. Centre for the Deaf trained both professional and voluntary
literacy workers with the deaf; the ILEA seconded one of its full-time members of
staff to advise the Adult Literacy Resource Agency on the special problem of
illiteracy of hearing-impaired adults. An indication of the City Lit.'s contribution
to the education of disadvantaged adults is given by the proportion of full-time
staff engaged in this work. In December 1979 eighteen of the thirty-five full-time
staff worked in the Centre for the Deaf. Another two were concerned with the
mentally handicapped and their tutors and with adults with severe reading and
writing difficulties; two others were attached to community studies in the training unit.

It would have been very easy for the City Literary Institute to have become
isolated from the rest of the London adult education service. Its advantages of
location, its own building and full-time staff, its distinctive curriculum and, at
one time in common with other literary institutes, a higher rate of pay for tutors,
set it apart from men's and women's institutes and, perhaps to a lesser degree,
from adult education institutes after the 1957–9 reorganization. Indeed, when
adult education institutes were permitted to offer subjects previously only available in literary institutes (and the special rates for literary institutes were
abolished), there was a good deal more interaction between the City Lit. and
other London adult education institutes. In the first place a *modus vivendi* between

the City Lit. and central London adult education institutes had to be developed in order to avoid uneconomic overlapping or competition. A co-operative scheme was worked out by the principals concerned with the City Lit.

The surge forward in adult education provision in London in the 1960s had led the ILEA to step up training of part-time tutors, vice-principals and principals. The weight of this extended training programme fell on the small team of further education inspectors concerned particularly with adult education institutes; they naturally tended to concentrate their individual efforts on training for their own subject areas. Towards the end of the 1960s it became apparent that training needed to be more broadly based, particularly for the growing number of full-time staff that were now being appointed to institutes. It was natural to turn to the City Literary Institute in which to establish a training unit. Dr South, then vice-principal, in the same session in which he was appointed principal (1967–8), began a series of four-week sandwich courses for principals and vice-principals from inner and outer London. These courses were at Diploma of Adult Education level. The ILEA's representative on the Extra-Mural Council of the University of London had been urging that this course should be offered by the University. Such a course was not to become available until 1972. In the meantime, more generalized training at a lower level was needed and, in 1970, a tutor-organizer was appointed to the City Lit. to establish a training unit and develop a training programme for the London service. If the unit was to succeed it had to be acceptable to the principals and staff of the adult education institutes and an advisory committee of principals and staff was set up to assist the tutor-organizer. Understandably, for the first few years the main effort of the unit was directed to vice-principals and full-time staff of adult education institutes with a gradual incursion into the part-time field.

In an adult education service as large as London, with some 7000–10,000 part-time tutors, the main impact of training for part-time tutors must be closely linked with the institutes themselves. The wealth of talent and specialized knowledge available to London through employment of part-time tutors makes it more difficult to develop a training programme for them. They are usually very busy people doing a full-time job in addition to their part-time teaching; many are experts in their subject and may have taught for many years. Nevertheless, many can be helped by training to be very much more effective in the conduct of a class and in the presentation of their material. Although it is generally believed that 'adults vote with their feet' and show their disapproval of a poor tutor by not attending, it is surprising what some adult students are prepared to suffer. Attendance at training courses by part-time tutors is voluntary. Although, since the late 1960s, the ILEA has paid the salary of a tutor who is unable to take his or her class because of attendance at a training course – there is no direct financial incentive to undergo training. Despite this, there is evidence of a remarkable response over the last fifteen years, particularly by tutors of crafts and what are generally known as women's subjects. One had only to see the results of the work done in the annual ten-day course for tutors in needlework crafts to see how readily they responded to new techniques and design. Nevertheless, those most in need were those that did not come to training courses.

The position was not quite the same with work with disadvantaged adults since, however knowledgeable the tutor in his or her subject, they were aware that a special approach was often required and were usually only too anxious to have whatever help was available. The second full-time appointment to the training unit reflected the growing involvement of institutes with the disadvantaged and, in 1976, a tutor in community studies was appointed to the unit. By 1979 the training unit had two full-time workers both directly involved in in-service education and two part-time workers, one working with tutors of mentally handicapped adults and the other concerned with administration. For several years it has run fifty to sixty short courses on a great variety of aspects of the service; physically, much of the unit's work had moved from the City Lit. into other institutions and centres. Despite the variety and extent of its programme, possibly for the reasons given above, there was little in its programme designed to help the general teaching and learning skills of inexperienced tutors.

In 1978 the Advisory Committee on the Supply and Training of Teachers (Department of Education and Science) proposed a three-stage plan for the training of tutors in adult education. In the spring of 1979 the ILEA mounted a pilot scheme in institutes in south-east London for the first stage, as suggested by the Advisory Committee's report. The pilot scheme was well received by the trainee tutors as well as the staff of the institutes involved and was considered by them to be extremely successful in engendering confidence and developing teaching ability. The ILEA went on, therefore, to offer two Stage 1 courses a year in each of the five regions of London. The courses are intended to further the understanding of adult students, increase pedagogic skill and any tutor of any subject may apply. Each course deals with such topics as student motivation, lesson planning and teaching methods and a genuine attempt is made to incorporate trainee requests and suggestions into the course content. There is no written work or required reading in Stage 1 and the tutor's teaching is not formally assessed. A certificate is, however, given to those who complete the course which lasts thirty-six hours, twenty-four of which are spent in attendance at seminars and discussions and twelve in visiting classes, supervised teaching and tutorials. Support tutors, usually full-time members of the staff from the same institute, are attached to each tutor on the course and play an important role in helping to link theory with practice.

Some Stage 2 courses began in 1980. They are about 100 hours in length and lead to a recognized award in the teaching of adults made by the City and Guilds of London Institute. There is a common core of sixty hours for everybody and a subject module of forty hours has to date been arranged for fashion, art, language and the education of the handicapped. Stage 3 involves the student in one-day-a-week attendance throughout the year at Garnett College or the University of London and these courses will be equivalent to normal teacher training programmes. Each stage is complete in itself. Stage 1 attempts to make tutors aware of the problems and possibilities inherent in teaching adults and to suggest appropriate methods. A vice-principal has been seconded to the training unit to co-ordinate and supervise courses; she acts as the course director and senior staff, from the institutes involved, lead seminars and are responsible throughout for a group of six trainee tutors. The response to Stage 1 courses suggests that there are a considerable number of the part-time tutors in the adult education service who are prepared to undertake a form of training which will supplement their specialist knowledge by helping them to improve their techniques of imparting it to others.

14.   Into the 1980s

In preparing its budget strategy for 1980–81 the ILEA faced the heavily increased financial limitations imposed by central government on the education service, as well as steeply rising costs. The restraints were such that a reduction of some £1,235,000 in the cost of operating the adult education service was judged to be necessary. A saving of this magnitude called for major policy decisions.

Despite increasing financial pressures since 1975, the ILEA had striven to maintain the policy it had represented to the Russell Committee of charging a fee to students of approximately 10 per cent of the economic cost. Fees in inner London were still generally well below those charged by LEAs in contiguous areas and the ILEA decided that the proportion of cost to be met by students in adult education classes should be raised from 10–15 per cent. The economic cost of a two-hour class for the session 1980–81 was estimated to be £85.70; 15 per cent of this would give a basic fee of £13 compared with £8.30 for the previous session. The fee for each additional class was also raised from £3 to £6. The estimated additional income from increased fees was £387,000. A further estimated saving of £575,000 was expected from the reduction of the educational year for mainstream classes from thirty-five weeks to thirty. Classes for the disadvantaged continued to operate for thirty-five weeks.

Charges for models in art and photography classes, previously borne by the ILEA, were met by students from the beginning of the summer term 1980. Institute term dates were adjusted so as to avoid meeting in school premises when the schools were closed for half-term and Christmas; this measure saved money on heating, cleaning, lighting and overtime payments. These savings, with a 10 per cent reduction in the maintenance grant allowances for institutes and a cut in the hours of canteen assistance, produced an estimated saving of an additional £200,000.

Regrettable as these reductions were, the ILEA nevertheless sought to preserve the essential fabric of the adult education service. Governors were reminded of their power to make up to 100 per cent remission of students' fees in case of hardship. The fee for classes for pensioners, the deaf and those in receipt of family-income supplement or supplementary benefit remained at £1 for any number of classes.

Under the London Government Act 1963 the ILEA had an obligation to admit students from the area of other LEAs in, or contiguous to, greater London. It was also generally envisaged (Section 31(8)) that there would be free movement across local authority boundaries and LEAs had an obligation to meet the cost of tuition

293

of any of their residents who chose to attend a class in an ILEA institute. The extra-Authority student paid the ILEA fee and the balance of the economic cost of the student's tuition, as determined by a nationally agreed recoupment rate for each student, was recovered from the student's home LEA. Each year the ILEA submits a 'recoupment return' and account to the LEAs concerned in respect of students from their area who have attended ILEA educational establishments. Many people who worked in London found it more convenient to attend ILEA classes near their place of work or on their way home. The fact that ILEA fees were lower generally than in contiguous areas was, if not a direct incentive, certainly not a deterrent to them to continue to attend. Although in broader areas than adult education there was a two-way traffic, in general, LEAs paid more to the ILEA in recoupment charges than they received. From 1975 onwards LEAs, subject to central government 'nil growth' rate-support grant, were looking for economies. Some, having increased student fees in their own establishments and cut back on the provision for adult education, began to look askance at the large bills presented by the ILEA for recoupment of tuition costs.

By 1979 four authorities, Berkshire, Essex, Surrey and West Sussex, had withdrawn from the free-trade arrangements for adult education classes and had decided not to meet recoupment charges for any students living in their areas who attended ILEA adult education classes. This meant that students from these areas had to pay a fee ranging from £44.30 – £90.80, according to the level of the class. All but a few were deterred from enrolling. From September 1980 a total of some fourteen Authorities had decided to withdraw from the free-trade arrangements. Barnet decided to pay recoupment for the majority of high-level courses at the lowest recoupment rate only, with the result that students from that area had to be charged a supplementary fee to cover the difference.

The action by these LEAs was certainly contrary to the intentions of the London Government Act and the Secretary of State for Education and Science was asked to give directions on the legality of their action. The ILEA, in the meantime, had no option but to charge students from these areas fees which would cover the cost. The financial implications for the ILEA were considerable. In 1977 – 8 recoupment income in respect of adult education classes at maintained and aided establishments amounted to no less than £1,816,300.

There were other implications, too. A survey in 1976 had shown that 21.1 per cent of students in adult education classes lived outside inner London, of whom 9.9 per cent worked there. The cessation of free-trade arrangements could affect substantially the total enrolment of some institutes on the periphery of inner London. Overall, it could either reduce the total enrolment or leave some 20 per cent more places for inner London residents. The impact, however, throughout inner London would be uneven and some institutes would be affected more than others.

The pattern of institutes in 1979 was largely that set in the 1957–9 reorganiza-tion. As we have seen, not only did the institutes soon outstrip the modest total-student enrolment envisaged in 1959 but they had also grown unevenly. The population of London in 1958 was 3.225 million; by 1978 it was 2.45 million. Again the decline had not been evenly spread and was much greater in some areas than in others. Not only had the population declined but, in a number of areas, it had changed in character. Some institutes had an area in which the age-profile of the population was unbalanced; others had a concentration of immigrant groups or a population in which one socio-economic group was predominant. The areas of institutes, determined in 1957–9, had been based on Development Plan Neighbourhood Units with the aim of catering for a cross-section of the commu-nity. Where neighbourhood areas had become ethnic-minority group areas and 'single-class' areas a comprehensive institute with a varied programme, which would attract a student body of a mixed-social class, became difficult if not impos-sible. Moreover, neighbourhoods took little or no account of borough bounda-ries. The growth of outreach and community education work throughout the 1970s had emphasized the need for a close working relationship between the ILEA's adult education service and voluntary and statutory services concerned with social welfare, health and employment. Most of these services were orga-nized on a borough basis and the fact that some boroughs were served by three or four institutes made consultation with borough-based services complicated. By 1979 it was clear that some revision of the pattern of adult education institutes was needed. Surveys in 1976 and 1977 had shown the uneven spread of accom-modation, wide variations in size and consequent numbers of full-time staff between one institute and another and, more particularly, in the extent to which resources were allocated for work with the disadvantaged.

Two factors determined 1980–81 as the year in which a reorganization should take place. The first was the impending retirement of a number of principals and vice-principals; the second was the ILEA's need to make further savings in the adult education sector in 1980–81 and 1981–2. The ILEA's budget strategy for 1980–81 provided for savings of £91,000 to be achieved by the reorganization of institutes. The full year saving was estimated to be £194,000. Although the need to make savings was a factor which affected the timing of the reorganization, set against savings by increasing fees (£387,000) and the reduction of the normal length of the session (£575,000), the saving element was relatively small.

The sub-committee (14 November 1979) authorized the Education Officer to proceed with further consideration of the reorganization of adult education institutes. In December he issued a consultative document to the academic boards and governing bodies of the ILEA's thirty adult education institutes, the City Literary Institute, Morley College and the Mary Ward Centre; central and local consultative committees for adult education; teachers' associations; inner London borough councils and the British Association of Settlements. This document noted the population over seventeen years of age in each of the twelve inner-London boroughs and the City of London as well as the population projections for 1986 and 1991. The figures showed a steady decline: 1978 – 1,957,000; 1986 – 1,930,000; 1991 – 1,899,700.

The Education Officer proposed twenty larger institutes to replace the existing thirty-one, on the grounds that larger institutes would respond to a wider variety of needs (including unpredictable needs) and would be more flexible in the use of academic staff. The larger institutes, it was argued, would enable a more even distribution of full-time staff and of accommodation. As was customary in ILEA reorganizations an assurance was given that no full-time staff, academic or non-teaching, would be made redundant and that all would be protected in their substantive grades. For the first time in any reorganization it was proposed that the City Literary Institute should assume responsibility for some of the general work of an adult education institute in addition to its work in specialist fields. It was also proposed that Morley College, an aided establishment, hitherto classified as a literary institute, should be given responsibility for an area and for the general adult education and community education work in that area.

The consultations showed that there was general acceptance that some modification of the existing pattern was necessary. Whilst some misgivings were expressed that large institutes might be insensitive to the requirements of local communities, the argument that larger institutes would give a better distribution of accommodation and a more even allocation of full-time staff was accepted. A number of the bodies consulted emphasized the need for well-supported small centres within the larger institutes. As was perhaps to be expected a good deal of discussion was concerned with the delineation of boundaries. There was a disposition to accept mergers rather than the break-up of existing institutes. Indeed, some of the more obdurate objections were eventually resolved by recognizing this and accepting constructive local variations of the original proposals. It is interesting to note the line-up of supporters and objectors on the proposal to give Morley College local-area responsibilities. The governing bodies of institutes in the area and the local adult education consultative committees opposed the proposal; the borough council, voluntary groups and Morley College council, however, strongly supported it. There was no support for the City Lit. to take on a more generalist role.

Towards the end of April 1980 the Education Officer was able to present to the Further and Higher Education sub-committee revised proposals (ILEA 0162)[1] which took account of the suggestions and objections. The sub-committee agreed to his proposal for nine institutes instead of the existing fourteen north of the Thames and ten, including Morley College, in place of the existing seventeen institutes south of the river, with the City Lit. remaining as it was. It was, however, apparent that more time was needed for the transition, involving as it did the setting-up of Formation Committees for the new institutes (representative of existing governing bodies) and the reallocation and appointment of staff. The teachers' organizations and many governing bodies had suggested January, 1981, rather than September 1980, as a more acceptable 'vesting' date. This was approved by the sub-committee, although it meant that the saving resulting from the reorganization in 1980–81 would be reduced to £39,000, leaving the Education Officer to find the remaining £52,000 from elsewhere. This decision allowed existing teams of staff to enrol students for the session 1980–81 in the normal way and gave more time for the other preparatory work which was necessary before the new institutes could be established.

ILEA 0162 was a remarkably comprehensive document which, in addition to reporting the result of the widespread consultations, also set out the boundaries of the new institutes and, for each institute, gave a detailed statement of the accommodation allocated to it and a suggested staffing structure. Crucial to the reorganization was the effective deployment and use of full-time staff. The 1980–81 reorganization was the first in which full-time staff, other than principals, were a factor. Twenty years before, the institutes were looking hopefully towards the possibility of full-time vice-principals which the larger institutes suggested might be justified. There is no doubt that the most important single development since those days has been the appointment of full-time staff to take charge of particular subject areas. At a time of stringent national economy which came close to matching that of the 1930s, it was clearly important to ensure the fullest possible use of full-time staff.

The improved deployment of full-time staff which the reorganization made possible was shown in the Education Officer's proposed staff structure for each institute which was to be considered by the Formation Committees and the academic boards. In the proposals eventually approved all institutes had more than ten full-time staff and fourteen institutes, excluding principals and vice-principals, had from ten to twenty full-time staff. Every institute had from two – nine full-time staff concerned with community education or the education of the disadvantaged. Seventeen had two or more full-time staff for English as a Second Language work and one or more staff for literacy. Fifteen had one or two community-education workers. Each institute had, for some years, had a media resources officer and the reorganized institutes were to retain this post and, in addition, an audio-visual aids (AVA) technician would be appointed to each institute. Two media resources officer posts were to be established to service the community resource units at the Chequer Street building of the former Central London Institute and at the former Frobisher Institute.

For the first time institutes had sufficient full-time staff to call for a more explicit organizational and management structure than may have been necessary or practicable in the past. Each new institute had one or more staff whose particular responsibility was the supervision of a centre and all had heads of department and other staff responsible for specialist subject areas. If the service was to continue to discover and meet the needs of all sections of the community and to implement the ILEA's policy of discrimination, not only had the specialist staff to be evenly deployed but the management structure of the new institutes had to be such as to extend as widely as possible their spheres of influence. The management structure had also to guard against the built-in danger that the larger establishment might become remote from the many local communities within their area. Moreover, they would need to provide a basis for further development and educational advance when the economic climate improved. In the guidance offered to formation committees and academic boards the Education Officer saw the need for a clarification of roles and organizational responsibilities, together with further training, if an effective relationship between generalists and subject specialists in the larger number of centres within each new institute was to be established.

The Changed Situation

In 1969 the number of full-time teaching staff in maintained adult education establishments was ninety-five (including nine full-time staff employed in HM prisons); in December 1979 it was 383 (including forty-three employed in prisons and a penal establishment for girls). Moreover, in addition to this fourfold increase in full-time teaching staff, thirty-two full-time administrative officers, some twenty clerical staff and thirty-seven audio-visual aids staff (thirty-one media-resources officers and six AVA technicians) had been appointed. The City Literary Institute had three librarians and a library assistant; the library facilities at adult education institutes are serviced from the central library resource centre.

Nevertheless, some 7000–8000 part-time teachers continue to be the main teaching force in adult education establishments. From the early 1960s, the LCC and the ILEA had recognized the substantial professional contribution made to the service by part-time teachers and had related their salaries to the nationally negotiated Burnham Further Education Committee Scales for full-time lecturer grades in vocational further education establishments, a practice which has now been adopted nationally. In the early 1970s a sick-pay scheme was introduced by the ILEA, whereby part-time teachers who have completed 240 hours of paid service in the previous year become eligible for sick pay on a specified scale up to a maximum entitlement of three weeks sick pay in any period of the one year. Following a major review of the conditions of service of part-time teachers, in association with teachers' organizations, the ILEA, in 1974, issued a code of practice on the renewal and termination of part-time teachers' engagements. The code removed a good deal of the difficulty inherent in engagements which depend largely upon the satisfactory level of student enrolment and attendance and the interpretation by individual principals of what constituted a 'satisfactory' period. Although an appeal procedure was embodied in the revised arrangements, the appeal tribunal has been used only twice since it was instituted.

The situation in respect of staff in 1979 was therefore vastly different from that in 1969. The advent of governing bodies and academic boards in 1974 brought a local policy-making infrastructure which has changed drastically the former isolation of the principal and exposed him or her to broader issues than might otherwise have been the case. Whilst some principals, initially, may have found it irksome to keep a chairman and governing body fully informed and others may have regarded a governing body as yet another body to which they were accountable, the majority have found them a welcome support and a strengthened link with the central policy-making process. Similarly, the local adult education consultative committees and the central consultative committee have widened the span of the consultative machinery and encouraged influences to be brought to bear which otherwise might have been lost. The extent to which adult education has permeated the inner London community is well illustrated by the fact that, in the reorganization of 1980, no less than 200 organizations were consulted compared with twenty-seven in the youth and adult education services review of 1973.

The battery of skills demanded of a principal of any one of the new reorganized institutes will therefore be greatly different from those required say, in 1969, when the principal was the sole full-time member of the institute staff. Then he/she was the one full-time professional leading a team of part-time teachers, making such consultative arrangements as were possible with local organizations and individuals. Now a principal is the director of a professional team, embodying a range of specialist skills which have to be brought to bear on a very much wider and complex community. Nevertheless, the aims of the adult-education institute remain the same as were stated in 1969. 'To develop the personality, satisfy creative needs and fulfil latent abilities, so that the student may become the best person, worker, home maker or citizen that he or she can be . . .; to provide the means for social intercourse with other people in the community' and 'to develop attitudes leading to greater social responsibility, social interaction and co-operation in living together in local groups and in the community at large.'[2]

The principals of 1980 have so much more − so very much more − at their command with which to try to achieve these objectives if the necessary financial support can be provided by the ILEA.

The number of men and women covered each year in the 1970s in the adult education establishments in inner London was roughly 13½ per cent of the population; an increase of some 6 per cent since 1969. The cost of the adult education service in 1969 represented approximately 2.2 per cent of the ILEA's budget; in 1980 it was 2.7 per cent.

15. A Proud Heritage

As an organization concerned solely with education, the School Board for London attracted a distinguished body of elected members who were primarily interested in education. They established a distinctive pattern of education over a densely populated area of the metropolis which, except for minor variations, was the same area administered by the LCC Education Department and by the ILEA today. Inner London, even today, remains a conglomerate of neighbourhoods which frequently do not respect the geographical boundaries of inner London boroughs but which, for a 100 years or more, have had, and expect to have, the same educational facilities which the resources of a large authority can give.

The educational administration of that area has continued to attract men and women of distinction as elected members, prepared to give a great amount of their time voluntarily as members of the Education Committee and its sub-committees. If they are chairmen of committees they give the greater part of their time. The inner London educational service has always attracted, too, professional staff of high quality. But officers and teachers can only operate effectively in a climate of enlightened policy-making by elected members. The history of London's adult education service is the record of a series of initiatives by individuals – elected members and professional staff – encouraged and supported by equally bold and enlightened policy decisions which provided the resources necessary to sustain them.

In an area as large and complex as inner London, individual initiatives could be tested in a particular locality before being applied generally. Advances made throughout the Authority's area were of a size and scale to make an impact on national development. In this way the School Board for London, the LCC and the ILEA have been pacemakers for a great deal of the development of adult education in this country. At a time when adult education was persistently conceived as higher education concerned primarily with the humanities and the universities, it was the LCC men's and women's institutes which pointed the way to the further education of ordinary men and women who had no initial aspirations to higher education. When the study of the humanities and other cultural activities were seen as the province of universities and voluntary organizations, it was the bold initiative of London literary institutes which established the local education authority's role in this field. When adult education was fast becoming a service for the 'educated', it was the ILEA which acknowledged the gap in its own service and set about making an education service for the whole community.

By its latest reorganization, the ILEA has opted for the larger unit as a means of bringing together teams of full-time staff. Whilst this may reflect the increasing pressure on the service of government cuts and the current economic climate of retrenchment, it must also be seen as the natural culmination of the growth of the adult education service over the last 100 years. The mark of maturity in any educational establishment is the extent to which it can support a team of full-time staff, with all that implies in the raising of standards and creativity which such staff can bring. In the inner London adult education service which depends so much on the part-time tutor, it has an even greater significance. The great strength of the service has been the ability to draw its part-time tutors from the remarkable pool of talented men and women who live in, or near, the great metropolis. To harness this great stream of some 8000 artists, musicians, linguists and craftsmen and deploy them to the greatest advantage demands the full-time energies of well-organized teams.

The LCC was the first to recognize the need for, and to appoint, full-time principals of evening institutes in the great reorganization of 1913. Their task was not simply to recruit and supervise part-time staff but to know their area, make contacts with schools, employers and local voluntary organizations and generally to be the organizer of cultural and recreational activity. To those who made this far-sighted decision must go the honour of giving to the service that distinctive mark which made it a social as well as an educational service for countless thousands of Londoners. Most of the principals of women's, men's and literary institutes were key figures in their locality who knew their areas and the people in them. They established a tradition of sturdy independence and dedicated service which their successors have maintained. They gathered around them bands of devoted part-time and, in many respects, voluntary workers, but they also developed close relationships with their fellow principals in their respective associations of principals of men's, women's and literary institutes.

The School Board for London, the LCC and the ILEA have all made the most of the advantages of large-scale operation and tried to minimize any disadvantages by built-in checks and consultative procedures. This is well illustrated in the operation of the adult education service. Members of the School Board were very much involved with the day-to-day administration of schools and the evening continuation schools closely linked with them. As we have seen the LCC style of administration was very different. Policy and broad lines of operation were determined at the centre and the principals given a good deal of automony in the day-to-day work of their institutes. From the earliest days of the LCC, the institutes were administered by a small management section at the central office and not as part of the divisional administration of schools. There has always been a substantial amount of consultation direct with individual principals as well as through local joint standing conferences of principals and principals' associations. These two factors — central administration and consultation with associations of principals – probably account for the close-knit nature of the adult education service.

It is difficult for those outside the London service to appreciate the strength of the close relationships which characterize the inner London adult education service. The support the London principals have given, and give, to each other, both personally and professionally, is immense. It has its origins, and some of its continuity, in the general lack of precedence given to non-vocational, compared with vocational education, and the need to secure accommodation in schools which, despite the Authority's policy, was often grudgingly made available. For many years, too, principals were the only full-time members of staff at institutes. This, together with the nature of their duties and their hours of work, made them 'a race apart' and called for men and women of independent mind and character. They came together, however, in their respective principals' associations. There were inter-association rivalries but, as a body, they were strongly supportive of each other. They generated a deep, almost family, pride in the London adult education service which, at its best, insisted on the highest standards from teachers and taught. At its worst it was slightly disdainful of anything which was not London born.

The appointment of full-time vice-principals and other staff and the overt recognition of institutes as adult education centres which followed the 1957–9 reorganization brought to an end the comparative isolation of principals. The inter-relationship continued and, with the wider career prospects which the London service could then offer, took on a more sophisticated pattern. Staff began to move from institute to institute and consultation and in-service training, below principal level, enabled specialist influences to permeate the service generally.

The successful evolution and implementation of the ILEA's policy depends on close collaboration with those who have to operate it. Consultation with associations of principals and other teachers' organizations have been a major means of this collaborative action. In more recent years, this consultative process has been extended to governing bodies, academic boards, local and central consultative committees and so on. Close collaboration, however, means more than consultation on specific issues. It is a continuing process and the adult education service has had, and still has, two aspects which help this. For many years day-to-day support and advice has been given to institutes by a small team of inspectors who, in addition to specialist-subject responsibilities, have pastoral responsibility for a number of adult education institutes. They work closely with the assistant education officer and staff of the branch concerned with adult education and are 'the guides, philosophers and friends' of the institutes in their care. They provide a valuable two-way channel for information and support between the central administration and the field.

Probably no other group of educational establishments has as many social events as adult education institutes. Exhibitions, demonstrations, open evenings, dress shows, plays, poetry readings, musical performances, keep fit displays etc., make a very great contribution to the social life of the institute and to the local community. Invitations to these events are given by the principals to elected members of the Authority and borough councils and to senior officers, inspectors and staff of the management branch. Not only are they enjoyable occasions, they are valuable insights into the work of the institutes and a valuable contribution to the collaborative process.

Every review of adult education in London throughout the last 100 years has emphasized the importance of accommodation which would give facilities for adequate storage of materials, for library or reading rooms and for the many social and extra-class club activities which are so important a part of adult education. A great deal has been done in inner London to ensure additional provision for adults in schools and in the allocation, wherever possible, of accommodation for the sole use of institutes which the increase in day classes has made even more important. The 1980–81 reorganization has made a more even distribution of accommodation but the problem of adequate accommodation remains. The advantages of accommodation for the sole use of adult education can be seen, *par excellence*, in the purpose-built premises of the City Lit., Morley College, and the former Stanhope Institute and in the adapted accommodation of a number of other institute centres. Any major advance in this respect depends on the allocation of redundant school buildings and on central government capital-building and minor-works programmes and calls for a general recognition of the place of adult education in the educational system – a practical recognition that has been notably absent from the progammes of successive governments.

There is no lack of demand for adult education. Throughout the years the demand has steadily increased. As more people have experienced full-time education, so more have responded to ways in which to continue it. As the ILEA said in its evidence to the Russell Committee – education begets education. Since, too, it is generally agreed that the best publicity comes from satisfied students, the more students there are, the more there will be who will wish to join them. The record of growth in 1960s illustrated this. The steady increase in 'welfare' classes throughout the 1960s and the conscious effort made in the early 1970s to reach out into the community and to those for whom education at school had not been a success, added a new dimension to the inner London adult education service.

The overall evidence is that, despite the falling population, demand exceeds the capacity of the resources available. The effects of 'nil growth' and restricted resources, shown in the steady fall in enrolment since the peak reached in 1975–6 when total enrolment reached 295,000, masks the latent demand. There is little doubt that greater demands will be made on the institutes to respond to the educational needs of the elderly, young mothers, the institutionalized and the unemployed. In a period of economic restraint such responses have to be made at the expense of the mainstream provision. The ILEA has tried to provide, in the larger institutes of 1981, a concentration of staff and resources to support and strengthen work in those areas which previously lacked full-time staff and a basis for future development which, hopefully, a more favourable economic climate will allow.

The record of the inner London adult education service shows, time and time again, that demand depends on facilities being made available and offered in a manner which is relevant to the needs and circumstances of the people it aims to serve. The great increase in welfare classes and in community-based adult education stemmed from the initiative of the ILEA, its officers and the principals and staff of its institutes. It was in the tradition of a service which made the educational advances which demonstrated what could be done by an education authority to improve the quality of life of ordinary men and women. Such initiatives are a vital part of the antidote to individual apathy and the frightening atrophy of an inner city. They have helped thousands of men and women to awaken to a new lease of life by developing latent interests and skills they did not know they had. It is a record of which the inner London service can be proud.

Appendix A

(i)   Diagram showing student admissions to evening schools (vocational and non-vocational classes), 1882-83 to 1911-12.

(i) (a)   Number of students admitted to evening schools (vocational and non-vocational), 1882-3 to 1911-12.

(ii)   Diagram showing student enrolment in non-vocational adult education classes, 1913-14 to 1950-51.

(ii) (a) Number of students enrolled in non-vocational adult education classes, 1913-14 to 1950-51.

(iii)   Diagram showing student enrolment in non-vocational adult education classes, 1950-51 to 1979-80.

(iii) (a) Number of students enrolled in non-vocational adult education classes, 1950-51 to 1979-80.

Note: Enrolment figures produced by the LCC and ILEA give the actual number of individual students. The term 'enrolment' is sometimes used in LEA and national adult education statistics to indicate the number of class or subject enrolments made by individual students. These are, of course, much greater than the number of individual students.

A (i)

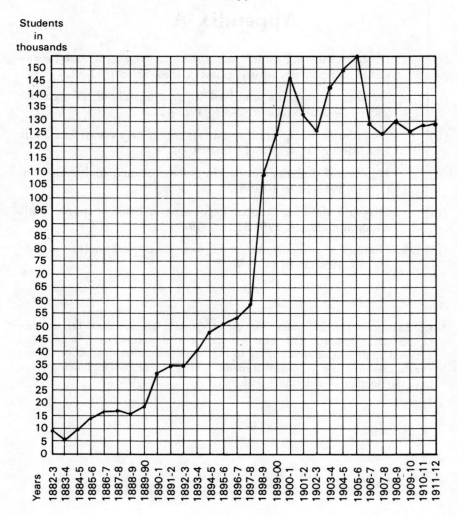

Reprinted from *Eight Years of Technical Education and Continuation Schools*, Report of the Education Officer to the Education Committee, 1912.

A (i) (a)
Student Admissions

Session	No. of schools	No. of pupils admitted throughout session
1882-3	83	9064
1883-4	74	5563
1884-5	84	9346
1885-6	114	13,968
1886-7	128	16,050
1887-8	128	16,320
1888-9	135	15,732
1889-90	159	18,268
1890-91	232	(a) 31,015
1891-2	239	34,562
1892-3	242	34,797
1893-4	265	40,858
1894-5	271	48,512
1895-6	271	50,218
1896-7	276	52,804
1897-8	280	57,586
1898-9	321	(b) 109,121
1899-1900	368	125,640
1900-01	395	146,971
1901-2	398	(c) 133,191
1902-3	376	(d) 126,753
1903-4	373	144,865
1904-5	373	150,605
1905-6	351	156,604
1906-7	327	(e) 127,130
1907-8	307	124,931
1908-9	299	130,087
1909-10	276	(f) 126,514
1910-11	280	128,464
1911-12	275	129,019

Notes:
(a) Changes in Code which provided for a more extended course of instruction
(b) Abolition of fees
(c) Uncertainty existed. Cockerton judgment
(d) Re-imposition of fees to pupils over sixteen
(e) Fee charged to pupils under sixteen except in cases of poverty
(f) Introduction of organized courses of instruction

Reprinted from *Eight Years of Technical Education and Continuation Schools*, Report of the Education Officer to the Education Committee, 1912.

A (ii)

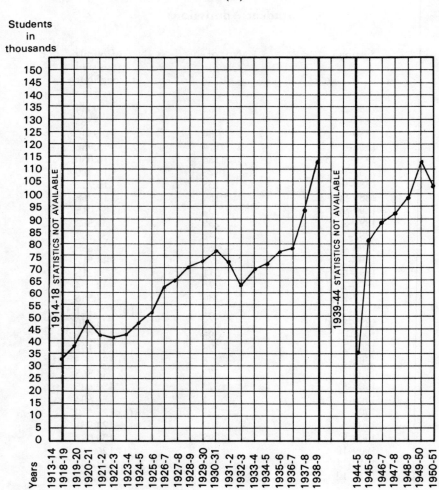

Students
in
thousands

Years

A (ii) (a)
Number of Students Enrolled

	Women's institutes	Non-vocational institutes	Free (men & mixed) institutes	Literary institutes	Men's institutes	Men's junior institutes	Affiliated club classes	Deaf	Total
1913-14(a)	13,364	1537	17.075	—	—	—		450	32.426
1914-18	STATISTICS NOT AVAILABLE								
1918-19	28,028	—	2541	(b)574	—	—		88	31,231
1919-20	31,680	—	3405	2582	—	—		213	37,880
1920-21	35,573	—	4531	4449	(c)2128	—		173	46,954
1921-2	27,936	—	4135	5901	2906	—		102	40,980
1922-3	27,435	—	3773	5181	3349	—		102	39,940
1923-4	27,296	—	4099	5464	4021	—		122	41,002
1924-5	29,928	—	4908	7055	4747	—		124	46,762
1925-6	30,194	—	4610	7914	5002	(d)2725		97	49,542
1926-7	32,113	—	4562	10,211	5830	4266	(e)3917	103	61,002
1927-8	32,893	—	4887	11,071	7522	4576	3748	73	64,770
1928-9	33,195	—	4546	12,044	8578	5747	3809	94	68,013
1929-30	34,449	—	4436	13,878	9460	6317	3961	131	72,632
1930-31	35,003	—	2875	14,805	10,993	7886	3573	205	75,340
1931-2	31,991	—	2175	12,820	10,767	8420	3348	149(f)	69,670
1932-3	28,194	—	1953	11,710	9,927	6963	3192	163(f)	62,102
1933-4	28,891	—	2249	12,052	14,091	7382	3200	75	68,040
1934-5	31,449	—	2202	11,810	14,796	8204	2973	181	71,615
1935-6	32,232	—	2266	12,968	14,517	9913	2940	201	75,037
1936-7	35,073	—	2319	12,289	14,404	10,453	2870	257	77,665
1937-8	43,922	—	2579	13,734	17,289	12,275	2793	303	92,895
1938-9	54,975	—	5004	13,715	23,835	14,133	2694	332	114,688
1939-44	STATISTICS NOT AVAILABLE (g)								
1944-5	18,567	—	—	5359	6044	4929	—	—	34,899
1945-6	46,831	—	—	12,589	13,086	6837	885	—	80,228
1946-7	49,135	—	—	16,061	15,574	6241	889	—	87,900
1947-8	56,014	—	—	16,804	18,463	—	974	—	92,255
1948-9	59,021	—	—	16,832	22,478	—	292	—	98,623
1949-50	71,133	—	—	17,806	24,091	—	299	—	113,329
1950-1	65,490	—	—	16,327	19,963	—	271	—	102,051

Notes:
(a) The first year after the 1913 reorganization
(b) First two literary institutes opened
(c) Five men's institutes opened
(d) Five men's junior institutes opened
(e) Although instructors had been supplied for many years to classes in voluntary clubs, the number of students in such classes included for the first time in published statistics for session 1926-7
(f) Economic crisis — cuts in public expenditure; high unemployment
(g) Although no published statistics are available for the sessions 1939-43 references to the number of students in reports to the Education Committee indicate that enrolments for 1944-5 were abnormally low due to 'flying bomb' attacks

A (iii)

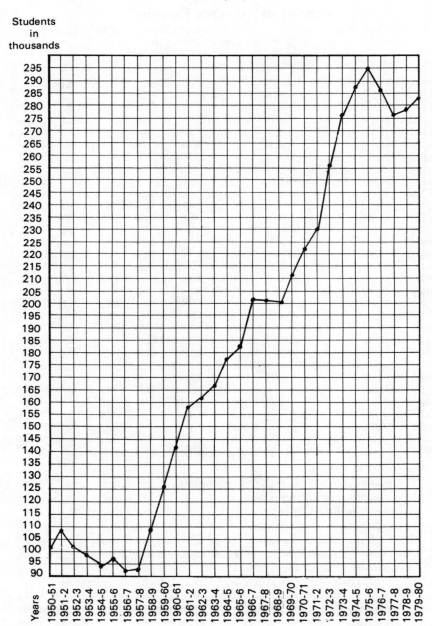

Students
in
thousands

A (iii) (a)
Number of Students Enrolled

	Women's institutes	Men's institutes	Affiliated club classes	Literary institutes	General/ adult-education institutes	Adult-education at aided establish-ments	Com-munity centres	Total
1950-1 (a)	65,490	19,963	271	16,327				102,051
1951-2	69,327	22,604	222	15,663				107,816
1952-3	64,813	22,152	(b) 299	14,992				102,256
1953-4	62,072	22,111		14,616				98,799
1954-5	59,237	21,683		14,547				95,467
1955-6	59,982	22,485		15,422				97,889
1956-7 (a)	54,543	21,845		15,053				91,441
1957-8	54,713	23,331		13,971				92,015
1958-9 (c)	5386	4904		12,738	85,270			108,298
1959-60				(d) 10,677	113,717			124,394
1960-1				12,100	128,879			140,979
1961-2				12,351	139,760	(e) 5497		157,608
1962-3 (a)				12,762	140,606	5210		158,578
1963-4				13,700	145,804	5202		164,706
1964-5				13,205	158,101	5158		176,464
1965-6				13,016	(f)165,850	5046		183,912
1966-7				13,322	178,672	(g) 10,343		202,337
1967-8 (a)				13,045	178,162	10,127		201,334
1968-9 (a)				12,785	177,721	9923		200,429
1969-70 (a)				13,144	187,848	10,132		211,124
1970-1			(City Lit only)	11,317	202,518	9828		223,663
1971-2				11,758	213,490	10,548		235,796
1972-3				11,777	239,119	11,292		262,188
1973-4				11,853	253,104	12,650		277,607
1974-5				12,691	260,529	13870		287,090
1975-6				12,050	266,779	14,634	1015	294,478
1976-7 (a)				12,226	260,221	11,013	2225	285,685
1977-8 (a)				12,593	251.370	11,512	1361	276,836
1978-9				12,294	(h) 252,103	11,667	1934	(h)277,998
1979-80 (a)				12,499	255,564	12,404	2399	282,866

Notes:
(a)   Increase in fees
(b)   After this year students enrolled at club classes were included in institute statistics
(c)   First year after the 1957-9 reorganization which merged women's and men's institutes into general institutes and abolished suburban literary institutes
(d)   The City Literary Institute and Marylebone Literary Institute
(e)   Although aided establishments such as Morley College, Mary Ward and Toynbee had provided adult education for many years the students enrolled had not previously been shown in published statistics for non-vocational institutes
(f)   'General' institutes re-named adult education institutes
(g)   Figures for Goldsmiths College adult education department, previously included in higher education statistics, now included with those for non-vocational institutes
(h)   Adjusted figure to include students from Wormwood Scrubs prison — published figures for 1978-9 omitted them

Appendix B

Number of Classes Held in Each Subject in Adult Education Institutes per week

Summary	1950-51	1960-61	1968-9	1974-5	1978-9
1 Animals	102	39	51	80	64
2 Art and Architecture	188	553	1556	2381	2426
3 Commercial Subjects	—	—	—	30	36
4 Cookery	327	355	502	614	623
5 Domestic Craft	2209	2380	3238	3650	3372
6 Drama	475	365	507	365	314
7 Languages	236	699	1911	2286	1941
8 Literary, Cultural and Historical Studies	188	185	444	521	358
9 Music	589	573	864	1005	943
10 Dancing	760	556	858	877	867
11 Games and Sports	702	1310	2296	3075	2914
12 Miscellaneous	276	246	652	903	702
13 Technical crafts	796	1084	1289	1395	1235
14 Basic Education	36	176	177	879	1552
	6884	8521	14,345	18,061	17,347

1. Animals	1950-51	1960-61	1968-9	1974-5	1978-9
Animal care and training dogs, pets, etc.	—	15	14	32	25
Aquaria	14	6	5	2	1
Bee-keeping	5	—	2	5	4
Birds — caged; ornithology	19	2	6	11	14
Horsemastership	—	—	10	12	4
Pigeons	12	12	12	15	14
Poultry-keeping	27	4	1	2	1
Rabbit-keeping	25	—	1	1	1
	102	39	51	80	64

2. Art and Architecture					
Antiques	—	—	63	78	59
Architecture	5	11	18	13	10
Art appreciation/history	21	35	82	106	86
Carving and sculpture	2	—	141	167	151
Costume — history of	3	—	—	2	1
Drawing, Painting, etc.	119	258	654	885	947
Enamelling	—	—	6	27	20
Handwriting/Calligraphy	—	6	20	25	21

	1950-51	1960-61	1968-9	1974-5	1978-9
Jewellery	—	44	63	194	214
Lithography	—	—	10	27	24
Modelling and Pottery	38	199	480	766	785
Mosaic	—	—	11	7	14
Porcelain	—	—	2	6	16
Silverwork	—	—	6	26	14
Silk screen printing	—	—	—	52	64
	188	553	1556	2381	2426

3. Commercial Subjects

	1950-51	1960-61	1968-9	1974-5	1978-9
Typing and shorthand	—	—	—	30	36

4. Cookery

	1950-51	1960-61	1968-9	1974-5	1978-9
Cakes, decoration of	—	—	63	—	—
pastries	—	—	14	110	132
confectionery	—	—	15	—	—
Chinese	—	—	—	3	15
Continental	—	—	75	65	49
Deep freeze	—	—	—	2	6
Dietetics, haute, nutrition	—	—	4	21	24
General	327	323	327	409	369
Vegetarian	—	2	4	4	19
Indian	—	—	—	—	9
Invalid	—	30	—	—	—
	327	355	502	614	623

5. Domestic Craft

	1950-51	1960-61	1968-9	1974-5	1978-9
Basketry and cane-making	—	64	51	36	68
Batik	—	—	—	3	21
Crochet	—	—	—	54	68
Dressmaking, pattern cutting and children's wear	998	1215	1576	1736	1492
Embroidery and needlework	211	154	117	134	119
Fabric and design	—	—	33	35	22
Flower arrangement	1	50	121	131	118
Flower making	—	8	14	23	5
Fur and fur renovations	—	—	7	—	1
General craft	690	416	623	731	789
Interior decoration, painting and repairs	29	37	57	30	49
Home furnishing, soft furnishings, etc.	42	149	191	210	144
Lace-making	12	15	15	21	10
Leatherwork	—	13	15	26	27
Lingerie	21	8	3	2	—
Macramé	—	—	—	11	21
Millinery	99	93	125	88	40

	1950–51	1960–61	1968–9	1974–5	1978–9
Miscellaneous	—	—	—	59	37
Tailoring	106	156	226	172	99
Toy-making	—	—	5	43	63
Weaving, knitting, spinning	—	2	42	64	142
Wine-making	—	—	17	41	37
	2209	2380	3238	3650	3372

6. Drama

	1950–51	1960–61	1968–9	1974–5	1978–9
Drama and dramatic art	354	251	275	202	227
Effective speaking	—	—	13	6	5
Films — appreciation of, making of, etc.	3	18	31	35	21
Mime and movement	—	7	16	28	10
Speech training and elocution	116*	89*	79	63	46
debates	—	—	21	—	—
conversation	—	—	8	—	—
public speaking	—	—	24	—	—
Stage make-up	—	—	1	9	—
Stage technique	—	—	37	17	—
Theatre, history of	2	—	2	5	5
	475	365	507	365	314

* Includes effective speaking.

7. Languages

	1950–51	1960–61	1968–9	1974–5	1978–9
Anglo-Saxon	—	1	1	—	—
Arabic	—	1	7	19	44
Bengali	—	—	—	—	56
Bulgarian	—	—	1	3	3
Chinese	—	—	2	20	11
Czech	—	—	—	1	3
Danish	—	—	8	11	10
Dutch	—	—	7	22	12
English	17	19	191	170	85
Esperanto	—	1	3	3	—
Finnish	—	—	—	2	28
French	142	290	558	720	594
German	31	140	351	504	348
Greek	3	8	41	65	47
Gujerati	—	—	—	—	6
Hebrew	—	2	40	31	28
Hindi	—	—	—	—	1
Hungarian	—	—	—	2	2
Irish	2	1	6	5	9
Italian	11	131	305	261	230
Japanese	—	—	2	17	13

	1950-51	1960-61	1968-9	1974-5	1978-9
Latin	5	4	2	—	—
Norwegian	—	—	6	10	6
Persian	—	—	—	3	4
Polish	—	—	3	7	10
Portuguese	—	—	12	14	15
Romance linguistics	8	2	1	2	—
Rumanian	—	—	—	2	1
Russian	—	24	82	70	32
Scottish Gaelic	2	5	3	—	1
Serbo-Croat	—	—	3	5	4
Slovene	—	—	1	7	—
Spanish	11	63	257	282	294
Swedish	—	4	8	10	8
Turkish	—	—	2	4	13
Urdu	—	—	—	9	18
Welsh	4	3	8	5	5
	236	699	1911	2286	1941

8. Literary, Cultural and Historical Studies

	1950-51	1960-61	1968-9	1974-5	1978-9
Archaeology	1	13	38	25	21
Anthropology	—	1	3	2	3
Astronomy	1	5	8	14	11
Civics	—	6	5	4	2
Economics	—	—	9	8	2
Egyptology	—	—	—	3	4
Geography	3	—	3	2	5
Geology	2	4	7	2	4
Heraldry — genealogy, brasses	3	6	7	10	9
History — English, European, local, London, world	26	13	101	96	126
Law	—	—	2	6	3
Literature	60	28	70	37	29
Maths — computer, metric system	15	1	38	42	20
Miscellaneous	5	23	6	85	28
Philosophy	16	13	17	28	20
Psychology	17	25	26	39	23
Religion and Church history	7	22	35	29	11
Science — biology, botany, etc.	5	6	11	9	4
Sociology and social affairs	27	19	58	80	33
	188	185	444	521	358

9. Music	1950–51	1960–61	1968–9	1974–5	1978–9
Appreciation and theory	98	66	96	104	123
Bands, orchestras, etc.	104	79	124	160	129
Guitar, banjo, violin, piano, etc.	120	157	294	384	322
Jazz	—	—	6	8	14
Opera	—	—	89	92	119
Vocal	267	271	255	257	236
	589	573	864	1005	943

10. Dancing					
Dancing — ballet	50	42	67	—	—
ballroom	357	182	331	—	—
folk, country, square, morris	32	16	26	386	313
Medau and eurythmy	—	25	80	65	121
Miscellaneous	—	87	45	36	62
Modern	28	14	16	60	80
National	124	77	128	68	116
Old-time	168	113	192	258	163
Stage	1	—	14	14	12
	760	556	858	877	867

11. Games and Sports, etc.					
Aikido	—	—	—	9	11
Angling	5	8	6	7	4
Archery	—	3	23	22	22
Badminton	4	218	545	633	576
Basketball	—†	—†	—†	60	40
Boxing	105	44	30	27	23
Canoeing	—	—	—	4	2
Cricket	1	3	2	8	16
Circuit-training	—*	—*	19	28	38
Cycling	—	2	1	1	1
Fencing	62	71	136	156	119
Fives	—	—	—	2	5
Flying (theory)	—	—	1	7	1
Fly fishing and Fly tying	—	—	—	5	4
Football	12	118	208	270	248
Golf	—	50	110	101	63
Gymnastics	—*	—*	—*	16	30
Hockey	—	—	2	1	2
Indoor lawn bowls	—	—	—	4	—
Judo	42	134	193	161	103
Karate	—	—	—	38	22
Keep fit	360	321	366	582	552
Kendo	—‡	—‡	—‡	10	11

	1950–51	1960–61	1968–9	1974–5	1978–9
Lacrosse	—	1	3	—	—
Miscellaneous	23	10	45	12	17
Mountaineering	—	—	3	3	1
Netball	5	22	31	4	5
Rowing	—	—	—	2	2
Rugby	—	—	—	5	5
Sailing and rowing	—	3	4	6	4
Skiing	16	—	24	17	24
Squash, fives, volley ball	—	—	14	17	26
Swimming	—	48	163	192	175
Sub-aqua	—	—	—	19	24
Table-tennis	7	121	151	185	131
Tennis	3	22	49	64	59
Trampoline	—	3	12	10	8
Volley ball	—	—	—	14	13
Weight-lifting	44	93	126	124	120
Wrestling	13	15	28	33	12
Yoga	—	—	1	216	396
	702	1310	2296	3075	2914

* Included in Keep fit.
† Included in Netball.
‡ Included in Judo.

12. Miscellaneous

	1950–51	1960–61	1968–9	1974–5	1978–9
Authorship, journalism, writing	25	30	54	56	43
Bridge	—	—	—	—	60
Business methods for the layman	—	—	—	—	3
Chess	—	—	14	30	23
Current affairs — discussion	30	40	29	105	54
Efficient studying	—	—	4	2	1
English for newcomers	—	—	63	162	57
Health subjects including child care	—	—	18	—	—
first-aid and home nursing	126	31	102	131	91
Field studies	—	2	1	1	—
Margaret Morris movement	—	—	—	—	9
Marriage and housewives course	—	—	7	2	3
Mothers' groups	—	—	—	—	3
Philately	—	—	1	4	2
Playgroup leaders' group	—	—	22	72	68
Poise, personality, good grooming, beauty care	5	77	10	87	66
Retirement, preparation for and living in	—	—	16	8	19
Special classes for deaf and blind	27	25	134	113	52

	1950-51	1960-61	1968-9	1974-5	1978-9
Special classes for stammerers	—	—	33	4	3
Stock exchange and investment	—	—	15	9	8
Taxation for the layman	—	—	—	1	6
Travel talks	34	41	45	41	40
Wine appreciation	29	—	11	16	18
Workshop projects not included elsewhere	—	—	—	59	73
	276	246	652	903	702

13. Technical Crafts

	1950-51	1960-61	1968-9	1974-5	1978-9
Bookbinding	3	—	12	22	27
Electricity	4	10	14	16	17
Horticulture and gardening	31	40	48	83	79
Metalwork and wrought-iron work	25	32	44	45	33
Miscellaneous	23	2	—	30	48
Model engineering (and aero)	19	21	18	13	15
Motors — cars and scooters maintenance	52	258	352	326	265
advanced driving	—	—	40	—	11
Learner driver	—	—	—	20	12
Photography	69	121	171	161	147
Picture-frame making	—	—	6	20	25
Radio — television	53	84	86	89	59
tape-recording			4		
Seamanship and navigation chartwork, pilotage,	9	20	44	65	59
meteorology	—	—	3	—	—
Sewing machine, care of	—	—	—	10	16
Shoe and boot repairing	85	36	8	8	6
Upholstery	45	39	57	121	131
Woodwork — cabinet making	378	404	11	—	—
boat building	—	17	31	—	—
general	—	—	340	366	285
	796	1084	1289	1395	1235

14. Basic education

	1950-51	1960-61	1968-9	1974-5	1978-9
English as a foreign language	—	—	—	337	724
Literacy schemes	—	—	—	197	541
General education (English and arithmetic	36	176	177	345	287
	36	176	177	879	1552

Appendix C

Chairmen of Committees (LCC and ILEA)
with responsibility for adult education 1892–1981

YEAR	COMMITTEE	CHAIRMAN
1892	Special Committee on Technical Education	Sidney Webb
1893	Technical Education Board (committee appointed by the LCC under the Technical Instruction Act 1889). 20 Members of Council and 15 members from outside the Council. Members included T. McKinnon Wood and Quintin Hogg (founder of Regent St. Polytechnic); General Moberley, Hon. E. Lyulph Stanley, Sir Philip Magnus and H. Llewellyn Smith were among those appointed from outside the Council.	
1893-7	Technical Education Board	Sidney Webb
1898	"	E. Bond
1899 June	"	Graham Wallas
Dec	"	T. A. Organ
1900	"	"
1901	"	Sidney Webb
1902	"	Henry Ward
1903	"	"
April	"	A. J. Shepheard
1904 March	Education Committee set up. 43 members of whom 38 were members of the Council and 5 were women* appointed by council.	

	EDUCATION COMMITTEE	POLYTECHNIC AND EVENING SCHOOLS SUB-COMMITTEE
1904	Sir W. J. Collins	Hon. F. Thesiger
1905 April	"	Lord Chelmsford
Nov.	"	John Piggott
1906	A. J. Shepheard	W. S. Saunders
1907	J. F. Taylor	Lord Henry Bentinck
	(Rev. Stewart Headlam became a member)	
1908	"	"
1909	Cyril Jackson	Lord Henry Bentinck

		HIGHER EDUCATION SUB-COMMITTEE
1910	"	H. J. Clarke
1911	Cyril S. Cobb	Hon. Gilbert Johnstone
Nov.	"	Miss A. Susan Lawrence
1912	"	H. C. Gooch

* Dr Sophie Bryant, Miss Margaret Eve, Mrs Homan, Hon. Maude Lawrence, Miss Susan Lawrence.

YEAR	EDUCATION COMMITTEE	HIGHER EDUCATION SUB-COMMITTEE
1913	John W. Gilbert	H. C. Gooch
1914	"	"
1915	"	"
1916	"	"
1917	"	"
1918	Sir Cyril Cobb	"
1919	"	"
1920	"	"
1921 Jan.	"	"
April	H. C. Gooch	Rev. Canon R. D. Swallow
1922	Sir Cyril Jackson	"
1923	Mrs Wilton Phipps	"
1924	"	"
1925	"	"
1926	W. H. Webbe	Capt. O. Wakeman
1927	"	Harold Swann
1928	Sir John Gilbert	"
1929	"	"
1930	"	Capt. Edward Cobb
1931	"	W. F. Marchant
1932	Capt. Edward Cobb	"
1933	"	Harold Swann
1934	Mrs Eveline Lowe	Charles R. Simpson
	(Herbert Morrison Leader of the Council)	
1935	"	"
1936	"	"
1937	Charles Robertson	Mrs E. M. Lowe
1938	"	"
1939	"	Mrs Helen Bentwich
	"	GENERAL COMMITTEE
1940-2		Thomas H. Jones
1942-3	"	"
	(Mrs Margaret Cole co-opted)	
1943-4	"	Mrs L'estrange Malone
	(Mr Harold Shearman co-opted)	
		HIGHER EDUCATION SUB-COMMITTEE
1944-5	I. J. Hayward	Mrs Helen Bentwich
1945-6	"	"
1946-7	"	Harold Shearman
		FURTHER EDUCATION SUB-COMMITTEE
1947-8	Mrs Helen Bentwich	R. McKinnon Wood
	(I. J. Hayward — Leader of the Council)	
1948-9	"	"

YEAR	EDUCATION COMMITTEE	FURTHER EDUCATION SUB-COMMITTEE
1949-50	R. McKinnon Wood	Mrs Margaret Cole
1950-1	"	"
1951-2	"	"
1952-3	"	"
1953-4	"	"
1954-5	Harold Shearman	"
1955-6	"	"
1956-7	"	"
1957-8	"	"
1958-9	"	"
1959-60	"	"
1960-1	"	R. McKinnon Wood
1961-2	Mrs Marjorie McIntosh	Mrs Margaret Cole
1962-3	"	"
1963-4	"	"
1964-5	Mr James Young (ILEA formed. Mr Ashley Bramall Chairman of the Authority.)	"

		FURTHER AND HIGHER EDUCATION SUB-COMMITTEE
1965-6	Mr James Young	Sir Harold Shearman
1966-7	"	"
1967-8	Mr Frank Abbot (also Chairman of the Authority)	Dr. Gerard Vaughan
1968-9	Mr Frank Abbott	Mr Michael Grylls
1969-70	"	"
1970-1	Mr John Branagan	Mr Alec Grant
1971-2	"	"
1972-3	"	"
1973-4	Mrs F. Whitnall	J. W. Straw
1974-5	Mrs Iris Bonham	Mrs Margaret Rees
1975-6	F. W. Styles	"
1976-7	Mrs Anna Grieves	"
1977-8	Mrs Leila Campbell	Ellis S. Hillman
1978-9	Louis Bondy	"
1979-80	David Chalkley	"
1980-1	Ted Walker	Ann S. Ward

EDUCATION OFFICERS

1904-24 — Sir Robert Blair	1951-56 — Dr John Brown
1924-33 — Sir George Gater	1956-71 — Sir William Houghton
1933-40 — E. M. Rich	1972-77 — Dr Eric Briault
1940-51 — Sir Graham Savage	1977- — Peter Newsam

Notes

1. Before 1870 — a Perspective

1. Sabine, C.G.H., *A History of Political Theory*, 1937 (4th edn, Dryden Press, 1973) p.456.
2. Pole, Thomas, *A History of the Origin and Progress of Adult Schools*, p.30.
3. Op. cit., p.75.
4. Op. cit., p.35.
5. Kelly, T., *A History of Adult Education in Great Britain*, pp.76-7.
6. Op. cit., p.97.
7. Op. cit., p.102.
8. Hudson, J.W., *The History of Adult Education*, Op. cit., 34.
9. Kelly, T., op. cit., p.121.
10. Op. cit., pp.121-2.
11. Hudson, J.W., op. cit., p.52.
12. Op. cit., p.19.
13. Op. cit., p.22.
14. Op. cit., p.vii.
15. Op. cit., p.189.
16. Lovett, William, *Life and Struggle*, vol. II, G. Bell & Sons, 1920, pp.253-5.
17. Hudson, J.W., op. cit., pp.212-13.
18. Edwards, H.J., *The Evening Institute*, p.16.
19. Op. cit., p.18.
20. Bartley, G.T.C., *Schools for the People*, pp.138-9.
21. Op. cit., pp.415-16.
22. Carpenter, Mary, *Reformatory Schools for Children*, p.118.
23. Bartley, G.T.C., op. cit., pp.385-6.
24. Cole, G.D.H. & Postgate, Raymond, *The Common People*, 2nd edn, Methuen, 1946, p.362.

2. The School Board for London: 1870-1904

1. Reay, Lord, School Board for London valedictory address, 28 April 1904.
2. Spalding, T.A., *The Work of the London School Board*, p.4.
3. Hansard, vol. 199, col. 439.
4. Eaglesham, Eric, *From School Board to Local Authority*, pp.11-2.
5. Bray, S.E., *The Work of the London School Board*, p.117.
6. Op. cit., p.117.
7. Op. cit., p.118.
8. Op. cit., p.119.
9. ibid.
10. ibid.
11. Op. cit., p.120.
12. School Board for London, Minutes, 6 November 1879.

13. Op. cit., 20 July 1882.
14. ibid.
15. ibid.
16. Bray, S.E., *The Work of the London School Board*, p.258.
17. Op. cit., p.259.
18. *Final Report of the School Board for London*, p.284.
19. ibid.
20. ibid.
21. 53 and 54 Vict. c.22.
22. *Final Report of the School Board for London*, p.288.
23. ibid.
24. Op. cit., p.289.
25. ibid.
26. Op. cit., p.290.
27. Bray, S.E., *The Work of the London School Board*, p.260.
28. ibid.
29. Op. cit., p.262.
30. ibid.
31. ibid.
32. Op. cit., pp.263-4.
33. ibid.
34. Op. cit., p.264.
35. ibid.
36. *Final Report of the School Board for London*, pp.290-2.
37. Op. cit., p.292.
38. ibid.
39. Op. cit., pp.297-8.
40. School Board for London, Minutes, 9 July 1891.
41. Rex *v.* Cockerton, L.R., 1901, 1 Q.B., p.322.
42. Garnett, W., *How the County Council became the LEA for London on 1 May 1904*, reprinted from Educational Record, April 1929.
43. *Final Report of the School Board for London*, p.276.
44. The events leading up to, and those resulting from, the Cockerton Judgment are fully discussed in *From School Board to Local Authority* by Professor Eric Eaglesham.

3. Towards a Comprehensive Education Service

1. Allen, Bernard, *A Memoir of William Garnett*, pp.78-9.
2. ibid.
3. Op. cit., pp.124-5.
4. Gibbon, Sir G. & Bell, R., *A History of the London County Council 1889-1939*, p.242.
5. ibid.

4. The London County Council as Education Authority

1. Webb, Sidney, *Daily Mail*, 17 October 1902.

2. Haward, Sir Harry, *The London County Council from Within*, pp.61-2.
3. ibid.
4. ibid.
5. *Eight Years of Technical Education and Continuation Schools*, Report of the Education Officer to Education Committee, Dec. 1912, p.104.
6. Op. cit., p.61, para. 3.
7. Op. cit., p.50, section XV (2).
8. Op. cit., p.27, section IX, para. 3.
9. Op. cit., p.50, section XV (1).
10. Op. cit., p.56.
11. Op. cit., p.76.
12. ibid.
13. Toynbee Hall, Oxford House (Bethnal Green), Cambridge House (Camberwell), Bermondsey Settlement, Passmore Edwards Settlement (WC), Browning Hall (Walworth), Christian Social Union Settlement (Hoxton), Ratcliff (Women's) Settlement, Women's University Settlement (Southwark), Lady Margaret Hall Settlement (Kennington Road), United Girls School Settlement (Peckham), Talbot House Settlement (Camberwell), St Mildred's Settlement (Bethnal Green), St Hilda's (Shoreditch), Creighton House (Fulham).
14. Op. cit., p.82.
15. Report of the Higher Education sub-committee (1.5.13) to Education Committee, Education Minutes, 7 May 1913.
16. ibid.
17. ibid.
18. ibid.
19. ibid.
20. ibid.
21. ibid.
22. ibid.
23. ibid.
24. ibid.
25. ibid.
26. ibid.
27. ibid.
28. ibid.
29. ibid.
30. ibid.

5. The 1914-18 War

1. Education Committee, Minutes, 11 November 1914.
2. Op. cit., 18 November 1914.

6. Post-War Reconstruction: 1919-29

1. Education Committee, Minutes, 10 March 1920.

2. Adult Education Committee of the Ministry of Reconstruction, Fourth and Final Report, HMSO, 1919.
3. ibid.
4. Report by the Education Officer to the Higher Education sub-committee, 22 January 1920.
5. Williams, T.G., *Adult Education*, vol. 27, no. 4, 1955.
6. ibid.
7. ibid.
8. Burbidge, Fred., (Principal of Plumstead & Woolwich and Eltham Literary Institute), Final report on retirement in 1933.
9. Williams, T.G., op. cit.
10. Op. cit.
11. Bettany, F.G., *Stewart Headlam — a Biography*, 1926, p.159.
12. Op. cit., p.162.
13. Op. cit., pp.162-3.
14. Op. cit., p.183.
15. Op. cit., p.184.
16. Education Committee, Minutes, 28 April 1920.
17. Myers, S., 'London Men's Institutes' in *Journal of Adult Education*, vol. 6, no. 4, April 1934, pp.426-7.
18. Op. cit., pp.428-9.
19. Op. cit., pp.429-30.
20. Board of Education, *The Work of Men's Institutes in London*, Pamphlet No. 48 HMSO, 1926, pp.3-4.
21. Op. cit., p.5.
22. Op. cit., pp.6 and 7.
23. Myers, S. & Ramsay, E., *London Men and Women*, p.30.
24. Op. cit., p.9.
25. Op. cit., p.12.
26. Myers, S., op. cit., p.433.
27. LCC, The London Education Service, 1925-6 et seq.
28. Board of Education, *LCC Men's Institutes, Junior*, Pamphlet No. 84 HMSO, 1931.
29. Op. cit., p.7.
30. Op. cit., p.13.
31. Op. cit., p.27.
32. Op. cit., p.23.
33. Op. cit., p.22, para. 25 and pp.24-5, para. 28.
34. Myers, S. & Ramsay, E., op. cit., p.12.
35. Lindsay, K., *Social Progress and Educational Waste*, Geo. Routledge & Sons, 1926, p.87.
36. Op. cit., p.110.

7. The Changed Scene: London in the 1930s

1. Llewellyn Smith, Sir Hubert, *The New Survey of London Life and Labour*.
2. Booth, Charles, *Life and Labour of the People of London*, 1889-1901.

3. Adult Education Committee, *The Scope and Practice of Adult Education*, HMSO, 1930.
4. Llewellyn Smith, op. cit., vol. 1, p.1.
5. Op. cit., vol. 1, p.2.
6. Pimlott, J. A. R., *Toynbee Hall*, p.5.
7. Llewellyn Smith, op. cit., vol. 3, p.11.
8. Op. cit., vol. 1, p.21.
9. Op. cit., vol. 1, p.227.
10. Report of the LCC Medical Officer for 1925, p.8.
11. Llewellyn Smith, op. cit., vol. 1, p.51.
12. Op. cit., vol. 1, p.50.
13. Op. cit., vol. 1, p.286.
14. Op. cit., vol. 1, p.394.
15. Op. cit., vol. 1, p.45.
16. Op. cit., vol. 1, p.293.
17. Op. cit., vol. 1, p.194.
18. Myers, S. & Ramsay, E., Op. cit., p.1.
19. ibid.
20. ibid.
21. Op. cit., p.2.
22. Op. cit., pp.3-4.
23. Llewellyn Smith, op. cit., vol. IX, p.271.
24. Myers, S. & Ramsay, E., op. cit., p.6.
25. Pimlott, J. A. R., op. cit., p.23.
26. Op. cit., p.262.
27. Llewellyn Smith, op. cit., vol. IX, p.114.
28. *The Scope and Practice of Adult Education*, op. cit., p.xi.
29. Op. cit., p.5.
30. ibid.
31. Adult Education Committee, *Pioneer Work and Other Developments in Adult Education*, HMSO, 1927.
32. *The Scope and Practice of Adult Education*, p.13.
33. Op. cit., p.28.
34. Adult Education Committee, *Adult Education and the Local Education Authorities*, HMSO, 1933, p.52.
35. ibid.
36. Williams, T. G., *The City Literary Institute — a Memoir*, 1960, p.23.
37. Op. cit., p.25.
38. Myers, S. & Ramsay, E., op. cit., p.23.
39. Op. cit., p.35.
40. Op. cit., p.37.
41. Education Committee, Minutes, 9 November 1938.
42. ibid.

8. The 1939-45 War

1. Education Committee, Minutes, 21 February 1940.

2. Dent, H. C., *Education in Transition, 1939-1943.* A sociological survey of the impact of war on English education.
3. Education Committee, Minutes, 21 February 1940.
4. Dent, H. C., op. cit., p.149.
5. Williams, T. G., op. cit., p.45.

9. The Post-War Period: 1946-57

1. Except where otherwise stated references to the Education Committee are taken from the Minutes of the Education Committee for the date stated.
2. LCC Scheme of Further Education 1949.
3. Op. cit., p.11.
4. Op. cit., p.13.
5. Op. cit., p.18.
6. Op. cit., p.56.
7. ibid.
8. ibid.
9. Op. cit., p.59.
10. Op. cit., p.60.
11. ibid.
12. ibid.
13. Op. cit., p.63.

10. The Reorganization of 1957-9

1. Report (Ed. 614) by the Education Officer to the Further Education sub-committee, 20 June 1957.
2. ibid.
3. ibid.
4. ibid.
5. Report by the Education Officer to the Further Education sub-committee 30 October 1957.
6. Education Committee, Minutes, 20 November 1957.

11. The Years of Fruition: the 1960s

1. Education Committee, Minutes, 23 November 1960.
2. Maclure, Stewart, *100 years of London Education 1870-1970*, p.144.

12. The Years of Enquiry and Review: 1969-73

1. Report (ILEA 388) by the Education Officer to the Further and Higher Education sub-committee, 10 July 1969.
2. ILEA evidence to the Committee of Enquiry (Russell Committee) into Adult Education in England and Wales. Published as an appendix to the agenda of the Education Committee, 18 February 1970.
3. Op. cit., pp.57-80.
4. Op. cit., para. 147.
5. Op. cit., para. 148.
6. Op. cit., para. 164.

7. Op. cit., para. 154.
8. ibid.
9. ibid.
10. ibid.
11. Op. cit., para. 155.
12. Op. cit., para. 157.
13. Op. cit., para. 157.
14. A reference to the Egremont Community School, Cumberland.
15. ILEA evidence, op. cit., para. 158.
16. Op. cit., para. 166.
17. Op. cit., para. 169.
18. Report (ILEA 839) by the Education Officer to the Further and Higher Education sub-committee, 25 February 1970.
19. Report by the Education Officer to the Further and Higher Education sub-committee, 15 July 1970.
20. *A Chance to Choose*, ILEA publication No. 7168 0423.9., 1973.
21. Op. cit., para. 84.
22. Op. cit., para. 105.
23. Op. cit., para. 108.
24. *The Social Structure of the Student Body in Adult Education Institutes*, ILEA publication No. 033541.56461, October 1973.
25. Op. cit., para. 22.
26. Op. cit., para. 23.
27. ibid.
28. Op. cit., para. 24.
29. Op. cit., para. 37.
30. Op. cit., para. 41.
31. Op. cit., para. 42.
32. Op. cit., para. 45.
33. LCC, *The London Education Service*, para. 58.
34. *The Social Structure of the Student Body in Adult Education Institutes,* para. 58.
35. Op. cit., para. 64.
36. Op. cit., paras. 60 & 62.
37. Op. cit., para. 63.
38. Op. cit., para. 72.
39. Op. cit., para. 75.
40. Op. cit., para. 99.
41. Op. cit., para. 100.
42. Op. cit., paras. 102-3.
43. Op. cit., para. 105.
44. Report (ILEA 718) by the Education Officer to the Further and Higher Education sub-committee, July 1973.
45. Report (ILEA 607) by the Education Officer to the Further and Higher Education and Schools sub-committees, 23 August 1973.
46. *An Education Service for the Whole Community*, ILEA publication No. 7168 0529, 4 November 1973, para. 1.
47. ibid.

48. Op. cit., para. 19.
49. Op. cit., para. 24.
50. Op. cit., para. 25.
51. Op. cit., paras. 26 & 27.
52. Op. cit., para. 55.
53. Op. cit., paras. 56 & 57.

13. Reaching out to the Community

1. Report by the Education Officer to the Further and Higher Education and the Schools sub-committees, September 1974.
2. ibid.
3. Report (ILEA 445) by the Education Officer to the Further and Higher Education sub-committee, June 1975.
4. Report (ILEA 587) by the Education Officer to the Further and Higher Education sub-committee, 14 June 1973.
5. Report (ILEA 455) by the Education Officer to the Further and Higher Education sub-committee, 7 June 1974.
6. Report (ILEA 493) by the Education Officer to the Further and Higher Education sub-committee, 27 September 1976.
7. Report (ILEA 770) by the Education Officer to the Further and Higher Education sub-committee, 20 January 1977.

14. Into the 1980s

2. Report (ILEA 0162) by the Education Officer to the Further and Higher Education sub-committee, April 1980.
2. ILEA evidence to the Russell Committee, paras. 12-14.

Selected Bibliography

School Board for London

The Work of the London School Board; prepared for the Paris Exhibition of 1900 (edited by Spalding, T. A.), P. S. King & Sons, 1900.

Final Report of the School Board for London 1870-1904, 2nd revised edn, P. S. King & Sons, 1904.

Technical Education Board

Annual Reports, 1893-1902-3.

London County Council

Minutes of the Education Committee, 1904-64.

Reports by the Education Officer to the Higher Education sub-committee, 1910-47.

Reports by the Education Officer to the Further Education sub-committee, 1947-64.

Eight Years of Technical Education and Continuation Schools, 1912.

The London Scheme of Further Education, 1944.

The Reorganisation of Men's, Women's and Literary Institutes, 1957.

Inner London Education Authority

Minutes of the Education Committee, 1964 to present day.

Reports by the Education Officer to the Further and Higher Education sub-committee, 1964 to present day.

Evidence to the Committee of Enquiry into non-vocational adult education in England and Wales (Russell Committee), published as an appendix to the agenda of the Education Committee of 18 February 1970.

A Chance to Choose, ILEA No. 7168 0423.9, 1973.

The Social Structure of the Student Body in Adult Education Institutes, ILEA No. 033541.56461, October 1973.

An Education Service for the Whole Community, ILEA No. 7168 0529, November 1973.

HMSO Publications

Final Report, Ministry of Reconstruction Adult Education Committee, 1919 (CMD.321).

The Work of the Men's Institutes in London, Board of Education, Educational Pamphlets No. 48, 1926.

Report on the LCC Men's Institutes (Junior) for period ending July 31st 1930, Board of Education, Educational Pamphlets No. 84, 1931.

The Scope and Practice of Adult Education, Paper No. 10 of the Adult Education Committee, 1930.

Adult Education and the Local Education Authorities, Paper No. 11 of the Adult
    Education Committee, 1930.
Evening Institutes, Ministry of Education, Pamphlet No. 28, 1955.
Adult Literacy, Reports 1975/6, 1976/7, 1977/8 to the Secretary of State for
    Education and Science by the Adult Literary Resource Agency.
Adult Education: A Plan for Development, Report by a Committee of Inquiry
    under the Chairmanship of Sir Lionel Russell, CBE, 1973.

General Works

Adult Education after the War, a report of an enquiry made for the British Institute
    of Adult Education with a preface by Viscount Sankey, President of the
    Institute, 1945.
Adult Education, journal of the National Institute of Adult Education, 1926 to
    date.
Allen, Bernard, *A Memoir of William Garnett*, W. Heffer & Sons, 1933.
Bartley, G. T. C., *Schools for the People*, Bell & Daldy, 1871.
Bettany, F. G., *Stewart Headlam — a Biography*, John Murray, 1926.
Burrows, John, *University Adult Education in London — a Century of Achievement,
    1876-1976*, University of London Press, 1976.
Carpenter, Mary, *Reformatory Schools, for the Children of the Perishing and Dangerous
    classes and for Juvenile Offenders*, 1851. (Reprinted as No. 2 in The Social History
    of Education series, Woburn Press, 1968.)
Clyne, Peter, *The Disadvantaged Adult*, Longmans, 1972.
Dent, H. C., *Education in Transition 1939-43*, Kegan Paul, Trench, Trubner, 1944.
Eaglesham, Eric, *From School Board to Local Authority*, Routledge & Kegan Paul,
    1956.
Edwards, H. J., *The Evening Institute*, National Institute of Adult Education, 1961.
Gautrey, T., *Lux Mihi Laus — School Board Memories*, Link House Publications,
    1937.
Gibbon, Sir G. and Bell, R., *A History of the London County Council 1889-1939*,
    Macmillan, 1939.
Harrison, J. F. C., *A History of the Working Men's College, 1854-1954*, Routledge &
    Kegan Paul, 1954.
Haward, Sir Harry, *The London County Council from Within*, Chapman & Hall, 1932.
Hudson, J. W., *The History of Adult Education*, 1851. (Reprinted as No. 5 in The
    Social History of Education series, Woburn Press, 1968).
Hutchinson, Enid & Edward, *Learning Later — Fresh Horizons in Adult Education*,
    Routledge & Kegan Paul, 1978.
Kelly, Thomas, *A History of Adult Education in Great Britain*, Liverpool University
    Press, 1970.
Llewellyn Smith, Sir Hubert (ed.), *The New Survey of London Life and Labour*,
    P. S. King & Sons, 1930.
Lowndes, G. A. N., *The Silent Social Revolution*, Oxford University Press, 1937.
Maclure, Stewart, *100 Years of London Education 1870-1970*, Allen Lane, 1970.
Myers, S. and Ramsay, E., *London Men and Women*, British Institute of Adult
    Education Life and Leisure Pamphlet, No. 3, 1936.

Pimlott, J. A. R., *Toynbee Hall*, J. M. Dent & Sons, 1935.

Pole, Thomas, *A History of the Origin and Progress of Adult Schools*, 1816. (Reprinted as No. 8 in The Social History of Education series, Woburn Press, 1968.)

Williams, T. G., *The City Literary Institute — a Memoir*, Catherine Press, 1960.

Index